18741

CAMBRIDGE STUDIES IN RELIGION AND AMERICAN PUBLIC LIFE

Between the Times

D0630590

Library
Oakland S.U.M.

Cambridge Studies in Religion and American Public Life

General Editor

Robin W. Lovin

Books in the Series

Merrill D. Peterson and Robert C. Vaughan: *The Virginia Statute for Religious Freedom*

Thomas G. Fuechtmann: *Steeples and Stacks: Religion and Steel Crisis in Youngstown*

18741

Library
Oakland S.U.M.

Between the Times

The Travail of the Protestant Establishment in America, 1900–1960

Edited by
WILLIAM R. HUTCHISON
Harvard University

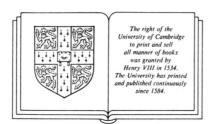

The right of the
University of Cambridge
to print and sell
all manner of books
was granted by
Henry VIII in 1534.
The University has printed
and published continuously
since 1584.

CAMBRIDGE UNIVERSITY PRESS

Cambridge

New York   Port Chester   Melbourne   Sydney

For Robert Wood Lynn:
"Guide, philosopher, and friend"

.

Published by the Press Syndicate of the University of Cambridge
The Pitt Building, Trumpington Street, Cambridge CB2 1RP
40 West 20th Street, New York, NY 10011, USA
10 Stamford Road, Oakleigh, Melbourne 3166, Australia

© Cambridge University Press 1989

First published 1989
First paperback edition 1990

Printed in the United States of America

Library of Congress Cataloging-in-Publication Data
Between the times : the travail of the Protestant establishment in
America, 1900–1960 / edited by William R. Hutchison.
p.   cm. – (Cambridge studies in religion and American public life)
Includes index.
ISBN 0-521-36168-0   ISBN 0-521-40601-3 (pbk)
1. Protestant churches – United States – History – 20th
century.   2. Sociology, Christian – United States – History – 20th
century.   3. United States – Church history – 20th century.
I. Hutchison, William R.   II. Series.
BR526.B47   1989
280′.4′0973 – dc19   89–31134

British Library Cataloguing in Publication Data
Between the times : the travail of the Protestant establishment
in America, 1900–1960.
1. United States. Protestantism, history
1. Hutchison, William R. (William Robert)
280′.4′0973

ISBN 0-521-36168-0 hardback
ISBN 0-521-40601-3 paperback

Contents

v

vi   *Contents*

Preface: From Protestant to Pluralist America

The phrase "between the times" has sometimes been used (as it was among European theologians in the 1920s) to convey a sense of alienation and despair. It may denote an acute societal "crisis of authority" or an anxious waiting for the Second Coming. But these words can also refer more neutrally, as they do in the title of this book, to a gradual and somewhat painful adjustment from one social reality to another.

American Protestantism underwent that sort of adjustment during the first six decades of the twentieth century. The so-called mainline denominations were compelled during those years to relinquish the comforts of an earlier taken-for-granted hegemony within American society. They were forced to confront a religious diversity that had been real, yet blithely or stubbornly unacknowledged, since at least the middle years of the nineteenth century.

By way of response, the churches strove to maintain their historic status and perform what they confidently believed were God-given responsibilities. One sees in retrospect, however, that they were also negotiating an epochal and quite fundamental transition, a transition from Protestant America to pluralist America.

The problem was not a loss of adherents. Proportional losses in relation to Catholics or non-Christians, particularly in urban centers, were among the facts of life that demanded recognition. But that phenomenon was not new, or even accelerated, in this era; far more startling changes in the statistics had occurred many years earlier, between the Revolution and the Civil War. Religious and other entities in a society, moreover, are not automatically in decline simply because others grow faster than they do. The more important question is what happens to the influence of a historically dominant religious body (or city or university or social class) as a result of such fundamental and material changes.

This was the distinctive issue, in the earlier twentieth century, for mainline Protestantism. Few besides radical nativists – those who wished to terminate immigration – thought much could be done about the changing numbers. What was at stake, for most Protestant leaders, was an established status that they were sure could and must be maintained despite the numbers. In short, the issue was hegemony. Seen from that perspective, the remarkable characteristic of the Protestant establishment, up to the 1960s and perhaps afterward as well, was not decline but persistence.

From the churches' own point of view, the issue was responsibility or, to put it precisely, custodianship. It requires only a bit of poetic license to say that the Protestant churches felt responsible for America: for its moral structure, for the religious content of national ideals, for the educative and welfare functions that governments would not (or, it was thought, should not) carry out. The agents of the Protestant establishment went on to ask, implicitly or otherwise, Who will do these things if we do not? Who else can run America?

Jews, Catholics, and others who considered themselves thoroughly accredited as custodians of American ideals found that stance at best disingenuous, at worst self-serving and outrageous; and today most mainline Protestants, along with nearly all secular commentators, would probably agree. Even the more fervid pleas, in recent years, for a restored public religion have commonly acknowledged that Protestant Christians can no longer presume to set the moral or public-policy agenda.

One can easily, and with justification, criticize mainline Protestantism for not recognizing such realities earlier, for having lingered between the times instead of seizing a new time – for having taken so long to discover America. Yet only the more facile or contemptuous of their critics would dismiss entirely what these churches attempted, or what they achieved, during an era of bewildering transformations.

Our purpose in this book is to initiate serious analysis of those attempts and achievements. We have tried to launch a close examination of the Protestant establishment's agenda for American society and the ways in which "others" related to it.

Although one might hastily assume that denominational Protantism has long since undergone this sort of scrutiny, we did not find that to be true. In recent years, especially, historians have paid far more attention to dissenters and other outsiders than to the more massive mainline religion they rejected, or from which they were excluded. Denominational history has not ranked high among our priorities. Some transdenominational movements, such as revivalism, have been studied extensively; others, such as the ecumenical movement, have remained relatively neglected.[1]

This is not because most interpreters have doubted the existence of something called mainline religion, or doubted its cultural significance. Far from it. One of the presenting problems, in fact, for projects like the one initiated with this volume is the constant, but usually vague and very general, allusion to such an entity in historical or sociological studies and in the media. More specifically, investigators and pundits have been reacting with pleasure or alarm to an allegedly sudden waning of old-line Protestant influence since the 1960s, but have been doing so without benefit of much serious analysis of the aims and status of Protestantism in the preceding decades.

To what extent did the major denominations and their leaders, before the much-discussed "watershed" of the sixties, actually call the tune for American Protestantism at large? for American religion? for the culture? The answers one finds imbedded in contemporary analyses or advocacies rest, as often as not, on inherited, relatively untested assumptions not entirely free of nostalgia.

If anyone needed to be blamed for this situation, it would not be the journalists or sociologists but, as already hinted, the historians of American religion. If excuses were then entertained, ours would be that we have been occupied with more pressing business; and we would add that mainline religion has, after all, enjoyed outrageously disproportionate attention in the past.

Both explanations may have merit. But we have mistakenly allowed ourselves to suppose, not only that our continuing analysis of outsiders can flourish while that of mainstream religion languishes, but also that the history of denominational Protestantism has been "done" – that we (both scholars and public) know all we really need to know. The resulting rationale for avoiding mainline history resembles that of a famous sports figure, Yogi Berra, who declined to take his friends to a certain restaurant: "Nobody goes there anymore. It's too crowded."

We have also, however, been unsure that if we did go there we would enjoy the company and conversation. The story of large standard Protestant denominations, we figure, is bound to be dull in comparison with that of, say, nineteenth-century Mormonism or present-day televangelism. The dullness, however, may be in ourselves if we have been failing to ask questions – quite different, perhaps, from those of traditional church history – that would lead to better understanding of what old-line Protestantism was and what it did or failed to do within American society.

One important deterrent to the framing of such questions has been a persistent lack of clarity about what one intends in using terms like "mainline," "old-line," "mainstream," or "central tradition." Are these terms meant to be merely descriptive, or somehow normative? If we speak of the mainstream religion of a particular time, or seem to assume the existence of such a thing, are we talking primarily about religious and cultural authority – about hegemony – or do we mean that this is where the vital juices were running? Are we discussing who was in charge, or offering assertions about the location, at a given time, of the "real" religion of Americans?

Because that important distinction has nearly always been blurred, any historian's perception that the larger white denominations were dominant has easily been misunderstood as some kind of assertion that they deserved to be dominant, and that those who stood at (or beyond) the periphery of power were peripheral, or of lesser significance, in other respects as well. Historians who assume the centrality or hegemony of denominational Protestantism have frequently been suspected of persisting in a discredited tradition of Protestant triumphalism. This has been true even when, like the late Sydney Ahlstrom in his *Religious History of the American People,* an author has expressed an almost virulent anti-triumphalist bias and given unprecedented coverage to nonmainline religion.[2]

Since terms like "mainstream" have been responsible for some of the confusion and avoidance, we have chosen in this project to emphasize such concepts as hegemony, power structure, and establishment – especially in designating the starting points for our inquiry. Those words and phrases, which are also imperfect, require working definitions, and the Introduction (Part I) attempts to provide them. For the moment, it is enough to say that our subject is the group of churches and network of leaders that appear, prima facie, to have dominated American Protestantism in the earlier twentieth century, and to have enjoyed considerable religious and cultural authority in the environing society.

When the authors do use necessary alternative terms such as "mainstream," they are employing those terms in the same sense – that is, as carrying no built-in assumption that the mainstream of power or of cultural authority was the main channel of dynamic historical development, or of faithfulness to religious and civic ideals. What would usually be called normative assessments of the establishment's aims and performance do of course arise within these essays. But language denoting centrality does not, so far as we intend or can tell, rest on prejudgments about who best represented "American religion."

The most intriguing issues are those that come into view when (and only when) one has distinguished between centers of power and centers of religious or social vitality. What need to be explored, in other words, are the relations between an establishment and its competitors (both religious competitors and "secular" ones), and the changes in these relations that occurred over time. So far as one can identify a mainstream of vital religious or theological development, to what extent was the establishment congruent with it? at what points alienated from it? If we are willing also to talk about a cultural mainstream or, more simply, about the apparent course of American history in a given era, in what ways was the Protestant establishment harmonious with that? in what ways out of touch with it or prophetically juxtaposed to it? In the now-current "Gramscian" terminology, an inquiry like the present one is working toward some understanding of the ways in which a dominant group exercised and refurbished its inherited authority, and the extent to which (if at all) a true "crisis of authority" occurred in the years under scrutiny.[3]

To suggest that in this volume we are even "working toward" such heady results may be foolhardy. As the authors met for conferences and consultations during the earlier years of this project, it became clear that we could attempt only a kind of reconnoitering in the broad forests and wetlands of Protestant "cultural authority." The most we could do, we concluded, was to gain some understanding of the establishment's program for American society, together with an initial grasp of the way that program was perceived, the challenges it faced, and some of the changes in direction that resulted. We have therefore concentrated on what we call the "Protestant Agenda," principally as articulated by the establishment itself (Parts II and III), but also as viewed and experienced by those who were total or partial outsiders (Part IV). Finally (in Part V), we have probed some ways in which the establishment was challenged by secularization, by religious pluralism, and – toward the end of this era – by "outside" forms of conservative evangelicalism.

Several alternative ways of gaining leverage on these concerns have struck us as promising and perhaps essential even though they were beyond our present capacities. (Most of these are being pursued in continuing studies of mainline Protestant history, under Lilly Endowment sponsorship, at Harvard and elsewhere.) One of the most important of these alternative approaches involves the establishment's complicated relationship to religious liberalism. Another – perhaps the most enticing of our neglected subjects – embraces the personal, local, and international dimensions of the Protestant establishment: a national leadership network that needs to be probed with the instruments of individual and group biography; local or regional establishments that so far have barely been touched upon in the sociological literature; overseas extensions or effects of the establishment that relate significantly to American foreign relations and the American impact abroad.

We are also quite aware, however, that we have scanted or telescoped the treatment of some subjects that do fall within our chosen areas of emphasis. At the conference that helped generate this volume, the educational arm of the establishment accounted for three papers – one each on the colleges and universities, the theological seminaries, and religious education; yet for the present publication we found it necessary to conflate those three subjects into one. In the same interest, that of limiting ourselves to a manageable number of chapters, we have here approached Catholic and Jewish relationships to mainline Protestantism through a study of one movement, the Goodwill Movement of the 1920s, in which both were involved. In general, the large and necessarily varied field of inquiry concerning "outsiders" – individual, denominational, or regional – is one to which, although we have ventured into it, we can hope at most to have opened gates and pointed directions.[4]

Some additional remarks are in order, finally, about our concentration upon the earlier part of the twentieth century.

To claim definitive status for the dates 1900 to 1960 would be unnecessary and would in fact mislead readers on a fundamental point. Although one may be able, for working purposes, to define "nineteenth-century America" and, at the other end of our period, a different society called "post-sixties America," the various forms of Protestant expression and influence did not follow the same schedule in moving from the first of those environments to the second; thus a fully logical scheme of periodization would have to vary with each subtopic we consider. Even then, one would need to comment on earlier and later happenings, since most significant change in any of these areas was gradual and evolutionary rather than cataclysmic. In asking the mainline Protestantism of 1900–60 to hold still long enough for historians to have a careful look, we are imitating the cinematographer who offers a freeze frame in the midst of an unfolding story.

Once this has been firmly acknowledged, however, it is possible to see the earlier twentieth century as an era in which, more than any other, the quest for cultural authority had become a matter of conscious intent and of programmed institutional expression. To be sure, the churches in the nineteenth century had pursued some explicitly "ecumenical" ventures embodying such aims; but these had been sporadic and relatively unsuccessful, largely because they had seemed unnecessary. The larger denominations had then been able to rely upon deep and truly vast reserves of inherited authority. They were central institutions in a society that before the 1830s had been overwhelmingly Protestant Christian, and that for all its vaunted diversities had been deeply grounded in English-speaking and Calvinistically derived traditions.

Not only had the challenges mounted and accelerated by the end of the nineteenth century; it seemed that the inherited capital, after so many decades of drawing against the account, had become less adequate for dealing with them. Yet the Protestant leadership and constituency were far from ready to relinquish control; and the American society, on the whole, was not yet demanding that they do so. Instead, the church leadership became quite explicit about the need both for aggressive denominational structures (already largely in place by the 1890s) and for the kind of joint effort represented in early twentieth-century moves toward federation.

Similarly, at the latter end of our era one can identify a complex and gradual, but still quite discernible, shift into a new mode – in this case a mode of greatly increased acceptance of diversity. Until about the 1950s, one rarely finds either insiders or outsiders using phrases like "triple melting pot," "post-Protestant America," or "third force" Christianity. Up to that time, the older churches, while recognizing unprecedented challenges to their authority and their power to do good in the society, had given virtually no thought to the notion that they must now do their work within a fundamentally altered – which is to say a truly pluralistic – framework.

These churches, in the era we consider, could not rebuild the populational and other foundations that had been gradually eroding. And they could not demand – on the whole could not even contemplate – the kind of constitutional recognition relied upon by many of their European counterparts. But they could, and did, work to shore up other parts of the superstructure of mainline Protestant dominance.

Our project was first formulated in the planning for a three-day meeting, in June of 1985, that involved some forty past and current members of the Harvard Colloquium in American Religious History (a fortnightly seminar, begun in 1972, principally for doctoral students and visiting scholars from several Harvard programs). From the thirteen papers presented at that conference, an editorial committee selected eight essays that in revised form would be appropriate for this first, definitional, volume; and we commissioned four additional articles on topics for which investigators were not to be found among the original conferees.

For any director and editor of collaborative work, the one nearly impossible task among many pleasant ones is that of ensuring that contributors discuss the same themes while retaining substantial freedom to discuss those themes in their own ways and to come to their own conclusions. The particular origins and procedures of this project may have enhanced the chances of producing a coherent volume, but they of course increased the risk that a party line would somehow be insinuated. Although only four of the authors (Voskuil, Schneider, King, and Wacker) were "my" doctoral students, most were longtime members of the Harvard Colloquium, and nearly all conferred repeatedly as the project unfolded.

The authors were, however, examining parts of the establishment phenomenon that simply *did* develop differently, and they reached disparate conclusions even as they strove to address common questions. One result is that, although my own introductory, concluding, and connective essays do seek to generalize about our findings, or about those of a given set of authors, those passages inevitably are infected with my own interpretation of what "we" have discovered. Any of my colleagues, it is safe to say, would have written them differently. All have had to be forbearing as I or some group of their coauthors have suggested new essay titles, or have otherwise presumed to tell them what their findings really mean. Wherever my summaries and extrapolations have not done justice to those findings, I hope the authors – and the reader – will practice forbearance just once more.

From the outset, the Protestant establishment project has enjoyed financial and other forms of support from the Lilly Endowment, which is also sponsoring the further investigations to which I have alluded; we owe special thanks to Robert W. Lynn, the Endowment's Vice President for Religion. Among the many others who have helped us, I must single out Marie Cantlon, who carried broad editorial responsibilities; David Emblidge, and later Emily Loose, at Cambridge University Press, who encouraged and guided us; Richard Seager, who managed most of the conferences and other meetings; Kay Shanahan, who provided clerical and many other kinds of support; and Erick Schenkel, who searched out musty volumes and distant archives for the book's illustrations.

I must also acknowledge a large debt to all those who, along with eight of the present authors, participated in our "Craigville Conference" of June 1985. Dorothy Bass, Grant Wacker, and John F. Wilson served with me on an executive committee that helped plan subsequent meetings and the volume itself. At an advanced stage in the book's development, Robin Lovin, Martin Marty, and other directors of the Chicago project on Religion and American Public Life offered further sponsorship, criticism, and assistance.

William R. Hutchison

NOTES

1 The exceptions have been tough-minded examinations of Protestant aspirations that deal to some degree with the twentieth century. See especially the books by Albanese, Handy, and Marty that are listed at the end of Chapter 1.

2 Sydney E. Ahlstrom, *A Religious History of the American People* (New Haven: Yale University Press, 1972), preface, introduction, and passim.

3 Antonio Gramsci, *Selections from the Prison Notebooks,* ed. and trans. Quintin Hoare and Geoffrey Nowell Smith (New York: International Publishers, 1971), 12, 210–11.

4 Benny Kraut, even as he gallantly accepted responsibility for the dual assignment on Catholic and Jewish relationships to the Protestant establishment, urged an additional chapter on Roman Catholicism. I now agree with him, not because of any deficiency in Kraut's presentation but because of my own heightened sense of Catholicism's importance to this entire story. In the case of regional establishments, we did hope and attempt to include an illustrative essay focused on the experience of Southern Baptists as outsiders to the establishment in the twentieth century. We were forced to postpone that task.

Contributors

Dorothy C. Bass, Associate Professor of Church History at Chicago Theological Seminary, has made numerous contributions to the study of religious education, the ministry, and women's history. She collaborated with Sandra Hughes Boyd in compiling *Women in American Religious History: An Annotated Bibliography and Guide to Sources* (1986).

Virginia Lieson Brereton, who received a doctorate in American history and education from Columbia University, teaches writing and history at Harvard. She is the author, with Christa Klein, of "American Women in Ministry" (in *Women of Spirit,* 1979), and of the forthcoming book-length studies, *Conversion Narratives of Protestant American Women, 1800–Present,* and *The Formation of the American Bible School, 1880–1940.*

Edwin S. Gaustad is Professor of History, Emeritus, at the University of California, Riverside. His books include *A Religious History of America* (1966, revised 1989) and *Faith of Our Fathers* (1988).

William R. Hutchison, Charles Warren Professor of the History of Religion in America, Harvard University, has written on religious liberalism, foreign missions, and the overseas impact of American religion and culture. In 1987 he published *Errand to the World: American Protestant Thought and Foreign Missions.*

William McGuire King has produced a dozen articles on American and European history, dealing primarily with religion in relation to social reform. His most recent contribution is "An Enthusiasm for Humanity: The Social Emphasis in Religion and Its Accommodation in Protestant Theology" (in M. J. Lacey, ed., *Religion and Twentieth-Century American Intellectual Life,* 1989). King is Associate Professor of Religion at Albright College.

Benny Kraut is a Professor and Director of Judaic Studies at the University of Cincinnati. His work as a scholar has focused on the relationships among Jewish, Christian, and other traditions. Kraut's study of Felix Adler, *From Reform Judaism to Ethical Culture*, appeared in 1979. His most recent book is *German-Jewish Orthodoxy in an Immigrant Synagogue: Cincinnati's New Hope Congregation and the Ambiguities of Ethnic Religion* (1988).

R. Laurence Moore, Professor of American History at Cornell University, published *Religious Outsiders and the Making of Americans* in 1986. He has also written on European and American socialism, and on spiritualist movements in the United States.

Robert A. Schneider, who received the Ph.D. in the study of religion from Harvard University, teaches in the American Studies program at Temple University. He is preparing a monograph on Rufus Anderson and the administration of the nineteenth-century mission enterprise.

Mark Silk, who took his Ph.D. at Harvard in medieval history, edited the *Boston Review* and is now a staff writer for the *Atlanta Journal and Constitution*. His books are *The American Establishment* (with Leonard Silk, 1980) and *Spiritual Politics: Religion and America Since World War II* (1988).

Dennis N. Voskuil is the author of *Mountains into Goldmines: Robert Schuller and the Gospel of Success* (1983), and is completing a study of Protestant neo-orthodoxy. He is Professor of Religion at Hope College.

Grant Wacker is Associate Professor of Religious Studies at the University of North Carolina, Chapel Hill. He has made extensive contributions to the interpretation of evangelicalism and pentecostalism in America. His book, *Augustus H. Strong and the Dilemmas of Historical Consciousness*, was published in 1985.

David W. Wills, who received his Ph.D. in Religion and Society from Harvard University, has written or edited a number of important works on black religion and the black churches in the United States, and is coeditor of a forthcoming documentary history of Afro-American religion. He is Professor of Religion at Amherst College.

I

Introduction

1

Protestantism as Establishment

WILLIAM R. HUTCHISON

Historians of American religion have generally taken for granted the existence of a Protestant establishment. Sydney Ahlstrom's *Religious History of the American People* used that terminology repeatedly. Robert T. Handy's arguments concerning an alleged "second disestablishment" of Protestantism after about 1920 (the first having occurred soon after the American Revolution) have been well received. Richard Neuhaus in the 1980s attributed the decline of religious influence in the civic order to, among other things, a "final disestablishment of mainline Protestantism." And E. Digby Baltzell, with a sociological more than religious definition in mind, used the term to identify certain breeding-grounds for anti-Semitism.[1]

Possibly such authors have alluded to something that, even if real, is not at all definable. Richard Rovere, who helped to give the term "establishment" the currency it enjoyed in this country after 1960, acknowledged that experts will always disagree about what a given establishment is and how it works, but he added that experts have also disagreed about the nature and operation of the Kingdom of God without on that account denying its existence. Leonard Silk and Mark Silk, in their volume of 1980, *The American Establishment,* acknowledged that the entity to which they had devoted their days and nights might be "a spirit, a ghost borne on the wind"; yet they remained convinced it was a reality.[2]

The Denominational Matrix

Plausible working definitions do, in any case, seem attainable with respect to religion. This is especially true if one begins, as we do in this volume, with the modest proposition that in the earlier years of this century an establishment, identifiable both as a group of denominations

3

and as a network of leaders in general connected with them, existed *within* American Protestantism. This intra-Protestant entity, if fuzzy at the edges and changeable over time, was not much more so than, say, the Republican Party or the American Federation of Labor (which as a federation provides a pretty good analogy). It was, at any rate, stable and definable enough to present one with an initial object of research, a starting point or base for inquiries into the dynamics of American religious and cultural history.

Let me be more specific. When historians, in their analyses of nineteenth-century religion, have used terms like establishment or mainline in a more-than-regional sense, they almost always have meant Congregationalists, Episcopalians, Presbyterians, and the white divisions of the Baptist and Methodist families. For the decades since 1900, the Disciples of Christ and the United Lutherans usually have been added, while the vast southern segment of the Baptists (unlike Southern Methodists or Presbyterians) has been seen as increasingly and intentionally removing itself from such a category.

These seven denominations represented well over half the constituency of the Federal and National Councils of Churches, supplied an overwhelming amount of their leadership, and to an amazing degree dominated the various enterprises ancillary to the main conciliar organizations. When "American Protestantism" dispatched delegates to the twelve-hundred-member World Missionary Conference at Edinburgh in 1910, all these groups except the Lutherans sent from 20 to 123 representatives. (American Methodists alone accounted for over 10 percent of the delegates at a gathering touted as broadly representative of world Christianity.)[3]

When the International Sunday School Council in 1922 formed an American subcommittee, these denominations provided at least 90 of the 109 members, and all of the fourteen officers. When American denominations in 1924 joined in establishing a National Council for the YMCA, it was these bodies (along with the Dutch and German Reformed churches and the Society of Friends) that made up the council. When John D. Rockefeller, Jr., and others in 1930 set in motion a "laymen's inquiry" into foreign missions, the same churches (minus the Lutherans) provided the ecclesiastical sponsorship. All of these churches (excluding the Disciples but including three different groups of Presbyterians) ranked among the top ten suppliers of Protestant missionary personnel; and all including the Disciples ranked in a top ten with respect to missionary budgets.[4]

The ability of the largest Protestant bodies to flood mission fields and international gatherings with their personnel, and to supply a huge proportion of the leadership, in some ways gave a distorted image of their position in American religious life. To speak only of numbers, their dominance among Protestants at home amounted to something like 60 percent, not 90 percent. But the resulting misperceptions, for example among European co-workers and observers, could in themselves work to strengthen the establishment's real authority, both at home and abroad. Exaggerated estimates, in other words, were to some extent self-fulfilling.

One can illustrate that phenomenon by reference to the period just after the First World War, when many people had come to think of "American Protestantism" as the principal creative and executive force in European reconstruction. In those years the Federal Council of Churches, which in its first decade (1908–18) had experienced only mixed success in unifying the American churches and directing their social outreach, gained enormously in international visibility, prestige, and prophetic standing. Europeans who admired "American religion" idealized the Federal Council both as a reliable representation of that larger entity, and as the leading model for structures of worldwide Christian unity and reconciliation. But even those who habitually distrusted American activism – and they were many – applauded the Council's insistent lobbying against the isolationist or recriminatory actions of Allied governments. Such American bodies and their leaders were viewed askance for undue paternalism and efficiency-mindedness, yet still admired extravagantly as religious America's rebuke to the United States Senate. These perceptions in turn helped produce the larger-than-life status that American "liberal" Protestantism was to enjoy in international settings for at least the next three decades.[5]

If the unity and effectiveness of the establishment could be exaggerated, especially from distant perspectives, so of course could that of any given denominational family within it. As an earlier allusion to three Presbyterian bodies indicated, several of these families – the Baptists, Lutherans, and Methodists as well as the Presbyterians – were exceedingly diverse. The number of ecclesiastical organizations "denominated" by the same name varied, as of 1920, from ten among the Presbyterians to twenty-two among the Baptists; and, except for an increase in Baptist groups, those numbers remained much the same in 1960. But any close look at relative numbers and resources within each denominational family will reinforce the conclusion that control was concentrated in a very few large bodies.[6]

One finds represented on the boards of the establishment organizations both those "family members" (United Presbyterian, Methodist Protestant) that eventually would merge with a more powerful sibling, and other Protestant bodies that were destined to maintain a separate identity (black Baptists, the Reformed churches, Quakers, Moravians). Yet the small scale of such representation, for example in the case of black church- es with huge constituencies, again underscores the establishment's domi- nance. Blacks, along with Mennonites, Free Methodists, and Seventh- Day Adventists, were represented at the Edinburgh meeting of 1910. But delegation size had been determined by the size of mission budgets, and these churches had been allotted only one to three delegates each.[7]

Not all the pieces in the mosaic of American institutional religion contribute in that way to the clarity of a central pattern. The establish- ment, though massive and seemingly very much in control, was not a monolith. Some American denominations that took no part in establish- ment enterprises – usually because they chose not to – could nonetheless boast competitive membership statistics, or a large degree of regional authority, or both. (The leading examples of "both" were the Southern Baptist Convention, the Missouri Synod Lutherans, and the Mormons.)[8] In any given area of activity, moreover, one or more "outsider" groups were likely to rank among a top ten or top twelve.

In foreign missions, the mainline churches shared prominence with outsider groups that specialized in such activity – especially with the Christian and Missionary Alliance and the Seventh-Day Adventists. In domestic social activism (judging from a longitudinal study, made in the 1950s, of the denominations' welfare enterprises), all except the Disciples ranked at the top; but the mainline churches were joined there by such specialists in city mission work as the Salvation Army and the Volunteers of America. When it came to concern for higher education (as reflected in official sponsorship of colleges and universities), this set of churches, minus the Episcopalians, again dominated the statistics, with the seven leading groups, at any given time, supporting over half of the Protestant institutions; but in this area they shared leadership with the Roman Catholics.[9]

The Establishment as a Personal Network

If these "Seven Sisters" continue, after careful nuancing of the description, to look like an established church operating without parlia- mentary sanction, that is partly because the American establishment was a personal network as well as a congeries of institutions. The historian James A. Field in the 1970s called attention to the familial, social, and old-school-tie relationships, in many areas of the world, not only among missionaries, but between the missionaries on one hand and en- trepreneurs, educators, philanthropists, and diplomats on the other. Such interrelationships had been visible in an earlier period when the medical missionary Peter Parker, whose wife was a Webster, held a series of diplomatic posts including, in the 1850s, that of American minister to China. By the twentieth century, partly because of what Field (a former naval officer) called "lack of intertheater transfer," mission-family dynasties had grown up in several areas of the world: Gulicks in Hawaii and Japan, Scudders in India, Underwoods in Korea, and many others.[10]

Field suggested that the situation in the Mediterranean world, where the "web of interconnected influence" had been established earlier than elsewhere, was an especially graphic single-theater epitome of more far-reaching networks extending across familial, occupational, and also national boundaries. And the overseas-based networks resembled, or actually extended, others that seem to have operated only on the national scene. The prospect therefore is that, just as historians of American foreign relations have had to take account of the interconnected influence of the Dodge, Stokes, Phelps, and Bliss families (with special attention to Woodrow Wilson's lifelong friend and adviser Cleveland Dodge),[11] so the aims and operations of the Protestant leadership at home probably will not be adequately understood until we have worked through the relationships, official and personal, of those who managed or supported the Protestant enterprise.

That word "work" should be emphasized. Historical name dropping, however intriguing and usefully suggestive, will tell us little about how the personal network operated – for example, about who influenced whom. We know already, however, that friendships like those linking the Fosdicks (Harry Emerson and his brother Raymond) with the Rockefellers, or the ecumenical executive John R. Mott with Woodrow Wilson, or Reinhold Niebuhr with leaders of the academic and foreign-policy establishment, figure in the stories both of mainline Protestantism and of its attempted cultural outreach and control. Mott's most exhaustive biographer, C. Howard Hopkins, scattered through his book references to Mott's interviews and other contacts with nine presidents of the United States. On one red-letter day in 1923, this particular lion of the religious establishment "began with William Howard Taft at 9:30, lunched with President Coolidge, and visited with his old friend Woodrow Wilson at 3:30."[12]

Similarly, biographers of the theologian Reinhold Niebuhr have documented his extensive and intimate involvement in secular branches of the establishment. Richard Fox, recounting Niebuhr's participation in a State Department consultation of 1949, surmises that

> both he and the assembled foreign-service officers and department specialists learned something of value from one another. No doubt too he and the State Department officials lent one

John D. Rockefeller, Jr. (*left*), and John R. Mott (*right*) at a testimonial dinner for Mott, 1946. Religious News Service photo.

another a certain amount of prestige: he basked in the aura of high affairs of state, they lingered briefly in the presence of a celebrity intellectual. They helped augment his standing as a significant Establishment figure, he helped elevate their own image as intellectually vigorous officials, not narrow-minded technicians. If Niebuhr did not influence government policy, he did participate in a system of influence in which some individuals and agencies established themselves as authoritative voices.

Two weeks later, according to Fox, Niebuhr learned that he was being seriously considered for a post "at the very summit of the Establishment," the presidency of Yale University. His sponsors included Jonathan Bingham, the lawyer and later New York congressman, Chester Bowles, who was then governor of Connecticut, and the historian Arthur Schlesinger, Jr.[13]

Reinhold Niebuhr testifying before a Senate committee on ethics in government, 1951. Religious News Service photo.

Such information – the kind that relates to well-known personages and is likely to be mentioned in printed sources – would be merely the tip of a vast iceberg. The personal network in question also operated through less official contacts, both among the preeminent lay and clerical figures and among the rank and file. To cite one example: If we are to understand more fully the tensions in mainline Protestantism before and during the fundamentalist–modernist controversy (c. 1910–30), we should learn not only how the various participants carried out their official duties, or what they said at conferences, but also how they spent their leisure time, and with whom.

The Presbyterian and ecumenical leader Robert E. Speer (a man often thought to have *had* no leisure time) spent part of most summers from 1901 to 1925 at Camp Diamond in northern New Hampshire, fishing and otherwise consorting with a number of persons whose names are well known to historians of missions or of Presbyterianism – with Robert Wilder, Charles Erdman, Henry Frost, the Hudson and Howard Taylors, and a great many others. As those same historians would know, Speer's fellow fishermen, and the organizations to which they were linked (the Student Volunteer Movement, Princeton Seminary, the China Inland Mission), played important and at some points sharply opposed roles in Speer's public career. The story of Speer's involvement in such a community could throw light on his willingness to be a contributor, along with Erdman and Frost, to the series of pamphlets that helped launch the fundamentalist movement. The circumstances, or just the fact, of his quitting Camp Diamond in 1925 (along with the Erdmans and the Wilders; the Frosts and Taylors stayed on) would at the least add dimension to what we know of the epochal falling-out, in the mid-twenties, between the fundamentalists on one hand, Speer and the Princeton Seminary moderates on the other.[14]

If such communities (the better known would include, for example, Silver Bay and Chautauqua in New York State, and Estes Park in Colorado) have their stories to tell of the religious establishment's less guarded moments, the more numerous "Pequod Islands," where members of *different* elites met and mingled, could tell us about its relations to the business, educational, and other secular worlds. The novelist John P. Marquand may well have based his evocation of Pequod Island, the beloved summer home of George Apley and his friends, on such real locations as Mount Desert Island, off the Maine coast. On Mount Desert, year after year, Browns and Peabodys of the religious establishment vacationed with Eliots, Rockefellers, and Peppers – that is, with educational, business, and political leadership. Although it was common in the languid, cheery recollections of these bucolic seasons to stress one's democratic or even egalitarian credentials (most memoirs include tributes to the sturdy locals and their ancestral wisdom), George Apley's poignant rumination is also apt: "Sometimes here on Pequod Island and back again on Beacon Street, I have the most curious delusion that our world may be a little narrow." A good many summer colonies were playgrounds, and to some extent workplaces, for a tight and well-defined social organization in which the leaders of mainline Protestantism were fixtures.[15]

Professor William Adams Brown, of Union Seminary in New York, devoted a section of his autobiography to "Forty Years of Mount Desert." Brown, a leading liberal theologian who during the First World War had been Speer's deputy in directing the War-Time Commission of the Churches, was prominent in both the intra-Protestant and the more general power structure. As a distant cousin to the Adamses of presidential lineage and a descendant of leading merchant bankers (Brown Brothers), he was a veritable embodiment of the network in its historical dimension; and his beloved summer place represented its contemporary form.

Brown's memoir mentions only the Mount Desert "names" that might be household words among the educated, rich, and famous – again, tips of an iceberg. But these are enough to make the point: univer-

Meeting of the trustees and officers of the General Education Board (which distributed Rockefeller monies for diverse educational purposes) at Hotel Samoset in Rockland, Maine, in July 1915. The group included three university presidents (Eliot of Harvard is third from left in front row), five prominent clergymen, and Rockefeller, Jr. (third from left, second row). For full identifications, consult footnote 16. Courtesy of the Harvard University Archives and the Rockefeller Archive Center.

sity presidents such as Eliot of Harvard and Gilman of Johns Hopkins; Professors Dana (Yale) and Peabody (Harvard); and Seth Low, the Columbia University president who was also a reform politician. There were Fords and Morgans as well as Rockefellers; Lord Bryce, the British ambassador, as well as Senator George Wharton Pepper of Pennsylvania.

Vacation communities, though undoubtedly good points of entry for an understanding of the religious power structure and its outer connections, would represent only one starting point. Investigators have, for example, long since detected the Protestant establishment's massive footprints in the biographical dictionaries. When C. Luther Fry, in 1931, surveyed the stated religious affiliations of *Who's Who* biographees, he found that among 16,600 who listed a preference, fully 7,000 were either Episcopalians or Presbyterians. Congregationalists, despite the smaller size of that denomination, numbered an equally astounding 2,000. Baptists, with Northern Baptists probably overrepresented, Southern and black Baptists undoubtedly underrepresented, came in at about 1,500. Unitarianism evoked Emerson's "congress of kings" by weighing in with 1,000 biographees. Catholics, Lutherans, Disciples, Jews, and Quakers, in that order, could claim from 750 to 180.[16]

Here again, in other words, the bodies we are concerned with ranked in a top ten. Some of them, obviously, ranked embarrassingly high, enough so that Fry wondered, as have others before and since, whether Episcopalianism made for leadership or leaders simply made for the Episcopal churches. For us it makes little difference, just as it makes little difference whether mainline male persons were enormously influential or were greatly overrecognized. (I think both explanations are correct.) Either way, we are dealing with a network of Protestant leadership that, whatever its degree of actual hegemony, lasted well into the era of the more differentiated mainstream (one including Catholics and Jews) that Will Herberg charted in the 1950s,[17] and possibly into the era, three decades later, when it became common to suppose that evangelical and "third force" Protestantism had subverted the influence of the old-line denominations.

Another dimension needing exploration is the one embodied in the structures of leadership and influence in local communities. Only after the completion of many new studies, chosen with attention to reasonable sampling criteria, will it be possible with any specificity to relate these local establishments to the ones that dominated nationally or regionally. Meanwhile, however, sociological descriptions of such communities as W. Lloyd Warner's "Yankee City" can at least be accepted as presenting "variations within a [national] type,"[18] and therefore as providing bases for some starting reflections.

This would seem to be true, at least, for communities in those regions that were well represented within the national religious establishment. The New England community selected by Warner and his associates in the 1930s contained fifteen congregations, of which eleven were Protestant Christian. Three of these churches were Congregational, while Presbyterians, Methodists, Baptists, and Christian Scientists had one apiece. The Episcopalians and the Unitarians each sponsored a church and a chapel.[19] Studies of the network of personal and institutional leadership in such towns, or of the mainline Protestant presence in more diverse communities such as the "Middletown" community studied by Robert and Helen Lynd would undoubtedly deepen our understanding of the national establishment, how it operated – and also how and why it changed.

In the midwestern "Middletown" of the 1920s, for example, the Lynds found, among both townspeople and ministers, evidence of decline in ministerial prestige. Despite "a widespread attitude of respect and in many cases warm affection and esteem" toward local ministers, "especially among the women," Middletown business leaders appeared to find excuses for excluding the clergy from the all-important Rotary Club. The Lynds gained "an impression of the ministers as eagerly lingering about the fringes of things trying to get a chance to talk to the men of the city who in turn are diffident about talking frankly to them."[20]

Whether such signs and complaints of alienation, even if common beyond Middletown, were in any way new to the 1920s is an extremely tricky question. Laments concerning "ministerial decline," laid end to end, would form a wide and solid line from 1630 to 1930 and, if valid, would document the ending of all ministerial influence in America sometime before the Revolution. It would be rash, moreover, to take exclusion from the Rotary Clubs of the 1920s, or terror in the face of such exclusion, as indicating permanent deterioration in ministerial standing. Clearly, the sociological data concerning denominational strengths and memberships, to say nothing of sociologists' "impressions" about local networks, will need to be treated comparatively, both over time and across the country.

The task, however, like that of inquiring into the nationwide web of individual relationships, becomes less formidable when one considers that at least some of the preliminary work – in one case local history and sociology, in the other case individual biography – has been done and sits waiting to be synthesized.

Liberalism and the Protestant Establishment

Of all the terms used in recent years for what we are calling the Protestant establishment, the one least likely to be employed in this book as an actual synonym is "liberal Protestantism." Liberalism in all the most usual senses – theological, social, and ecumenical – was undeniably an important element in the common life of these churches, as well as in their doctrinal development and their bureaucratic and other leadership. But the habit of designating the Protestant mainline churches simply as "liberal," which is at least understandable if one has in mind the alignments of the 1970s and 1980s, is problematic for earlier periods.

The churches, church constituencies, and leaders we are talking about, when forced to choose between modernism and fundamentalism, or between the social gospel and more individualistic modes, did tend strongly to make the more "liberal" choice; and the fact that they did so is a vitally important part of their story. In making such choices, however, they were not in all instances – probably not in most instances – opting for what those churches and people would have spoken of as liberalism, to say nothing of modernism.

The Protestant establishment can in fact be understood as a "broad church" that held together, and exercised whatever cultural authority it did enjoy, precisely because it retained the adherence, at all levels, of many besides liberals. While it is probably true that few who called themselves fundamentalists were able to remain comfortably in these churches after about 1930, all the evidence indicates that "liberal" was rarely a preferred term outside the theological seminaries and the more sophisticated periodicals. (During the time of neo-orthodox reaction against conventional liberalism – that is, between 1930 and 1960 – such terminology was a bit suspect in those precincts as well.) Most establishment leaders and people, if forced to use limiting terms, were likely to designate their own positions as evangelical, confessional, progressive, or – calling on that all-time favorite among weasel words – moderate.

One can refuse to take such protestations seriously. We might insist that most of the so-called moderates, and most of those in furious neo-orthodox revolt, were in fact liberals – that "establishment" and "liberalism" are in the end best understood as synonymous terms. The habit of equating them developed, after the 1950s, largely because many evangelicals, along with nearly all fundamentalists, did make exactly that assertion about the old-line churches, and particularly about their intellectual and bureaucratic leadership. It became common to insist that those establishment functionaries, whatever fancy or fudging names they might give themselves, were all basically liberals. It was also charged that much of the rank and file, in failing either to speak out in their denominations or to defect from them, were fellow-traveling liberals as well.

Among a number of evangelicals who built polemics and programs on such allegations, one of the more discriminating was James DeForest Murch. Just after the period considered in this book, Murch sought to rally true Christians against a liberal superchurch that he thought was conspiring, especially through the ecumenical movement, to impose liberal and collectivist thought all across American culture. "It needs to be made clear," he explained in the first pages of *The Protestant Revolt* (1967), "that there is a liberal ecclesiastical establishment which sets the tone for and influences the direction of modern institutional Protestantism."[21]

Murch, far from assuming that all adherents of the old-line churches deserved to be branded as liberals, asserted that "thousands upon thousands" within those churches had discerned the contrast between true Christianity and "the pronouncements and practices of the Councils of

Churches and the Liberal Establishment." Multitudes, he thought, were ready for active revolt. Even within the "small body of 'key men'" who managed the selection of "the 'right people' to all important positions in the ecclesiastical machine," many would not call themselves liberal. These leadership groups, he conceded, included "theologians of various persuasions (except 'fundamentalists')." The liberal establishment, in other words, was made up, basically, of just two kinds of people: Although doubtless controlled by actual liberals, it included all too many others who merely tolerated their thinking and connived in their machinations.[22]

Perceptions of an essentially liberal establishment and its dangers, while perhaps most intense at this moment of renewed evangelical consciousness, were by no means new. In 1923, as the fundamentalist controversy heated up, the periodical *Ministers' Monthly* (founded a year earlier to counter the "controlled press" of the major denominations) devoted two articles to "the flood tide of liberalism." This tide, it was said, had engulfed not only the theological seminaries, but also foreign missions, the religious press, and "the ecclesiastical machinery in nearly all of the leading denominations." J. Gresham Machen, chief scholarly mentor of the fundamentalists, sounded some of the same notes in his *Christianity and Liberalism* (also 1923), and the plaint could be heard amid the rhetoric of the Scopes trial two years later. The allegation that liberalism was taking over was in fact as old as the reactions, early in the century, to denominational "social creed" legislation and to the formation of the Federal Council of Churches. It was as venerable as fundamentalism itself.[23]

Card-carrying liberals, especially if social action was foremost in their religious thinking, acquiesced readily enough in this equation between "mainline" and "liberal"; and the tendency to make such an identification was strengthened accordingly. But the degree to which liberal ideas actually had come to pervade the establishment and its strategies remains an important open question.

What are we justified in assuming, meanwhile, about liberalism's importance in the twentieth-century development of these denominations? Estimates by such historians as C. Howard Hopkins and the present author may be reliable so far as they go: Hopkins identified very strong social gospel influence, and official denominational acceptance, in all of our seven bodies and nine others.[24] My own *Modernist Impulse* was inclined to see roughly as much liberal and modernist commitment within mainline Protestantism as conservatives found there (and in the same places: among the intellectual and bureaucratic leadership). The subject is, however, sufficiently complex that one will need to look behind the statistics, public pronouncements, and informed impressions on which such accounts have relied. In the meantime (and perhaps afterward as well), "liberal" must remain a term that, while it clearly helps to define the establishment, in no sense exhausts its definition.

Whatever the case with other establishments, this one was not a "ghost borne on the wind," but was defined concretely in the management of American Protestant life. The nature of its extension outward, its interconnection with other organizations and elites, is bound to remain somewhat more elusive. Even harder to answer definitively are questions of "influence" and of broad cultural authority – how much of the earlier hegemony endured or was successfully refashioned in the new conditions of the twentieth century. The difficulty of drawing the final and comprehensive map is not an excuse for failing to explore a few specific and vital territories. The essays that follow attempt to do that.

NOTES

1 Sydney E. Ahlstrom, *A Religious History of the American People* (New Haven: Yale University Press, 1972); Robert T. Handy, *A Christian America: Protestant Hopes and Historical Realities* (New York: Oxford University Press, 1971), Chapter 7; Richard John Neuhaus, *The Naked Public Square: Religion and Democracy in America* (Grand Rapids, Mich.: Eerdmans, 1984), ix; E. Digby Baltzell, *The Protestant Establishment: Aristocracy and Caste in America* (New York: Random House, 1964).

2 Richard Rovere, "The American Establishment," *Esquire,* 57 (May 1962), 106; Leonard Silk and Mark Silk, *The American Establishment* (New York: Basic Books, 1980), 328.

3 World Missionary Conference, 1910, *History and Records and Addresses* (Edinburgh: Oliphant, Anderson & Ferrier, 1910), 51–63.

4 Herbert H. Smith (ed.), *Organized Sunday School Work in North America, 1918–1922: Official Report of the Sixteenth International Sunday School Convention* (Chicago: International Sunday School Council, 1922), 4–6; S. Wirt Wiley, *History of Y.M.C.A.-Church Relations in the United States* (New York: Association Press, 1944), 115; William E. Hocking et al., *Re-Thinking Missions: A Laymen's Inquiry After One Hundred Years* (New York: Harper, 1932), v–vi, ix–x; James Dennis et al. (eds.), *World Atlas of Christian Missions* (New York: Student Volunteer Movement, 1911), 16–29; Joseph I. Parker (ed.), *Interpretative Statistical Survey of the World Mission of the Christian Church* (New York: International Missionary Council, 1938), 43–5.

5 Adolf Keller, *Dynamis: Formen und Kräfte des amerikanischen Protestantismus* (Tübingen: Mohr, 1922), Chapter 5; Karl Bornhausen, *Der Christliche Activismus Nordamerikas in der Gegenwart* (Breslau: Alfred Töpelmann, 1925).

6   *1919 Year Book of the Churches* (New York: Federal Council of Churches, 1919), 196 and 205; *1962 Yearbook,* 249 and 254. See generally the Federal and National Council of Churches *Yearbooks,* published since 1916. (Cited hereafter as *Yearbook* or *Handbook* with date.)

7   World Missionary Conference, 1910, *History,* 55, 58, 51.

8   *1962 Yearbook,* 8, 249–54; *1951 Yearbook,* 2, 234–9; *1941 Yearbook,* 88, 129–35; *1931 Handbook,* 160, 259–63.

9   Parker, *Survey,* 43–45; *1919 Yearbook,* 211–14; *1934 Handbook,* 208–81; *1935 Yearbook,* 14–17; Horace R. Cayton and Setsuko Matsunaga Nishi, *The Changing Scene: Churches and Social Welfare,* vol. 2 (New York: National Council of Churches, 1955), 180–214; *1916 Yearbook,* pp. 43–157; *1933 Yearbook,* 103–216; *1951 Yearbook,* 210–19.

10 James A. Field, "Near East Notes and Far East Queries," in John King Fairbank (ed.), *The Missionary Enterprise in China and America* (Cambridge, Mass.: Harvard University Press, 1974), 51 and 23–55 passim; Edward V. Gulick, *Peter Parker and the Opening of China* (Cambridge, Mass.: Harvard University Press, 1973).

11 Field, "Near East Notes," 53–5.

12 C. Howard Hopkins, *John R. Mott, 1865–1955* (Geneva: World Council of Churches, 1979), 665.

13 Richard Wightman Fox, *Reinhold Niebuhr: A Biography* (New York: Pantheon, 1985), 239.

14 Helen Waite Coleman, *The Camp Diamond Story,* privately printed, n.d. (c. 1942); William R. Hutchison, *Errand to the World: American Protestant Thought and Foreign Missions* (Chicago: University of Chicago Press, 1987), 164–75.

15 William Adams Brown, *A Teacher and His Times* (New York: Scribner's, 1940), 144–55.

16 *1933 Yearbook,* 311–16. Methodists, more proportionately, numbered 2500. The gentlemen assembled at Rockland were: (Front row) President Alderman of the University of Virginia; the Rev. Frederick T. Gates, Executive Assistant to John D. Rockefeller, Sr.; President Eliot; President Judson of the University of Chicago; and the Rev. Wallace Buttrick, Chairman of the GEB; (Middle row) Wickliffe Rose, General Agent for the Peabody Education Fund; the Rev. Hollis Frissell, Principal of Hampton Institute; John D. Rockefeller, Jr.; the Rev. E. C. Sage, Assistant Secretary of the GEB; Albert Shaw, Editor of *Review of Reviews;* and Abraham Flexner, Assistant Secretary of the Carnegie Foundation for the Advancement of Teaching; (Back row) George Vincent, President of the Chautauqua Foundation, the Rev. Anson Phelps Stokes, author, Secretary of Yale University; Starr Murphy, philanthropic advisor to John D. Rockefeller, Sr.; and Jerome Greene, Secretary of the Rockefeller Foundation.

17 Will Herberg, *Protestant-Catholic-Jew: An Essay in Religious Sociology* (New York: Doubleday, 1955).

18   W. Lloyd Warner and Paul S. Lunt, *The Social Life of a Modern Community*
      (New Haven: Yale University Press, 1941), 5.
19   Ibid., 188–93.
20   Robert S. Lynd and Helen Merrell Lynd, *Middletown: A Study in Contempo-
      rary American Culture* (New York: Harcourt, Brace, 1929), 349–50.
21   James DeForest Murch, *The Protestant Revolt: Road to Freedom for the Ameri-
      can Churches* (Arlington, Va.: Crestwood Books, 1967), 25.
22   Ibid., 27–8.
23   William R. Hutchison, *The Modernist Impulse in American Protestantism*
      (Cambridge, Mass.: Harvard University Press, 1976), 260 and Chapters 6–8
      passim.
24   C. Howard Hopkins, *The Rise of the Social Gospel in American Protestantism,
      1865–1915* (New Haven: Yale University Press, 1940), 280–98.

SELECT BIBLIOGRAPHY

Albanese, Catherine L. *America: Religions and Religion*. Belmont, Calif.:
      Wadsworth, 1981.
Brown, William Adams. *A Teacher and His Times: A Story of Two Worlds*. New
      York: Charles Scribner's Sons, 1940.
Field, James A., Jr. *America and the Mediterranean World, 1776–1882*. Princeton,
      N.J.: Princeton University Press, 1969.
Handy, Robert T. *A Christian America: Protestant Hopes and Historical Realities*.
      2nd ed. New York: Oxford University Press, 1984.
Herberg, Will. *Protestant-Catholic-Jew: An Essay in American Religious Sociology*.
      New York: Doubleday, 1955.
Hopkins, C. Howard. *John R. Mott, 1865–1955: A Biography*. Geneva: World
      Council of Churches, 1979.
Hutchison, William R. *Errand to the World: American Protestant Thought and Foreign
      Missions*. Chicago: University of Chicago Press, 1987.
      The Modernist Impulse in American Protestantism. Cambridge, Mass.: Harvard
      University Press, 1976.
Lynd, Robert S., and Helen M. Lynd. *Middletown: A Study in Contemporary
      American Culture*. New York: Harcourt Brace, 1929.
Marty, Martin E. *Righteous Empire: The Protestant Experience in America*. New
      York: Dial, 1970.
Murch, James DeForest. *The Protestant Revolt: Road to Freedom for American
      Churches*. Arlington, Va.: Crestwood, 1967.
Warner, W. Lloyd, and Paul S. Lunt. *The Social Life of a Modern Community*.
      New Haven, Conn.: Yale University Press, 1941.

II

The Protestant Agenda: Old Business

The essays in this section explore early twentieth-century developments in three traditional staging areas for Protestant influence in American society: the local congregation, the educational arena, and what would later be called "the media." In each, Protestantism's dominant position had been challenged, well before 1900, by the industrial and scientific accelerations of the late nineteenth century; by the drifting of more and more churchly or clerical functions toward "secular" sponsorship; and, looking further back, by the drastic reduction in Protestantism's numerical advantage (from over 95 percent of the population in 1790 to roughly 60 percent after 1860). And in each area one can readily discover a full spectrum of responses, from capitulation or abdication at one extreme to denial or studied obliviousness at the other. In between, occupying the largest space, are the many forms of attempted adjustment.

The drama of the establishment's resistance, persistence, and adjustment was played out most poignantly in American congregational life. Edwin S. Gaustad, viewing that huge and crowded stage, places the spotlight on preaching and the other functions of parish ministry. Pastors struggled both to meet the traditional requirements of personal ministry and to help the church and its people reach out to a larger society and more encompassing social problems. Having taken their place between the "little flock" and the great world, they experienced the dilemmas of the Protestant establishment itself. While fearing a loss of effectuality and "outside" status if they declined to engage their society directly, they also knew beyond doubt that such engagement risked the widening (or just the increased visibility) of the ancient gap between clergy and laity. The choice often seemed a cruel one – between nurturing the little flock and "leading" where few of that flock would follow.

The altered conditions for Protestant influence were more difficult for anyone to ignore in relation to education and publishing (which soon included broadcasting). As Dorothy Bass makes clear, Protestant control of higher education had already diminished drastically by the turn of the century; and the churches' influence had been threatened seriously, if less directly, by the new questions being forced upon Sunday schools and theological seminaries. In the world of newspapers and magazines, where Dennis Voskuil's story begins, religious and therefore Protestant publication had occupied a steadily decreasing portion of the field since at least the mid-nineteenth century.

New modes and instruments for a Protestant voice had to be found, or grasped when offered, and the religious leadership committed itself to finding them – on the whole cheerfully and with confidence. At some points, notably in the liaison that was forged between religion and a powerful new medium, radio, the Protestant establishment found both a voice and, for the time at least, a reaffirmation of its special position.

2

The Pulpit and the Pews

EDWIN S. GAUSTAD

In the first two generations of the twentieth century, the local churches and parishes of establishment Protestantism still thought of themselves largely as guardians of the moral and spiritual treasure carefully cached away by ancestors centuries before. The inevitable corollary of such guardianship was a sense of responsibility for the centuries yet to come. Despite the double shock of Darwin and the biblical critics, despite Comte and Freud, the leadership in America that counted was still assumed to be in good hands. Mainline Protestants continued to believe that when God chose to speak directly, it was to the Fosdicks and Coffins, to the Niebuhrs and the Tillichs, that the words were delivered. The churches between 1900 and 1960 were challenged, but not threatened; their agenda were crowded, but not trivialized. These large denominations saw the nation's destiny, the community's welfare, as peculiarly and inescapably *their* concern. Public schools were still *their* institutions, war (either its purposes or its abolition) still a matter of *their* decision. And the quality of life in general, morals and manners, depended chiefly on *their* leadership. Or so they earnestly believed and regularly assumed.

A Protestant Nation?

Immigration had greatly altered the demographic reality, but the newest immigrants were viewed, to a considerable extent, only as the newest challenge to evangelism. Although intellectual authority was passing from the sacred to the secular, the parishes had scarcely noticed. Mission boards and denominational staffs had struggled mightily with schism and recrimination, but the establishment endured. Earthquakes of enormous magnitude may have rocked institutional headquarters, but by the time the tremors reached the grass roots, the shaking – with few exceptions – could be ignored.

When, amid much noise and clamor, a dissident faction called the Orthodox Presbyterian Church launched its separate ecclesiastical ship in 1937, the much-touted schism accounted for less than 1 percent of the Presbyterian establishment. Northern Baptists shook more vigorously and bled more profusely, but the surviving leadership (which, after all, still included the Rockefellers and the presidents of such institutions as Brown and the University of Chicago) continued to count in establishment ranks. The Disciples of Christ, America's very own denominational creation in the 1830s, ruled from the heartland of the Midwest, while Episcopalians ruled from the corporate board rooms of the Northeast. Congregationalists, heirs of a New England mind that had become virtually a national academic mind, spoke with quiet, potent authority. Methodism expressed its leadership most conspicuously in the arena of social reform, seeking to ameliorate the grinding force of industrial power and the corrupting effect of urban blight. Lutheranism, still badly divided along ethnic and national lines in 1900, sixty years later spoke in accents more distinctly American if not quite in total unison.

As late as 1960 the establishment continued to think of its cultural authority as largely unshaken. Superficially, statistics gave some comfort as one surveyed the preceding sixty years. In approximate numbers, Congregationalists had grown from just above one-half million members to over two million, that growth resulting in part from mergers with smaller denominational entities in 1931 and 1957. Disciples, surviving the schism of the Churches of Christ at the beginning of the century, increased from three-quarters of a million to two million. Episcopalians, whose time of schism was still to come, jumped from less than a million in 1900 to over three million in 1960. In that same time period Lutheranism, the Missouri Synod branch aside, grew from less than two million to over five million. Methodism spurted from five million to over twelve million, about two million of the latter figure being in separate black bodies. (In 1939, the northern and southern branches of Methodism healed their pre-Civil War schism.) Northern (or American) Baptists, suffering as noted above from the modernist–fundamentalist acrimony, grew only modestly from under a million to less than one and one-half million. Northern Presbyterians (U.S.A.) on the other hand moved from about one million to over three in the same time period, that upward surge being augmented by a 1958 merger between the Presbyterian Church (U.S.A.) and the United Presbyterian Church of North America.

Indeed, the first half of the twentieth century witnessed a broad rever-

sal of the all-American trend toward repeated schism and endless proliferation, the older and larger churches choosing to seek commonalities
rather than magnify differences. All together, the "Seven Sisters" of the
Protestant establishment increased their numbers from around ten million in 1900 to something over twenty-six million two generations later.
Growth charts arched only upward, instilling confidence or at least de-
laying painful and searching self-examinations. Only if one compared
more carefully the mainline Protestant growth with the population
growth of the nation did one discover that the establishment was just
barely keeping up. And if one further compared growth rates with such
non-establishment bodies as the Mormons, the Adventists, the Southern
Baptists, and the Pentecostals, then these statistics lost virtually all power
to comfort and reassure.

In the period from 1900 to 1960, WASP had nonetheless not yet become a four-letter word and the Protestant ethos pervaded not only the
local churches themselves but to a degree shaped the towns and suburbs
in which Protestant churches found themselves. Mainline Protestantism
was not insular, neither an ethnic enclave nor a refugee from persecution
and societal distrust. Rather, these large denominations participated fully
in the larger society, believing that they bore the heaviest responsibility
for guiding the nation, sustaining both its moral vision and its watchful
walk along the paths of righteousness. This chapter will examine modifi-
cations and adjustments in that assumption as cultural authority gradually shifted its locus from the sacred places of traditional Protestantism to
the marketplaces of a burgeoning secularism.

Pulpit and the Word, or Words

"Goin' to preachin'," though a rural colloquialism, nonetheless
pointed to the most conspicuous feature of almost all Protestant worship
in these years. With the exception of the Anglo-Catholic wing of the
Episcopal Church, the pulpit, not the altar, was the focus of action and
often of architecture as well. To a disturbing degree, Protestant churches
rose or fell in membership, succeeded or failed in finances, expanded or
shrank in influence, largely as a result of the energy and personality of the
minister. The public spoke not so much of magnificent buildings as of
"great pulpits," Theodore Roosevelt's metaphor of a "bully pulpit"
being readily understood by all. Pulpit power could galvanize the parish,
and often resound far beyond those parochial walls.

In 1924 Charles Clayton Morrison conducted a wide-ranging poll to
determine "the twenty-five most influential and representative living
preachers of our time." The poll was of Protestantism only, but with an

The *Century*'s peerless preachers, 1925. From *Christian Century* XLII (January 8, 1925):54–5.

effort to reach all sections of the country and all segments within American Protestantism. Around ninety thousand ballots were dispatched and over twenty thousand returned. The results, published the following year, not only named the preachers but in turn gave each of the twenty-five clergymen the opportunity to select his favorite sermon, the message "which springs from your own heart of hearts, and expresses what you consider to be . . . the characteristic note of your ministry." Morrison's volume, therefore, is doubly representative: in the persons chosen, and in the words spoken. What are the results?

First, the gentlemen are in fact all gentle*men* and all are white; no female cleric, no black spokesman emerged to the fore. Second, the Northeast is heavily overrepresented. Two of the twenty-five clergymen were from the South (Nashville and Dallas), with seven from the Chicago-Detroit area. Only two ventured west of Chicago, one guiding a church in Seattle, the other briefly in San Francisco. Two may be classified as itinerant preachers. Third, the leading denominations were, in order, Presbyterian, Methodist, Congregationalist, Baptist, and Episcopalian (one). Neither the Disciples nor the Lutherans were represented; even more significantly, no denomination outside of the establishment seven was included, although one clergyman (Frederick F. Shannon) moved from Methodism through the Reformed Church to Chicago's Orchestra Hall and a radio ministry.

With respect to the content of their sermons, one finds a similarity that gives further force to the "establishment" claim. All were biblical, with the King James Version resisting such possible competitors as the English Revised Version or the American Standard Version or the newly published translation by Edgar Goodspeed. All proceeded from a text to an exposition of the biblical circumstance, then to an application of the biblical truth. One would gain from these sermons little sense of the American scene in 1925: virtually no attention to race, class, economic warfare, sectarian strife, Bolshevism abroad or heresy at home. Almost without exception, the sermons were personal, devotional, irenic, stressing the sensitivity and growth appropriate to the Christian. One sermon on the Virgin Birth (by Mark A. Matthews, Seattle Presbyterian) did throw down the gauntlet with respect to that doctrine, while another (by Ernest F. Tittle, Evanston Methodist) addressed itself to the subject of evolution and religion in tones of quiet moderation. The pervading flavor, however, is indicated by such titles as these: "Character and Work," "Shining Stars of Expectation," "Christ, Our Religion," "Walking in Galilee," and "The Old Rugged Cross."[1] At this level of popularity and fame, the biblical centrality of the Protestant sermon would seem to justify Arthur Sullivan's hymnodic refrain: "We are not divided; all one body we."

Like most such polls, what this one really measured was not so much influence or representativeness as sheer popularity. And popularity in general rested not on engagement with political and social questions but on rising above controversy: preaching about the "shining stars of expectation" and "the old rugged cross." No divisiveness or alienation there. In a great many Protestant parishes of the day, however, less highly visible pastors did confront urgent political and social issues, did dare to transport biblical criticism from the restricted study to the inclusive pew. Some preachers were accused of becoming more like sociologists and politicians, less like proud proclaimers of sacred truths. Others appeared to undermine their very authority by questioning the Bible rather than preaching it. As early as 1909, a Lutheran clergyman-professor in Ohio, troubled by the impact of higher criticism on the pulpit, declared that it was not the minister's task to carry a lot of critical apparatus with him into the pulpit: "The responsibility placed upon him is not to dissect the Word, but to hold it forth before a sinful world, as its only hope of healing. It must be preached in its grandeur, and with its reach of thought from eternity to eternity. The man who stands in the pulpit must be a positive man."[2]

Two decades later, a Methodist minister bemoaned the apparent necessity for the preacher to spend so much time indicating what he did not believe, parading his rejection of orthodoxy and abandoning his proper calling. "Is social service to take the place of the preached word as the mightiest of elevating forces known to man?" True, the severest economic depression the nation had ever known brought much uncertainty and challenged virtually all authority. But the preacher may still proclaim a knowable and lovable personal God; he may still, despite all that biblical scholarship and students of world religions had to say, affirm Jesus Christ as "finally the ultimate revelation" of that God; and he may still find in human personality that which must be aided on its way to fulfillment and abundance. Above all else, today's preacher, like all great preachers of the past, must concentrate not on religion's theoretical and metaphysical queries but on the solid, pressing duty of applying religion to practical problems: "making men better persons to live in a better world."[3] We have had quite enough of "the subjunctive Protestant pulpit," a pulpit all too ready to substitute a sterile rationalism for revealed religion, all too eager to throw "a veil of rational mist over Mount Zion, thus obscuring its rugged beauty."[4]

With only a couple of exceptions the most popular preachers in the mid-1920s were those who followed the advice concerning the practical application of religion offered above. Revelation, not reason, reigned. Practical application rather than metaphysical musing prevailed. But basic cultural shifts and pressing social issues could not everywhere be ignored. The criticisms noted demonstrate that in many Protestant pulpits across the land, those shifts and those issues were in fact not ignored. So far as the words preached in these pulpits were concerned, the most disturbing feature to many a critic – both clerical and lay – was the declining authority of the Bible. Over the course of sixty years, at least four factors combined to erode the biblical force of the Protestant pulpit. First, of course, was the direct challenge to the historicity and reliability of the Bible itself. On this very point, the dramatic trial on a charge of questioning "the inerrancy of Holy Scripture" of Presbyterian professor C. A. Briggs (Union Theological Seminary, New York City) in the final decade of the nineteenth century only presaged the turmoil that would afflict every major denomination, to one degree or another, in the twentieth century. And although most pulpits did not themselves turn hot with controversy, many cooled their use of "Thus saith the Lord." Second, as indicated, many preachers identified so closely with current causes (World War I, for one example; pacifist crusades in the 1920s, for another) that they lost something of biblical time frames and worldviews.

But social activism had its precise opposite in a kind of social insulation that concentrated on, above all else, personal improvement and self-help. Although this trend reached an apogee in the 1950s with Norman Vincent Peale, the wide strain can be traced back readily at least to Baptist Russell H. Conwell's famous "Acres of Diamonds," a lecture first delivered in 1890 and repeated thereafter with such frequency and effect as to enable Conwell to establish the college that became Temple University. Conwell, under the influence of New Thought's transcendental optimism, concentrated on the psychological more than the theological or biblical: You too can find health, happiness, and prosperity – especially prosperity. Prosperous Christians, Conwell argued, can do more for the world than impoverished ones, so it is a Christian's duty to get rich. Fourth and somewhat subtler in its impact was the gradual displacement of "preachin'" by the more carefully and self-consciously constructed service of worship. In the process, all across the country the pulpit, and its conspicuously large Bible, were moved off to the side, both literally and figuratively, to be replaced by altar or table, stained glass or baptistry, cross or reredos, flags or flowers.

It is true that countervailing forces could also be found to keep the preached Word from slipping off stage altogether. By the end of the 1920s, at least, the "acids of modernity" began to acquire a most un-

pleasant taste, certainly for such influential communicators as Harry
Emerson Fosdick and Walter Lippmann. It seemed to many critics that
the remnant to be saved by science made Calvinism's estimates look
generous. Pinning one's hopes on the triumphs of psychology and sociology, they thought, resulted in rhetoric that had begun to sound
unconvincing, or worse. So one might return to biblical preaching if
only because the Bible's flaws no longer looked unique. Additionally,
biblical translations of the sort that would reach both pulpit and pew
enlivened interest in the Book. An American Standard Version aroused
some parishes at the beginning of the century, although it did not dis-
lodge the KJV from its authorized throne. But the preparation of the
Revised Standard Version in the 1940s and 1950s, then a purely Protestant effort, drew the establishment together not only in defense of the
translation but, perhaps more surprisingly, in its pervasive use. With the
Bible grabbing newspaper headlines, the pulpits found that book harder
to ignore. Indeed, biblical scholars turned from criticism to reconstruction, leading to a "rediscovery of the Bible" in both classroom and
church, among both laity and clergy. Fosdick's widely read *Modern Use
of the Bible* (1924, with many subsequent reprintings) greatly assisted in
popularizing this "rediscovery" so that "adult Bible class" was no longer
a contradiction in terms. The sermon, despite the many criticisms and
controversies, never totally lost its biblical base, nor the parish its biblical
loyalty. Yet by 1960 it was no longer sufficient to quote the Bible as
though all argument could in this way be settled, nor could all of the
establishment's responsibility be discharged in sentimental retreats to
private piety or nineteenth-century hymnody.

The Minister's Status

What suffered even more in these sixty years was the image of
the minister: his role, his function, his self-esteem, his social standing, his
political and economic clout. If the Sacred Word lost authority, so inevitably did the dispenser and interpreter of that Word. No one was prepared to denounce the minister, as religion was still deemed a "good" in
American society and religious leaders still rated as most trustworthy in
public-opinion polls, especially in the postwar revivalism of the late
1940s. While many preachers continued to win loyal and devoted follow-
ings, others wrestled with the question of their central and defining
function. Was the preacher chiefly a truth-revealer, a counselor, an administrator, a scholar, a fund-raiser, or a community leader? Churches
too grappled with this question, sometimes assisting the clergyman in his
struggle, sometimes aggravating and intensifying the conflict. Churches

with a strong liturgical tradition (Episcopalians and Lutherans, for example) found themselves less tossed about, even as their clergy found themselves less susceptible to every wind of doctrine – or of politics. Others, in the "free" and often freewheeling churches, searched for some assurance of what, above all else, the minister should be. Of course, part of his duty was to visit the sick, marry the young, bury the old, oversee the "physical plant," and address the local Rotarians. But these duties spoke not to the essence, only to the accidents of being a Protestant minister in twentieth-century America.

The older image lingered: The minister was primarily a preacher, perhaps a prophet, possibly even a theologian. From his training in the past and his sermon preparation in the present, he was to be God's spokesman to his own faithful flock. This, after all, was his presumed area of expertise – and the twentieth century worried more and more about expertise. Not politics or business or medicine or social reform represented his special authority, but he (or gradually she) should be weighed and hired according to his ability to interpret, defend, and apply the truths of the Christian religion. In denominational journals, much attention was given to the minister's continuing education, to his library, and to his understanding of contemporary theology if not his contribution thereto.

While early theological liberalism may have accentuated the freedom from biblical language and dogma, neo-orthodoxy reversed this trend within the establishment. As Lloyd Averill noted, the preacher influenced by Barth, Niebuhr, and others returned with new confidence and conviction to "the biblical record as the only source of our knowledge of God's [saving] act done once for all." With an eye cocked at the liberal pulpiteers, Averill added: "This means, then, that biblical preaching will displace preaching in which the primary appeal is made to generalized human experience, for the simple reason that such generalized experience cannot yield God's saving action."[5] In these circles, the pulpit was expected to echo less of rationalism and social activism, speak less in the subjunctive mood and more in the mood of proclamation of the great biblical themes of incarnation, atonement, justification, and sin.

In choosing their clergy, as most of these Protestant churches continued to do, the laity intended that the clergyman (and his wife) be something of a moral model. Religion and morality were closely tied, nowhere so closely as in the sometimes unreal expectations concerning the standards for clerical behavior. In the earlier decades, divorce was unthinkable, adultery (rumored or real) unforgivable. Honesty in both language and deed was required, and perfect humility appropriate. Some denominations worried about the example set in the consumption of

alcohol and use of tobacco, the former especially when prohibition sentiment was at its height, the latter particularly in regions whose economy
did not depend on cultivation of the leaf. Others, scorning the private
sins singled out by lingering blue laws, asked for moral achievement in
fighting community crime, ignorance, ill health, and poverty. The pastor in any case should not be seen as passively reflecting the ever-declin-
ing standards around him; above all, he must not be indifferent to the
necessity of "taking a stand," wherever the line might be drawn, whatever the issue at stake.

In the search for function, the minister was sometimes in danger of
becoming the Universal Friend, the ever-ready volunteer, the community's one-man United Way. Some clergy plunged happily into such activity, even as many of the laity reveled in their minister's high visibility
in this area. One layman in 1924 put it bluntly: "An excellent way to
choose a minister . . . would be to send him down on Main Street and
around to the school buildings to chat with the business men and the
children about politics, civic affairs, football, and geography, and then
let the business men and the children vote on him."[6] No irony was
intended. Others spoke with suitable vagueness of community leadership, outgoing nature, memberships in clubs, lodges, and business
associations. Although membership in PTAs was predominantly female
across America, such male membership as could be found was primarily
clerical. Many clergy saw the true test of their leadership and authority to
be not in the pulpit or parish but in the wider circle of school boards,
chambers of commerce, directors and trustees and toastmasters. In general, the faithful flock who called him and paid him felt not neglected
thereby but vindicated.

A major shift in the period from 1900 to 1960 was from preacher to
counselor. A whole field of new training and literature sprang into being
that turned counseling from a casual sideline into a primary pastoral
preoccupation. Clergymen were urged to talk less and listen more, to
augment their study of the Bible, the church, and theology with study of
the individual personality and the forces that directed its development.
Elwood Worcester, an Episcopal clergyman, in 1906 launched the Em-
manuel Movement, which dedicated itself to bringing the insights of
psychology into an active relationship with religion at the parish level.
Anton T. Boisen unleashed a barrage of new journals aimed at making
pastoral psychology (a phrase used as the title of one such journal) a
routine part of the clergyman's job description. And Seward Hiltner,
with both theological and psychological insight, tried to rescue "spiritual
healing" from the edges of America's religious life and place it at the
center. In saving others, the minister risked losing himself, or at least

replacing a spiritual depth with a pop psychology surface. As E. Brooks Holifield points out, the path from salvation to self-realization is not all upward or noble. "Most sermons that masqueraded as personal counseling probably collapsed in banality." Adjustment often meant success rather than reform, and self-realization could be discussed and marketed quite apart from the Christian religion. Pastoral counseling was most appropriate, Holifield concluded, but it should not be "exalted as the paradigm of clerical activity."[7]

Finally, in all the concerns about what his true role should be, the clergyman struggled to maintain his professional status among the other professions. For a century or more, America had indulged in an orgy of growing professionalism, with respect and rewards growing accordingly. The clerical profession, which had enjoyed such great prestige in the colonial period, found itself in contest with, and largely defeated by, the other newer professions. When clergymen became somewhat self-conscious about the perquisites of their profession – the railroad passes and tax exemptions and charitable gifts of goods or services – they often chose to relinquish these, but rarely with any compensating elevation of rewards. Haggling about salary suggested a preoccupation with material matters that was unseemly in a minister. Maintaining clergy on a level with doctors and lawyers, managers and corporate presidents, suggested a cost that was unacceptable to the laity. The earlier concern of the radical reformers about a "hireling ministry" resulted in a strange sort of compromise in the Protestant establishment: Ministers shall be paid, but not much.

Denominational organs reported surveys that showed clerical salaries falling behind not only those of professionals but often of craftsmen and merchants as well; they then reported on the exodus from the ministry to better-rewarded areas of employment; they then reported that no one paid much attention. Although salary variations did exist among the leading denominations, those variations were negligible compared with the great gap between the pay of the clergy as a class and that of doctors, lawyers, jurists, academicians, engineers, and many civil servants. In 1923, the *Literary Digest* noted that the weekly salaries of Protestant ministers (e.g., Congregationalist, $28.86; Northern Methodist, $29.44) ranked considerably below those of plumbers ($47.17), masons ($51.57), plasterers ($55.79), and bricklayers ($55.92).[8] More than two decades later, the U.S. Bureau of the Census noted that between 1939 and 1949, clergy dropped from the highest 30% of salaried workers to the lowest 30%. The median annual income for clergymen rose in that period from $1,264 to $2,319, a gain of 83%; the gain for all other white-collar professions in that same period averaged 122%.[9] In the struggle over image, the clergyman unsure of his role as prophet or moral leader, as citizen or therapist, found little reassurance in observing the swift deterioration of his economic and professional standing.

The Laity: Leadership and Devotional Life

Although many of the Protestant bodies vociferously rejected an authoritarian, sacramental priesthood, the expected elevation of the laity did not regularly or readily emerge as the clear consequence. The "priesthood of all believers" (or, as James Luther Adams has it, the "prophethood of all believers")[10] often turned out to be more cant than clear achievement. By 1900 the professionalism of the clerical class, the pervading reality in all seven denominations, threatened to increase the distance between pastor and people. Educational standards still varied, and social standing shifted not only from denomination to denomination but from region to region and even from parish to parish. Nonetheless, among all the Sisters an imaginary iconostasis separated the altar/table from the pew. If conscious and timely efforts were not made to involve the laity in meaningful ways, the laity did not protest so much as simply opt out. In general, such newer sectarian groups in America as Jehovah's Witnesses, Pentecostals, and Mormons came much closer to achieving a priesthood and prophethood of all their members than did those denominations well on their way from the status of sect to that of church.

Women and men in the pew were not ignored since the church's very survival depended upon their goodwill and support. The absence of all governmental subsidy or support in American religion stimulated each local church, when confronted with a sea of empty pews, to take quick and energetic remedial action. But the involvement of the laity tended to be episodic, restricted, and at a level that virtually guaranteed a growing gap between leadership and membership. Sometimes the clergy took deliberate steps to narrow that separation, and sometimes the laity seized the initiative. A Baptist church in Pasadena, California, for example, decided in 1921 that its pastors had become too casual about the historic affirmations of the Christian faith and instructed its pulpit committee to recommend only such candidates as were willing to subscribe to that local church's own detailed confession of faith. Lutherans found this action so commendable that they urged it on their own communion: "Here is a congregation that does not shift the responsibility for maintaining the faith upon the theologians and educators of the Church, but itself assumes that responsibility and declares the faith to which it adheres and stands pledged." Enough of unsupervised pulpit performance, the *Lutheran* editorially concluded.[11]

Much of the private piety of the membership, however, remained just that: private, in the home, within the family, at the table, by the bedside. The phenomenally successful Methodist publication, the *Upper Room,* suggested how large that hidden piety might be. Launched in 1935, this Protestant "Book of Hours" reached a circulation of over three million within a single generation. Guiding the faithful in a regimen of daily Bible reading, meditation, and prayer, the *Upper Room* represented the most successful venture in encouraging young and old within the churches to do more than occupy a pew one hour per week. Religious best-sellers like *The Nazarene* (1939) by Sholem Asch and *The Robe* (1942) by Lloyd C. Douglas expressed as well as enhanced this devotional side of American religious life. And the greatest best-seller of all, the Bible, appeared along with study outlines, concordances, commentaries, atlases, and aids without number that found a market far beyond that of the seminary student or the clerical class. To look only at the decade of the 1920s as an instance of this Protestant vigor in biblical translation, these major efforts may be noted: "An American Translation" of the New Testament by Edgar J. Goodspeed (Baptist) in 1923; *The Riverside New Testament* that same year by William G. Ballantine (Congregationalist); the first modern-speech translation done by a woman, Helen Barrett Montgomery (Baptist) in 1924; a new translation in 1927 of the Old Testament (and four years later the entire Bible) under the guidance of J. M. P. Smith (Baptist); also the completion in 1927 of Congregationalist Charles Foster Kent's six-volume *Student's Old Testament Logically and Chronologically Arranged.*

In the twentieth century and among establishment Protestants, a near-universal literacy could be assumed, as could a near-universal familiarity with the Bible or biblical materials. Rarely was the immediate leadership of the minister deemed a necessary condition for this quietly pervasive devotion and understanding. Biblical language, biblical history, biblical anecdote and epigram constituted the common frame of discourse, as Giles Gunn has shown for arts and letters and James T. Johnson for law, politics, and rhetoric.[12]

One of the happy by-products of "liturgical renewal" that followed World War II was that in many instances it resulted in a greater involvement by the laity in public worship. Conscious efforts elevated formal participation through congregational responses and affirmations, or through prescribed leadership in the service of worship. In some traditions lay participation was more spontaneous than planned, whereas in others the role of the laity in public worship was long established but restricted. The sort of movement that all the world could watch in Roman Catholicism after Vatican II had been going on, unevenly, within the Protestant establishment for a generation or two before. In general, the Protestants moved from *ex cathedra* to *intra cathedra,* from a single voice to many voices. Of course, the laity, both male and female, had long been active behind the scenes: on boards and vestries, in committees and societies, directing campaigns for membership and funds, encouraging missionary activity and supervising local charity. Important symbolic significance, however, accompanied the systematic effort to make public worship more a partnership and less a performance, to create a broader understanding of what a service of worship was supposed to do and what riches of tradition waited to be tapped. The real value here as elsewhere, however, depended on making certain that the increased role for the laity never declined to the status of the merely token, that increased participation also resulted in increased understanding and authority.

Even the ecumenical movement, often perceived as the special preserve of only top-level clerical bureaucrats, turned out at voting time to involve far more than those ministers who had been elevated to "headquarters." The lesson came late for some, but eventually to all, that ecumenical successes required educational labors at the grass roots. Persons who had not in their lifetime been asked to think about the nature of the church, the orders of ministry, the efficacy of the sacraments, were by the 1930s being asked to think, reflect, and decide. Instant courses in church history and denominational polity informed and involved the laity so that they could become participants in a genuine dialogue rather than passive observers in a process far beyond their ken. Whether any particular ecumenical proposal succeeded or failed, the result tended to be the same: a more sophisticated and educated congregation, both in head and in members.

Each of the seven denominations with which we are concerned gave much attention to active merger proposals. Congregationalists, Methodists, Lutherans, and Presbyterians all succeeded in consummating significant unions or reunions: Congregationalists in 1957, Methodists in 1968, the Lutherans in 1960 and 1962, the Presbyterians in 1958. (In the case of Lutherans and Presbyterians, even more significant mergers were to follow in the 1980s.) Over a period of many years Episcopalians carried on conversations with Eastern Orthodoxy, Lutheranism, and Roman Catholicism, while Baptists held discussions with the Church of the Brethren. Disciples, whose very origin lay in a concern for church unity, joined with many others in promoting greater cooperation; naturally, they found the Consultation on Church Union, proposed in 1960, congenial to their heritage and mission. This Consultation, set in motion by the Presbyterian Eugene Carson Blake in the Episcopal cathedral of Bishop James Pike in San Francisco, soon involved all major Protestant denominations except the Lutherans.

Aside from private devotion and public worship, along with the occasional bursts of involvement that ecumenical decisions required, lay activity undergirded and often directed the educational and service dimension of the local church. Historically in America, the Sunday school frequently preceded the formal organization of a church, part of the reason being that only lay leadership was necessary for the former. With an ordained clergy often unavailable, lay women and men could and did create their own ecclesiastical forerunner or substitute. Lay domination of the Sunday school movement continued through much of the period under review. In some situations, "adult Bible classes" took on a life of their own, enjoying such success that renting movie houses and lodge halls became necessary. In other cases, laity-led youth programs (Sunday evenings as well as Sunday mornings) proved the chief method of recruiting and retaining an age group that had persistently challenged or defied the church. Many saw the Sunday school as the necessary complement to the public school, and equally urgent in the process of Americanizing and Christianizing the nation. In the eyes of the Religious Education Association (REA), founded in 1903, the churches bore responsibility for the religious instruction "not only of their own children, but also of the American people as a whole." At that time concern was expressed that only 60–70 percent of America's children were in Sunday schools, a figure that deteriorated rather than improved.[13] The ambition was great, and the laity carried the greater burden.

In general, the educational arm joined the ministerial arm in cooperative endeavor. When, however, religious education began to develop its separate agenda – summer camps, weekday schools, graded lessons, "a conduct curriculum," national and international agencies – some clergy nervously wondered if they were still in charge of what went on in their own churches. In 1930 one minister asked, "Is there a danger that the program of religious education will tend to supplant the pulpit or to undermine its place of influence and importance in the Church?" He proceeded to answer the question in the negative, but only by arguing that the pastor must "take his rightful place in the more complete program of the local Church." Pastor and people must work together more closely, neither exercising a monopoly in its own sphere, but each strengthening and supporting the other.[14]

Others worried about the undifferentiated nature of a so-called religious education that seemed inclined to leave biblical truths behind for a kind of behaviorism or humanism that either conflicted with the church's own heritage or abandoned the "religious" in religious education. We must ensure a Christian education, some argued, and to do that we must educate within the boundaries of a specific tradition. Six years after the founding of the REA, a Lutheran academic declared that the church school must not be guided by the university and the trends of the larger society. Quite the contrary, its purpose was to transmit that truth placed peculiarly in its charge. "The Lutheran Church has the most scriptural body of doctrine in Christendom. Why then should not all her schools inculcate that doctrine and defend the truth? . . . Why then should [truth] be thrust aside or ignored simply because it is not included in the programs of would-be leading educators of the time?" Our church schools, he concluded, should be Lutheran in particular, Christian in general, and worldly not at all.[15]

If creating "the Democracy of God" (the phrase is from George Coe, long-time president of the REA and professor of Psychology of Religion at Union Seminary and Columbia University) remained the grand goal of the REA at the national level, the goal at the local level was to see that clergy and laity worked not against but with each other in their efforts to mold young minds and hearts to embrace those verities that the older generation honored.

Churches Beyond the Parishes

The church, however, also faced a larger community that, as circumstances might require, it could serve or correct or uplift. At the parish level, several issues pushed the churches beyond their own walls into and among the multitudes. Prohibition occupied much Protestant attention not only in the passage of the Eighteenth Amendment but during all the years of its operation, in the election of 1928, in the crisis of repeal, and well beyond. When local churches lost the national option to prohibit the sale of alcohol, they fought for the local option, as the American map took on a crisscross pattern of wet and dry counties. Often in these struggles laity surrendered their political innocence and churches their credibility. Temperance crusades and temperance pledges accompanied or substituted for political maneuvering, until the drive to rid the nation of alcohol seemed not so much a manifestation of the social gospel as a subversion of it. Paul Carter concluded: "Only rarely did the dry leaders understand how much they were advancing the secularist bias of the rising generation by causing it to associate the Church simultaneously with a joyless legalistic morality and with dubious ethical practices in its achievement – in short, with hypocrisy."[16]

The churches also wrestled with the fact of immigration and eventually confronted the First Disillusionment, namely, that all those millions who emigrated to America did not thereby become converts to Protestantism. Ugly manifestations of nativism in the nineteenth century led to unequal exclusions of foreigners in the twentieth. Much of the new policy of immigration was designed to preserve the old dominance of Protestantism in America. Non-Protestant countries were by definition backward, undemocratic, and likely to send to America persons more difficult to assimilate into the social whole. So immigration must be slowed or stopped, and the task of converting those aliens already here must be accelerated. "Never has the foreign-born or alien problem confronted us so seriously," the *Lutheran* reported in 1920. "The 17,000,000 foreign-born in our midst, and the aliens arriving in our ports, now at the rate of 5000 daily," and with millions more poised to come, forced the "old stock" either to decide whether to flee from the cities where immigrants settled, or to join with them in the great task "of Christianizing, Americanizing the non-Christian and the un-American."[17] "Home missions" in the first quarter of the twentieth century meant above all else a mission to the immigrant.

The concern for this foreignness in the American midst could turn into a concern about racial intolerance and bigotry. In relating to the newly arrived Jewish immigrants, for example, perhaps understanding and acceptance more than mission and conversion should define the goal. Establishment Protestantism, at both local and national levels, pledged itself to resist the anti-Semitism typified by Henry Ford's *Dearborn Independent* in the 1920s. Ministers signed up for the cause, and local churches conducted educational campaigns against a social sin that did not die with Henry Ford. Denominational and ecumenical leaders said what needed to be said; genuine "conversion" to an inclusive humanitarianism was more difficult to measure. The Ku Klux Klan, an institutionalization of the resentment against and hostility toward Jews, blacks, and Catholics, divided many local churches into pro-Klan and anti-Klan factions, such division being by no means limited to the South.

Liberal Protestantism, always in danger of being an elite Protestantism, did not establish an enviable record with respect to blacks in the first sixty years of this century. Negroes were preponderantly Protestant (chiefly Baptist and Methodist), but this religious commonality proved incapable of transcending racial diversity. For the most part blacks maintained separate denominations and whites segregated worship. Resolutions were passed, lynching was denounced, integrated meetings – with some tentativeness – were held, and commissions on race relations were appointed. Little of all this filtered down to the parish level, however, with any genuine effectiveness, or with any radical reversal of traditional patterns of voting, schooling, worshiping, dining, dating, and thinking. With a few daring exceptions, such as Clarence Jordan's Koinonia Community in Georgia and certain Pentecostal sects in their formative stages, "race relations" persisted in being more a topic to discuss than a reality to reform. Only in the 1960s did parishes become significantly involved; only then did they discover that they were in fact on the front lines.

On the broader issues of economic and social justice, of industrial democracy and grinding poverty, the local churches could not remain immune to the nation's problems nor to their own. In the aftermath of World War I, clergy and laity together reflected on the limits and actual effects (as opposed to purposes) of war. Pacifism reached the pews as Peace Sundays were declared and peace messages heard. The only rearmament worth talking about was moral rearmament, announced Lutheran Frank Buchman in the 1930s in words that reached far beyond his own circle. The Disciples leader Kirby Page, using language that had no denominational limit or label, wrote in 1937 that "the way of Jesus and the method of war stand in utter opposition to each other." Methodists, Episcopalians, Baptists, Congregationalists, and Presbyterians all joined in celebrating Armistice Day in their own communions and communities as a day to declare "war no more." In a poll conducted in 1934, over 60 percent of the nation's clergymen maintained that the churches should go on record as "refusing to sanction or support any future war." Another instance of social concern had penetrated into the pews.[18]

The depression of the 1930s made it impossible to dodge questions concerning capital and labor, means of production and distribution, distances between rich and poor, and the appropriate role of both government and the churches. By 1932, churches as well as banks were closing, as parish budgets declined or collapsed, as ministers (until they lost their own jobs) tried to help church members keep theirs. It was time to give charity until it gave out; then it was time to ask what, fundamentally, was wrong with the system.[19] Although there was plenty of social gospel theory available from earlier decades, the theory had tended to attract attention only in those communities where bitter strikes or lockouts polarized a church. In the thirties, however, all were affected to some degree and all gave more interested attention to economic issues. This is not to say that establishment Protestantism urged its followers with one voice away from capitalism and toward socialism. In fact, the voting evidence in 1932 and 1936, though not definitive, suggests that the Republican candidates in those years received the greater support from this particular establishment.[20] John C. Bennett in 1939 complained that the New Deal, if it succeeded at all, would have to do so against the opposition of most Protestant churches.[21] Yet denominational journals gave ever-increasing coverage to economic and social questions, for these issues had become the bread-and-butter, the roof-and-heat questions for many American families.

In these large questions as well as in those that followed World War II, one distressing development became ever clearer: The perceptions and position of clergy and laity were moving further and further apart. Perhaps too much was happening too soon, perhaps clergy spent too much time at headquarters and not enough at home, perhaps a non–circuit-riding membership had far more invested in the status quo than a mobile (not necessarily upwardly) clergy did. Perhaps, as one disenchanted observer noted, preaching produced more and more irritation, less and less conviction. Whatever the case, by the 1960s it was obvious that the clergy often did not speak for their churches, and that headquarters often spoke only for headquarters.

In *The Gathering Storm in the Churches,* published at the end of the 1960s, Jeffrey Hadden cited a variety of surveys, not always precisely comparable, that revealed the gap between clergy and laity in doctrinal and social issues, in attitudes toward civil rights demonstrations and ecumenical proposals. While similar surveys do not exist on prohibition issues in the twenties or pacifist hopes in the thirties, my own surmise is that pastor and people then spoke more nearly in unison than was the case a generation later. The implications of this variance in perception and conviction for establishment Protestantism are many, but among them is the uneasy suspicion that many churchmen and -women felt bereft of or betrayed by leadership. Evangelism seemed to have been abandoned or downplayed; foreign missions had become more fruitless or pointless than in an earlier age. Many among the laity might well have asked, What is the point in keeping the club going when we can no longer agree either on constitution or on bylaws? This portrayal might be far too grim, but at a minimum one can argue that these deep divisions within the local fellowships – once the sixties had ended – made the very perpetuation of those fellowships more problematic.

A Secular Nation against a Protestant Ethos

After the Civil War, northern Protestantism (which at that point surely was establishment Protestantism) seized the opportunity to redeem the South and make America whole. Congregationalist Lyman

Abbott asked, "[What are] we going to do with the conquered territory?" And the "we" meant the Protestantism of the Northeast: its task with respect to the emancipated slave and to those churches that had "preached their congregations into rebellion." Reconstruction meant among other things "the establishment of free churches and the proclamation of a full gospel"; this was a task not for government to perform but for those Christian churches whose special relationship to the nation uniquely qualified them for the task.[22] When at the end of the nineteenth century the Spanish-American War was fought and quickly won, Protestants worried about their ability to lead and mold a republic now become a world power. They also worried about the annexation of the Philippines, a predominantly Catholic country, and about the necessity for Protestant missionaries to turn the people to a more American form of Christianity. In World War I Protestant clergy joined together under a Presbyterian president to spread throughout the Western world the blessings of their religion and form of government.

Sometime between the end of that war and the 1960s, the Protestant establishment suffered its Second Disillusionment, namely, the realization that no one was any longer watching the nameless city set upon the no-longer-existing hill. Like the New England Puritans after Cromwell, establishment Protestants after the Holocaust and Hiroshima no longer pursued their errand into the wilderness with the same conviction and intensity. In his 1951 survey of the first half of the twentieth century, *Christian Century* editor Paul Hutchinson wrote that men and women no longer seemed to have control over their own destinies. Impersonal forces had grown too vast, moral decisions too remote from the power brokers. Once, Hutchinson wrote, "the Protestant church press" had been "one of the most potent elements in the nation's journalism." Once denominational colleges had shaped higher education in America. Once church hospitals and other church social agencies had been the chief instruments of social welfare. Once Protestants shaped America's cities, but now they have fled the cities. And once Protestant voices made a difference in national concerns, "but Protestant influence on public affairs is by no means as direct or as confident as it was fifty years ago."[23]

Similarly, churchman Theodore O. Wedel at midcentury found that the peculiar emphasis within Protestantism upon the sermon, and a biblical sermon at that, had given way to a Sunday service where pulpit authority disappeared. The brevity of the modern sermon suggested that, among other things, not much remained to be said. So much of the church's activity had become an end in itself and could claim no loftier goal than perpetuating an existence without direction or delight. In short, "We're not sure why we are here, but let's make certain that we all come back next week."[24] By the end of the 1960s, statistics no longer

Varieties of religious experience. "Voluntary prayer" after the Supreme Court's 1962 decision. Religious News Service photo.

gave comfort to establishment Protestantism, nor did the declining enrollments in Sunday schools and seminaries. Social engineering supplanted evangelism in the churches, Professor Donald G. Bloesch (Dubuque Theological Seminary) complained, just as "group dynamics has edged out common prayer and Bible study." "Ministers today are espousing a secular religion that has no anchorage in the sacred."[25] And so it appeared that secular forces had everywhere taken charge, that pluralism was no momentary aberration, that hands were no longer clean, nor were godly-nation models any longer available. Protestantism did not equal the whole of Christianity, and Christianity did not equal the whole of religion, and all of religion in the nation did not equal the American way of life.

In much of the sixty-year period under study, however, the language of Christian nation and the hope of Protestant destiny lingered. The public schools came in for about as much attention in those years as they did before 1900 and as they would again after 1960. Catholics since the nineteenth century had charged that the public schools were essentially a Protestant enterprise. Protestants had vigorously denied the allegation, and just as vigorously pursued the goal. Public-school teachers, principals, and superintendents were regularly Protestant – or at least not Catholic. Protestant Bibles were read, Protestant prayers offered, Protestant hymns sung. And as this gradually began to change, Protestant churches argued for an even closer alliance with "their" schools.

In 1920 the official organ of the United Lutheran Church reported with joyous approval a Bible study plan adopted in Atchison, Kansas, for use in the public schools. The Bible, the editor noted, was appropriately studied in the schools for "its truths are objective, as are the truths of history and science, and it asks no favors from the teacher." The editor did note, however, that "a proper person, that is a Christian," should have charge of this elective course.[26] The Disciples in 1921 gave space to an Arkansas editor who, vowing his loyalty to the principle of separation of church and state, declared in the spirit of Horace Mann that "our Public School needs the influence of, and the spiritual uplift of, Christianity minus any touch of sectarianism." It should also be minus, he made clear, any touch of "popery." "Protestant America must be alert and active in promoting, making more efficient, and influencing the public school."[27]

In the 1930s, a Methodist publication surveyed all the encouraging signs of close cooperation between Protestantism and the public schools. An Indiana county had, since 1921, offered Bible courses in all ten of its high schools; North Carolina in 1944 had Bible courses in one hundred towns reaching some twenty thousand students. An Iowa pastor reported that the clergy in his town visited all rural and elementary schools providing lessons of "moral guidance" based on the Bible. In Kalamazoo, Michigan, daily Bible reading was offered in all classes, with daily devotions, religious drama, and Bible memory work being part of the regular program.[28]

The International Council of Religious Education, speaking for much if not all of establishment Protestantism, at midcentury called on the public schools to offer "a theistic interpretation of reality in those communities where this interpretation of life is held by the vast majority of persons." Protestant churches had a right "to expect that the school will not teach a materialistic atheism," wrote Gerald E. Knoff of the Council staff, adding: "I believe schools and churches can work together much more closely than they customarily do."[29] A generation later such sentiments would be identified with the new Christian Right, but in the earlier decades of the twentieth century they were commonplace among virtually all Protestants. Also commonplace were the united efforts to see that no tax monies reached the Roman Catholic parochial schools.

When in the early sixties the United States Supreme Court at last struck down the practice of (Protestant) religion in the public schools, the widespread condemnation of those decisions revealed the pervasive if unexamined assumption of a cozy connection between the religious establishment and public education.[30] At that point, many Protestant denominations decided that parochial education deserved more serious attention than they had heretofore been willing to give it. As Bishop James A. Pike noted in 1952, "If no other way can be found for a Christian orientation in our schools, we have no other alternative but to pull out lock-stock-and-barrel and develop as effective a school system as our consecrated devotion and sacrifice can provide."[31]

If Protestants by 1960 had essentially given up on the public schools, what of the nation itself? Had it too been turned over to the secularists? Had it too become the agent of materialistic atheism? Here, understandably, Protestants revealed greater ambivalence, since it was difficult to conceive of pulling out of the nation "lock, stock, and barrel." Here also much sophisticated and even agonized attention focused on the churches' involvement in politics, the extent to which direct political action was appropriate, the degree to which "moral man" may reshape "immoral society."

Presbyterian Life in 1948 sponsored a symposium on "the role of the church in the civic life of our democracy." Most participants emphasized the subtle but strong leavening power of Christian principles as lived out in every sector of society as opposed to direct endorsement of candidates or programs. (One spoke of the Eighteenth Amendment as a "disastrous defeat" for American Protestantism.) The New Testament Church, argued Clarence Macartney, "was not given a commission to reconstruct human society or to change the form of the world's political institutions." On the other hand, declared Robert W. Frank, "the Church should put on the whole armor of God and be foremost in the struggle for a more decent, a more just, a more Christian social order." Somewhere in between these poles, Elizabeth R. Steele observed that "when the Christian Church educates the conscience and inspires the will to righteousness, it is doing more to reform the social order than if it were to speak out on every public question."[32] Although the parishes were not certain just where lines of political commitment should be drawn, they in general showed more hesitancy and uncertainty than did the national bodies speaking in their behalf.[33]

During the turbulent decades between 1900 and 1960, many Protestant leaders interpreted the cacophony of events more in terms of challenge than of defeat. Protestantism was being called to ever-larger tasks, was being asked to assume larger burdens. Yet while the challenges took on ever more Bunyanesque proportion, the solutions shrank and withered before such towering might. The Protestant establishment still spoke with authority for Protestantism and perhaps for much of religion besides. But as a cultural authority in a nation of growing diversity and indifference, mainline Protestantism exerted an influence, as Paul Hutchinson wrote in 1951, "by no means as direct or as confident as it was fifty years ago."

When after 1960 the discussion of Protestantism and American democracy shifted to the softer ground of "civil religion," this new terminology represented, at least in part, a recognition that establishment Protestantism no longer directed the destiny of the nation. It appeared to be having enough difficulty with its own destiny. Proponents of civil religion hoped, however, to plumb the nation's past in such a way as to rescue essential religious insights, a covenantal relationship, for example, or a sense of Providence's grand design, in order to assist a nation and a people skimming without rudder or ballast across a dangerous sea. Yet a religion beyond and above all denominational expressions of religion intrigued academia far more than it did ecclesia. Sitting in the Protestant pews (or absenting themselves from them), many devout and troubled church members simply wondered where their Protestant America had gone.

NOTES

I wish to express appreciation to Ray F. Kibler III for his able and timely research assistance.

1 C. C. Morrison, *The American Pulpit* (Chicago: Christian Century Press, 1925).
2 L. H. Larimer, "The Need for Positive Preaching," *Lutheran Quarterly* 30 (January 1909): 94.
3 C. A. Jackson, Jr., "The Call to Preach – Model 1930," *Christian Advocate,* May 1930, 650–1.
4 Marcus L. Gray, "The Protestant Pulpit: A Study," *Christian Advocate,* February 28, 1930, 265.
5 "Proclamation and Ministry," *Foundations: A Baptist Journal of History and Theology* 2 (July 1959): 227.
6 A Layman, "Some Thoughts on Preaching," *Christian Advocate,* May 9, 1924, 587.
7 E. Brooks Holifield, *A History of Pastoral Care in America* (Nashville: Abingdon Press, 1983), 221, 356.

8   The *Literary Digest* sparked this discussion in its December 15, 1923, issue. For denominational comment on these data see, e.g., W. A. Tyson, "Ministerial Support," *Christian Advocate,* January 11, 1924, and February 1, 1924.

9   The Religious News Service picked up the Bureau of the Census report, thereby ensuring a wide coverage in the denominational press. See, e.g., *The Christian-Evangelist,* November 16, 1955, 1126.

10 See the anthology of Adams's writings edited by George Beach, *The Prophethood of All Believers* (Boston: Beacon Press, 1986).

11 Unsigned editorial, "A Pulpit That Is Wedded to a Faith," *Lutheran,* February 10, 1921, 16; quoting from the Baptist periodical, *The Watchman-Examiner.*

12 Giles Gunn, *The Bible and American Arts and Letters* (1983); James T. Johnson, *The Bible in American Law, Politics, and Political Rhetoric* (1985), both volumes published jointly by Fortress Press (Philadelphia) and Scholars Press (Chico, Calif.). For more data on biblical translations, see Ernest Frerichs, *The Bible and Bibles in America,* especially the chapters by Keith R. Crim and Harold P. Scanlin (Atlanta: Scholars Press, 1988).

13 Presidential address of George A. Coe, in *Religious Education* 5(1910–11): 1–5.

14 *Christian Advocate,* February 14, 1930, 200–2.

15 Holmes Dysinger, "Our Church Schools: Their Object and Their Method," *Lutheran Quarterly* 39(July 1909): 426, 429.

16 Paul A. Carter, *The Decline and Revival of the Social Gospel* (Hamden, Conn.: Archon Press, 1971), 44.

17 S. D. Daugherty, "Fleeing From God's Work," *Lutheran,* October 21, 1920, 5.

18 Kirby Page, *Must We Go to War?* (New York: Farrar & Rinehart, 1937), 182–6. On Frank Buchman and his message, see his *Remaking the World* (1947; reprint London: Blandford Press, 1961).

19 Paul Carter, *Decline and Revival,* Chapter 11. For a useful instance of the social gospel working itself out at the parish level, see D. G. Paz, "The Anglican Response to Urban Social Dislocation in Omaha, 1875–1920," *Historical Magazine of the Protestant Episcopal Church* 51(June 1982): 131–46.

20 See Robert M. Miller, *American Protestantism and Social Issues, 1919–1939* (Chapel Hill: University of North Carolina Press, 1958), Chapter 8.

21 Quoted in Robert M. Miller, *How Shall They Hear without a Preacher? The Life of Ernest Freemont Tittle* (Chapel Hill: University of North Carolina Press, 1971), 372. In 1935 President Franklin D. Roosevelt appealed directly to the nation's clergy (in a mailing of over 120,000 letters) for their help in identifying the most pressing social and economic problems in their own communities. "Tell me where you feel our government can better serve our people," he wrote. The file of replies (over 30,000), now at the Roosevelt Library in Hyde Park, has not, as far as I know, been fully exploited. For attention to the replies from the Episcopal clergy, see Monroe Billington and Cal Clark, "The Episcopal Clergy and the New Deal," *Historical Magazine of the Protestant Episcopal Church* 52(September 1983): 293–305.

22   Lyman Abbott, "Southern Evangelization," *New Englander* 23 (1864): 699ff.
23   Paul Hutchinson, "American Protestantism at the Mid-Century Mark," *Religion in Life* 20(Spring 1951): 191–2. Nor did the author find any great comfort in the assertion of the respected Abraham Myerson (of the Harvard Medical School faculty) that he would continue to treat "the evolved theology of professional religionists" as a subject for abnormal psychology: "That which was holy in less critical times has become psychiatric in our own day" (201).
24   Theodore O. Wedel, "The Lost Authority of the Pulpit," *Theology Today* 9(July 1952): 165–6.
25   Donald G. Bloesch, "Why People Are Leaving the Churches," *Religion in Life* 38(Spring 1969): 93, 98.
26   "Religion in Public Schools," *Lutheran*, September 30, 1920, 3.
27   Herb Lewis, "Christianity and the American Public School," *Christian-Evangelist,* July 14, 1921, 837.
28   W. S. Fleming, "At Last Religion Returns to the Schools," *Christian Advocate,* September 14, 1944, 1146–7.
29   Gerald E. Knoff, "The Aims of Religious Education," *Christian Advocate,* September 21, 1950, 1132–3.
30   *Engel* v. *Vitale* (1962) and *Abingdon* v. *Schempp* (1963).
31   Quoted in *Foundations* 4(January 1961): 31.
32   "The Church and Politics: A Symposium," *Presbyterian Life* 1(1948): 14–18.
33   See Charles Y. Glock et al., *To Comfort and to Challenge* (Berkeley: University of California Press, 1967). This study was undertaken on behalf of the Department of Christian Social Relations of the National Council of the Protestant Episcopal Church.

SELECT BIBLIOGRAPHY

Carter, Paul A. *The Decline and Revival of the Social Gospel: Social and Political Liberalism in American Protestant Churches, 1920–1940.* Ithaca, N.Y.: Cornell University Press, 1954.
  The Spiritual Crisis of the Gilded Age. De Kalb, Ill.: Northern Illinois University Press, 1971.
Cauthen, Kenneth. *The Impact of American Religious Liberalism.* New York: Harper & Row, 1962.
Douglas, Mary, and Steven M. Tipton, eds. *Religion in America: Spirituality in a Secular Age.* Boston: Beacon Press, 1983.
Handy, Robert T. *A Christian America: Protestant Hopes and Historical Realities.* 2d ed. New York: Oxford University Press, 1984.
Holifield, E. Brooks. *A History of Pastoral Care in America.* Nashville, Tenn.: Abingdon Press, 1983.
Hudson, Winthrop S. *American Protestantism.* Chicago: University of Chicago Press, 1961.
Marty, Martin E. *Modern American Religion: The Irony of It All, 1893–1919.* Chicago: University of Chicago Press, 1986.

Righteous Empire: The Protestant Experience in America. New York: Dial Press, 1970.

Meyer, Donald B. *The Protestant Search for Political Realism, 1919–1941.* Berkeley, Calif.: University of California Press, 1960.

Michaelsen, Robert S., and Wade Clark Roof, eds. *Liberal Protestantism: Realities and Possibilities.* New York: Pilgrim Press, 1986.

Miller, Robert M. *American Protestantism and Social Issues, 1919–1939.* Chapel Hill: University of North Carolina Press, 1958.

Nash, Arnold S. *Protestant Thought in the Twentieth Century: Whence and Whither?* New York: Macmillan, 1951.

Wells, David F., and John D. Woodbridge, eds. *The Evangelicals: What They Believe, Who They Are, Where They Are Changing.* Nashville, Tenn.: Abingdon Press, 1975.

3

Ministry on the Margin: Protestants and Education

DOROTHY C. BASS

In the closing months of 1899, messianic predictions about various aspects of life in the coming century were not uncommon, particularly on the part of America's Protestant establishment leaders. William Rainey Harper, president of the University of Chicago, biblical scholar, Sunday school superintendent, and Baptist, extolled the messianic role of the university. Although the university and Christian cultures had long had a close and complex relationship, lately a new form had evolved, consistent with developments in the intellectual life of an increasingly secular Western culture. The university, Harper declared, should be the prophet, the priest, and the sage of modern society. Through its functions of scholarship, teaching, and service, a "religion of democracy" could be advanced. In anticipation of "the day when the universal brotherhood of man will be understood and accepted by all men," Harper heralded "the university spirit which, with every decade, dominates the world more fully."[1] Emboldened by modernist theology to celebrate the scholarly scrutiny of all aspects of life and the extension of God's redemption from the church to society itself, he confidently embraced an idealized institution that was in principle free from the constraints of Protestant hegemony. Harper even attributed a transcendental quality of its own to the university.

Harper did not live to evaluate the modern American university's success in promoting a religion of democracy, nor will that task be attempted here. His sense that the university occupied the place of central importance in the educational life of the American people, however, does provide a beginning point for considering the cultural authority of the Protestant establishment in the earlier twentieth century. American education had long been a mainstay of Protestantism's commanding cultural influence. Thus, while Protestant leaders joined in the celebration of the

48

university's ideals, some ought to have wondered what impact the university system would ultimately have on Protestantism's public presence. If Harper's confidence in the ultimate harmony of denominational Protestantism with the transcendent university were mistaken, or if real universities did not live up to his high hopes, the Protestant establishment could find its leadership diminished, not just in education but also in the larger culture.

A continuum of Sunday schools, denominational colleges, and theological seminaries provided the basic agencies of education for the establishment denominations, socializing the churches' own members and leaders and promoting their influence in the larger society. As historian Lawrence Cremin has noted, however, schools can pursue their goals only within a larger ecology of education, which holds "educational institutions and configurations in relation to one another and to the larger society that sustains them and is in turn affected by them."[2] For Protestant educators, the rise of the university constituted a decisive ecological shift. Sunday schools, denominational colleges, and theological seminaries continued, but all three were strongly affected by the university system's ideals of science, professionalism, standardization, and cosmopolitanism. Simultaneously, their share in the general education of the American public decreased. As the new educational forces came to bear upon each kind of Protestant school, the ability of each to contribute to the vitality of the Protestant establishment changed. Examining these changes may shed light on the character of Protestantism's authority in twentieth-century American culture.

The Authority of the University in Higher Education

The fact that Protestantism's role in higher education changed dramatically during the period under consideration is readily established by statistics. At the beginning of the twentieth century, almost half of all undergraduates attended church-related colleges, the majority of which were affiliated with the seven denominations of the Protestant establishment. By 1965, two-thirds of all undergraduates were enrolled in government-supported institutions. Only half the remaining third were in church-related schools, and among these 41.5 percent were Roman Catholic, while only 33 percent were establishment-sponsored.[3]

The extraordinary growth of higher education under the auspices of other institutions (governments or non-establishment religious groups) accounts for most of this quantitative change. But the fact that other kinds of institutions throve can account neither for decline in the absolute

numbers of colleges affiliated with these denominations nor for the recurrent crises of identity that have plagued them and their sponsors
throughout the century. Colleges tied to the leading Protestant denominations not only showed quantitative losses in the earlier twentieth
century, they also lost the authority to define the character of higher
education, even for themselves. This loss, well under way by 1900, was
clear by 1925.

Denominational colleges had flourished during the nineteenth century,
when westward expansion, denominational assertiveness, and flexible
academic standards provided opportunities and demand for founding
numerous small institutions. What linked such colleges to their sponsoring churches were a common ethos and constituency, expressed in religious activities on campus and shared visions of the world beyond it.
Official sponsorship, reflected in varying degrees of financial assistance
and policy control, was often regional rather than national. The presence
of sizable numbers of clergy on faculties further enhanced the connection. Located in "college towns" of manageable size and drawing students and faculty from a like-minded social group, these schools, which
rarely had more than a few hundred students, offered a fixed curriculum
and a strong communal life. The nineteenth century was "the age of the
college."

By the early twentieth century American universities, in the prevailing
view of education historians, had completed the impressive emergence
begun after the Civil War. Emulating the research universities of Ger-
many and explicitly differentiated by their leaders from "the old-time
college," the great private and state universities of the age promoted a
model of academic enterprise that was specialized, secular, and attuned to
national and international communities of scholarship. A new breed of
professors appeared, members of the newly founded disciplinary guilds
that corresponded to the now segmented departments of the university,
and at least as committed to advancing knowledge as to teaching undergraduates. For students, the elective system, the introduction of professional studies and the practical sciences, and the larger size of the university added elements of freedom and vocational utility to the college
years. Moreover, university builders of the late nineteenth century were
prone to assert that denominationalism and the new scholarship were
incompatible. President Charles W. Eliot of Harvard announced in 1891
that "it is impossible to found a university on the basis of a sect"; President Andrew D. White of Cornell took sides against religious emphasis in *The History of the Warfare of Science with Theology* (1896); and the
ceremony opening Johns Hopkins in 1876 included neither prayers of
invocation nor benediction. In instance after instance, the new
universities dissociated themselves from the values and practices that

had characterized American higher education in the era of Protestant hegemony.[4]

During the first quarter of the twentieth century, many of the distinctive standards of the modern research university came to exercise substantial influence not only within institutions like Harvard, Chicago, and Johns Hopkins but also in colleges throughout the land. The interventions of two leading philanthropic foundations were crucial in promoting this expansion of the university's influence. Their activities by no means single-handedly wrested educational authority from the denominations. Yet a consideration of the policies of these foundations, exemplifying the quest for national order and standards shared by reformers in various fields of American life at the time, discloses the vigor of cultural trends that would finally effect the displacement of the Protestant establishment denominations from a central and formative role in American higher education.

The experts to whom Andrew Carnegie and John D. Rockefeller entrusted several hundred million dollars for distribution to colleges and universities believed that a "comprehensive system of higher education in the United States" was sorely needed. Universities had been added to the previous constellation of unregulated colleges. Demarcations between graduate and undergraduate education as well as between secondary and collegiate education were obscure. Many schools were built on shaky financial ground, and academic standards, whether for freshmen or faculty, varied widely. These two great fortunes, the experts determined, could provide the means of bringing order to a chaotic system.

The key episode in this story opened in 1905, when Andrew Carnegie gave $10 million to support professors' pensions. Although the philanthropist stipulated no restrictions in this attempt to advance education, the policymakers at the new Carnegie Foundation for the Advancement of Teaching quickly discerned that "there would be involved in the administration of this gift a scrutiny of education which would not only be desirable in the granting of pensions, but would go far to resolve the confusion that then existed in American higher education."[5] The foundation's early reports explicitly announced the intention of limiting participation in the pension plan to selected colleges and universities that were willing to serve as models of the foundation's plan for standards in higher education. State institutions, which executives of earlier foundations had found to be uncooperative, were excluded.[6]

Standards for participation in the Carnegie pension program, therefore, were conceived as an indirect means to improve higher education as a whole. Historians of higher education treat the Carnegie initiatives as the culmination of efforts to standardize entrance requirements and accreditation that had been underway for more than a decade and judge that the strategists achieved their goals.[7] Carnegie guidelines required colleges to be clearly differentiated from secondary schools, to have minimum endowments of $200,000, and to have at least eight full professors with earned doctorates, including all department heads.

Historians of American religion are more likely to be interested in the fourth Carnegie rule: the clear exclusion of denominational colleges and universities from the plan. Placing institutions along a spectrum with five points from "absolute denominational control" through "no formal connection . . . but a strong sympathetic one," the foundation excluded colleges in the first four categories and required colleges in the fifth to certify by trustee resolution that no distinctly denominational tenets influenced admission, instruction, or the choice of trustees, officers, or faculty.[8]

About fifteen denominational colleges and universities severed ties with their denominations in order to participate in the Carnegie pension fund, including Wesleyan, Drury, Drake, Coe, Dickinson, Goucher, Swarthmore, Bowdoin, Rochester, Occidental, Rutgers, and Brown.[9] Many, probably most, other denominational colleges would not have been accepted by Carnegie even if they had been willing to disaffiliate, since other measures of excellence were also applied. Some historically church-related colleges (particularly Congregational ones) were already sufficiently free from denominational control to qualify for the plan; Oberlin is a leading example.

Such changes naturally evoked criticism of the foundation's arrogance. A Baptist expressed his resentment of the implicit pressure on colleges to disaffiliate "after the prayers, and the tears, and the sacrifices of the Church have brought the college an endowment," while an editorial in the *Independent,* a liberal Protestant nondenominational weekly, objected to the power of a private fortune to "effect profound changes in the constitution and management of our colleges, severing venerable denominational ties, tightening up requirements for admission, differentiating the college from the University, systematizing finances, raising salaries, and in more subtle ways modifying the life and work of thousands of educators."[10] On the other hand, many liberal Protestants welcomed the advent of higher standards for the colleges. For instance, President Henry Churchill King of Oberlin College, a leading Congregationalist, served as an adviser to the Carnegie Foundation. In his view, true religion would be furthered by the application of the highest standards of scholarship. Not denominational ties but high ideals of inquiry within a general collegiate ethos of "moral and religious conviction and purpose" should typify the Protestant contribution to higher education.[11]

By the early twentieth century, the faculties of the best denominational colleges included many modern scholars like King, who possessed an M.A. from Harvard and had studied with Adolf von Harnack at a prototypical modern university in Berlin. Trained themselves in research universities and sharing in the valuation their era placed on standards, excellence, expertise, and order, this new breed of professor would presumably welcome Carnegie interventions in their own institutions. In some cases of disaffiliation, such as Swarthmore, strong forces within the college were already advocating the kinds of changes the foundation required. On the other hand, changing educational ideals probably were not the only reasons for disaffiliation given the expense of higher education and the difficulty of finding funds for support in that age as in our own. At Brown, for instance, the trustees admitted that the financial attractiveness of pension fund participation was a reason for disaffiliation but denied that it was the chief one; instead, Carnegie money had given them a lever for liberalization that they already had been seeking.[12]

Denominational affiliation, or its abandonment, had a wide variety of meanings for different colleges, depending on peculiarities of denominational polity and institutional tradition. Before the establishment of national denominational boards of education, which came in the early twentieth century as a response to the perceived crisis in church-related higher education, ties were usually local or regional, expressed through a stable constituency and the predominance on boards and faculties of a particular Protestant church membership. Disaffiliation did not necessarily break all these ties; surely disaffiliated schools with strong traditions, such as Oberlin and Swarthmore, continued to have a distinctive religious tone in the ensuing decades. Nor did continued affiliation necessarily guarantee that a school's religious commitment would be unmistakably manifest, as numerous twentieth-century studies seeking to discover the distinctive religious mission of church-related colleges reported. Rather, the new climate of authority in higher education – a climate governed by the sun of national standards and the winds of university research – altered in important ways the ecology within which all colleges would henceforth have to live. A few who adapted remarkably well rose to national prominence; most others were probably strengthened in many aspects of instruction, but at the cost of having to adhere more closely to homogeneous, secular norms.

The other great fortune that shaped higher education in the first decades of the century belonged to a devout Baptist, John D. Rockefeller, and was thus somewhat differently administered. Even so, the Rockefeller-supported General Education Board shared the Carnegie Foundation's high esteem for "a comprehensive system of higher education," as well as its judgment that the proliferation of weak denominational colleges was a chief cause of the prevailing chaos. "Rival religious bodies have invaded fields fully – or more than fully –occupied already," the board's initial report declared in 1902; "misguided individuals have founded a new college instead of strengthening an old one." The policy of the board was to support excellent denominational institutions, hoping that weaker ones would die.[13]

Rockefeller funds were consistently available to a wider range and number of colleges and universities than were Carnegie funds. In 1919, for instance, $50 million were made available in matching grants to endow faculty salaries to 203 colleges and universities, among them six state institutions, forty secular private ones, and a diverse range of others including thirty-six black, forty Methodist, thirty-five Baptist, thirty Presbyterian, and fifteen Congregational colleges. (Some of these, unable to raise matching funds, lost the grants.) Despite such liberality and a disavowal of any wish to influence grantees, however, the General Board was as prone as the Carnegie Foundation to use financial inducements as a method of enforcing national standards in higher education.[14]

In setting standards for colleges, the board may well have drawn on the extensive involvement of its benefactor and staff with the University of Chicago, the most unusual example of higher education under Protestant establishment auspices. The university drew heavily on Rockefeller funds administered through the American Baptist Education Society, and the charter, adopted in 1890, required that the president and two-thirds of the trustees be Baptist. Even so, university leaders always avoided a sectarian stance, courting support from a wide public, displaying unusual religious and ethnic tolerance, and apparently aspiring to win the esteem of international scholars more than that of American Baptists. (Perhaps the religious tone and explanatory epistles of William Rainey Harper, the dynamic president of the university from 1890 until he died of cancer in 1906 at the age of forty-nine, assuaged the doubts of some Baptists.) When the American Baptist Education Society was transformed into the General Education Board in 1902, many principles of the older body were retained, with Chicago in some sense providing a standard for the new generation of grants. The university's influence probably worked to promote the nationwide application of essentially secular standards rather than to boost the overall position of denominational institutions in the comprehensive system then emerging under foundation guidance.[15]

The policies of the Carnegie Foundation and the General Education Board did not substantially reduce the number of colleges and universities affiliated with Protestant establishment denominations. In fact, it has

John D. Rockefeller, Sr., with President Harper of the University of Chicago. Courtesy of the University of Chicago Archives.

been argued that, despite expectations, Rockefeller support of the stronger colleges freed denominational funding for the weaker ones, reports of whose death had been greatly exaggerated.[16] Yet the foundation-supported triumph of a national comprehensive system of accreditation, entrance requirements, and faculty expertise marked a major change in the climate of cultural authority prevailing among almost all institutions of higher education. Denominational colleges seeking to measure up to the new standards necessarily gave relatively less attention to their traditional aims and constituencies. This shift had far greater import for the Protestant establishment presence in higher education than the pension chasing of some fifteen newly disaffiliated schools.

Black colleges were affected by the shift in educational authority in distinctive ways. In 1940, the pattern of black higher education was similar to what the predominant pattern had been in 1900: one-half of the undergraduates were in church-supported schools, of which about half were affiliated with the Protestant establishment denominations. Forty percent of all black college presidents were clergymen; 75 percent of those in the denominational schools were. Through these colleges, the churches had an opportunity for broad impact in the larger black community, even though less than a quarter of the students were members of the sponsoring establishment denominations. Yet the relative strength during this period of these colleges' church relationships was counterbalanced by their marginalization from the now–dominant national comprehensive system. The great majority were not accredited at the highest level. These colleges did not have the financial resources to make a free choice between denominationalism and membership in the new system.[17]

During the years after the First World War, numerous pressures – including financial opportunities other than those from foundations – contributed in individual cases to the transformation of predominantly white colleges. Institutions that drew on urban wealth and reflected the new national orientation became more successful, but those that continued to rely on traditional local and ecclesiastical sources of support and control gave up apparent opportunities to grow and thrive. Although the leadership and constituencies of many colleges continued to reflect the membership of particular denominations, this fact increasingly denoted less particularity than previously. The forces of standardization and nationalization pushed secularization of some crucial aspects of a college's program, even if not official disaffiliation. Moreover, constant unaccustomed pressure from state departments of education and regional accrediting agencies to conform to changing standards raised new uncertainties, exerting pressure on both the budgets and the spirits of many colleges.[18]

In the meantime, other changes also marked the declining influence of old-line Protestantism in higher education. In 1925–6, for instance, a wave of student-led challenges to compulsory chapel attendance swept the nation, although requirements of some kind persisted at most schools at least until World War II.[19] More powerful than student protest in almost every case, however, was trustee policy, and there was a precipitous decline in clergy presence on the boards of the flagship universities of the land. A 1935 study of thirty leading institutions (fourteen of them state supported, but several others – Yale, Princeton, Brown – pillars of the nineteenth-century Protestant establishment) found only forty-eight clergy among the trustees, and most of those were bishops serving the Catholic University of America. These figures contrast sharply with those of the preceding century, when no other group outnumbered the clergy in service as trustees. Between 1884 and 1926, the number of clergy trustees declined by 50% at Amherst, 60% at Yale, and 67% at Princeton; at fifteen other private colleges, clergy trustees declined from 39% in 1860 to 23% in 1900 to 7% in 1930.[20] In addition, a third measure by which nineteenth-century colleges had traditionally shown their respect for religious leadership had also virtually disappeared. Harvard had its last ordained president in 1869, Denison in 1889, Illinois in 1892, Yale in 1899, Princeton in 1902, Marietta in 1913, Wabash in 1926, and Oberlin in 1927.[21]

By the 1920s, the denominations that had so dominated the vanished "age of the college" could acknowledge the necessity of re-visioning their role in higher education. The Baptists and Presbyterians faced some distinctive problems in this decade as the fundamentalist–modernist controversy wracked their colleges and seminaries. By the 1930s they were once again immersed in dilemmas common to other groups.[22] In an effort to meet perceived challenges, the staffs of denominational boards of education, formed earlier in the century, were strengthened through internal reorganization and interdenominational coordination in the Council of Church Boards of Education.[23] Support of church-related colleges continued to be high on the agendas of these agencies. But new plans were being laid to foster a religious presence in other academic institutions as well.

Tacitly conceding to other agencies the authority to shape the most important features of higher education, representatives of the Protestant establishment sought fresh means to influence students and faculties. In particular, three initiatives in higher education on the part of the Protestant religious establishment stand out as exemplary efforts to redefine and regain their influence in the colleges and universities in a new era. These initiatives were campus ministry at secular institutions, promotion of the academic study of religion, and efforts to raise faculty consciousness about the religious and ethical dimensions of higher education.

Strategies of Protestant Influence, 1925–60

Around the turn of the century, denominations began to develop a new form of presence in higher education by placing on or near university campuses ministers whose special calling was to serve Christian students at secular institutions. The social analysis and basic strategy of this movement were expressed in the title of a 1938 book by Clarence P. Shedd, a professor at Yale Divinity School: *The Church Follows Its Students*. Shedd, the key figure in the professionalization of campus ministry in the second quarter of the century, urged churches to recognize that the demography and spheres of influence in higher education had radically changed. The rise of state and other secular universities and the overall increase in the number of young people attending college, he argued, meant that tax-supported institutions now demanded a major share of the churches' attention. Moreover, state schools would likely offer fruitful fields of ministry: YMCA and YWCA work had thrived there for years, chapel was often still available, and many of the students came from pious homes. Christians interested in influencing higher education were being old-fashioned and irresponsible if they overlooked this rich field, Shedd concluded.[24]

The development of university pastorates was led and dominated by the denominations of the Protestant establishment. The Presbyterians were the pathbreakers, founding programs at the universities of Kansas, Illinois, Wisconsin, Colorado, Arkansas, and Nebraska between 1905 and 1909. The other denominations moved more slowly, but some characteristic steps were taken as Episcopalians decided to base campus work at local parishes, Methodists invited students to fellowship at newly formed Wesley Foundations, and Baptists funded university pastors through state associations in the Midwest. After two decades of modest growth, campus programs expanded more rapidly during the 1920s, with funding reaching a peak between 1925 and 1930. Active denominations acquired buildings near campus to house their work, and national denominational student organizations came into being. Such programs continued to grow through the 1950s.[25]

The influence of the two hundred university pastors who were active in 1938, as well as that of their successors in the field, on students and universities can hardly be assessed. But it is clear that their work had considerable impact on the perceptions of higher education held by religious leaders in this arena, whose imagination had earlier been focused almost exclusively on church-related institutions. Shedd's argument about shifting demographics in higher education was essentially correct, and by 1960 one of his heirs could repeat it with even more conviction: during 1958–9, there were four times as many Methodists in Iowa's three state schools as there were in Iowa's four Methodist colleges. The church should follow its students.[26]

A second initiative by the Protestant establishment in higher education, the promotion of the academic study of religion, expanded rapidly in the 1920s. Drawing leaders from colleges and universities rather than from denominational structures, this initiative presupposed the existence of "an intellectually respectable, modernist and liberal, scholarly and scientific approach to religion on campus, which would take all that science had to offer and come back for more, and which would move on a level beneath but respectful to all faiths," as one of them put it. Those who advocated this initiative were themselves scholars trained in such an approach; in most cases they were also committed members of Protestant establishment denominations. In effect, their efforts to seek a larger presence for religion in higher education simultaneously eased the transition toward a more pluralistic vision that would ultimately further diminish the hegemony of the churches from which they came.[27]

Merrimon Cuninggim, a Methodist involved in this movement during the midcentury decades, characteristically both judged that "secularization" had triumphed in higher education between 1900 and 1918 and assessed the future prospects of religion in higher education with remarkable optimism. Other significant leaders at midcentury concurred: The 1920s had been a low point of religious influence, but the situation had improved substantially since then. An important turning point came in 1922, when Charles Foster Kent, a longtime professor of biblical literature at Yale, founded the National Council on Religion in Higher Education. Kent's express hope was that religion could "once again" attain a significant place in college and university life, a place he believed must be won through the intellectual and educational respectability of religious studies. By 1946, thanks in part to the council's efforts, a sizable increase in the academic study of religion in fact had occurred, with two-thirds of all accredited colleges reporting departments of religion, including 100 percent of church-related colleges and 30 percent of state-supported schools. However, another study at midcentury disclosed that religion was usually either ignored or treated with positivist hostility in the textbooks most widely used in courses offered by other departments.[28] Apparently another feature of the modern university – the specialization of knowledge – helped secular institutions to resist at a fundamental level the rapprochement proposed by religious academics.

Whatever the curricular impact, the National Council on Religion in Higher Education did call forth a network of concerned educators who, well into the 1960s, dominated Protestant reflection on the religious and ethical dimensions of higher education. With institutional bases in a Society of Fellows, in the Edward W. Hazen Foundation, and later in the Danforth Foundation, this network also was chiefly responsible for the third initiative of this era: raising the consciousness of faculty, administrators, and promising graduate students about the importance of religion and values in higher education. This initiative originated among liberal academics within the Protestant religious establishment, that is, among leaders like Kent who were disturbed by what they saw as decline in religion's presence in colleges and universities. Significantly, however, these same leaders acknowledged that religion's academic future did not lie with the old establishment; membership in the organizations they founded was open to persons of all faiths.[29]

If the university pastorate movement was funded and shaped by denominational boards eager to extend their institutional influence, the other two initiatives arose from within the academy and were more difficult to link to any specifically ecclesiastical agenda. All three demonstrated, however, that the standards of the modern university now drummed the beat to which the Protestant establishment's religious presence in higher education must march. Protestants responded sensibly to the changing ecology of American education, seeking new forms of effectiveness through all three initiatives. Yet it was hardly possible for them to have a formative impact amid the extraordinary growth of higher education under the auspices of other groups, a growth governed by the university's standards of science, specialization, and secularity.

As institutions concerned with both scholarship and the church, theological seminaries occupied an important place in the shifting relationship between religion and education. Slower than colleges to be absorbed into the national comprehensive system of education, seminaries nonetheless experienced pressures from the university. In 1936, accreditation guidelines adopted by the American Association of Theological Schools in the United States and Canada sought to enhance the seminary's status as a "graduate professional school," with tougher admissions policies, higher levels of faculty expertise, and firmer bases of financial support.[30] And at midcentury, a study of Protestant theological education by H. Richard Niebuhr, Daniel Day Williams, and James M. Gustafson discovered a trend toward greater affiliation with universities and greater interest in the graduate character of theological education. Moreover, as theological faculties came increasingly to be composed of professors holding research doctorates, a small number of university-related divinity schools emerged as important centers indirectly shaping the fundamental programs of most denominational seminaries.[31]

However, seminaries were also well positioned to transfer some of the university system's cultural authority to the credit of the churches. By defining ministry as a profession entered through specialized graduate training, the seminaries helped to stake the churches' claim to intellectual currency and social esteem in twentieth-century America. In addition, some Protestant educators hoped, a new breed of professional church leaders could work to extend the new models through the religious education movement into local congregations. From this movement emerged some of the central issues to confront the Protestant establishment in the age of the university.

The University Meets the Sunday School

As important as colleges and seminaries were in educating lay and clerical leadership for Protestant establishment churches, another school was closer to the hearts and more influential on the minds of their millions of members. The Sunday school, run by laymen and -women in almost every congregation, had taken hold during the nineteenth century and become a characteristic feature of American Protestantism, displaying and deepening a people's love for Bible stories, rousing songs, and moral verities. As public schools and higher education changed around the turn of the century, however, the Sunday school did not; innocent of new research in developmental psychology and biblical criticism, it continued to operate in ungraded classes, with uniform lessons, under amateur direction. The new breed of Protestant educational leaders were embarrassed by this homey institution and the "Sunday school faith" it fostered; yet they were reluctant to relinquish the educational potential it represented – a potential that made the Sunday school, in the 1910 remark of President William Howard Taft, "one of the two or three greatest instrumentalities for making the world better, for making it more moral, and for making it more religious."[32] Less sanguine than Taft, the reformers nonetheless hoped that the Sunday school, renovated in accordance with new standards of scholarship and infused with appropriate measures of expertise, could still play a useful part in the churches' educational mission.

The movement to reform the Sunday school emanated from the Religious Education Association (REA), an organization that included presidents and professors from colleges, seminaries, and universities, as well as leaders concerned with youth work, Sunday schools, and the religious presence in public schooling. Indeed, the impressive list of participants in the first convention, called together by William Rainey Harper in 1903, demonstrates the density of the Protestant establishment's educational network at the century's inception. The REA, however, was not generally representative of Protestant educators, at least not once its leaders' agenda became evident. The organization may have included the "best" church educators of its time, as one historian has noted, but it did not include the "most."[33] It was a base for advocacy, fashioned by liberal Protestants to bring the findings of modern scholarship to bear on the educational activities of the churches, while at the same time strengthening what they saw as the waning educational influence of religion in the larger society. "The Association," Harper declared, "will propose to make new contributions to the cause of religious and moral education, and this will be done through the light of scientific investigations."[34] Ironically, it sought to recruit the ideas and practices of the university, which were undermining denominational colleges, to the task of renewing Protestant hegemony in education.

During the first half of the century, the REA provided through its journal and conventions a forum for a broad range of educational concerns. Its membership was drawn almost entirely from the denominations of the Protestant establishment. (Only a very few Jews, members of black denominations, and Catholics were involved, until the last became a major presence after Vatican II.) The transformation of colleges and seminaries, new patterns of student work, and other matters were frequently discussed. But the institution that stood at the center of REA concern – and more important the institution that the REA not only discussed but also substantially influenced – was the Sunday school. Or, as many reformers liked to call it, the church school.[35]

Early twentieth-century reformers of church education held two images clearly in mind: the image of the "old" Sunday school, where a "collection of indifferent children and ignorant teachers [met] in the church auditorium or basement," as REA executive secretary Henry Cope put it,[36] and the image of the "new" public school, where progressive educational methods drew each child into a democratic learning process suited to his or her stage of development. The "old" was dominated by the curriculum of the International Sunday School Lesson Committee, which provided short Bible passages to be studied "uniformly" by all scholars on a given Sunday, in China or in Connecticut, at age six or at eighty-six. Used in the great majority of Protestant establishment congregations since its development in 1872, the Uniform Lesson Series simplified educational planning and teacher training at the local level and provided a hospitable setting for the contributions of thousands of lay volunteers. The "new," on the other hand, could be observed in the best public schools of the age. Transformed by the scientific research of psychologists and the philosophy of John Dewey, the curriculum was devised for the distinctive capabilities of each age group and directed to the flourishing of individuals within an educational environment integrally related to society as a whole.

Shailer Mathews, a professor, and later dean of divinity, at the University of Chicago, had been exposed to the Uniform Lessons during a Baptist boyhood, and he summarized the case against them at the first

REA convention. The lessons forced students at various stages of mental development to study the same lesson; the lessons lacked pedagogical movement; the lessons ignored the particular needs of adolescents in spiritual crisis. Clearly a new, graded curriculum would be far less simple than this; it would have to be devised, supervised, and perhaps even taught by persons knowledgeable in the latest psychological research. Moreover, Mathews pointed out, there was another flaw in the old curriculum: it used the Bible poorly.[37] Short excerpts of text – sometimes chosen because they were thought to interest children or in response to temperance or other pressures on the International Lesson Committee – provided the weakest method of understanding Scripture, in the reformers' view. Curriculum must also be revised in light of recent developments in the higher criticism of the Bible.

In their celebration of modern scholarship, professional leadership, and secular progressive education, the new breed of Protestant educational reformers both expressed and contributed to changing patterns of authority in American education as a whole. Challenging the hold of pious laity on the popular transmission of the fundamental text of the faith, religious educators sought to reshape content and reassign responsibility in accordance with norms developed in powerful cultural institutions that lay well beyond most laity's reach or ken. Ideally, these reformers hoped, a professional specialist in religious education – the director of religious education – would be hired to take on the task of transformation in the local congregation. The minister (specially trained in the religious education courses proliferating in the seminaries) could do so if a congregation could not afford a second professional.

In a movement parallel to that governing denominational involvement in higher education, denominational boards of education were organized to raise the educational quality of church schools, working together after 1910 in the Sunday School Council of Evangelical Denominations. Advocates of "religious education" were heavily represented and were also the dominant force in the successor organization founded in 1922, the International Council of Religious Education. In 1929, the Council published its "International Standards," a document that, consolidating early attempts at standardization, listed and elaborated ten desirable church school characteristics.[38] All of these initiatives represented a significant transformation of images of church education in the national organizations of the Protestant establishment, where growing professional staffs did the hard work of developing and promoting educational material.

The impact of this transformation at the local level, where Sunday schools actually functioned, was much less far-reaching. Although it is difficult to assess change of this kind, the clarity of the new norms in religious education did enable reformers to investigate the issue of local compliance with national expectations. In 1930, a survey of 746 church schools disclosed that only a slight majority (55%) were using graded rather than uniform lessons. Adoption of other reforms was even lower: 72% spent less than $1.25 per pupil per year (and that from special offerings rather than from the church budget), and less than half conducted teacher-training sessions, kept good records, maintained a library, were governed by a congregational committee, or attained an average attendance of 70%. These figures are the more remarkable when it is taken into account that the churches surveyed ought to have been particularly favorable to reform: All had seminary graduates as ministers, and on the whole they were larger, more urban, and more prosperous than average. Five Protestant establishment denominations – Baptist (Northern), Methodist (Northern), Presbyterian (U.S.A.), Christian (Disciples), and Congregational – accounted for 84% of the churches surveyed.[39]

Persisting in the local churches, the Yale-based researchers concluded, was "the presence of a Sunday-school stereotype much older than the International Standard and not as yet greatly affected by it." With an optimism characteristic of their liberalism, they blamed the disappointing facts on "the recency of these new standards and the comparative slowness with which any traditional pattern is superseded by new practices."[40] As a matter of fact, however, the movement was not just beginning its ascent; it was entering a period of decline. Reform – always a more expensive business than stasis – was in part set back by the Great Depression. Sales of new curricular materials, for instance, could not fare well in an age of congregational belt-tightening. Directors of religious education, who from the beginning had faced the uphill battle of convincing the laity to pay for nonclergy professional leadership, were also often displaced from church budgets. (That most of them were women likely added to the churches' reluctance to value their contributions.) And the effects of the nationwide "religious depression" among establishment denominations were also felt; between 1926 and 1936, Sunday school enrollment dropped by 34% among the Methodists, by 23% among the Disciples, and by 18% among the Presbyterians, whereas fundamentalist and charismatic groups made major gains.[41]

Although the chief focus and impact of the religious education movement (however far it fell below its founders' hopes) were on the churches' schools, the most articulate and visionary of the movement's leaders had always intended their efforts to extend well beyond this narrow scope. "To inspire the educational forces of this country with the religious ideal; to inspire the religious forces of this country with the

George A. Coe, innovator in religious education. From the George Albert Coe Papers. Manuscript Group. No. 36, Special Collections, Yale Divinity School Library.

educational ideal": these were the stated goals of the REA.[42] Considerable concern for religion's broad educational impact in American society – a call to consider the most expansive public implications of religious education in all its forms – was a strong feature of the movement. In part, this was a comfortable inheritance from the previous century, when the privileged position of the Protestant establishment in the shaping of public schools and other educational agencies had been clear. Yet in this new century the old theme was voiced in the fresh tones of modernist theology. Open to social science, rejecting doctrinal imperialism within a diverse nation, and emphasizing the immanence of the divine throughout society, liberal religious leaders hoped to share the responsibility of meeting the educational challenges of industrial mass society with secular progressive educators.

George A. Coe, the era's leading spokesman for the public mission of religious education as well as one of its most gifted academic theorists, led the drive for unity between religious and secular forces in education, discerning in modernist theology and progressive education the compatible sensibilities of which good marriages are made. A religion of democracy would be their offspring. Coe's visionary proposals were, however, difficult for the less inspired educators who actually had to apply them to the mundane realities of running schools. And so a range of more practical proposals for increasing the public impact of religious education, which reformers knew could hardly accomplish its mission in one poorly organized hour on Sunday mornings, also appeared during the first quarter of the century: released or shared time for religious instruction, in-school study of religions as aspects of human culture, or after-school programs through which churches could supplement the Sunday class hour. All these programs were vigorously debated not only when proposed but for decades thereafter. While some were actually implemented in scattered locations, no large-scale, unified strategy to increase the educational impact of the churches emerged. There was one modest exception: week-long Vacation Bible Schools, conceived early in the century, attained substantial popularity by midcentury.

By 1940, the denominations of the Protestant establishment found their educational programs for children in turmoil on two fronts. First, even as the public school moved into a more dominant position in the overall ecology of education, public schooling increasingly reflected less consistency with Protestant church education and more direction from forces other than the Protestant establishment, although the rate and extent of this shift showed regional and local variations. To be sure, Protestants did expend considerable energy combating Catholic educators' efforts to draw on public funds. Yet they may have done so, as religious educator F. Ernest Johnson of the Federal Council of Churches suggested in 1940, in the "naive assumption that if the public schools could be protected from Catholic encroachment through drawing off funds for parochial schools or influencing school policies in other ways, the religious interests of the community would be well served." A corresponding program of positive Protestant involvement in public education was lacking. As Johnson noted, there had been "little serious consideration in Protestant circles of the effects of secularism in education on religious attitude and outlook." Many Protestant leaders, perhaps most, shared Johnson's concern about public education's secularist trend; when it came to public policy, however, such leaders in effect opted for the secularization of the public school rather than the public financing of Catholic education.[43] This secularization, a departure from the educational arrangements of earlier times, surely hastened the decline of Protestant establishment cultural authority.

Second, the attempted transformation of the Sunday school, far from unifying church education into a modernized national system as good as secular schooling, increased division and uncertainty. The failure of the religious education movement to carry the day (in spite of its significant influence in many quarters) is not itself a sign of loss. Indeed, an argument could be made that the persistence of an ethos of lay biblicism enabled these churches to remain stronger than they would otherwise have been. But the gap between national leadership and local laity on the crucial matter of how the formative tradition ought to be taught to the new generation cannot have been healthy for these institutions. The new generation of reformers who seized the initiative around midcentury – neo-orthodox "Christian educators" eager to correct the theological mistakes of their liberal predecessors – hoped to heal the gap, sharing as they did the laity's emphasis on the centrality of the Bible to church education. Professional ethos set even them apart from the lay culture of the old-time Sunday school in many communities, however, and the pattern of estrangement continued. As one national educational movement followed another, the Sunday school remained, constant in its essential features. Unlike Protestant institutions of higher education, it was in a position to evade the long arm of the standardized university system. The Sunday school was, after all, an identifying feature of the American Protestant congregation and, at the least, secure in its function as the domestic "nursery of the church."[44]

Resistance to educational professionalism in the life of the local congregation not only indicated a widespread lay refusal to yield to the wisdom of high-level church educators; it also marked resistance to major developments in twentieth-century American education. Local communities of Protestants, grounded in the habits of persistent traditionalism, intended to go on reading the Bible for themselves. They claimed authority over one aspect of the transmission of culture. And they did so within a context in which other important agencies for culture's transmission – schools, colleges, universities, seminaries – had become part of a "national comprehensive system" formatively shaped by the values and practices of the modern university.

In contrast, higher education was the realm of Protestant establishment cultural activity most heavily influenced by the dominant ideals of science, professionalism, standardization, and cosmopolitanism. By virtue of their own training and theological inclinations, Protestant establishment leaders in higher education more often than not shared these ideals, and there can be little doubt that many of the institutions under their stewardship were academically strengthened when the ideals were adopted. Yet at midcentury it would have been difficult to find a Protestant leader as optimistic about the religious opportunities inherent in the prevailing pattern as William Rainey Harper had been in 1899. Two generations after Harper, those concerned with sustaining a religious

68	*Dorothy C. Bass*

presence in higher education had come to agree with him that the university had to stand at the center of their vision; the church-related college now occupied a less prominent place both in their thinking and in the large and still growing world of higher education. Far from finding the modern university a powerful force for religion, however, they had learned that specific strategies had to be undertaken to alert it to the importance of religion in human affairs. And so denominations positioned ministers at the edges of campuses, departments offered elective courses in religious studies, and voluntary societies sponsored seminars on values.

In the context of the university system within which they developed, these very strategies both acknowledged the displacement of religion from the core of educational value and opened a hopeful pathway to the affirmations of religious and educational pluralism that would come to prominence in the later twentieth century. In reality, the university ideals that shaped the history of American education in the twentieth century had already won the day in 1899. By the 1960s, some leaders of disestablished Protestantism were at last ready to concede that their ministry in education lay "on the margin," where, they hoped, a new sort of freedom to witness and serve could be found.[45]

NOTES

1 William Rainey Harper, "The University and Democracy," in *The Trend in Higher Education* (Chicago: University of Chicago Press, 1905), 34.
2 Lawrence A. Cremin, *Public Education* (New York: Basic Books, 1976), 36.
3 William C. Ringenberg, *The Christian College: A History of Protestant Higher Education in America* (Grand Rapids, Mich.: Eerdmans, 1984), 132; Manning M. Patillo and Donald M. Mackenzie, *Church-Sponsored Higher Education in the United States: Report of the Danforth Commission* (Washington, D.C.: American Council of Education, 1966), 21.
4 Hugh Hawkins, "The University-Builders Observe the Colleges," *History of Education Quarterly* 11(1971): 354–8; Mark A. Noll, "Christian Colleges, Christian Worldviews, and an Invitation to Research," in Ringenberg, *The Christian College,* 26, 29.
5 Henry S. Pritchett in the Carnegie Foundation's *Thirteenth Annual Report* (1935), quoted in Ernest Victor Hollis, *Philanthropic Foundations and Higher Education* (New York: Columbia University Press, 1938), 37; Ellen Condliffe Lagemann, "The Politics of Knowledge: The Carnegie Corporation and the Formulation of Public Policy," *History of Education Quarterly* 27(1987): 210.
6 Hollis, *Philanthropic Foundations,* 34–8.
7 Laurence R. Veysey, *The Emergence of the American University* (Chicago: University of Chicago Press, 1965), 31ff.; Frederick Rudolph, *The American College and University: A History* (New York: Knopf, 1962), 432–5.
8 Paul M. Limbert, *Denominational Policies in Support and Supervision of Higher*

Education (New York: Bureau of Publications, Teachers College, Columbia University, 1929), 56.

9   I have found no exhaustive list but have combined data from Limbert, *Denominational Policies,* 57; Hollis, *Philanthropic Foundations,* 54; Rudolph, *American Colleges and Universities,* 433; Merrimon Cuninggim, *The College Seeks Religion* (New Haven, Conn.: Yale University Press, 1947), 8; and W. Bruce Leslie, "Localism, Denominationalism, and Institutional Strategies in Urbanizing America: Three Pennsylvania Colleges, 1870–1915," *History of Education Quarterly* 17(1977): 248.

10 W. S. P. Bryan, *The Church, Her Colleges, and the Carnegie Foundation,* and *Independent* 66(June 17, 1909): 153–4, quoted in Hollis, *Philanthropic Foundations,* 55, 52.

11 Henry Churchill King, "Religion in Our Colleges," address to the National Council of the Congregational Churches, *Report of the Sixteenth Regular Meeting* (Boston: Office of the National Council, 1915), 142–3.

12 Leslie, "Localism, Denominationalism, and Institutional Strategies," 248 ff.; Hollis, *Philanthropic Foundations,* 54.

13 The "comprehensive system" phrase is also from the 1902 report; both are quoted in Hollis, *Philanthropic Foundations,* 36.

14 Leslie, "Localism, Denominationalism, and Institutional Strategies," 246; Hollis, *Philanthropic Foundations,* 198, 271, 133.

15 Limbert, *Denominational Policies,* 224, 41; Veysey, *The Emergence of the American University,* 373–5.

16 David B. Potts, "American Colleges in the Nineteenth Century: From Localism to Denominationalism," *History of Education Quarterly* 11(1971): 375; Limbert, *Denominational Policies,* 225.

17 Richard I. McKinney, *Religion in Higher Education among Negroes* (New Haven, Conn.: Yale University Press, 1945).

18 This is the argument of W. Bruce Leslie's study of Swarthmore, Bucknell, and Franklin and Marshall, "Localism, Denominationalism, and Institutional Strategies."

19 A 1940 study showed that compulsory chapel of unspecified frequency and content, was still operative at 91% of church-related colleges, 56% of independent colleges, and 11% of state colleges and universities. Dean R. Hoge, *Commitment on Campus: Changes in Religion and Values Over Five Decades* (Philadelphia: Westminster Press, 1974), 135; Cuninggim, *The College Seeks Religion,* 301.

20 Hubert Park Beck, *Men Who Control Our Universities* (New York: King's Crown Press, 1947), 55–6; Ringenberg, *The Christian College,* 127; Veysey, *The Emergence of the American University,* 350.

21 Ringenberg, *The Christian College,* 127; Rudolph, *The American College and University,* 419.

22 Potts, "American Colleges in the Nineteenth Century," 370–2; Limbert, *Denominational Policies,* 67–73.

23 *Christian Education* 7(1924): 311–28, and Limbert, *Denominational Policies,* 226.

24 Clarence P. Shedd, *The Church Follows Its Students* (New Haven: Yale Uni-

versity Press, 1938), 7–11; on Shedd's importance, see Cuninggim, *The College Seeks Religion*, 4, and Amos N. Wilder, *Liberal Learning and Religion* (New York: Harper, 1951), 13.

25 Shedd, *The Church Follows Its Students*, 13–73, 167–219; Rudolph, *The American College and University*, 459; Daniel E. Statello and William M. Shinto, *Planning for Ministry in Higher Education* (New York: United Ministries in Higher Education, n.d. [1970s]).

26 Shedd, *The Church Follows Its Students*, 219; Robert Michaelsen, "Religious Education in Public Higher Education Institutions," in Marvin J. Taylor (ed.), *Religious Education: A Comprehensive Survey* (New York: Abingdon Press, 1960).

27 Thornton W. Merriam, "Religion in Higher Education Through the Past "Twenty-five Years," in Wilder, *Liberal Learning and Religion*, 7. Merriam, former executive director of the National Council on Religion in Higher Education, was here describing the vision of Charles Foster Kent.

28 Cuninggim, *The College Seeks Religion*, 13–14, Merriam, "Religion in Higher Education," 6; Virginia Corwin, "The Teaching of Religion," in Wilder, *Liberal Learning and Religion*, 169; and Howard B. Jefferson, "The Present Religious Situation in Higher Education," in Christian Gauss, *The Teaching of Religion in American Higher Education* (New York: Ronald Press, 1951), 86, all agree that the situation at midcentury was an improvement over a low point around 1920. On Kent, see Merriam, 5; 1946 figures are from Cuninggim, *The College Seeks Religion*, 300, 151. *College Reading and Religion: A Survey of College Reading Materials Sponsored by the Edward W. Hazen Foundation and the Committee on Religion and Education of the American Council on Education* (New Haven: Yale University Press, 1948).

29 Hugh Hartshorne, Helen R. Stearns, and Willard B. Uphaus, *Standards and Trends in Religious Education* (New Haven: Yale University Press, 1933), 193; Merriam, "Religion in Higher Education," 3–23. In spite of these organizations' policy of inclusivity, my strong impression, based on names appearing in publications, is that members of the denominations of the Protestant establishment continued to dominate them.

30 Robert W. Lynn, *Why the Seminary? An Introduction to the Report of the Auburn History Project* (unpublished manuscript, 1979), pp. 93–7.

31 H. Richard Niebuhr, Daniel Day Williams, and James M. Gustafson, *The Advancement of Theological Education* (New York: Harper, 1957), 52, 213.

32 Quoted in Jack L. Seymour, *From Sunday School to Church School* (Washington, D.C.: University Press of America, 1982), 80.

33 Robert W. Lynn, *Protestant Strategies in Education* (New York: Association Press, 1964), 28.

34 Religious Education Association, *Proceedings of the First Annual Convention, 1903* (Chicago: Religious Education Association, 1903), 237.

35 Stephen A. Schmidt, *A History of the Religious Education Association* (Birmingham, Ala.: Religious Education Press, 1983).

36 Seymour, *From Sunday School to Church School*, 82.

37 REA, *First Convention*, 186–99; Robert W. Lynn and Elliott Wright, *The Big Little School*, 2d ed. (Nashville: Abingdon Press, 1980), 104, 116.

38   Seymour, *From Sunday School to Church School,* pp. 93–4, says that these organizations were "mainline Protestant," although he does not name the denominations included. The International Council of Religious Education became the Department of Christian Education of the National Council of Churches of Christ in 1952.

39   Hartshorne, Stearns, and Uphaus, *Standards and Trends in Religious Education.*

40   Ibid., 58, 107.

41   Lynn and Wright, *The Big Little School,* 133; on professional religious educators, see Elizabeth Howell Verdesi, *In But Still Out: Women in the Church* (Philadelphia: Westminster Press, 1973).

42   These goals, adopted in 1905, are quoted in Lynn, *Protestant Strategies in Education,* 27.

43   F. Ernest Johnson, *The Social Gospel Re-Examined* (New York: Harper, 1940), 175–6, quoted in Lynn, *Protestant Strategies in Education,* 39; Leo Pfeffer, *Church, State, and Freedom* (Boston: Beacon Press, 1953), 292.

44   The domestication of church education is a central theme in Jack L. Seymour, Robert T. O'Gorman, and Charles R. Foster, *The Church in the Education of the Public* (Nashville: Abingdon, 1984).

45   Robert W. Lynn, "A Ministry on the Margin," in Kenneth Underwood (ed.), *The Church, The University, and Social Policy,* vol. 2 (Middletown, Conn.: Wesleyan University Press, 1969), 19–24. The author wishes to thank Dr. Lynn for his permission to borrow this title and for his helpful conversation during the preparation of this essay.

SELECT BIBLIOGRAPHY

Cuninggim, Merrimon. *The College Seeks Religion.* New Haven: Yale University Press, 1947.

Lynn, Robert W. *Protestant Strategies in Education.* New York: Association Press, 1964.

Lynn, Robert W., and Elliot Wright. *The Big Little School.* 2d ed. Nashville: Abingdon Press, 1980.

Ringenberg, William C. *The Christian College: A History of Protestant Higher Education in America.* Grand Rapids, Mich.: Eerdmans, 1984.

Rudolph, Frederick. *The American College and University: A History.* New York: Knopf, 1962.

Seymour, Jack L., Robert T. O'Gorman, and Charles R. Foster. *The Church in the Education of the Public.* Nashville: Abingdon Press, 1984.

Shedd, Clarence P. *The Church Follows Its Students.* New Haven: Yale University Press, 1938.

Taylor, Marvin J. (ed.). *Religious Education: A Comprehensive Survey.* New York: Abingdon Press, 1960.

Veysey, Laurence R. *The Emergence of the American University.* Chicago: University of Chicago Press, 1965.

Wilder, Amos N. *Liberal Learning and Religion.* New York: Harper, 1951.

4

Reaching Out: Mainline
Protestantism and the Media

DENNIS N. VOSKUIL

The advent of radio broadcasting during the early twenties provided the Protestant establishment with a remarkable new means of broadening the base of support for modern and ecumenical Christianity. Certainly many mainline Protestants agreed with a 1923 *Christian Century* editorial predicting that the "radiophone" would stimulate a general improvement in preaching, encourage positive changes in religious values, and contribute appreciably to the dismantling of "sectarianism."[1]

The promise of radio, however, would remain unrealized. Comfortably in control of the religious press well into the twentieth century, members of the Protestant establishment do not appear to have taken full advantage of the emerging electronic media. Ironically, the mainline Protestants, who were most appreciative of modern science, most ebullient about the potential for human progress, and most willing to accommodate theology to modern thought forms, did not successfully exploit the new technologies of mass communication. A further irony, perhaps, is that fundamentalists and Pentecostals, avowed theological antimodernists, eventually became the juggernauts of the electronic media. By the eighties, religious television had become almost exclusively the domain of flamboyant right-wing televangelists such as Jimmy Swaggart, Jerry Falwell, and Jim Bakker. Partly as a result of their halting participation in the communications revolution, establishment Protestants had been moved to the very edges of what Robert Lynn has aptly described as the "Media Society."[2]

Arthur M. Schlesinger has written that "power in America today is control of the means of communication."[3] The measure of cultural authority exercised by establishment Protestants between 1900 and 1960 was directly related to their ability to control, or at least gain access to, print as well as electronic media. The battle for control was waged on

72

two fronts. On the one hand, mainliners fought the fundamentalists and other conservatives in an effort to retain a major share of the specifically "religious" media – the religious press, as well as religious radio and television. On the other hand, they fought to gain influence in the marketplace of the "secular" media. In this respect, there was an ongoing effort to recreate a nineteenth-century model of "Protestant America." At stake on both fronts was the exercise of power or influence, the ability to give shape to the social and religious agenda for America.

The Religious Press

The religious press in America had experienced its heyday much earlier, in the early and middle decades of the nineteenth century. In addition to a full complement of magazines and journals, weekly religious newspapers, in those years, were rolling off the presses in increasing numbers. By 1850 at least 181 religious periodicals were being published in this country, about half of them newspapers. The Congregationalists alone produced at least twenty-five periodicals.[4] In general, the religious press of the "national period" competed head to head with the secular press for readership, often providing full coverage of political, economic, and social events as well as religious news. The Protestant perspective, at this time pervasively evangelical, reached to the very center of national life; and Protestant journalists took all of society to be their "beat."

By the end of the nineteenth century the religious press had been moved toward the margins of the publishing industry. As the cultural ethos of America shifted and as the news business became more demanding and competitive, few distinctively religious newspapers survived. To be sure, religious periodicals continued to flow from the Protestant presses, but more and more they tended to be specialty items – missionary magazines, Sunday school papers, scholarly reviews, and so forth – with narrow readerships. Moreover, once-independent journals became house organs, reporting denominational news and boosting denominational causes. While these journals were often well written and visually attractive, they could not compete successfully in the nonreligious publishing market.

By 1900, then, the specifically Protestant press was struggling to maintain a distinctive voice in a society that was becoming increasingly pluralistic and secular. The *Outlook* and the *Independent* were two of just a handful of Protestant papers that managed to retain significant readership well into the twentieth century. Incorporated as the *Christian Union* by Baptists shortly after the Civil War, the *Outlook* soon came under the editorship of Lyman Abbott, a brilliant associate of Henry Ward Beecher who later succeeded the famous preacher in the pulpit of the Plymouth Congregational Church in Brooklyn. Over time Abbott altered the scope of the *Outlook* but not its basic religious perspective. In an editorial penned in 1897, Abbott affirmed his belief

> in the immortality of the spirit and in change of forms, in the old religion and in a new theology, in the old patriotism and in new politics, in the old philanthropy and in new institutions, in the old brotherhood and in a new social order.[5]

Organized by antislavery congregationalists, the *Independent* was edited for a time by Henry Ward Beecher and staffed by such luminaries as Washington Gladden, but the paper owed its success to longtime publisher and editor Henry Bowen. According to Frank Luther Mott, a historian of American publishing, the *Independent* was just one of "a very small group of religious papers to hold a comparatively general audience in a period which saw most such periodicals degenerate into denominational news letters." In 1928 the *Independent* and the *Outlook* were merged.[6] By this time neither paper retained a strong religious identity.

If few Protestant periodicals attracted general readerships after 1900, the Protestant perspective continued to be read in nonreligious papers and journals. Members of the establishment edited and published many of the most prominent journals in this country. Often they reflected a distinctly establishment ethos. Moreover, periodicals such as the *North American Review, Harpers, Scribners,* and the *Atlantic Monthly* commonly contained articles and editorials that explicated Protestant establishment concerns. The decline of the religious press, therefore, may represent a change in modes of influence but not an actual loss of cultural authority.

An ideological shift within Protestantism during the early decades of the twentieth century also came to have considerable bearing upon establishment control of the media. Initially evangelical in theological temperament, certain denominations gradually came to embrace a moderate form of theological liberalism. Many Protestants, of course, resisted the liberal movement and began to identify themselves in opposition to the growing liberalism in particular denominations. For the liberals it was not merely a question of maintaining media influence in secular society; it was also a matter of retaining control of the Protestant share of the religious media in the face of conservative evangelical activity arising within the establishment and to some extent beyond it.

In terms of general cultural influence the nineteenth century may be regarded as the golden era for the Protestant press, but well into the twentieth century an astonishing number of periodicals were still being produced by the establishment churches. The *New Handbook of the*

Churches, published in 1931, listed a total of 542 Protestant denominational journals and magazines.[7] Many, of course, were state and diocesan publications. There were also many foreign language monthlies, Sunday school weeklies, and missionary reviews. All of these were targeted to a very particular and local denominational readership. Nearly all denominations also produced more widely read national papers and journals, such as the *Congregationalist,* the *Baptist,* and the *Lutheran.*

It is significant that among the 542 periodicals listed in the 1931 *Handbook* more than half were published by establishment denominations. Although these establishment churches represented a mere fraction of the 143 Protestant groups in this country, they produced 272 of the periodicals listed. Again, especially among the Northern Baptists, Disciples, and Episcopalians, these constituted many small local enterprises. The establishment share of the periodical market in 1931 reflects quite accurately the numerical strength of these mainline denominations at this time. Of the estimated thirty-one million Protestants in America more than half (over sixteen million) were members of these churches in 1931.[8]

The number of periodicals published by establishment denominations declined significantly during the mid-twentieth century. The *Yearbook of the American Churches* issued for 1961 listed just 75 mainline publications, and more than 30 of these were local United Methodist journals. This means that less than 15 percent of the 504 periodicals cited in the 1961 *Yearbook* were published under establishment auspices. It is apparent that non-establishment groups, generally those that were rigorously conservative or evangelical, by then dominated whatever there was of a "Protestant press." In a general way, the publishing decline is reflected by the overall membership statistics. Between 1931 and 1961 the mainline churches grew from sixteen million to more than twenty-four million members. Yet, during the same period, the overall number of Protestants increased from thirty-one million to sixty-four million.[9] By 1961, then, the establishment churches could claim only 38 percent of American Protestants. Certainly it might be argued that the decline in the number of establishment periodicals cannot be tied only to these less dramatic membership figures. The consolidation of ethnic and language groups had obviated the need for foreign-language journals; the economic depression of the thirties weeded out weaker periodicals; church mergers led to the elimination of overlapping periodicals; and, of course, this decline occurred in the midst of an electronic revolution when radio and television forced changes in all phases of the publishing industry. Still, it should be noted that the drastic decline in mainline publishing occurred at the very time in which evangelical publishers were expanding their markets.

The Christian Century: first issue under the new name.

Does the dwindling of the establishment share of the religious publishing market attest to a concomitant loss of cultural authority? Not necessarily. The number of periodicals published by the establishment groups cannot be assumed to reflect accurately their actual influence in America. Even circulation figures do not provide a full and accurate reading of a journal's cultural sway. Although challenged by evangelicals, certain establishment periodicals have maintained a high degree of cultural visibility and influence. The history of the *Christian Century* is illustrative.

The *Christian Century* was initially published in 1884 at Des Moines, Iowa, under the denominational auspices of the Disciples of Christ and entitled the *Christian Oracle.* Soon the publication moved to Chicago where a group of liberal Disciples headed by Professor Herbert L. Willett, a prominent exponent of biblical higher criticism who taught at the University of Chicago, took over the editorship. Following a name change in 1900 that reflected a mood of expectant optimism about the approaching century, the journal struggled through years of financial difficulty before being literally taken off the auction block in 1908 by

Charles Clayton Morrison, the young paster of Monroe Street Christian Church in Chicago. Despite his own financial strains Morrison gradually transformed this tiny organ of the progressive wing of the Disciples into a broad-based nondenominational liberal journal, accurately described by one of its own chroniclers as "the most influential Protestant magazine of its time."[10] During Morrison's thirty-nine-year editorship, the *Century* came to be regarded as the interpretive standard of the Protestant establishment.

Toward the end of our period the *Century* sustained losses in its always rather modest circulation list.[11] Still, its influence continued to be felt in and out of ecclesiastical circles. One of the first religious publications to be included in the selective *Readers Guide to Periodical Literature*, the *Century* was placed on the shelves of public and academic libraries, and provided an establishment interpretation of religious events and movements. Researchers regularly looked to the *Century* as an opinion maker. In this manner the *Century* continued to shape American religious self-understanding. For many years the *Guide* balanced the inclusion of the *Century* and a few other mainline Protestant journals with important Roman Catholic and Jewish journals. Only after 1960, however, was a self-defined evangelical journal added to the review list.

The maiden issue of *Christianity Today* came off the presses in October of 1956. The initial editorial explained that "theological liberalism," the dominant religious movement of the twentieth century, had "failed to meet the moral and spiritual needs of the people." The new journal, therefore, would offer "historical Christianity" to a generation that had "grown up unaware of the basic truths of the Christian faith taught in the Scriptures and expressed in the creeds of the historic evangelical churches." It would provide "a clear voice" for a segment of American Christianity that long had been "neglected, slighted," and "misrepresented."[12] *Christianity Today* thus presented itself as one of the early entries in an expanding evangelical market that came to include such diverse journals as *Eternity, Decision, Sojourners,* and the *Wittenburg Door.*

One can gain further insight into the visibility and influence of the Protestant establishment by studying the "religion section" of *Time* and *Newsweek* over a span of six decades (see Table 4.1). From the beginning, both publications included religious news in their weekly issues. Evaluation of the stories covered by these magazines reveals not only what a large share of Americans read about current events but, even more, which religious concerns the editors of *Time* and *Newsweek* considered to be newsworthy.

Before the sixties, nearly one-half of all the religious stories covered by *Time* and *Newsweek* were either directly or indirectly related to one of the

Table 4.1. *Frequency of religious references in selected volumes of* Time *and* Newsweek, *1933–84*

	Time						Newsweek					
	T–33 (vols. 21–2)	T–43 (vols. 41–2)	T–53 (vols. 61–2)	T–63 (vols. 81–2)	T–73 (vols. 101–2)	T–83 (vols. 121–2)	N–36 (vols. 7–8)	N–44 (vols. 23–4)	N–54 (vols. 43–4)	N–64 (vols. 63–4)	N–74 (vols. 83–4)	N–84 (vols. 103–4)
Establishment and other denominations												
Northern Baptists (American Baptist)	2	2	5	0	0	0	1	1	0	1	0	0
Congregationalists (UCC)	2	1	0	0	0	0	1	0	0	0	0	0
Disciples of Christ	0	0	0	0	0	0	0	0	0	0	0	0
Episcopalians	9	13	5	1	2	0	1	7	4	7	2	0
Methodists	4	5	8	2	0	0	5	3	1	2	0	0
Lutherans	2	1	4	3	1	0	0	1	3	3	0	0
Presbyterians	5	4	14	1	2	0	5	3	4	2	1	1
Totals	24	26	36	7	5	0	13	15	12	14	3	0

Others

Anglicans	3	14	5	4	0	2	1	11	7	2	1	0
Quakers	0	2	2	0	0	0	0	1	0	0	1	0
Unitarian/Universalists	1	1	3	0	0	1	0	0	0	1	0	0

Religious Topics

Total citations recorded	80	127	183	105	69	32	73	82	87	98	41	31
Specified mainline Protestants (U.S.)	24	26	36	7	5	0	14	14	12	14	3	0
Implied mainline Protestants (U.S.)	13	29	24	32	7	4	19	18	20	19	5	2
Roman Catholic (U.S. and non-U.S.)	19	29	53	30	20	14	26	17	20	35	9	10
Jewish (U.S. and non-U.S.)	2	2	13	4	4	1	0	3	2	7	2	0
Fundamentalist and/or evangelical (direct and implied)	1	4	15	15	9	5	2	5	6	5	9	6
No religion section in issue	2	1	0	1	16	25	8	6	3	5	22	32

Protestant leaders on the covers of *Time,* 1951–61. Clockwise from upper left: Henry Knox Sherrill, Henry Pitney Van Dusen, Theodore Adams, Eugene Carson Blake, Paul Tillich, Franklin Clark Fry. Copyright 1951–61 Time, Inc. All rights reserved. Reprinted by permission.

mainline Protestant denominations. Although a large percentage of the remaining coverage went to Roman Catholicism, a relatively small number of stories were written about non-establishment Protestant groups. By the 1970s *Time* and *Newsweek* had trimmed back their coverage of religious stories, often going three or four weeks without publishing a "religion section"; the number of stories related to establishment Protestantism had clearly declined. At the same time, those about fundamentalists, Pentecostals, and other conservative groups had risen sharply.

It is evident that between 1900 and 1960 the Protestant establishment not only lost much of its control over the religious press but also ceased to be viewed by the secular press as the exclusive or primary representative of American Protestantism. In America, where secularization has been accompanied by religious fractionalization, fundamentalists, Pentecostals, and other non-establishment groups came to share the publishing power with once dominant mainline Protestant churches.

Religious Radio

Modern broadcasting can be traced to 1912 when the United States Congress passed and President Taft signed the initial radio licensing law. The first voice broadcast, however, had been achieved six years earlier by Reginald Aubrey Fessenden, a Canadian who successfully transmitted a Christmas Eve service to ships at sea along the east coast of the United States. In addition to a selection from the Gospel of Luke, radio operators picked up a woman's voice singing Handel's "Largo" and a violin solo of Gounod's "O Holy Night" played by Fessenden himself.[13] Religion and radio have long been wedded.

During the following decade the radio industry made great strides in technology, and President Wilson signaled the promise of the medium when he broadcast his famous Fourteen Points across the Atlantic to the German people in January 1918. The first non-experimental regular radio broadcasts came in 1920 when Westinghouse Electric and Manufacturing Company established station KDKA in Pittsburgh. KDKA went on the air on November 1, 1920, just in time to broadcast the Harding-Cox election returns. Two months later KDKA carried the first regular radio broadcast of a church service. A Westinghouse engineer received permission from his rector, the Reverend Edward Van Etten, to broadcast a vesper service from Calvary Episcopal Church in Pittsburgh. Two other Westinghouse engineers, one Jewish and the other Roman Catholic, dressed in choir robes, handled the technical aspects of the program. Van Etten previously had arranged to have his associate conduct the January 2 vesper service, so the Reverend Lewis Whittemore became the first radio preacher. Van Etten confessed later that he had been unaware of the significance of the occasion.

> The whole thing was an experiment, and I remember distinctly my own feeling that after all no harm could be done! It never occurred to me that the little black box was really going to carry out the service to the outside world. I knew there was such a thing as a wireless, but somehow I thought there would be some fluke in the connection, and that the whole thing would be a fizzle![14]

KDKA's success was quickly emulated as stations sprang up across the country. In 1922, 382 stations were already in operation. By 1927 the number swelled to 732! During these years the number of receiving sets jumped from 60,000 to 6,500,000. The early stations generally consisted of small transmitters owned by electrical companies, radio shops, department stores, colleges, chambers of commerce, and other organizations that sought "to capitalize upon the novelty of the radio." The churches got in on the ground floor of radio braodcasting. Of the 600 stations operating in 1925, it is estimated that 63 were church owned.[15] Local congregations purchased these stations to enhance their ministries and, for the most part, operated only on Sundays. Few church-owned stations survived the depression era. The Radio Act of 1927, an attempt to control the chaos in the radio industry, led to the adoption of new technical standards (assigned frequencies, regular schedules, better equipment) for operating stations. Unable to afford the required equipment or personnel, religious stations sold off their licenses to private owners.

Few mainline Protestant churches owned and operated their own radio stations at this time. Most were content to participate in interdenominational efforts to secure broadcast time on local stations and network systems. It was the policy of the Federal Council of Churches of Christ, representing about twenty-five Protestant denominations in the twenties, to encourage local councils of churches to develop cooperative radio ministries. The earliest and most notable example of such cooperation occurred in New York City, where Frank C. Goodman, supported by the Greater New York Federation of Churches, developed a schedule of three weekly programs. One of these, "National Radio Pulpit," featuring popular Brooklyn pastor, Dr. S. Parkes Cadman, first aired May 3, 1923, on WEAF. The feature became so popular that when the National Broadcasting Company (NBC) was formed with WEAF (now WNBC) as the flagship station, Cadman's program became network radio. "National Radio Pulpit" set a standard for the religious market as a procession of great preachers, including Ralph Sockman, David H. C. Read, Harry Emerson Fosdick, and Norman Vincent Peale, succeeded Cadman.[16]

Now that a nationwide network of stations had been established, NBC naturally turned to the Federal Council to develop religious programming. Such an arrangement made it easier for NBC to control program content and to avoid providing the many Protestant denominations with "equal time." Similar arrangements were later made with representative Roman Catholic and Jewish groups, the National Council of Catholic Men, and the Jewish Theological Seminary in America.[17] In 1928 NBC established a Religious Advisory Council, and asked Charles S. Macfarland, the General Secretary of the Federal Council, to join Catholic and Jewish counterparts in an effort to bring religious broadcasting into harmony with network concerns. The council formulated four policies that shaped religious radio for decades:

1 Religious groups should receive free time, but pay for production costs.

A KDKA radio preacher, 1923. Courtesy of Radio Station KDKA, Pittsburgh.

2 Religious broadcasts should be nondenominational.
3 Network programs should use one speaker for continuity.
4 Broadcasts should employ a preaching format, "avoiding matters of doctrine and controversial subjects."[18]

These policies served as general Federal Council, and hence mainline Protestant, policies until 1944 when Everett Parker organized the Joint Religious Radio Committee of the Congregational Christian, Methodist, Presbyterian (U.S.A.), and United Church of Canada denominations. Convinced that the preaching format did not appeal to a broad base of listeners, Parker's group began to produce more creative and dramatic programs. These programs were so well received that the Radio Commission began to review its long-standing format policies. In 1948 the Protestant Radio Commission of the Federal Council merged with the Joint Religious Radio Committee. In 1950, when the old Federal Council became the National Council of Churches of Christ in the United States, its Broadcasting and Film Commission functioned much like the earlier Federal Council Radio Commission. Although they cooperated in these ecumenical efforts, mainline denominations (notably the Methodists, Episcopalians, and Presbyterians) developed their own innovative radio programs.[19] The many local programs, with rare exceptions, broadcast traditional preaching and worship services.

The partnership of NBC and the Federal Council tended to give the Protestant establishment control over religious network broadcasting. It was an arrangement that involved "sustaining" or free air time. This broadcasting hegemony was threatened in 1927 when the Columbia Broadcasting Service (CBS) network was formed. Needing revenue to survive during its infancy, CBS accepted payment from non-establishment groups until 1931. After the embarrassment caused by the political extremism of its client Father Charles Coughlin, CBS adopted a "sustaining time" policy and refused to sell time for religious broadcasting. CBS followed a policy of developing its own programs but did invite the Federal Council to supervise Protestant broadcasts. When ABC, actually the old "Blue Network" of NBC, was formed during the forties, it too adopted a policy of giving air time only to mainline Protestant groups. The Mutual Broadcasting System, formed during the mid-thirties, followed an early policy of providing *only* purchased time to religious broadcasters. This practice of course allowed non-establishment groups to build national audiences. Charles Fuller's "Old-Fashioned Revival Hour" was Mutual's largest customer during the early 1940s, a time when one-quarter of Mutual's revenues were obtained from religious broadcasts. In 1944 Mutual shifted its policies, restricting religious broadcasting to

Sunday mornings, cutting program length, and forbidding the solicitation of funds over the air. Mutual quickly lost many of its religious customers.[20]

The Communications Act of 1934 empowered the Federal Communications Commission (FCC) to license local stations to broadcast in a particular area over a given frequency. Based on the principle that the airways belong to the people, the act also stipulated that the stations must operate in the interest of the listening public in the broadcast area. The FCC's suggestions regarding public-interest programming often included "religion." Rather than risk having licenses revoked, station owners tended to set aside free air time for religious broadcasting. This "sustaining time" was normally made available on Sunday mornings, a time of few listeners and therefore of low advertising revenue.

In 1960 this situation began to change as the FCC concluded that the public would not be served by distinguishing, in the evaluation of a station's performance, between "sustaining time" programs and commercially sponsored ones. As long as the required proportion of public-interest programs were broadcast – whether these programs were free or sponsored – the stations would be meeting their public-service obligations. This change in policy had a dramatic impact on religious broadcasting.[21] The establishment Protestants who had cooperated with the broadcast companies in producing "sustaining time" programs were now thrust into an open market.

The open market, of course, had long been controlled by nonestablishment groups who had been paying for broadcast time since the early days of network radio, and who, quite naturally, had opposed the long-standing relationship between the Federal Council and the national networks. These groups, mostly fundamentalists and evangelicals, not only resented the implicit assumption that the Federal Council represented normative American Protestantism, they were convinced of a conspiracy to keep them off the air altogether. When the non–establishment groups perceived that they were being denied the right to buy time, they began to marshal forces against their perceived enemy, the Federal Council (later the National Council).[22]

When the National Association of Evangelicals (NAE) was organized in 1942 one of its immediate concerns was to counter the influence it believed the Federal Council exercised in network religious broadcasting. Anxious about access to the airwaves, representatives at initial meetings of the NAE quickly passed a resolution calling for the establishment of a radio committee "in order to help in securing a fair and equal opportunity for the use of radio facilities by evangelical groups and individuals." In 1944 evangelical broadcasters established the National

Religious Broadcasters. Although officially separate from the NAE, the National Religious Broadcasters remained closely tied to the philosophy and goals of the NAE.[23]

Despite apparent disadvantages during the early decades, the non-establishment broadcasters gradually gained control of religious radio. If a few conservative Protestants initially resisted the medium, fearing that radio was Satan's accomplice, they soon wholeheartedly embraced radio as a primary vehicle for spreading the Gospel. One student of American evangelicalism claims that the emerging strength of the movement was due in no small part to a core of influential religious broadcasts: "The Lutheran Hour" (Walter Maier), "The Old-Fashioned Revival Hour" (Charles Fuller), "The Back-to-God Hour" (Christian Reformed), "Back to the Bible" (Theodore Epp), "Haven of Rest" (Bob Myers), "National Radio Chapel" (Paul Rader), and "The Radio Bible Class" (M. R. DeHaan).[24] Featuring dynamic personalities and effective speakers, these broadcasts captured and sustained large audiences. Forced by early policies of the networks to pay their way into radio, the evangelical entrepreneurs learned well the lessons of media marketing.

As late as 1956 mainliners sought to prop up an earlier version of "Protestant America." The Broadcasting and Film Commission of the National Council of Churches issued a policy statement advocating that stations and networks provide free time and refuse to sell commercial time for religious broadcasting. At this juncture the policy was rejected by radio executives as well as evangelicals.[25] Times had changed. The alliance between the networks and mainline Protestantism had fallen apart. The Protestant establishment, which once had had a market monopoly on religious radio, had become barely audible. By itself this did not prove a loss of cultural authority; religious radio has never attracted more than a relatively small percentage of the total radio audience. Still, a potential vehicle for cultural influence had been virtually lost to establishment Protestantism.

Religious Television

Religious television can be traced back to Easter Sunday, 1940, when separate Roman Catholic and Protestant services were telecast for those in New York City who owned primitive receiving sets. In keeping with the vision of America as a nation of tripartite faith, a Jewish Passover service was telecast a month later.[26]

Following a precedent established during the early years of radio, the television networks sought at the outset to deal primarily with "the reputable and mainline religious groups." In fact, the television producers simply adopted those groups that had been advisers and sponsors of religious radio – the National Council of Catholic Men, the Jewish Theological Seminary in America, and the Federal Council of Churches. The networks assisted in the shaping of these early programs by making production facilities, technical services, and even some financial resources available to these groups who then produced their own programs. In some cases, networks used religious consultants for their own productions that were then fed to stations for airing on "sustaining" or public-service time. Local stations often made similar arrangements for producing and airing local religious programs.[27]

The established religious groups generally benefited from these arrangements, and the fifties became "the heyday of the network mainline religious programming." Long-running and award-winning programs originated during this period: "Lamp unto my Feet" (CBS), "Directions" (ABC), "Frontiers of Faith" (NBC), and "Look Up and Live" (CBS). While these ecumenical, network-sponsored programs were high-quality productions, they tended to express rather broad religious truths rather than raise pointed economic, social, or theological issues. Noting this deficiency, a few of the larger denominations, especially those not represented by the Federal Council, began to develop their own syndicated programs, some of which were then granted free air time by local stations. Despite high production costs, Southern Baptists syndicated "The Answer," Seventh-Day Adventists produced "Faith for Today," and the Lutheran Church-Missouri Synod presented "This Is the Life." Therefore, as television moved into the 1960s, four types of religious telecasting existed: (1) network sustaining-time programs; (2) syndicated sustaining-time programs; (3) local programs (mostly sustaining time); and (4) paid-time audience-supported syndicated programs. The last type came eventually to dominate religious television.[28]

Although Oral Roberts and Rex Humbard began their television ministries during the fifties, the real explosion of paid-time religious programming occurred after the late 1960s. Often called "the electronic church," these predominantly evangelical and fundamentalist programs were to develop into a multimillion dollar industry.[29] In 1959 purchased airtime accounted for 53 percent of religious telecasting. Some three decades later the figure would be 92 percent. Paid-time programming, moreover, would nearly eliminate local religious programming as stations sought both to maximize their revenues and to fulfill public-service obligations by selling religious broadcast time to the highest bidders.[30] With the possible exception of Robert Schuller's "Hour of Power," none of the top-rated paid-time programs of this later period would maintain a mainline Protestant profile.

As the evangelicals came to dominate the television market, establishment Protestants were even less visible on television than they were audible on radio. The mainline churches seemed little inclined to spend the money and expend the effort to compete with the electronic evangelicals. But, again, one must question whether this was incontrovertible evidence of the decline of the mainline. Television, some suggested, was not a good medium for communicating the more subtle Christian truths generally held by members of the Protestant establishment. Effective television, they said, required more unambiguous and immediate forms of communication. But if the mainliners had refused to bend their message to the "logic of television," they had also virtually abandoned the field to those who were not only willing but eager to proclaim a repetitive and unambiguous message. Having lost control of religious television, the establishment Protestants had, at the least, lost some of their power to shape Christian identity.

Conclusion

By 1900, members of the Protestant establishment already sensed that they were losing some of their sway over the publishing market in America. Even before the turn of the century the editor of a Protestant paper argued for a strong religious press, because "the standpoint of the leading non-religious Journals is no longer avowedly Christian."[31] Still, while the patterns of immigration and the process of secularism may have dimmed once-bright hopes for the establishment of "Protestant America," mainline Protestants certainly felt that they held enough cultural influence to be a "leaven in the loaf" of the print media. After all, members of this group were well placed throughout all segments of society. Certainly, during the early decades of the twentieth century, members of the establishment were confident that theirs was the normative Protestant voice in America.

As the church entered the electronic age it was only natural for the emerging radio networks to turn to the Federal Council of Churches in Christ, the ecumenical establishment, to represent the interests of Protestants. The cozy relationship that developed between the national networks and the Federal Council (later the National Council) tells us that the mainline churches were regarded, at least by radio executives, as the standard-bearers of Protestantism. The establishment groups baptized the radio industry and the radio industry helped to promote an official nonsectarian version of Protestantism. Robert Lynn argues that during the thirties and forties, the thinking of mainliners about radio was in "the spirit of Christendom."[32] To some degree, all of this carried over into the relation of the establishment churches to television.

Despite relatively easy access, however, mainline Protestants were never very comfortable with the electronic media. Already during the forties Charles Crowe, a Methodist pastor in St. Louis, complained to readers of the *Christian Century* that "in spite of the fact that radio affords the most powerful medium of mass influence in history, with opportunity to reach a vast, heterogeneous audience untouched by conventional church activities, its use by religious leaders has been lamentably unintelligent and ineffective." Crowe was convinced that the standard preaching format failed to take advantage of the medium. "Regardless of how popular the preacher may be, these programs often lack the common touch, the dramatic, mass appeal which is the genius of radio."[33] Crowe was undoubtedly aware of the fact that non-establishment fundamentalists and evangelicals, even though hamstrung by having to pay for broadcasting time, could boast of several successful radio programs that deviated from the straight preaching format. Indeed, the non-establishment groups were in the process of claiming the religious airwaves. As the televangelists later took control of the television market, it seemed apparent that the evangelicals were far more able than establishment Protestants to take advantage of the electronic revolution.

Seeking to explain the phenomenon of television to readers of the *Christian Century*, Harvey Cox suggested in the 1960s that the liberal church had not learned to contend with "postliterate society." In moving us from written to visual electronic communication, television had helped change the culture's way of perceiving reality.[34] And James Taylor, editor of a mainline journal, later explained what this had meant for the establishment churches:

> Television is a captive of time and space; words are not. Words are reflective; television is experiential. . . . The liberal churches depend on words. They offer carefully reasoned theologies. They publish magazines. They write letters. When the liberal churches dip into the experiential world of television, their programs often manage to be, at the same time, secularly acclaimed critical triumphs and spiritual disasters.

Wedded to the written and spoken word, the establishment churches could not compete with the experiential evangelicals. The future, according to Taylor, was therefore ominous for mainline Protestantism:

> Today, we're in a new Reformation. I see nothing that the liberal churches can do to stop it or change it. We might as well face the fact that more and more people who would otherwise have belonged to our churches are going to be born again out of television's experiential womb.[35]

By the late eighties, a period of stability in the mainline churches and turbulence for televangelists, none of this seemed quite so predictable.

Between 1900 and 1960, however, the influence the Protestant establishment exercised over the media, both religious and nonreligious, declined. On the one hand, the cultural forces of pluralism and secularism eroded the Protestant base of support in the open media markets. On the other hand, emergent non-establishment evangelical groups competed vigorously for the religious markets, especially radio and television. One must be cautious, however, not to overstate the degree of establishment decline. Even at its apex the Protestant mainstream was not as dominant as is usually suggested to students in introductory American religion courses. A mainstream, yes, but non-establishment groups always claimed and found access to the media. Similarly, the later renaissance of evangelicalism was probably less dramatic than most observers assumed. The establishment denominations have always contained a large percentage of evangelical moderates who have supported both establishment and non-establishment religious media. In a similar way moderates who have not been identified with establishment denominations have embraced a broad range of religious media. After 1960, the Protestant establishment in America continued to draw its membership from and be characterized by the "moderate middle" of a wide range of denominations.[36]

NOTES

1 "The Radiophone in Preaching," *Christian Century* 40(March 22, 1923): 355.
2 Robert W. Lynn, "The Unnoticed Revolution: Mainline Protestantism and the Media Society" (unpublished manuscript, presented in 1974 at Claremont, Calif.), 20.
3 Arthur M. Schlesinger, cited in Theodore H. White, *The Making of the President 1972* (New York: Atheneum, 1973), 245.
4 Lynn, "Unnoticed Revolution," 29; and Judith S. Duke, *Religious Publishing and Communications* (White Plains, N.Y.: Knowledge Industry Publications, 1981), 161–2.
5 *Outlook* 45(January 2, 1897): 15; and Frank Luther Mott, *A History of American Magazines, Vol. III, 1865–1885* (Cambridge, Mass.: Harvard University Press, 1957), 422–35.
6 Mott, *A History of American Magazines, vol. II, 1850–65,* 367–79.
7 See Charles Stelzle (ed.), *The New Handbook of the Churches* (New York: J. E. Stohlman, 1931), 89–156.
8 Ibid., 259–64.
9 Benson Y. Landis (ed.), *Yearbook of American Churches, 1961* (New York: Office of Publication and Distribution, National Council of Churches, 1960), 12–105.

10 See Charles Clayton Morrison, "The First Twenty Years," *Christian Century* 45(October 11, 1928): 1220–2; "Looking Ahead," *Christian Century* 55(October 5, 1938): 1185–8; and Linda-Marie Delloff, "C. C. Morrison: Shaping a Journal's Identity," *Christian Century* 101(January 18, 1984): 43–7.

11 See Duke, *Religious Publishing,* 165.

12 "Why Christianity Today?" *Christianity Today* 1(October 15, 1956): 20.

13 J. Harold Ellens, *Models of Religious Broadcasting* (Grand Rapids, Mich.: Eerdmans, 1974), 14–15.

14 See Jeffrey K. Hadden and Charles E. Swann, *Prime Time Preachers: The Rising Power of Televangelism* (Reading, Mass.: Addison-Wesley, 1981), 72–3; Ben Armstrong, *The Electric Church* (Nashville: Thomas Nelson, 1979), 19–20; Eric Barnouw, *A Tower of Babel: A History of Broadcasting to 1933* (New York: Oxford University Press, 1966), 71, and Spencer Miller, Jr., "Religion and Radio," *Annals of the American Academy of Political and Social Science* 177(January 1935): 135–40.

15 Herman S. Hettinger, "Broadcasting in the United States," *Annals of the American Academy of Political and Social Science* 177(January 1935): 1–3; Miller, "Religion and Radio," 135–40; and Ellens, *Models,* 16.

16 Ellens, *Models,* 16–18; William F. Fore, "A Short History of Religious Broadcasting," in A. William Bluem, *Religious Television Programs: A Study in Relevance* (New York: Hastings House, 1969), 203–11.

17 Hadden and Swann, *Prime Time Preachers,* 74–8; Ellens, *Models,* 18–20; and Peter G. Horsfield, *Religious Television: The American Experience* (New York: Longman, 1984), 12–15.

18 Fore, "Short History," 203–4; and Hadden and Swann, *Prime Time Preachers,* 77.

19 Ellens, *Models,* 32–7; Fore, "Short History," 204–5; and Horsfield, *Religious Television,* 3–7.

20 Ellens, *Models,* 18; Hadden and Swann, *Prime Time Preachers,* 77; and Daniel P. Fuller, *Give the Winds a Mighty Voice* (Waco, Texas: Word Books, 1972), 155–6.

21 Horsfield, *Religious Television,* 13–15.

22 See "The Scramble for Radio-TV," editorial, *Christianity Today* 1(February 18, 1957): 20–23; and Lowell Sperry Saunders, "The National Religious Broadcasters and the Availability of Commercial Radio Time" (Ph.D. diss., University of Illinois, 1968).

23 Quoted in Hadden and Swann, *Prime Time Preachers,* 80. See also Saunders, "Religious Broadcasters," 32–40.

24 For fundamentalist objections to radio evangelism, see Wendell P. Loveless, *Manual of Gospel Broadcasting* (Chicago: Moody Press, 1946), 15–17. For radio's contribution to burgeoning evangelicalism, see Joel A. Carpenter, "Fundamentalist Institutions and the Rise of Evangelical Protestantism, 1929–1942," *Church History* 49(March 1980): 62–75, and "From Fundamentalism to the New Evangelical Coalition," in George M. Marsden (ed.), *Evangelicalism in Modern America* (Grand Rapids, Mich.: Eerdmans, 1984, 3–16.

25 See Saunders, "Religious Broadcasters," 150–8.

26 Hadden and Swann, *Prime Time Preachers,* 81.
27 Horsfield, *Religious Television,* 1–3.
28 Ibid., 5–6.
29 Ibid., 8–10; Hadden and Swann, *Prime Time Preachers,* 17–45; 100–2; and Charles E. Swann, "The Electric Church," *Presbyterian Survey* 69(May 1979): 9–16.
30 Horsfield, *Religious Television,* 9–10, 101–10; and William Martin, "The Birth of a Media Myth," *The Atlantic* 247(June 1981): 7, 10–11, 16.
31 Cited by Theodore Peterson, "Estates in Conflict," *Christian Century* 79(July 18, 1962): 883.
32 Lynn, "Unnoticed Revolution," 24.
33 Charles W. Crowe, "Religion on the Air," *Christian Century* 61(August 23, 1944): 974.
34 Harvey Cox, "The Gospel and Postliterate Man," *Christian Century* 81 (November 25, 1964): 1459–61.
35 James A. Taylor, "Progeny of Programmers: Evangelical Religion and the Television Age," *Christian Century* 94(April 20, 1977): 379–82.
36 See, e.g., Richard G. Hutcheson, *Mainline Churches and the Evangelicals* (Atlanta: John Knox Press, 1981), 165–80.

SELECT BIBLIOGRAPHY

Barnouw, Eric. *A Tower of Babel: A History of Broadcasting to 1933.* New York: Oxford University Press, 1966.

Duke, Judith S. *Religious Publishing and Communications.* White Plains, N.Y.: Knowledge Industry Publications, 1981.

Ellens, J. Harold. *Models of Religious Broadcasting.* Grand Rapids, Mich.: Eerdmans, 1974.

Fore, William F. "A Short History of Religious Broadcasting." In A. William Bluem, *Religious Television Programs: A Study in Relevance,* 203–11. New York: Hastings House, 1969.

Television and Religion: The Shaping of Faith, Values, and Culture. Minneapolis: Augsburg, 1987.

Frankl, Razelle. *Televangelism: The Marketing of Popular Religion.* Carbondale, Ill.: Southern Illinois University Press, 1987.

Hadden, Jeffrey K., and Charles E. Swann. *Prime Time Preachers: The Rising Power of Televangelism.* Reading, Mass.: Addison-Wesley, 1981.

Horsfield, Peter G. *Religious Television: The American Experience.* New York: Longman, 1984.

Hutcheson, Richard G. *Mainline Churches and the Evangelicals.* Atlanta: John Knox Press, 1981.

Marty, Martin E. "The Protestant Press." In Martin E. Marty, John G. Deedy, Jr., David Wolf Silverman, and Robert Lekachman, *The Religious Press in America,* 5–63. New York: Holt, Rinehart, and Winston, 1963.

Mott, Frank Luther. *A History of American Magazines.* 4 vols. Cambridge, Mass.: Harvard University Press, 1957.

III

The Protestant Agenda: Matters Arising

As establishment churches and their people, trying to adjust to twentieth-century conditions, pursued traditional responsibilities in new ways, they were also led to undertake projects that at least seemed significantly new – and of course to undertake these with some show of allegiance to their heritage.

The two endeavors we have chosen to emphasize as prime items of new business on the establishment's agenda are their organized, self-conscious approaches to Protestant ecumenism and to social reform. For both of these, and for the two of them as connected efforts, there had been sporadic but highly significant nineteenth-century precedents in the work of such collaborative agencies as the Evangelical Alliance.

Like the movements analyzed in the following essays, these prototypes had tried to combine unifying, evangelizing, and reforming objectives. They had responded to a changing religious demography, and especially to the dramatic increase in Roman Catholic population, with programs that can be seen as defensive – a circling of the wagons – or as embodying genuine determination to transcend denominational differences and work for broad societal objectives. Like the twentieth-century embodiments of the ecumenical and social movements, they had seemed to produce the unwanted effect of distancing Protestant leaders and theorists from their prime constituents – the people in the pews.

So then, what was new? What was new was the central (and, detractors thought, overweening) importance now accorded to the federative and social emphases. In the thinking that informed these enterprises, moreover, both friends and foes heard a different tone, if not always different words, when it came to the relationship between evangelism and social action. Church-based reformers in the mid-nineteenth century had nearly always wanted reform to serve the purposes of evangelism.

With the rise of the social gospel at the end of the century, and then its wholesale adoption by the Federal Council of Churches (FCC) after 1908, the establishment churches became more vulnerable to charges that they were scanting personal evangelism in favor of direct reform of the structures of society.

Robert A. Schneider's essay describes the new federative ventures (principally the FCC) that thus found themselves attempting more than one difficult act of amalgamation: not only must they link the denominational bureaucracies, with their divergent aims and histories; they were also pressed to synthesize traditional conceptions of Protestant responsibility with freshly minted responses to the urban industrial society.

William McGuire King examines the social emphasis during the later decades of our era – a time when a somewhat seasoned "reform establishment" ventured into a world political arena where, King believes, it gained a long-sought public visibility while losing much of what had been most prophetic in the earlier social enthusiasm.

5

Voice of Many Waters: Church Federation in the Twentieth Century

ROBERT A. SCHNEIDER

"It is the voice of many millions that speaks here today like the voice of many waters." Speaking for the first time, early in the twentieth century, the Federal Council of the Churches of Christ in America did not quite claim that as the voice of the people it was the voice of God; but the Council spoke confidently, certain that the sentiments it voiced had long been shared by "the larger Protestant Churches of the country, holding to historical and evangelical Christianity." Those churches were joined by others for the constituting meeting in 1908, and all expected that soon the majority of Protestant denominations that "hold to Christ as the head" would belong to the Council. The new organization, "conscious of the numbers and potency of the religious forces represented in its membership," declared itself "profoundly impressed with the present opportunity for coordinating the churches in the interest of wider and larger service for America and for the Kingdom of God."[1]

Forty-two years later, toward the end of the era treated in this volume, the founders of the National Council of the Churches of Christ in the United States of America expressed similar feelings of promise and responsibility. Because "the American Churches, of which the Council is one of the visible symbols, are in their true estate the soul of the nation," the new body would be "an organ through which the will of God may become effective as an animating, creative and unifying force within our national society."[2] Such statements, by both councils, reflect pretensions to virtual establishment status. Although the United States could have no legally recognized state church, the ecumenical organizations claimed for themselves the role of an informal national establishment. Assuming a continuity of beliefs and purposes that ran from individual church members through denominational structures to cooperative agencies, the Federal and National councils grounded their public claims to authority

The establishment lines up. A session in Westminster Hall, Philadelphia, of the first Federal Council meeting, December 1908. From Elias B. Sanford, *Federal Council of the Churches of Christ in America: Report of the First Meeting . . . Philadelphia, 1908* (New York: The Revell Press, 1909), p. 8.

in their representative nature and the size of their constituencies. Thus the executive committee of the Federal Council asserted in 1908 that any body representing "to any extent" over seventeen million church members and "a family and individual constituency" of half the nation's population "can but receive world-wide recognition from those who thoughtfully watch the trend of national and international affairs." And the first National Council delegates, informing President Truman during the Korean crisis that they supported the United Nations and prayed for him, also noted that they represented twenty-nine denominations and over thirty-one million Americans.[3]

The organizations of the Protestant ecumenical movement, of which the Federal and National councils are merely leading examples, have not received from historians the attention they deserve. Summary judgments abound, testifying to the widespread perception that the councils exercised or at least were intended to exercise Protestant power. There has been little systematic analysis of the evidence supporting that perception. This brief essay is not a comprehensive interpretation of Protestant cooperative organizations – that remains to be undertaken – but simply a thematic overview of the relationship between these organizations and the Protestant establishment in the earlier twentieth century. That the relationship was a close and vital one is clear from the number of references to ecumenical agencies in the other essays in this book.

The cooperative organizations that merged in 1950 to form the National Council of Churches, and especially the most prominent of them, the Federal Council, were dominated by the denominations we are calling the Protestant establishment. Federal Council traits and tensions, consequently, reflect those of the establishment, and the Council's stated purposes reveal the establishment's agenda. Although the Council failed to create a Protestant united front, it did retain the loyalty of a substantial number of Protestant denominations. For member churches, the Council functioned as an "established church" of which they were a part. It embodied in a single institution the authority, interests, and activities of a religious establishment otherwise incorporated only in particular denominations. The Council provided practical services to its members, and facilitated their access to centers of political and economic power. It also served, like any established church, as a symbol of basic values, a constant reminder to the faithful of their duties to God, church, and society. When they repeatedly emphasized the two broad purposes of the Federal Council – to both manifest Protestant unity and reform American society – Council leaders implied that the organization possessed the comprehensive range of concerns of a religious establishment. And this embodiment of a diffuse establishment, like any national church, produced an elite that interacted with political and economic elites. The limits of the fragmented establishment's authority are suggested by the pattern of Federal Council achievements and failures: The Council succeeded most often when its efforts were perceived as appropriate by those in political or economic power, or when it acted in concert with other religious interest groups. It was most influential when both conditions were fulfilled.

Cooperative Organizations and the Establishment

The bewildering array of establishment-affiliated cooperative organizations in the late nineteenth and early twentieth centuries can be sorted out most easily if the organizations are characterized by their final relationship to the National Council of Churches after 1950. A first category consists of the organizations that formed the core of the Council. The Federal Council of Churches was unique among these agencies because it was a representative federation of denominations. The other parent organizations were almost all special interest groups made up of denominational executives with the same areas of responsibility in different churches. The Foreign Missions Conference of North America grew out of an 1893 meeting of the foreign mission board officers from twenty-three denominations. Administrators of home mission, educational, stewardship, and media programs – along with the leaders of women's mission boards – created similar organizations. Although independent of each other, and varying widely in the number of member churches, these groups were all initiated and dominated by establishment denominations (the Home Mission Council, for example, originally consisted of Northern Baptists, Congregationalists, Evangelical Lutherans, northern Methodists, northern and southern Presbyterians, United Presbyterians, Dutch Reformed, and German Reformed). The agencies formed a coalition of cooperative organizations with different concerns but essentially the same controlling constituencies.[4]

In 1908 this coalition was confronted with a new Federal Council of Churches. Created by the coalition's parent denominations, the Council united not simply board officers but the churches themselves. Here was the core around which other organizations could gather in a more comprehensive and centralized Protestant cooperative complex. "Consultative member" status in the Federal Council for each group was accompanied by increasingly close coordination among all the agencies. The Council's impulse was to be comprehensive, but it soon relinquished some fields of interest, such as foreign missions, to the appropriate organizations. Agencies dealing with central Council concerns, however, were usually brought into a close – and potentially subordinate – relationship. Within five years of the Council's founding, for instance, the Home Missions Council and its officers were listed in the Federal Council's reports, identified as a cooperating body but implicitly part of the Council's structure.[5] In 1950 the sprawling complex of eight interacting, establishment-related cooperative organizations – offering activities ranging from high-level strategic consultations of executive officers to the mass ecumenical rituals of the Federal Council's assemblies – was consolidated into a single body, the National Council of Churches, "the most complex and intricate piece of ecclesiastical machinery this planet has ever witnessed."[6]

The second category of cooperative organizations comprises those that predated the complex that would become the National Council, or originated outside of it, but that merged with an agency of this complex or, later, joined the National Council. In the third category are organizations that avoided inclusion either in the original complex or in the Council. The organizations in these two categories originated as pre-1880 voluntary societies, pre-1880 general cooperative bodies, or post-1880 "movements." There seems to be no clear correlation between an organization's origin and its eventual relationship to the National Council.

Three venerable voluntary societies survived from the early days of evangelical activism into the late nineteenth century. One, the American Tract Society, retained its evangelical orientation when the establishment became "liberal," and eventually associated itself with the conservative Protestant churches aligned with the National Association of Evangelicals. The International Sunday School Association, on the other hand, united with the Sunday School Council of Evangelical Denominations (an old coalition special interest group) and thereby entered the cooperative complex. The American Bible Society followed a middle path, avoiding entangling alliances with the "complex" organizations but maintaining close ties with the establishment churches. To maintain those ties it had to adjust to the Federal Council (dropping its insistence on the King James Version, for instance, as a result of the popularity of the Council-sponsored Revised Standard Version).[7]

One of the pre-1880 general cooperative bodies, the Evangelical Alliance, was the most immediate forerunner of the Federal Council and eventually disappeared into it; the other two bodies, the Young Men's and Young Women's Christian Associations, were among the Council's strongest competitors. The Evangelical Alliance for the United States of America functioned briefly in the late 1840s and was revived after 1866. The program of common action through which it sought to advance evangelical unity – a "practical" orientation typical of American Protestant ecumenism – made it part of the evangelical crusade for a Protestant America: it forwarded "religious liberty" by supporting Protestant minorities in Roman Catholic countries, and promoted "Christian union" in the United States by voicing anti-Catholic and nativist concerns about immigration and urbanization. After 1886 the new Alliance general secretary, Congregationalist Josiah Strong, prodded the organization to reform society as well as to demonstrate evangelical solidarity. Strong combined the convictions of the "social gospel" (that sin was social as well as individual, and that the gospel of Jesus Christ was the only adequate response to the problems of an urban, industrial, and capitalist society) with a vision of Christian cooperation on the congregational level. He moved too far too fast, however. Local cooperation threatened denominational leaders, and the social gospel alienated conservative Alliance members; in 1898 Strong resigned from the Alliance.[8]

The Alliance leaders who drew back from social action also did not endorse the growing interest among church people in federation. The Alliance survived in name until 1944, when its records and assets were given to the Federal Council, but the most active Alliance leaders had long since transferred their attention, as well as their social gospel and federative interests, to the church federation movement. There was a direct, often unrecognized connection between the Evangelical Alliance and the Federal Council; there was also an important parallel. The Council inherited the ambitious goal of balancing the dual purposes of Josiah Strong's Alliance: to manifest Protestant unity and to apply the social gospel.

The Young Men's and Young Women's Christian Associations were also changed by social gospel influence. They expanded their focus from the Christian nurture of young adult workers to a full range of social service activities, while remaining independent, lay-controlled organizations, "intimately allied with the churches, and generally regarding themselves as carrying on a program on behalf of the churches in the community."[9] The Associations tried to cooperate rather than compete with the Federal Council, but the latter seemed to them an uncertain, narrowly church-bound undertaking. The surprisingly small role played in the Federal Council by John R. Mott, undoubtedly the most famous Protestant ecumenist of the early twentieth century, is explained in part by his close identification with the YMCA's views.[10]

The significance of the Council of Churches as a concept and an actual institution became apparent during World War I, when the Christian Associations' efforts to act as official military social service agencies representing the Protestant churches were rebuffed by the denominations.

From that point on, organizations with formal ecclesiastical connections – in this case the General War-Time Commission of the Churches and the Federal Council that sponsored it – replaced the Associations as the primary agents of establishment cooperation and social action.[11]

Among the new Protestant organizations that continued to spring up in the late nineteenth and early twentieth centuries were a series of supposedly informal, spontaneous, lay-led "movements." Most familiar is the Student Volunteer Movement for Foreign Missions, formed in 1888, but similar campaigns devoted to the support of seminarians and to coordinated denominational fund-raising were organized early in the new century. Two became formal organizations (the Missionary Education Movement and the Inter-Seminary Movement) and were among those merged into the National Council. The Student Volunteer Movement followed them in 1959. But the Interchurch World Movement of 1919, rather than giving way to the Federal Council-oriented complex, almost succeeded in replacing it.

Following a well-received joint Protestant wartime fund-raising drive, establishment leaders, with the support of John D. Rockefeller, Jr., launched a massive campaign for a unified education and evangelism budget. This movement "represented, potentially, the formalization and institutionalization of a quasi-Protestant establishment in the United States. The thirty denominations participating in the joint budget represented about sixty percent of Protestant church membership in America."[12] When the Interchurch Movement sought official denominational endorsement and control it became a direct competitor of the Federal Council. Council income and prestige suffered from the Movement's well-publicized activities.

The movement overreached itself, however, and its collapse in 1920 left the churches in debt. The Federal Council's slower, less flamboyant style of cooperation was vindicated. The Council "emerged from the Interchurch experiment as the central unifying agency of American Protestantism."[13] Ironically, the Council and the churches continued quietly to imitate the movement's utilization of business techniques and bureaucratic procedures.

The Structure of the Federal Council

What was this Federal Council of Churches that reoriented the cooperative coalition around itself, replaced the Evangelical Alliance, forced the American Bible Society, the YMCAs, and the YWCAs to adjust to its presence, and outlived the sensational Interchurch Movement? The origins of the Federal Council are usually traced to the late

nineteenth-century movement for church federation. Promoted by societies of interested individuals and congregations, this movement proposed to counter the increasing diversity of American Protestantism with
a federal union, in which churches would commit themselves to cooperative action without surrendering their autonomy (as opposed to the
more radical approach of corporate union, which in the twentieth century would produce denominational mergers and the Consultation on
Church Union). The federative ideal became reality in 1908 when numerous churches accepted a plan produced by the 1905 Interchurch Conference on Federation. But the federative movement got as far as it did
because denominational leaders also wanted union. They used the movement to prod the churches toward federation and then brought the
movement under denominational control.[14] The result, therefore, was
not another voluntary society, but an impressive federal council of
churches.

At its birth in 1908 the Federal Council consisted of thirty-three Protestant denominations. Of these, fewer than one-third were part of the
establishment; and five more non-establishment churches joined later
(including the Syrian Antiochian Orthodox Church, the first non-Protestant member, which came aboard in 1938). So the dominating position of
mainline bodies was of course never advertised in Council rhetoric. Yet,
for at least four reasons, that dominance was effective and evident.

Establishment leadership was effectual, first of all, because of a certain
preselection or preestablished harmony: churches at the extremes of the
theological spectrum were not involved in the Council. The most liberal
ones were excluded when only those churches "already in fraternal relations" and "in substantial agreement" as to basic Christian doctrine were
invited to the 1908 meeting. The American Unitarian Association had
responded positively to an invitation to the 1905 conference, only to be
informed that it had been sent by mistake.[15] The members of the new
Council made their theological boundaries even more explicit in 1908
when they inserted in the constitution a description of Jesus Christ as
"their Divine Lord and Saviour," knowing that this would prevent Unitarian and Universalist membership in the Council.

Several conservative denominations, on the other hand, avoided the
Council for their own reasons, thereby keeping a substantial number of
Protestants out of the Council's orbit. These included the large Southern
Baptist Convention – then encroaching on the northern Methodists'
status as the largest single Protestant denomination in the United States –
the majority of Lutherans, and the rapidly growing Holiness and Pentecostal groups.

Second, a closer look at the Council's members throughout the twentieth century reveals that, in addition to the nine original establishment

members, ten of the other charter members would merge with one of those establishment denominations at some point after 1908.[16] Furthermore, four of the original non-establishment members left the Council within five years, and two more left later. Two of the five smaller bodies that joined after 1908 also remained only a short while.[17] Finally, of the eight non-establishment members belonging to the Council from its beginning to end, four were close to the larger denominations in many ways (the Society of Friends, the Seventh-Day Baptists, the Moravian Church, and the Reformed Church in America); four more constituted the "black religious establishment" (African Methodist Episcopal [AME], African Methodist Episcopal Zion, Colored [after 1956, Christian] Methodist Episcopal churches, and the National Baptist Convention).

Third, since the establishment denominations were the largest, their delegates dominated the Council numerically – the size of each denomination's representation at Council meetings and on the executive committee being determined by national membership statistics. The largest delegations in 1908 were the northern Methodists, northern Baptists, northern Presbyterians, Disciples of Christ, Congregationalists, and southern Methodists. Then came the largest black denominations, the National Baptist Convention and the AME Church. Throughout the life of the Council, the northern Methodists at first and then the reunited Methodist Church (northern, southern, and Methodist Protestant in 1939) outnumbered the next largest delegation by half again as many representatives. In 1908 61 percent of the 413 delegates to the Council were apportioned to the nine establishment churches. By 1932, with the number of Council members reduced by mergers and withdrawals to twenty-four, the seven of the establishment were represented by 70 percent of the delegates.[18] Although the major denominations were relatively lax about attendance at Council meetings, establishment delegates still outnumbered the representatives of other churches.

A fourth reason for the dominance of mainline denominations was their capacity to supply Council officers and employees. Of the fifteen Council presidents, symbolic leaders who could shape the organization if they so desired, all but one were from the major denominations, as were most of the professional employees – generally ordained ministers – who guided the daily operations of the Council. The only black executive, George E. Haynes, was a Congregationalist layman. Alone in his status as both a layman and a member of a non-establishment denomination was Moravian Benson Y. Landis of the Department of Research and Education.

The men involved in Council committees and projects as speakers or officers were also predominantly from the establishment. The roster included conservatives – northern Presbyterians J. Wilbur Chapman,

William Jennings Bryan, John Wanamaker, and John Converse – as well as liberals – Baptists Walter Rauschenbusch and Harry Emerson Fosdick, Disciple Charles C. Morrison, Episcopalian George Hodges, and Methodist E. Stanley Jones.

Many of the prominent laymen associated with the Council were politicians. Bryan spoke to the 1914 meeting as the Secretary of State, and ten years later, a year before the debacle of his battle against evolution at the Scopes trial, he supported the Council's international peace efforts. Presbyterian John Foster Dulles chaired the Commission on a Just and Durable Peace throughout World War II, before becoming Secretary of State in 1953. The election of Episcopal layman Charles P. Taft as council president followed his service in several government positions during the war. It is noteworthy that the only laymen to serve as president were Robert E. Speer, a professional religious administrator, and Taft, son of a former United States president and brother of a United States senator.

The decision makers in the Council were not only "established," white, and ordained, they were also predominantly male. Although a large number of women, of unknown religious affiliation, worked for the Council as office secretaries and assistants, and female delegates grew slowly in number over the decades, the first woman was elected to office in 1948, when Congregationalist Mildred Horton became vice president. Before that time, interestingly enough, the few female leaders had been selected from the less dominant churches. Nannie Burroughs of the National Baptist Convention, for instance, had held a number of committee positions.

Clearly, the "churches of Christ in America" that spoke through the Federal Council were not quite as inclusive a group as the name suggested. Because only Protestants were represented in the Council until 1938, because substantial segments of American Protestantism did not participate, because the establishment denominations provided the majority of Council leaders, the Federal Council did not speak with a united voice for "the Churches of Christ" or even the Protestants in the United States. Rather, it expressed the interests and concerns of one part of American Protestantism: the dominant churches and those that chose to associate with them. Despite its representative structure, and despite repeated efforts to include smaller members as equal partners, the Council was inevitably a reflection of mainline Protestantism.

All this is not to say it was monolithic. Delegates and officers from establishment churches did not share a single viewpoint simply because they came from a very few denominations. But their overwhelming affiliation with those denominations at least meant that the ambiguities, inconsistencies, and tensions visible in the Council, as well as the agreements among its participants, reflect the characteristics of the American Protestant establishment in the early twentieth century.

The Purposes of the Federal Council

By the same token, the Council's stated purposes articulated an establishment's view of its special responsibilities both to its own traditions and to society – an establishment agenda. From the start the Federal Council had two explicit purposes, described in the preamble to its constitution as "more fully to manifest the essential oneness of the Christian churches of America in Jesus Christ as their Divine Lord and Savior," and "to promote the spirit of fellowship, service and cooperation among them."[19]

For many of the Council's founders and supporters the real function of the new organization was the first of these: to demonstrate the actual unity, despite obvious diversity, of American Protestant Christianity. From the Evangelical Alliance they inherited the assumption that common action for the evangelization of non-Protestants (or at least non-churchgoers) was the best foundation for the consolidation of Protestantism. William Roberts, one of the ecclesiastical politicians who helped bring the Council into existence, illustrates the importance of traditional Protestant ecumenism in that process. The Princeton Seminary librarian, a former Lane Seminary professor and Stated Clerk of the General Assembly from 1888 to 1920, was a conservative Presbyterian who evidently believed that in the Federal Council he was helping to create an improved Evangelical Alliance. He did not approve wholeheartedly of the social service and peace activities immediately undertaken by the new Council, and the Commission on Evangelism created in 1912 (and chaired by Roberts) may have been the result of his desire to balance those "liberal" emphases.[20]

Yet the impulse to influence society along social gospel lines was clear in the earliest statements and actions of the Council. The organization aimed "to bring the Christian bodies of America into united service for Christ and the world," and "to secure a larger combined influence for the churches of Christ in all matters affecting the moral and social condition of the people, so as to promote the application of the law of Christ in every relation of human life."[21] That final phrase, especially, reveals the presence of social-reforming attitudes. And in the popular mind, if not in the minds of all its founders, the Federal Council quickly became "a sort of official keeper of the Social Gospel."[22]

At its first meeting the Council accepted the report of its Committee on the Church and Modern Industry. Presented by Frank Mason North,

Symbol of the establishment's social reform agenda: Labor Temple in New York City (at 2nd Avenue and 14th Street), 1913. From Harlan Paul Douglass, *The New Home Missions* (New York: Missionary Education Movement, 1914), facing p. 102. Used by permission of the National Council of Churches.

this report incorporated a statement of "social ideals" originating with the social gospel activists of the Methodist Federation for Social Service, adopted by the northern Methodist Church, and soon permanently associated with the Federal Council as "the social creed of the churches."[23] The Council established the Commission on the Church and Social Service, with North as chair.

Interpreters have variously suggested that the Council adopted the social gospel as its ideology because no other interdenominational group was tackling social issues; or because, in line with earlier cooperative efforts, action was a more realistic ground for union than doctrine.[24] Both views seem correct: Social gospel advocates used the pragmatic bent of Protestant ecumenism to turn the Council into a vehicle for reform. In so doing they gave it a clear purpose for existing, and may have ensured its survival, but they also lost the support of a sizable body of Protestants. Four churches withdrew from the Council before 1913 in reaction to its liberalism. And theological and social conservatives in denominations remaining with the Council constantly complained that their values and goals – William Roberts's values and goals – were neglected.

When the old evangelical community divided roughly down the middle, the Council was certainly influenced more by the liberal than by the conservative side. Yet its leaders always envisioned the Council as more than a social action agency, and as connected to a far wider group than just those Protestants willing to let themselves be labeled "liberal." From 1908 to 1968, supporters of the Federal and National councils insisted that the organizations successfully balanced efforts for Protestant unity (which were stereotyped as a "conservative" concern) and programs for social reform (thought to be a "liberal" interest).[25] The councils engaged in both cooperative evangelism and collective political lobbying. This perceived comprehensiveness – the desire of the councils to be all things to all Protestants – is one of the basic components of their establishment mindset.

The Development of the Federal Council

The designers of the Federal Council sought a true federal union of churches, a strictly representative organization closely tied to the constituent denominations. Three factors conspired, however, to make the Council more of an independent entity than its creators envisioned. Two were restrictions built into the constitution: The Council had "no authority to draw up a common creed or form of government or of worship," and it could not "in any way limit the full autonomy of the Christian bodies adhering to it." All that was expected of it, therefore, was the "expression of its counsel," and the recommendation "of a course of action in matters of common interest to the Churches, local councils and individual Christians."[26]

Apparently perceived in 1908 as ensuring that the Council would be an obedient servant of the churches, these restrictions in fact guaranteed that in order to survive, the Council would have to find a separate identity. By barring consideration of doctrine, polity, or worship, the churches pushed the Council in the direction of "action," where the social gospel awaited. By denying the Council any authority over its members, they made it possible for the Council to take positions and actions that would have been unacceptable had the churches been responsible for the Council's theology or bound by its decisions.

The third factor that made independence inevitable was the churches' failure to support the Council they had created. When the denominations did not fulfill their financial commitments the Council sought other sources of income. The 1912 Commission on Peace and Arbitration secured individual and foundation funding, setting a pattern that persisted throughout the life of the Council: Denominational grants covered central administrative expenses, whereas private donations financed special programs. Thus the churches could fund the Council as a manifestation of Protestant unity and liberal leaders could use private support to initiate controversial projects aimed at changing society.

The Federal Council was born with a full complement of executive officers, including thirty-three denominational vice presidents and a fifty-seven-member executive committee, and seven commissions or committees with a total of 179 members. The concerns indicate the intended comprehensiveness of the Council: literature and education; church and social service; temperance; family life; Sunday observance; foreign missions; and home missions. Commissions on evangelism and on peace and arbitration were added in 1912. Committees on relations with Japan (later, the Orient) and on the church and country life appeared a year later. The entire Council met every four years, the executive committee convened annually, and the Council's regular operations were actually managed by an administrative committee of twenty-five or so members and the secretarial council made up of the general and commission secretaries. Efforts were made to ensure that the administrative committee, meeting monthly in the Council's New York offices, would be representative of all the member denominations, but it inevitably included the most prominent Council members.

By 1918 nearly all commissions were employing paid secretaries (male executive officers) as well as female office secretaries. A commission on interchurch federations had been formed, as had new committees to deal with ministerial relief, Negro churches, Army and Navy chaplains, religious work in the Panama Canal zone, and Christian relief in France and Belgium. The Joint Executive Committee of the World Alliance for Promoting International Friendship through the Churches had been organized with the National Committee on the Churches and the Moral Aims of the War. The world war brought international concerns to the center of the Council's attention, where they remained throughout the 1920s. The Council continued to advocate American membership in the League of Nations long after most Americans had lost interest, and disarmament and a world court became important Council themes.[27]

The war not only made the Federal Council a leading American source of internationalist sentiment, it also turned a struggling federation into a viable and vital national public presence. Council bureaucracy and programming expanded rapidly and its prestige soared as it actually became the liaison between churches and government that the YMCA and YWCA only aspired to be. Improving the military chaplaincy had been a Council project since 1913, and advocates believed they had had some success. In 1917 General Secretary Macfarland on his own initiative and authority arranged with the armed services to have the Council's new General Committee on Army and Navy Chaplains "investigate and nominate" all candidates from Protestant churches.[28]

By the fall of that year the General War-Time Commission of the Churches had evolved from a Council initiative. Chaired by Robert E. Speer, the Commission was independent of the Council but closely associated with it; the chaplaincy committee became part of both agencies. The monopoly on Protestant chaplains, Speer's diplomatic skills, and government recognition of the War-Time Commission motivated the YMCA and YWCA and churches not normally affiliated with the Federal Council – Lutherans, the Christian Reformed Church, and the Southern Baptist Convention – to join the Commission. The staunchly conservative Calvinists of the Christian Reformed Church even went so far as to join the Federal Council itself (they withdrew in 1924). Black Baptists believed that it was only through their Council membership that they were allowed official military chaplains.[29]

The Federal Council "entered the war as a small, obscure organization and it emerged as perhaps the most influential organization in American Protestantism, or indeed, in the entire American religious scene."[30] The Council's status among the denominations was growing; it was accepted as the official representative of "Protestantism" by Roman Catholic and Jewish groups as well as by the federal government. After the demise of the Interchurch World Movement in 1920 the Federal Council was unquestionably the giant among cooperative Protestant organizations in the United States.

By 1928 the Council had offices in Washington and Chicago as well as New York, employed fifty-two executive officers and administrative staff, and proposed a $365,000 budget for 1929. Its areas of concern reflected the concentration on social issues, the achievement of national prohibition, and the increasing integration of the cooperative complex. Gone were literature and education, Sunday observance, and missions; new sections focused on goodwill between Jews and Christians, the religious press, relations with Eastern churches, and mercy and relief.[31]

In 1932 the Council was restructured to increase both efficiency and responsiveness to denominational desires. A large-scale evangelism project, the National Preaching Mission, began four years later. World War II again brought special ministries to the fore, and Council membership rose once more. During the war the coalition agencies also began to consider consolidation. A 1941 study conference proposed the creation of an "inclusive cooperative organization which will provide for the continued, expanded, and more effective coordination and integration of our respective Councils." Nine years later the National Council came into being.[32]

The institutional history of the Federal Council after 1918 was one of constant growth. The Council's public image did not, however, fare as well. Opposition to the Council's pro-labor and internationalist "radicalism" – always present among economic and political leaders inside and outside of the Council's constituency – escalated into a steady barrage of virulent conservative criticism of Council domestic and foreign policy. The judgment of later observers that the Council was not really radical, that it depended on educational rather than coercive approaches to social change, does not negate the fact that after World War I the Council was widely identified by friend and foe with the social and political liberalism of any given decade.[33]

Controversy took its toll and the earlier widespread Protestant endorsement of the Council faded away. Theological and political family quarrels within the variegated establishment began to show quite clearly through cracks in the facade of Protestant cooperation. Henry Pratt suggests that the restructuring of 1932 and the National Preaching Mission reflected a shift away from controversial social issues and toward the other old Council interests, "personal religion" (the 1930s liberal equivalent of evangelism) and Protestant solidarity. He attributes this to the status anxiety of ecumenical leaders as Protestant prestige in American society waned. Council churches suffered from their association with prohibition and the Republican party; membership and attendance declined noticeably. Furthermore, the social gospel was faltering, and the Council was working ever more closely with cooperative organizations more evangelical than itself. Positively, social policies championed by the Council became less controversial as they became more familiar, and many of them were implemented in the New Deal. Council apologists were fond of quoting President Roosevelt's quip, when charged with radicalism, that he was "as radical as the Federal Council of Churches."[34] In foreign policy, which Pratt does not consider, the earlier strong Council position was undermined by the growth in the 1930s of militarism overseas. Internationalism and pacifism were pried apart as it became apparent that just relations among nations might require the use of force. Ironically, the military chaplaincy that had been the Council's springboard to prominence in 1918 became a sore point in the 1930s, assailed by pacifists as providing religious sanction for war. Such developments combined, according to Pratt, to produce a more cautious Council. It identified more closely with the member churches, tended to promote social change by appealing to them rather than to the government, and in general tried to avoid any appearance of radicalism.[35]

External assaults and internal tensions diminished during World War II, but it had become evident that the Federal Council did not, on any given issue, necessarily represent the views of even a majority of Protestants. It was never quite clear whom the Council *did* represent: It claimed to speak for the churches; the denominations officially backed it; non-member Protestants denounced it and in the 1940s created counterinstitutions; vocal groups within Council churches campaigned to leave it. The complex relationships of Protestant churches with the Federal Council illuminate the ambivalent impulses of the Protestant establishment.

The Churches and the Federal Council

One of the clearest evidences of the failure of the establishment's cooperative organizations to capture the loyalty of all Protestants was the emergence of competing agencies. Conservative Protestants were not willing to leave Protestant cooperation to the liberals. Fundamentalist extremist Carl McIntire organized the American Council of Christian Churches in 1941 and two years later a wider coalition of conservatives, many now calling themselves "neo-evangelicals," formally constituted the National Association of Evangelicals (NAE).

The evangelicals, by far the larger and more effective conservative voice, conceded that the Federal Council in its early years had been "somewhat of a reflection of the church life of America" and that "while majoring in social programs it did not neglect evangelism." Yet since at least the 1920s religious liberals "very definitely came into control of Council leadership, policy and program." The Council had "departed from the faith of Jesus Christ," and the new Association was formed to "provide a medium for voluntary united action among the several groups of Evangelical Christians of America."[36]

The National Association of Evangelicals was not technically a federation of churches – it was open to organizations and individual congregations as well as denominations – but its "fields of endeavor" and its administrative structure mirrored the Federal Council's. The conservative competitor promptly opened a Washington office, formed a commission on military chaplaincies (which won from the government the right to endorse chaplains from Association denominations), and proceeded to lobby alongside (and usually against) the older organization. By the 1960s the Association's early defensiveness and residual separatism had given way to the confident establishmentarian rhetoric so familiar in the Federal and National councils. "All major denominations in America (Baptist, Methodist, Presbyterian, Lutheran, Christian, Congregational, etc.) are represented. . . . The 24,000,000 orthodox Protestants in the denominations outside the National Council of Churches find in the NAE their most effective instrument in time of need."[37]

These self-conscious evangelicals did not capture the denominational hierarchies or the ecumenical superstructure of the old establishment, nor did the conservative cooperative complex that grew up around the Association put the Federal Council "ecclesiastical octopus" or National Council "superchurch" out of business. In proclaiming themselves the only true Protestants – a sizable group deserving the same social and political prerogatives as the churches of the Councils – they did achieve considerable public prominence. The National Association of Evangelicals became "a major symbol and coordinating center" of resurgent evangelicalism, and the public response to the renewed conservative presence "encouraged postfundamentalist evangelicals to feel like part of the 'establishment' again."[38]

The Federal and National councils survived conservative competition because they were many different things to different people. Henry Pratt, treating the two councils as functionally continuous, suggested that the "selective incentives" – tangible goods and services available to members – offered by the councils gradually increased until they were valuable enough to offset the churches' dislike of Council social policies. So long as the benefits of membership were minimal, before the 1930s, denominational loyalty to the Federal Council was weak and internal criticism loud and strong. By the end of our period, however, officials saw so many "genuine advantages in remaining in the federation and numerous and serious costs in withdrawing from it" that even the churches most disgruntled with the National Council's new political involvement in the civil rights movement would not terminate their membership.[39]

This interpretation recognizes the validity of the councils' constantly reiterated assertion that their controversial social policies were only part of their total program. Any evaluation of the influence of the councils on "religion" in the United States must include the impact of "steady day-by-day services to the member denominations in their basic tasks of evangelism, education, missions, and social welfare."[40] That impact varied by program, period, and denomination; overall there is little question that through their conferences and workshops, publications, public lobbies, service agencies, and consultants, the councils made themselves useful to the churches. In the process they changed the way American Protestant churches operated, and the way they related to one another.

At higher levels, however, the Federal and National councils came to embody the Protestant establishment. For an establishment that was essentially a broad consensus among separate denominations, the council of churches provided a single concrete and visible institution through which that consensus could be expressed, to which outside groups could turn, and over against which dissenters could identify themselves. The councils were structurally linked to the churches and partook of their authority, but they were also separate from the churches, a total that was more than the sum of its parts, the establishment's answer to denominationalism.

The Federal Council functioned as a state church by providing its members access to decision makers in government and business, and by speaking with a common voice more easily heard in public debate than the multiple voices of denominations. The Federal and National councils always received a respectful hearing from government officials, though control of access to government seems to have been greatest during World War I. The captains of industry were less respectful – the Federal Council's social gospel stance set it at odds with unrepentant capitalists – but the ending of the twelve-hour steel mill shift in 1923 was widely credited to the Council. Most dramatically, the monopoly of both councils, from the 1920s to 1960, on the free airtime of three of the four national radio networks strengthened their establishment status and brought loud protests from non-Council Protestant dissenters.

The original Federal Council purposes of manifesting Protestant unity and changing American society were always central to both councils, at the programmatic and at a deeper, symbolic level. The goal of unity, for example, was pursued at the practical level when the councils functioned (in Henry Pratt's terms) as "Protestant defense groups," turning to politics only "when the issue was posed in the narrow terms of protecting Protestantism's good name in American life." Thus they opposed the appointment of a United States ambassador to the Vatican and countered accusations of communist influence on the churches and the ecumenical movement.[41]

On a more profound level the councils, simply by existing, kept the great ideal of Christian unity before the eyes of American Protestants. That important role is illustrated in the relationship of the Reformed Church in America to the councils. The Dutch Reformed were charter members of the Federal, National, and World councils (and in 1985 would provide the National Council with its new general secretary, Arie R. Brouwer). In the 1930s, however, fundamentalist influence and a renewed sense of denominational identity prompted conservatives in the church to begin the first of many campaigns for withdrawal from the councils. All were rebuffed. The majority position was stated in 1934 when the church warned the Council that "there is a point beyond which cooperation cannot go," nevertheless asserting that it would be improper for the church to dissociate itself from a body that in many ways represented the "united Protestant Churches of America in the great Christian enterprise of the Kingdom of God."[42] The theological liberalism and social activism of the Federal Council offended many of the Dutch Reformed, but the church saw its participation in the Council as a statement about its commitment as a church to Protestant unity and Christian service.

The desire to change American society was evident in the councils' programs, and "social action" almost completely dominated their public image. At the practical level the councils' commitment to social action and social change alienated some members and appealed to others. Black Baptists, for example, "did not desire 'church union,' but they were impressed by the 'humanitarianism' of the ecumenical bodies."[43] The symbolic function of the councils with regard to social action provides an important insight into the nature of the Protestant establishment. In 1941 Federal Council interpreter John A. Hutchison observed that the general "Calvinist" conviction that "the church was charged with a responsibility for the spiritual and moral welfare of the community" was shared by all Council denominations.[44] The history of the most conservative establishment church reveals the power of that conviction. The southern Presbyterian Church in the United States withdrew from the Federal Council in 1912 in reaction to its social program, but returned the next year. A 1931 Council report cautiously approving the use of birth control methods by married couples sparked a controversy over the Council's right to speak in matters about which its members had not reached a consensus. From that debate emerged the standard defense of Council "radicalism": ecumenical organizations had the responsibility to speak *to* the churches prophetically as well as the authority to speak *for* them.[45] This crisis, and fundamentalist accentuation of theological issues, carried the Presbyterians out of the Council again. By the early 1940s, they were back, expressing their need to demonstrate a commitment to "inter-church co-operation and united action in matters which were for the welfare of church and state."[46]

The absence of that Calvinist sense of social responsibility helps explain the Lutheran reticence to join ecumenical organizations. The Lutheran Church, General Synod, was a charter Federal Council member but withdrew in 1917, when it merged into the United Lutheran Church. Five years later that church became a consultative member only, and no other Lutherans participated in the Federal Council. (They were, however, founding members of the National Council.) For the Lutherans the Federal Council "claimed unity where there was none, mixed church and state, violated the church's true task by attempting political reform, underemphasized spiritual regeneration in favor of social regulation, stressed statistical and social success, and had a materialistic conception of the mission of the church."[47]

A sense of responsibility for the spiritual and moral welfare of the community would seem to be a fundamental element of an establishment mentality. Consequently Lutherans were on the fringes of the Protestant establishment, and the uncertainty felt by others was strongly affected by this consideration. Southern Presbyterians were torn between the regional evangelical establishment of which they were a part – which preached the separation of religion and politics – and the felt obligation to participate in the cooperative religious care of society. Establishment churches without a specifically southern identity, like the Northern Baptist Convention, were also seriously divided over membership in the councils.[48] The Federal and National Councils of Churches were constant reminders of the Christian, Protestant, and establishment values of unity and responsibility. The churches might dispute the councils' interpretations or implementation of those values, but they could not deny the ideals or totally ignore the Councils' attempts to realize them.

Thus far this analysis of Protestant cooperative organizations has focused on institutional aspects. Institutions of this sort are, of course, simply groups of people. In any group and any kind of "establishment," the individuals in positions of leadership come to personify the organization and exert power and authority on its behalf. Not unlike the hierarchy of an established church, the officers and high-level employees of the ecumenical councils joined prominent denominational leaders and theologians to form the Protestant establishment's religious elite. We do not know enough about these people or how they worked. Prosopographical investigation of ecumenical personnel would help demonstrate in what ways "the American establishment was a personal network as well as a congeries of institutions," and in what ways that network overlapped with those of social, economic, and political elites.[49] How did the personalities and personal relationships of the long-term professional employees of the councils shape those organizations? What connections made possible – or were forged in – groups like the General War-Time Commission, the roster of which reads like a Who's Who of the Protestant religious and political establishment in the World War I era? What was the real nature and impact of the involvement of laymen like John D. Rockefeller, Jr., or John Foster Dulles, in ecumenical affairs? We will better understand the workings of the Protestant establishment when we can get beyond the pious accolades and hostile allegations to uncover personal networks of friendship and enmity, patterns of mutual interest, mutual influence, and mutual profit.

The Establishment Embodied

There is as yet little concrete evidence for any of the conflicting conclusions about the influence of the Federal and National councils on American public life. What *is* evident is that many Protestant religious leaders, both supporters and opponents, *perceived* the councils to have considerable authority with those in positions of power. Even the evangelical critics ridiculing Council "illusions of greatness" feared that such pretensions were taken all too seriously by important people.[50]

Judging by the standards of Protestant inclusivity, interfaith cooperation, and direct influence on government, the General War-Time Commission in particular and the Federal Council more generally during World War I probably came the closest of any entity in the first half of the twentieth century to exercising the authority of a Protestant establishment. During the war the leaders of cooperative Protestantism discovered that if they acted together, they could exert considerable influence on the federal government and military authorities. Protestant strategies also learned the limits of their authority: Each success required a major organizational and lobbying effort to overcome governmental inertia and resistance.

The presence of one or both of two factors seems to have contributed to ecumenical success in exercising influence, from the birth of the Federal Council to the end of our period and beyond: recognition by those in power of the appropriateness of an organization's involvement, and cooperation with other religious interest groups – non-Council Protestant, Jewish, or Roman Catholic. In 1918 the military chaplaincy was an obviously legitimate concern of the churches – and of the Catholic and Jewish organizations also lobbying the government. The crucial event in the 1923 campaign against the twelve-hour shift was a forceful joint statement by the Federal Council, the National Catholic Welfare Conference, and the Central Conference of American Rabbis.[51] The control of free radio airtime was a gift from the networks, and again, part of a tripartite arrangement. In fact, World War I did for the Catholic Church in the United States and for American Jewish leadership exactly what it did for Council Protestants: The government's desire to deal with a single agency for each religious tradition taught the value of cooperation and organization. The National Catholic Welfare Conference (originally the War Council) and the Jewish Welfare Board were started during the war and went on to play important roles as national organizations.[52] Despite the pervasive Protestant tone of American culture, cooperative organizations embodying a diffuse establishment that was only part of the Protestant community had little real power by themselves. The Protestant religious establishment in the twentieth century, as reflected in the ecumenical councils, was always part of a larger "triple establishment" of Protestant, Catholic, and Jew.

Ecumenical Protestantism changed a great deal after 1960. The National Council of Churches no longer called itself "the churches working together for a Christian America." Certainly the old Federal Council purposes remained: the National Council was to be "a community through which the churches can make visible their unity given in Christ, and can live responsibly in witness and service."[53] But the establishment mentality was gone, at least from official rhetoric.

In 1950, however, the first National Council assembly met in a Cleveland auditorium decorated with groupings of the United States, United Nations, and Christian flags. "Above the proscenium in great shining letters was the theme phrase of the Convention and the Council – 'THIS NATION UNDER GOD.' "[54] Before his election as the first Council president, Episcopal bishop Henry Knox Sherrill proclaimed that "the Council marks a new and great determination that the American way will be increasingly the Christian way, for such is our heritage. . . . Together the Churches can move forward to the goal – a Christian America in a Christian world."[55]

Scholars tell us that in the first half of the twentieth century Protestant identity, power, and social standing in the United States were declining steadily. Perhaps it was to counteract that decline that mainline Protestants sought to make their "establishment" more visible and vocal by embodying it in numerous ecumenical agencies, and then melding them into one massive National Council. In any case, at its birth in the exact middle of the century, the organization that was heir to the tradition of Protestant cooperation thought and spoke like a religious establishment.

NOTES

1 Elias B. Sanford (ed.), *Federal Council of the Churches of Christ in America: Report of the First Meeting of the Federal Council, Philadelphia, 1908* (New York: Revell Press, 1909), 207, 321–2, 12, 508; hereafter cited as *FCC 1908*.

2 *Christian Faith in Action: Commemorative Volume: The Founding of the National Council of the Churches of Christ in the United States of America* (National Council, 1951), 152.

3 *FCC 1908*, 18; *Christian Faith in Action*, 148.

4 On cooperative organizations, see Samuel McCrea Cavert, *The American Churches in the Ecumenical Movement 1900–1968* (New York: Association Press, 1968), and *Church Cooperation and Unity in America: A Historical Review: 1900–1970* (New York: Association Press, 1970).

5 *Federal Council Annual Report, 1913*, 123.

6 Quoted from an unidentified source by Henry Pitney Van Dusen, *One Great Ground of Hope* (Philadelphia: Westminster Press, 1961), 101. The National Council incorporated the Federal Council, Foreign Missions Conference of North America, Home Missions Council of North America, Missionary Education Movement of the United States and Canada, International Council of Religious Education, National Protestant Council on Higher Education,

United Council of Church Women, and United Stewardship Council. After
its founding the Council was joined by Church World Service, the Inter-
seminary Committee, the Protestant Radio Committee, the Protestant Film
Commission, and the Student Volunteer Movement for Foreign Missions.

7   Creighton Lacy, *Word Carrying Giant: The Growth of the American Bible
Society (1816–1966)* (South Pasadena, Calif.: William Carey Library, 1977),
161, 256–7.

8   Philip D. Jordan, *The Evangelical Alliance for the United States of America,
1847–1900: Ecumenism, Identity and the Religion of the Republic* (New York:
Edwin Mellen Press, 1982), 99–142.

9   Cavert, *American Churches*, 24.

10   C. Howard Hopkins, *John R. Mott, 1865–1955: A Biography* (Grand Rapids,
Mich.: Eerdmans, 1979), 284–5.

11   S. Wirt Wiley, *History of YMCA-Church Relations in the United States* (New
York: Association Press, 1944), 168–78, 197.

12   Eldon G. Ernst, *Moment of Truth for Protestant America: Interchurch Campaigns
Following World War One* (Missoula, Mont.: Scholars Press, 1974), 73.

13   Ibid., 168.

14   John Abernathy Smith, "Ecclesiastical Politics and the Founding of the
Federal Council of Churches," *Church History* 43(1974): 350–65.

15   *FCC 1908,* 5; Charles S. Macfarland, *Christian Unity in the Making: The First
Twenty-five Years of the Federal Council of the Churches of Christ in America,
1905–1930* (New York: Federal Council, 1948), 32.

16   Establishment members: Methodist Episcopal Church; Methodist Episcopal
Church, South; Presbyterian Church in the United States of America
("northern"); Presbyterian Church in the United States ("southern"); Congregational Churches; Disciples of Christ; Northern Baptist Convention;
Lutheran Church, General Synod; and the Commission on Christian Unity
of the Protestant Episcopal Church (rather than the Church itself). Merging
later: Methodist Protestant Church; Evangelical Association; United Evangelical Church; United Brethren in Christ; United Presbyterian Church;
Welsh Presbyterian Church; American Christian Convention; Evangelical
Synod; Reformed Church in the United States ("German Reformed"); and
Free Baptists.

17   The Congregational Methodist Church, Primitive Methodist Church, Re-
formed Presbyterian Church, and Swedish Lutheran Augustana Synod left
by 1913; the Mennonite General Conference in 1917; and the Reformed
Episcopal Church in 1945. Joining later were the Christian Reformed
Church, 1919–24; General Eldership, Churches of God, 1919–33; Syrian
Antiochian Church, 1938; Church of the Brethren, 1944; and the Evangelical
Unity of the Czech-Moravian Brethren in North America (now the Unity
of the Brethren), 1945.

18   *FCC 1908; Federal Council Annual Report,* 1932.

19   *FCC 1908,* 512.

20   John A. Hutchison, *We Are Not Divided: A Critical and Historical Study of the*

Federal Council of the Churches of Christ in America (New York: Round Table Press, 1941), 272.

21 *FCC 1908,* 513.

22 Hutchison, *We Are Not Divided,* 99.

23 On the "Creed" see Creighton Lacy, *Frank Mason North: His Social and Ecumenical Mission* (Nashville, Tenn.: Abingdon Press, 1967), 129–35.

24 Cavert, *American Churches,* 54; Hutchison, *We Are Not Divided,* 28–30; John F. Piper, Jr., "The Formation of the Social Policy of the Federal Council of Churches," *Journal of Church and State* 11(Winter 1969): 63–5.

25 Hutchison, *We Are Not Divided,* 25, 271–2; Cavert, *American Churches,* 36, 57.

26 *FCC 1908,* 513.

27 Cavert, *American Churches,* 105.

28 John F. Piper, Jr., *The American Churches in World War I* (Athens: Ohio University Press, 1985), 110; *Federal Council Annual Report,* 1917, 77.

29 James D. Bratt, *Dutch Calvinism in Modern America: A History of a Conservative Subculture* (Grand Rapids, Mich.: Eerdmans, 1984), 90; J. Deotis Roberts, "Ecumenical Concerns among National Baptists," in *Baptists and Ecumenism,* ed. William Jerry Boney and Glenn A. Igleheart (Valley Forge, Pa.: Judson Press, 1980), 46.

30 Hutchison, *We Are Not Divided,* 175.

31 *Twenty Years of Church Federation: Report of the Federal Council of the Churches of Christ in America, 1924–1928* (New York: Federal Council, 1929), 321–40.

32 *Work Book for the Constituting Convention, National Council of the Churches of Christ in the United States of America* (New York: Planning Committee for the NCC, 1950), 4.

33 Hutchison, *We Are Not Divided,* 96, 305; Henry J. Pratt, *The Liberalization of American Protestantism: A Case Study in Complex Organizations* (Detroit: Wayne State University Press, 1972), 16, 141. See also Pratt's "Growth of Political Activism in the National Council of Churches," *Review of Politics* 34(July 1972); 323–41, and "Organizational Stress and Adaptation to Changing Political Status: The Case of the National Council of the Churches of Christ in the USA," *American Behavioral Scientist* 17(1974): 865–83.

34 Cavert, *American Churches,* 143; Hutchison, *We Are Not Divided,* 121.

35 Pratt, *Liberalization,* 27–31, 50.

36 James DeForest Murch, *Cooperation without Compromise: A History of the National Association of Evangelicals* (Grand Rapids, Mich.: Eerdmans, 1956), 40–1; *Evangelical Action! A Report of the Organization of the National Association of Evangelicals for United Action* (Boston: United Action Press, 1942), 101.

37 James DeForest Murch, *The Protestant Revolt: Road to Freedom for American Churches* (Arlington, Va.: Crestwood Books, 1967), 254.

38 Joel A. Carpenter, "From Fundamentalism to the New Evangelical Coalition," in *Evangelicalism and Modern America,* ed. George Marsden (Grand Rapids, Mich.: Eerdmans, 1984), 13, 15.

39 Pratt, *Liberalization,* 257–8.
40 Cavert, *American Churches,* 244.
41 Pratt, *Liberalization,* 263, and "Organizational Stress," 872.
42 General Synod, Reformed Church in America, *Minutes,* 1934, 702; quoted in Herman Harmelinck III, *Ecumenism and the Reformed Church* (Grand Rapids, Mich.: Eerdmans, 1968), 72.
43 Roberts, "Ecumenical Concerns," 46.
44 Hutchison, *We Are Not Divided,* 91.
45 Cavert, *American Churches,* 151–2.
46 Murch, *Protestant Revolt,* 210.
47 Fred W. Meuser, "Facing the Twentieth Century, 1900–1930," in *The Lutherans in North America,* ed. E. Clifford Nelson (Philadelphia: Fortress Press, 1975), 387–8.
48 W. Hubert Porter, "Ecumenical Concerns among American Baptists," in Boney and Igleheart, *Baptists and Ecumenism,* 30–2; Pratt, *Liberalization,* 73–8.
49 William R. Hutchison, "Protestantism as Establishment," Introduction, this volume.
50 Ernest Gordon, *An Ecclesiastical Octopus: A Factual Report on the Federal Council of the Churches of Christ in America* (Boston: Fellowship Press, 1948), 76; Murch, *Protestant Revolt,* 56–9.
51 Cavert, *American Churches,* 111.
52 Piper, *American Churches in World War I,* 190–7; Sydney E. Ahlstrom, *A Religious History of the American People* (New Haven, Conn.: Yale University Press, 1972), 890–1.
53 National Council, *The National Council of Churches: The Churches Working Together for a Christian America* (New York, 1962); *Triennial Report, 1982–84,* 1.
54 *Christian Faith in Action,* 13.
55 Ibid., 11.

SELECT BIBLIOGRAPHY

Cavert, Samuel McCrea. *The American Churches in the Ecumenical Movement 1900–1968.* New York: Association Press, 1968.
    Church Cooperation and Unity in America: A Historical Review: 1900–1970. New York: Association Press, 1970.
Ernst, Eldon G. *Moment of Truth for Protestant America: Interchurch Campaigns Following World War One.* Missoula, Mont.: Scholars Press, 1974.
Hutchison, John A. *We Are Not Divided: A Critical and Historical Study of the Federal Council of the Churches of Christ in America.* New York: Round Table Press, 1941.
Johnson, Douglas W. "Program Dissensus between Denominational Grass Roots and Leadership and Its Consequences." In *American Denominational Organization: A Sociological View,* ed. Ross P. Scherer, 330–45. Pasadena, Calif.: William Carey Library, 1980.

Michaelson, Robert S., and Wade Clark Roof, eds. *Liberal Protestantism: Realities and Possibilities.* New York: Pilgrim Press, 1986.

Roof, Wade Clark. "America's Voluntary Establishment: Mainline Religion in Transition." In *Religion and America: Spirituality in a Secular Age,* ed. Mary Douglas and Steven Tipton. Boston: Beacon Press, 1982.

Szasz, Ferenc Morton. *The Divided Mind of Protestant America, 1880–1930.* Tuscaloosa: University of Alabama Press, 1982.

Toulouse, Mark G. *The Transformation of John Foster Dulles: From Prophet of Realism to Priest of Nationalism.* Macon, Ga.: Mercer University Press, 1985.

6

The Reform Establishment and the Ambiguities of Influence

WILLIAM MCGUIRE KING

Did the social and political impact of the Protestant establishment decline between 1900 and 1960? The answer to this question depends at least in part on the kind of impact being considered. On the one hand, the increasingly pluralistic and secular character of American culture undermined many of the informal and indirect public controls wielded by nineteenth-century establishments, especially at the local level. On the other, the loss of such traditional influence led the establishment denominations to develop more direct and structured forms of action that gave their social programs greater visibility and broader national scope.

Beginning with the social gospel movement of the first decade of the twentieth century, this systematic and coordinated social effort tended to transfer leadership within the Protestant establishment from enthusiastic amateurs to reform specialists: college and seminary educators, denominational executives, and professionally trained researchers and community activists. These individuals did not work in isolation. They formed an interlocking network of agencies and leaders that, like the spider's web, was strung of "gossamer threads that spanned indifferent space and derived whatever tensile strength they had from the fact that they were joined to one another."[1] Whether this circle of reformers represented the views of the majority of Protestant clergy and laity in the country is a moot point. What is certain is that it constituted a powerful "reform establishment" within Protestantism. It is this reform network that one must examine in order to assess the Protestant establishment's social and political impact in the twentieth century.

Paradoxically, although the reform establishment hoped to forestall the secularization of American culture, secular agencies supported and promoted its influence. Secular reformers and public officials accepted –

and at times even welcomed – Protestant social intervention, believing that denominational establishments could tap social resources not easily mobilized by public channels alone. Secular leaders knew that the Protestant churches could serve as useful laboratories in which to test public sentiment on pressing issues. Indeed, Protestant reform leadership played a prominent role in municipal and civic reforms during the Progressive Era; in public campaigns for the extension of rights to labor, racial minorities, and political dissidents during the twenties and thirties; and in national debates over foreign policy during the forties and fifties. Even after 1960, public agencies turned to the reform establishment to help formulate public policies on a wide range of issues regarding technology and human values.

Such public involvement makes it dangerous to speak glibly of a decline in the social and political impact of the Protestant establishment. On the contrary, the relatively cordial relationship between secular and religious agencies remained a remarkable feature of American public life from 1900 to 1960.

At the same time, the Protestant reform establishment's image of itself was seriously battered by twentieth-century developments. Protestant activists began the century confident that they articulated the core values of both the American churches and the secular culture. By 1960 this self-assurance was considerably eroded. Secular culture had reduced the role of Protestant reform to that of a special interest group, to one voice in a chorus. Protestantism no longer set the terms of public discussion and debate. Unable to monopolize the public arena, the Protestant reformers learned to share the stage with non-Protestant, non-Christian, and non-mainstream religious players. As a result, the Protestant establishment became uncertain about its social role and hesitant in its public actions.

The Reform Outlook

An inside look at the operation of the Protestant reform establishment will clarify these conclusions. One place to begin is an examination of Protestant efforts on behalf of the "world order" movement in the 1940s. Since World War I, Protestant social activists had been strongly interested in international issues of peace, justice, militarism, and social change. During the 1930s, internal dissension regarding pacifism and radicalism created confusion among the reformers and raised public doubts about the establishment's claims to represent Protestant opinion in America. By 1942 Protestant social leaders believed that the time had come to speak decisively once again on policy issues and reassert the relevance of a Christian perspective on world affairs. "Let us have an end of this Protestant inferiority complex," wrote Walter Van Kirk, of the Federal Council of Churches. Protestants, he warned, should stop complaining of their own ecclesiastical impotence. They should "rise up like men of God and, with vision and daring, create new and more effective instruments of Protestant strategy."[2]

An event in the early 1940s aptly illustrates this resurgent Protestant activism. On March 3, 1942, nearly four hundred denominational leaders gathered at Delaware, Ohio, on the campus of Ohio Wesleyan University for a three-day national study conference to formulate the Protestant response to America's entrance into the war. The Federal Council of Churches' Commission on the Bases of a Just and Durable Peace, whose chairman was Presbyterian layman John Foster Dulles, called the Delaware Conference in the hopes of rebuilding a consensus within Protestant social leadership in America.

Conference delegates were in a somber mood, believing that they must resist the prevailing winds of war fever and uncritical nationalism. Despite internal disagreements over pacifism, they shared a desire to exercise a restraint on public sentiment and to focus public attention on plans to rebuild international relations after the war. In projecting the possibility of a postwar "new world order," the delegates spoke in tones that echoed the ideals of two generations of Protestant reform.

The delegates' intellectual outlook was rooted in the social gospel movement that had dominated the Protestant reform establishment at the beginning of the century. Social gospel leaders had been convinced that Protestantism could not fight the forces of modern secularity armed with a gospel concerned primarily with private salvation and personal morality. They believed that the Christian gospel spoke of God's intention to redeem and refashion all areas of historical life and that the churches participate in God's work by applying a Christian vision to the solution of social problems. This effort would fulfill the ideals of both the Christian gospel and American civilization.

Although public enthusiasm for the social gospel waned after 1920, Protestant educators and reformers continued to stress the relevance of Christian social ideals and the imperative of direct Christian social action. The social gospel tradition thus became an important part of the Protestant establishment in America, reflected in the training of ministers, the staffing of denominational agencies, and the operations of the Federal Council of Churches, whose presidents were all drawn from its ranks. Although the social gospel found its largest following among Congregational, Methodist, Disciples, and Presbyterian leaders, it made inroads in the Episcopal, Baptist, and Lutheran denominations as well. Part of the social gospel's appeal was an explicit repudiation of denominationalism and ecclesiastical rivalry. The Protestant reform establishment was committed to ecumenical cooperation and church unity, believing that only a unified Protestantism could successfully resist the secularization of American culture. In fact, by the 1920s Protestant activists looked beyond the confines of American denominationalism and took a prominent role in international ecumenical discussions. This step enabled the reformers to present their message as an expression of the mind of the entire Christian church.

Social gospel advocates after 1918 stressed the linkage between domestic and international questions. Even moderate church leaders like John R. Mott, addressing the Student Volunteer Movement in 1920, spoke of the opportunities to build a new world order based on Christian social principles now that the foundations of the old order had been shaken by World War I.[3] Throughout the decade, representative Protestant agencies emphasized the importance of international questions regarding peace and justice. In 1925, for example, 160 official representatives of twenty-eight Protestant denominations met in Washington, D.C., at the National Study Conference on the Churches and World Peace. They summoned the churches to acknowledge that "economics and industry, social welfare and progressive civilization, morality and religion, all demand a new international order in which righteousness and justice between nations shall prevail and in which nation shall fear nation no longer, and prepare for war no more." The delegates called for an end to economic imperialism and Western colonialism, to racial discrimination and immigration restrictions, and to "economic and social oppression of minority racial groups within nations."[4] Rather than being isolationists, Protestant activists attempted to nurture a global perspective within the churches. The Federal Council's Department of International Justice and Goodwill, the *Christian Century,* and peace groups like the Fellowship of Reconciliation were all committed to an internationalist social gospel.

Most of the delegates who gathered in Delaware, Ohio, in 1942 belonged to this social gospel tradition. They wanted to speak with a politically independent, prophetic voice, applying the social convictions of Christianity to the urgent problems of war and peace. Although the American churches are "powerful social institutions," they declared, Christians must remember that they are members of one "ecumenical, supranational body, separate from and independent of all states." Even during wartime, Christianity's social vision must look beyond the claims and interests of any particular sovereign state. The paramount duty of Protestantism in times of national crisis, they maintained, is to challenge its own members and the leaders of political, economic, and cultural life with moral claims that transcend national, racial, or class self-interest.

The delegates argued that despite the nation's preoccupation with the war, the time had come to demand changes of national policy and they declared that such changes could not wait until the war's conclusion. The United States must be prepared now to subordinate "immediate and particular national interests to the welfare of all." Motives of vengeance or retribution must be renounced in favor of actions that could build a peaceful world order. Since nationalism was the primary force wreaking havoc in the modern world, the goal of U.S. policies should be to end "the sovereign power of the nation-state" and to lay the foundations for a genuine world government, having the necessary administrative, legislative, judicial, and military competence to function as a world peacekeeper.

They warned, moreover, that this world government must check the unbridled power of capitalism and related forms of economic nationalism. Instead, the postwar world should be prepared for "experimentation with various forms of ownership and control, private, cooperative and public." Economic systems should be flexible and responsive to human needs. They should recognize the need for a redistribution of the world's resources, for full industrial democracy, for universal opportunities for educational advancement, for the right to find employment "consistent with human dignity and self-respect," and for the support of traditional forms of agriculture "as a basis of family and community life."

Above all else, such a world government should respect cultural diversity and fundamental human rights. "The rights and duties of peoples to maintain their full cultural freedom must be preserved," the delegates noted. "All racial groups have contributed outstanding cultural gifts to civilization," and "the exchange of such gifts has enriched all mankind." Consequently, all racial and cultural minorities must have equal status and treatment before the law. And before the United States can promote this goal with any honesty, the American government and churches must put their own houses in order. "Justice in race relations," the conference declared, requires not only an absence of overt discrimination, but also the employment of Negro Americans in government agencies and their inclusion in the administrative personnel and fellowship of the churches, local and national. The United States should therefore assume the initiative in creating the international machinery that will establish a "true community of nations" and guarantee "autonomy for all subject and colonial peoples."[5]

Taken one by one, none of these propositions was new in itself. Each was rooted in the demands of the social gospel tradition in the 1920s and 1930s. Yet by packaging them together in this way, under the rubric of a world government, the Protestant reform establishment gave them great coherence and urgency. Many of the delegates at the Delaware conference thought Protestantism had finally found its vitality again. "This is the most distinguished American church gathering I have seen in 30 years," remarked a prominent Methodist bishop. Conference participants believed they were speaking not merely on behalf of the American churches but also on behalf of the ecumenical church. And, in a sense, they were. The organizers of the Delaware conference would become leaders in the World Council of Churches: John Foster Dulles, G. Bromley Oxnam, Walter Van Kirk, Henry P. Van Dusen, John Bennett, Georgia Harkness, Kenneth Scott Latourette, Henry Leiper, Ernest F. Tittle, Roswell Barnes, William Ernest Hocking, and E. E. Aubrey.

The delegates were speaking *to* American Protestantism as well as *for* it. They did not expect their recommendations to be well received, and they were not disappointed. *Time* magazine ridiculed what it called "organized U.S. Protestantism's super-protestant new program," and castigated the conference for waxing "hot and heavy" while "the japs [*sic*] were taking Java." In particular the magazine took offense at statements about the "shame and humiliation" of the United States in the area of race relations. The only positive thing *Time* could say about the conference was that it failed to move as far to the left "as its definitely pinko British counterpart" (the Malvern Conference).[6]

The Search for Relevance

How effective was the Protestant reform establishment in communicating this message to the rank and file of the denominations? Not very. When the Federal Council sent out teams of speakers to tour the United States and drum up support for the church's "Mission on World Order," they were met with stony indifference. When the Methodist bishops launched a "Bishops' Crusade for a New World Order," covering seventy-seven cities, they were greeted with contempt, at least judging from the letters to the *Christian Century,* the journalistic voice of the Protestant reform establishment. By March 1944, the Federal Council's peace commission was so discouraged that it sent a delegation headed by Dulles and Methodist bishop G. Bromley Oxnam to the White House to "warn the President" about "the misgiving which is growing within church circles regarding the probable nature of the coming peace." An editorial, "Toward Disillusion," appeared in the *Christian Century* lamenting that the prospect for a *Christian* world order "looks more discouraging with every passing week."[7] Protestant leaders were thus reminded that a consensus within their own ranks did not automatically translate into public influence. Even within the churches, cultural authority was not a birthright but a function of persuasiveness and timeliness.

After the war, however, the standing of the Protestant reform establishment changed dramatically. Protestant leaders discovered that subtle adjustments in their message could win over significant sectors of American public opinion. They began to stress a point John Foster Dulles had been making since 1940. According to Dulles, the disorder of the modern world was a product, not simply of economic injustice, but of "evil faiths," totalitarian and secular ideologies that were expansionistic in intent and unconcerned about human values. Dulles argued that only a correspondingly strong faith in the core values of a Christian civilization could prevent the fall of the West to such rival ideologies. "It is our lack of impelling faith that has weakened us," warned Dulles in a Federal Council pamphlet. Secular faiths "will arise to attack us . . . [and] we will succumb," he insisted, unless the West developed an even stronger religious faith that united all cultures "as never before, in common and constructive purpose."[8] Book after book appeared at the end of the war in which Protestant reformers reiterated this line of argument: Only a renewed commitment to Christian social ideals could save both Western and non-Western civilizations from the moral devastation of secular and idolatrous political faiths.

A further change of emphasis occurred as the Protestant reform establishment moved away from demands for sweeping social change and focused on the practical task of mobilizing public support for the establishment of a United Nations organization and the creation of a World Council of Churches. In January 1945, the Commission on a Just and Durable Peace voted to recommend that the churches support the Dumbarton Oaks Proposals "as an important step in the direction of world cooperation." Although these proposals stopped short of its own Christian vision of a new world order, the commission argued that "an idealism which does not accept the discipline of the achievable may lose its power for good and ultimately lend aid to forces with whose purposes it cannot agree."[9] Concern over loss of power and the fear of rival social ideologies reflected the changed perspective of the Protestant establishment, a perspective more in line with public sentiment.

A few months later, as John Foster Dulles was leading the drive for support of the United Nations within the American churches, he wrote to his good friend Bishop Oxnam concerning the international viewpoint of the Protestant reform establishment now that the Soviet leaders had revealed expansionistic intentions. Dulles explained that he had only recently come to comprehend Soviet foreign policy. And he suggested to

Oxnam that the Federal Council's Committee of Direction begin evaluating "the Russian problem" and answer the challenge of communism.[10] Indeed, within the next few years, Oxnam and other activists in Protestantism published numerous books and statements explaining the incompatibility of Christian and communist "faiths."

The fortunes of the Protestant reform establishment were changing. Support for a new world order based on the Christian perspective of the West was a message that suited the postwar interests of American policymakers and the concerns of American public opinion. By 1948, the Protestant reform establishment had become a participant in the Western policy establishment in ways unimaginable in 1942.

Popular magazines now gave generous space and serious attention to the words of Protestant leaders. In 1948, *Time* ran feature articles on Dulles, Oxnam, Reinhold Niebuhr, and the World Council of Churches. Perhaps it was merely coincidental that the issue asking the sobering question "Is Protestantism Slipping?" had a cover drawing of Karl Marx, glaring menacingly at the reader from behind a boiling cauldron, hammer and sickle looming in the background. The issue covering the formation of the World Council of Churches was particularly interested in the assembly's economic pronouncements, which rejected "the ideologies of both communism and laissez-faire capitalism." *Time* applauded the Council's call for "Christians to seek new creative solutions which never allow either justice or freedom to destroy the other." In an article on Oxnam, the magazine praised the bishop's forthright attack on communist views of human nature and his contention that economic justice was the best antidote to communism.[11] In fact, in a private conversation with Oxnam, Henry Luce, editor of *Time,* remarked that he was pleased with "the new field of force" that the Protestant social leaders had entered. According to Oxnam's recollection, Luce promised him that "men of power in business had decided to prove to the world that our scheme of things can work."[12]

It is no wonder the Protestant reform establishment believed it was helping to rebuild the world order. For example, when the European Recovery Plan was proposed in Congress, the Federal Council held a series of seminars to generate popular Protestant support. Large rallies were held at the New York Avenue Presbyterian Church and at the Washington Cathedral, attended by members of Congress, the president, and crowds of over two thousand. Both General Marshall and Dulles spoke. Their message was the need for action by the churches to alter the prevailing mood of the American people and lessen the danger of another war. Bishop Oxnam, who had been transferred to Washington, D.C., in order to take advantage of his political connections,

President Truman and Bishop Oxnam, 1946. Religious News Service
photo.

presented Congress with a petition signed by more than seven hundred
prominent churchmen in favor of the recovery plan. A delegation from
the Federal Council, led by Walter Van Kirk, met with President
Truman in the Oval Office to offer him their ardent support.

In the meantime, Oxnam was privately promising John Foster Dulles
that he would rally the power of the Methodist Board of Bishops behind
Dulles's policies, should Dulles become secretary of state in a Dewey
administration. This support, Oxnam reassured his friend, would be
quickly diffused throughout the boards and agencies of Protestantism's

largest denomination. In another letter on July 1, Oxnam asked Dulles to arrange a private meeting between presidential candidate Dewey and four or five prominent bishops. Oxnam hastened to explain that he did not wish to cross the line separating church and state; but he laid his reservations aside with the knowledge that such a meeting would serve the national interest rather than enhance the personal power of the bishops. In contrast to Roman Catholicism, wrote Oxnam, Protestantism wanted no advantages from the state. Nevertheless, since Dewey was appallingly ignorant in religious matters, argued the Methodist bishop, the candidate really ought to familiarize himself with the virtues, viewpoints, and organizational strengths of Protestantism.[13]

In many respects, Oxnam's relationship with Dulles symbolized the relationship that developed between the Protestant reform and political establishments after the war. Less than a month before the 1948 election, Oxnam again contacted Dulles. He pointed out that it was extremely hard for church leaders to supply local churches and community leaders with adequate political advice when they had so little access to the Department of State. Oxnam reminded Dulles that there was an influential group of churchmen just waiting to be mobilized and suggested that informal monthly meetings take place between the (future) secretary of state and prominent Protestant leaders. This would benefit the entire nation, the bishop maintained. Thirty key church leaders might be a conduit to thousands of communities across America and thereby aid in preserving the democratic way of life. Once again Oxnam admitted that this suggestion seemed to raise church–state objections; but since no sectarian preferences were being shown and the purpose was the public good rather than ecclesiastical preferment, he saw no practical harm in it.[14]

Oxnam renewed this request before the 1952 election. Although there is no evidence that Dulles ever seriously entertained these suggestions, he did meet regularly with Oxnam throughout the 1950s. In fairness to Oxnam, it must be noted that he frequently disputed Dulles's reasoning on foreign policy issues, especially in the later years of the 1950s. He persistently urged both the Truman and Eisenhower administrations to drop their support of right-wing dictatorships, and he tried to convince the secretary of state of the wisdom of recognizing the People's Republic of China. Moreover, the bishop continually reminded Dulles that the communist challenge demanded the active pursuit of economic justice and insisted that economic experimentation with mixed economies was most suitable in developing nations.[15] Oxnam believed that he was fulfilling a prophetic role, one that had been sketched out in 1942. His actions may or may not have been consistent with a prophetic stance. What is striking, however, is the almost total absence of critical reflection

on the part of either Oxnam or Dulles about the appropriate role of the
churches in politics.

Uncertainties of Political Advocacy

The operation of the Protestant reform establishment in the
1940s illustrated some of the limitations implicit in Protestant claims to
cultural authority and social influence. In the first place, actual authority
rested more on pragmatic considerations than on any clearly defined
place for reform leaders in either organized Protestantism or American
public life. Second, the nature of the influence exerted by the reform
establishment was ambiguous. What had originally started out in 1942 as
a "prophetic" – even radical – voice of nonconformity became gradually
assimilated into the general moral and political orthodoxy of the late
1940s. Establishment leaders assumed that they could influence the policies and decisions of major social and political agencies without bending
to popular sentiment. Yet their influence depended as much on an ability
to generate a public consensus as on moral authority. Protestant leaders
thus tended to vacillate between claims to prophetic stature and claims to
representativeness. Both perspectives were important, but they were not
necessarily compatible in practice. The confusion was common even in
the early decades of the social gospel when the Protestant reform establishment spoke ambiguously of America as already "Christianized" and
as a society standing in need of more radical Christianization.

Because the Protestant social leaders had no way to resolve this central
ambiguity, they tended to operate intuitively, without a clear perception
of the extent of their cultural authority. For example, the reform establishment functioned without a strong theoretical understanding of
church–state relations. This was not because individuals and organizations were insensitive about the issue; on the contrary, they were frequently interested in rebutting charges of impropriety. However, the
line between acceptable and unacceptable activity was gauged pragmat-
ically, by the barometer of public opinion. This was a matter not of
opportunism but of unclear guidelines.

Protestant social leaders certainly recognized the political dilemmas
confronting them. "The trouble is," wrote F. Ernest Johnson, of the
Federal Council of Churches, "that when we go after political ends we
usually become less a church and more a political instrumentality."[16] Yet
how could the church make an effective social impact without becoming
implicated in "politics"? The reformers sensed they walked a fine line. In
the early 1930s, for example, the editors of the *Christian Century*
protested the location of the Methodist Board of Temperance in Wash-

ington, D.C., across the street from the Capitol. Such action, said the liberal and prohibitionist journal, "has led the Methodist church [*sic*] suspiciously far into the field of political action." If such a precedent continued to be followed, "democratic government would be vitiated by ecclesiasticism. Clericalism would be rampant and dominant – unless, indeed, it thereby reduced itself to ridiculous impotence." Church agencies, the *Century* continued, should "refrain from establishing any working relation between their churches and the government, or the appearance of desiring to do so."

Careful reading, however, indicates that the real objection of the *Century* was less a matter of abstract principle than a fear that the clumsy assertion of ecclesiastical authority would bring public odium upon the church's social witness in general. Indeed, the *Century* admitted that it saw nothing amiss in church agencies lending their support to the Anti-Saloon League, even though it too had headquarters on Capitol Hill. The editor suggested, somewhat lamely perhaps, that by supporting "nonecclesiastical instrumentalities," church agencies could thereby "express their civic ideals and purposes at Washington without enmeshing the machinery of the church with the machinery of the state."[17]

The *Century* was appealing to a distinction between direct and indirect political involvement, rejecting the former as an inappropriate form of social action by the churches. The reform establishment frequently resorted to this line of reasoning. In actuality, however, the difference was insignificant, amounting to a question of appearances rather than of principle. The *Century*'s warning that the church should not be "a political partisan agency on behalf of any cause however ideal and desirable" simply did not ring true. It had fought for legislation protecting the rights of labor and for the extension of civil rights in the area of race relations. Charles Clayton Morrison, the editor of the *Century,* was himself lobbying hard for the "outlawry of war." And shortly thereafter the *Century* ran an important article by one of its associate editors, Reinhold Niebuhr, "The Church and Political Action," which repudiated the fiction of political neutrality by the church and called upon reform leaders to make their political convictions even more explicit.[18]

The reform establishment used the distinction between direct and indirect political action to lessen political backlash when a consensus within the churches was lacking. F. Ernest Johnson, in a candid discussion of this problem, acknowledged that despite strong verbal commitment to a sharp separation of church and state, "the separation that has been practiced is less the result of a considered philosophy than of opportunism." Johnson surmised that Protestant complaints about the political influence of the Roman Catholic Church reflected the fact that "many Protestant ministers would give all they possess to be as influential in the field of political ethics as Catholics are." Johnson too advocated a kind of "indirect" approach to Christian political action. He believed the churches should concentrate on the political education of individual members, letting small crusading groups of Christians pursue "a much more inclusive and thoroughgoing embodiment of Christian ideals in political action."[19]

As late as 1958, the discussion of these issues in Protestant establishment circles had not advanced much further than Johnson's discussion thirty years earlier. In that year Christian social ethicist John Bennett published *Christians and the State,* reiterating the point that the churches as a whole are better off focusing on the political education of their own constituencies. Direct political action by religious agencies was unwise because it could be counterproductive. "The most important type of impact of the Church on society or the state is indirect." Nevertheless, Bennett had to admit, on some political issues – where a sufficient consensus within the churches exists or where the principles involved require urgent action – direct involvement by the churches may be necessary. On thinking it over, Bennett finally admitted that "the distinction between direct and indirect action by the Church is not an absolute one."[20]

One probably will not find any more theoretical consistency than this within the Protestant reform establishment, which is not surprising considering the complexity of the issues. What is important, however, is that a lack of theoretical consistency frequently accounts for inconsistency in practice. While worrying about the propriety of direct political action, the Protestant reform establishment certainly sought to maintain a strong voice in matters of public policy. The result was a tendency to rely more on appearances and public sentiment as political guidelines, rather than on clear-cut policy. The simplest way to maintain the appearance of political restraint in the public eye was to construe the political realm in the narrowest possible way as "partisan" (party) activity. So long as partisan politics were avoided, every other sort of action or recommendation could be presented as nonpolitical or as only indirectly political.

The Irony of Success

Finally, what makes the cultural authority of Protestant reform difficult to assess precisely are the inherent tensions in the establishment's position in American public life. Its authority was limited by the fact that once the Protestant social leaders tried to influence the public arena, they were necessarily drawn into a dialogue, or rather, a trialogue. Reformers

Launching the Commission of the Churches on International Affairs, 1946. Clockwise from upper left: O. Frederick Nolde, John W. Decker, Henry Smith Leiper, Reinhold Niebuhr, John Foster Dulles, Walter W. Van Kirk. From O. Frederick Nolde, *The Churches and the Nations* (Philadelphia: Fortress Press, 1970), facing p. 8.

had to balance their own convictions with the claims of various religious constituencies and secular authorities. In order to be effective they had to accommodate the expectations of those they were trying to influence.

The influence exerted by the reform establishment in the late 1940s, for example, derived less from an inherent cultural hegemony than from the new prestige accorded by public opinion. Important secular and political agencies had come to regard ecumenical Protestantism as a vital force in the West's geopolitical struggles. The Protestant establishment's authority was dependent, in part, on its role as a highly visible and useful special interest group.

This observation does not denigrate the genuine moral convictions that Protestant leaders held. But the way in which the Protestant ecumenical reform establishment operated in this period virtually ensured that it would interpret its social responsibilities in ways that would serve the broader political establishment in which it had become enmeshed.

A good illustration of the way in which the structure of establishment agencies reinforced this tendency is the work of the Commission on International Affairs. The Commission was, in essence, the administrative arm of the World Council of Churches, functioning as "a source of stimulus and knowledge" to the World Council and "a medium of common counsel and action" for "formulating the Christian mind on world issues and in bringing that mind effectively to bear upon such issues."[21] The Commission wanted to provide an independent Christian voice in international affairs. The United States' members on the Commission in 1950 included John Foster Dulles, G. Bromley Oxnam, Reinhold Niebuhr, Richard Fagley (executive secretary), and Frederick Nolde (director). The Commission also worked closely in the United States with Walter Van Kirk and the newly organized National Council of Churches.

From the beginning, the Commission maintained an intimate relationship with United Nations organizations and accepted the perspective of the Western bloc nations. According to Alan Geyer, the Commission chairman Sir Kenneth Grubb complained about the undue power and influence of the American leaders, who "set the nature and shape the rules of international ecumenical discussion."[22] The Commission was granted observer status at all open meetings of UN agencies and consultative status with UNESCO, the Economic and Social Council, and the Food and Agriculture Organization. Commission officers cultivated close ties with UN delegates and received all unrestricted UN documents, maintaining an updated index file of these documents "for use by the staff in the preparation of reports" and for use "by church agencies and leaders for reference purposes."[23]

Indeed, the list of activities by the officers of the Commission reveals extensive involvement in UN conferences and commissions. According to Commission reports, these formal and informal contacts have "made access to officials of many governments possible, both on issues of general international import and on issues relating peculiarly to the life and work of the churches." On June 5, 1951, for example, Commission officers met with the UN Secretariat at UN headquarters for group consultation. The Commission delegates explained that the great advantage of such arrangements was that they testified to "a Christian interest in the problems facing government delegates" and contributed "further information about the views held by Christians throughout the world."[24]

The positions thus developed by the Commission in such consultations were in turn relayed to the American churches through the agencies of the National Council of Churches. American church leaders and agencies were encouraged to rely on the files of the Commission for information. The Commission was proud that American Protestant leaders could depend upon receiving "for their benefit background memoranda on international issues of major concern to the churches." The National Council in turn arranged study conferences for selected religious and political leaders. One such conference was held at Buck Hill Falls, Pennsylvania, in April 1951, to develop a set of findings concerning "The American Churches and Overseas Development Programs." According to Commission reports, conferences such as these enabled the National Council of Churches to convey to governmental leaders "the views of the churches related to the United Nations . . . [and] various problems of foreign policy."[25]

In essence, the whole process of information and consultation was circular and restricted to a fairly small leadership network. The opinions of the churches were being shaped by the very agencies to which the churches were to speak "prophetically." An example of such circularity appeared in a letter on current disarmament proposals that the Commission sent to national church leaders in 1950. The letter explained that the proposals being made "fitted closely with Soviet proposals" that had already been "rejected in the United Nations Atomic Energy Commission," and expressed the view that the outlawing of atomic weapons as suggested in the proposals was not desirable. "Peace requires a workable means of restraining every aggressor, no matter whether he uses atomic or other instruments of destruction, or measures of coercion or infiltration." The letter concluded that "the starting point for reduction of all kinds of armaments under the United Nations must be the development of international security." Although church leaders would have to make up their own minds, the Commission urged them "to be on guard against the possibility that their utterances might be used for [communist] propagandist purpose quite different from those they intend."[26] The point is not whether such recommendations were wise or unwise, but rather that the Protestant reform establishment had come to think of its social witness in terms congruent with the foreign policy concerns of the Western bloc nations in the UN.

A different sort of problem facing the reform establishment was the authority it exerted over its own Protestant constituency. For several decades the reformers themselves had lamented that "the following which these progressive leaders of the Church have among their own laity is questionable."[27] Most acknowledged doubts about "whether many of our social creeds are really expressive of more than minority opinion."[28] As the social policies of the churches fell more and more into the hands of specialists and internationalists, the distance from the local church increased.

In order to bridge this gap, the National Council of Churches adopted a new procedure in the 1950s. No longer would policy decisions be the

monopoly of leadership elites. Social statements would now be formulated after consultation with representatives "of business and management, labor, various segments of agriculture, and with economists and
theologians and pastors."[29]

The result, however, was to make National Council pronouncements,
like the 1951 statement on "Christian life and work," even more vague
and consensus oriented than earlier pronouncements. One statement, for
example, merely reaffirmed Christian faith in the democratic system and
stressed the importance of saving Western democracy by "injecting
Christian convictions in it." It called for a "concern for human values,"
for steadfast "loyalty to the United Nations," and for continued resistance through collective action to military aggression.[30] Nowhere in
the statement was there a critique of the concept of national sovereignty
or warnings about the perils of nationalism, as in the 1942 Delaware
resolutions.

Similarly, the National Council's statements regarding the economy
merely summarized popular views. They supported a variety of practical
welfare measures and condemned communism, but stopped short of any
criticism of American capitalism. The churches were urged to solve the
problems of social injustice by preaching love and humility.[31] Nowhere
were the earlier concerns of the reform establishment aired: the need for a
redistribution of wealth, the necessity of industrial democracy, the need
to restrict the profit motive, or the importance of maintaining a global
perspective on questions of peace and justice.

The argument that these statements were more practical and "realistic," and therefore more influential, than the social gospel emphases
overlooks the fact that the purpose of earlier pronouncements was to
educate the Protestant constituency and not just speak for it. Statements
representing popularly accepted views were not needed. John Bennett's
assessment in 1958 that "the only pronouncements or resolutions which
are worth the paper they are printed on are those which . . . represent
the kind of consensus which I have described" is thus hard to understand.[32] The Protestant reform establishment had become uncertain
about how to exert cultural authority and had sacrificed incisiveness for
unanimity. Indeed, by 1960 some members of the Protestant establishment were beginning to suspect that Protestant reform had won the right
to speak in the councils of the mighty, only to discover that there was no
longer much to say.

The limitations inherent in Protestant establishment claims to cultural
authority had become evident by the 1960s. The role of the Roman
Catholic Church, the black churches, and other religious groups in
American public life was coming to the fore. Within a few years, the

very concept of an "establishment" became anathema to a younger generation of Americans. Once again, as in the 1930s, the Protestant reform establishment found itself uncertain about its role in American public life. Protestant reform leaders realized that they had to do more listening and less speaking. The issue was not whether the Protestant establishment would somehow monopolize public debates. The issue was how Protestantism would share in creating a vision of society that could again be both credible and prophetic.

NOTES

1 Charles Chatfield, *For Peace and Justice: Pacifism in America, 1914–1941* (Knoxville: University of Tennessee Press, 1971), 129.
2 Walter Van Kirk, *A Christian Global Strategy* (New York: Willett, 1945), 101.
3 "The World Opportunity," in *North American Students and World Advance,* ed. Burton St. John (New York: Student Volunteer Movement, 1920), 17–23.
4 Benjamin Winchester (ed.), *The Handbook of the Churches* (New York: J. E. Stohlmann, 1927), 61–3.
5 "The Churches and a Just and Durable Peace," *Christian Century,* March 25, 1942, 390–7.
6 "American Malvern," *Time,* March 16, 1942, 44–8.
7 *Christian Century,* March 8, 1944, 295–7.
8 John Foster Dulles, "The American People Need Now to Be Imbued with a Righteous Faith," in Dulles et al., *A Righteous Faith for a Just and Durable Peace* (New York: Federal Council of Churches, 1942), 11.
9 Luman Shafer, "Necessary Reorientations in Thought and Life," in *The Gospel, The Church, and The World,* ed. Kenneth Scott Latourette (New York: Harper, 1946), 180–1.
10 John Foster Dulles to G. Bromley Oxnam, May 9, 1946, Oxnam Papers, Library of Congress, Washington, D.C.
11 "Is Protestantism Slipping?" *Time,* February 23, 1948, 72; "The Bishop's Challenge," *Time,* May 10, 1948, 54–6; "The First World Council," *Time,* August 30, 1948, 59; and "No Pentecost," *Time,* September 13, 1948, 50–5.
12 Oxnam, diary entry, November 18, 1948, Oxnam Papers.
13 Oxnam to Dulles, July 1, 1948, Oxnam Papers.
14 Oxnam to Dulles, October 19, 1948, Oxnam Papers.
15 Oxnam to Dulles, August 13, 1958; report of conversation with Dulles, November 3, 1958, Oxnam Papers.
16 F. Ernest Johnson, *The Church and Society* (New York: Abingdon-Cokesbury Press, 1935), 134.
17 "The Methodists at Washington," *Christian Century,* March 4, 1931, 294–6.
18 August 1, 1934, 992–4.
19 Johnson, *Church and Society,* 124, 137.'

20 John Bennett, *Christians and the State* (New York: Scribner's, 1958), 278–81.
21 *Commission of the Churches on International Affairs, 1947–1949* (London: World Council of Churches, n.d.), 2.
22 Alan Geyer, *Piety and Politics* (Richmond: John Knox Press, 1963), 123.
23 *Commission of the Churches on International Affairs, 1949–1951* (London: World Council of Churches, n.d.), 17.
24 Ibid., 20.
25 Ibid., 13.
26 Ibid., 27–8.
27 Ralph Read, "The Tragedy of the Christian Church," in *The Younger Churchmen Look at the Church,* ed. Ralph Read (New York: Macmillan, 1935), 7.
28 Johnson, *Church and Society,* 86.
29 Bennett, *Christians and the State,* 277.
30 "The National Council of Churches Views Its Task in Christian Life and Work," adopted by the General Board, May 16, 1951.
31 "Christian Principles and Assumptions for Economic Life," adopted by the General Board, September 15, 1954.
32 Bennett, *Christians and the State,* 283.

SELECT BIBLIOGRAPHY

Bennett, John. *Christians and the State.* New York: Scribner's, 1958.
Chatfield, Charles. *For Peace and Justice: Pacifism in America, 1914–1941.* Knoxville: University of Tennessee Press, 1971.
Fox, Richard. *Reinhold Niebuhr: A Biography.* New York: Pantheon, 1985.
Geyer, Alan. *Piety and Politics: Protestantism in the World Arena.* Richmond: John Knox Press, 1963.
Handy, Robert T. *A Christian America: Protestant Hopes and Historical Realities.* New York: Oxford University Press, 1971.
Handy, Robert T. (ed.). *The Social Gospel in America.* New York: Oxford University Press, 1966.
Hopkins, C. Howard. *The Rise of the Social Gospel in American Protestantism, 1865–1915.* New Haven, Conn.: Yale University Press, 1940.
Meyer, Donald B. *The Protestant Search for Political Realism, 1919–1941.* Berkeley: University of California Press, 1960.
Miller, Robert Moats. *American Protestantism and Social Issues, 1919–1939.* Chapel Hill: University of North Carolina Press, 1960.
Piper, John Franklin, Jr. *The American Churches in World War I.* Athens: Ohio University Press, 1985.
Toulouse, Mark. *The Transformation of John Foster Dulles: From Prophet of Realism to Priest of Nationalism.* Macon, Ga.: Mercer University Press, 1985.
White, Ronald C., and C. Howard Hopkins (eds.). *The Social Gospel: Religion and Reform in Changing America.* Philadelphia: Temple University Press, 1976.

IV

Outsiders and "Junior Partners"

Outsiders to an establishment – those not equally empowered – are readily enough identified, yet difficult to generalize about. In their great number and variety, outsiders may be such because of exclusion, or because of self-exclusion – or both. Their alienated or separate status may be based on differences in doctrine, race, region, ethnicity, socioeconomic status, or gender. They may well represent some mix of these and still other differentiating features.

The fate of outsiders, in real life or in historical memory, is equally hard to capture in generalizations. As a matter of theory and of national ideology, especially in America, the outsider's status has generally been an honored one. But in actual day-to-day experience, even much-admired "religious dissenters" have faced condescension or worse in their own times, and they have not always fared better in the history books.

We have chosen to inquire into the experience of two groups, women and blacks, who as partners in the enterprise of Protestant Christianity had a vested interest in determining its destiny; and of two others, Roman Catholics and Jews, who were far from sharing that interest yet did share involvement in what came to be called the Judeo–Christian tradition.

These four groups, for all their obvious prominence among the many that deserve attention (and perhaps just because of this prominence), cannot serve adequately to illustrate the varieties of outsider status. Yet they do, as it happens, illustrate very different degrees of outsider "intentionality." Women were married to the establishment, in both real-life and symbolic ways. Their outsidership, their exclusion from recognition and control, can scarcely be called intentional. Catholics and Jews, nearly at the other pole, desired recognition for themselves and an equal stand-

141

ing in American society, but in no sense sought election to the Protestant directorate. Blacks, and black churches, would seem to have stood somewhere between these poles, claiming their place and rights as sizable segments in the Protestant constituency, but also very ready, especially toward the end of the period we examine, to insist upon a separate identity.

Virginia Lieson Brereton analyzes the experience of United Church Women, the broadest and perhaps most important of the many women's organizations that, although they sought loyally to serve church and society, at the same time worked zealously to effect women's acceptance (as more than undersecretaries and assistants) in the boardrooms of the establishment.

Blacks, whether individually or as organized in congregations and denominations, were in general denied even junior partnerships in the firm, and were only very selectively admitted to the other subordinate positions that women held. David Wills, surveying the variety of black responses to that situation, highlights the experience of some who chose to wage the battle by utilizing such insider status as they were able to win; and of other black leaders or organizations that relied instead (or also) upon the advantages of relative independence from an implacably white power structure.

For Jews and Catholics, religiously the "true outsiders" in this company, choices among accommodation, collaboration, and resistance were of course presented in a quite different context, but one that serves especially well to highlight a general truth about the establishment's relation to American society. A recurrent difficulty about collaboration, as Benny Kraut's examination of the Goodwill Movement demonstrates, was that the motives and assumptions of Protestant outreach to other faiths were still at base conversionary, and still infused with a territorial imperative. For this kind of outsider the problem, sometimes imaginary or exaggerated, yet fundamentally and pervasively real, was the degree to which the Protestant establishment, as late as the 1920s, still expected to write and control the common agenda.

In that light, one of the more thought-provoking features of interfaith relationships was the countervailing Roman Catholic hope, not merely for the conversion of Jews and Protestants, but for a (usually) modest Catholicizing of American culture. That the Catholic Church, with a constituency almost equal to that of the Federal Council, should harbor such ideas ought not to be surprising. What should provoke thought is that it usually *was* considered surprising (and to a great extent still is) – that Protestants who could tolerate such ideas were nonetheless inclined to think them, if not dangerous, then just a bit quaint.

7

United and Slighted: Women as Subordinated Insiders

VIRGINIA LIESON BRERETON

In the early fifties Mildred McAfee Horton, a prominent educator and churchwoman, was attending a meeting of the National Council of Churches' Division of Christian Life and Work; a colleague asked for "Dr. Horton's" opinion on an issue under discussion. She responded, "I really don't know what it is. He is at home doing the breakfast dishes so his wife can attend this meeting. But *Mrs.* Horton thinks . . ." and went on to outline her opinions. Horton's denial of the title "doctor" is surprising here. Since she held a number of honorary degrees, the ascription was accurate enough. True, she lacked an earned doctorate, but then so did her husband. And her husband's status scarcely needed highlighting. The Reverend Douglas Horton was a moderator of the International Congregational Council, served on the Central Committee of the World Council of Churches, and would shortly become dean of the Harvard Divinity School.

His wife's preference for the title of "Mrs." to that of "Dr." was not unusual in the fifties; most married women chose to go by their husbands' names. The Reverend Mossie Allman Wyker, a prominent Disciples leader, was quoted as saying she wanted to be called Mrs. James D. Wyker, "because my husband is a wonderful man. I'd rather do my work in his name." What gives greater pause in Horton's case is that she had not come to prominence as "Mrs. Horton." She had married in 1945, at age forty-five, after she had already achieved a distinguished career as dean of women at Oberlin, president of Wellesley, and commander during World War II of the newly formed WAVES. Nevertheless, on this occasion she chose pointedly to highlight her identity as wife.

Horton's remark cuts both ways. In part it bespeaks wifely subordination fifties-style, but it also reveals that her husband was at home doing the dishes, obviously supportive of his wife's public activities. (And she

Mildred McAfee Horton. Religious News Service photo.

wanted her colleagues to know this.) The husband's dishwashing role does not sound like a traditional arrangement. Indeed, after her marriage Horton continued in leadership roles and vigorously championed the cause of an equal role for women in the church. Furthermore, she took her own service to the church very seriously. In the late forties she had been elected the first female vice-president of the Federal Council of Churches; as a lay consultant to the first Assembly of the World Council of Churches in Amsterdam in 1948 she had been one of a small number of women to address a plenary session of delegates. When the National Council of Churches was formed in 1950, she served as a vice-president and as vice-chair of the Division on Christian Life and Work. She took a leadership role in the secular sphere, as well; she was, among other positions, chairwoman of the National Social Welfare Assembly, member of the U.S. Commission for UNESCO, and the first woman on the boards of the New York Life Insurance Company, NBC, and RCA.

The point of this anecdote is that even Horton's situation contained ambiguities. On the face of it, her experience proved that a woman, given the right natural gifts and the requisite circumstances, could achieve insider status in the middle decades of the twentieth century. She was born into a prominent Presbyterian family (her father, Cleland McAfee, was a pastor, professor, and denominational leader); she graduated from Vassar; she married well. Although many of her achievements were in what one might call the "female public track" – dean of women, president of Wellesley, head of the WAVES – she had also risen to eminence in the traditionally male world of the Protestant ecumenical establishment. Yet the prominent positions she achieved in the church agencies were so frequently "firsts" that she often was viewed as an oddity and exception.

When, as the only officer present, she had presided at a Federal Council committee meeting, a "male dignitary" complimented her, "You did that well – as if you had been doing that sort of thing all your life. I had no idea a woman could handle things so smoothly." This was of course meant as praise; yet it was a total misreading of Horton's career, for she *had* been doing "that sort of thing" all her life. And it suggested that as a woman her acceptance into male church circles would depend upon her ability to deliver an outstanding performance.

Then there is the matter of her emphasis on her domestic role. Was she simply radiating happiness at recently found domestic bliss, or exhibiting a becoming modesty that rested easily on a bedrock of well-earned self-assurance? Was she trying to tell those assembled that, despite the prominent public role she was playing, her peculiarly female role was intact? They might know her as a church leader, but her deepest loyalties lay at home. This may seem to strain the limits of a casual remark, except that nearly every married woman leader in the church at this time, no matter how far-flung and prominent her public activities, insisted that she was first and foremost a homemaker.[1]

Women as Outsiders and Insiders

If there was a hint of ambiguity even in Horton's "insidership," it was much more pronounced in the lives of churchwomen whose family connections were less prominent and whose public achievements were less illustrious. Conditioned by the feminist movement, we are of course predisposed to see the ways in which churchwomen have been outsiders. By 1900, to be sure, women had at least advanced to the point where most people agreed they should have some voice in the church, Pauline passages to the contrary. But that voice was still to be ladylike and severely circumscribed. Most of the Protestant churches of the twentieth century were slow to grant women the right to participate in denominational policy-making bodies, and even when these lay rights were granted the numbers of women in governing groups remained small.

The Presbyterians (PCUSA) in 1930 voted to ordain women as elders in the churches, and five attended the next year's General Assembly as "commissioners." Left to right: B. J. Silliman, Utah; Lena Jennings, Ohio; O. G. Roberts, Pennsylvania; Helen B. Logsdon, California; Mary A. Yielding, Oklahoma. From James H. Smylie, *American Presbyterians: A Pictorial History*, published as *Journal of Presbyterian History* 63:1 and 2 (Spring and Summer, 1985):194. Courtesy of the Office of History, Presbyterian Church (U.S.A.).

Full ordination rights for women, of course, came even more slowly than lay rights. And ordination rights entailed the requisite education; only slowly during the course of the twentieth century did female aspirants to the ministry gain admittance to seminaries on an equal footing with men.

The fact of outsidership was no less true in the ecumenical councils of the church. The Federal Council of Churches, which had a reputation for championing liberal causes, showed no great hospitality toward women's leadership, remaining throughout its history a largely male and clerical bastion. (Even its commissions and committees on matters such as family and marriage were usually headed by men!)

Excluded from the centers of authority and education in the churches in the early twentieth century, women continued to be most active and successful in the separate and parallel organizations they had established during the nineteenth century. These national and regional organizations, chiefly devoted to home or foreign missions, raised enormous amounts of money and showed much skill in publicizing the missionary cause. Beginning in the 1880s, women also had set up educational institutions of their own, religious-missionary training schools to prepare them for service in the church, especially as teachers and missionaries.

As Laurence Moore has argued, outsidership has sometimes conferred certain benefits on outsider groups. In the case of women, these were a sense of identity as women, a degree of autonomy, and a power base. By the early twentieth century women had established a significant presence for themselves outside the normal ecclesiastical structures. This mode of operation often failed to satisfy churchwomen, however, and on occasion they protested publicly. Belle Harris Bennett, pleading for lay rights before the Methodist Episcopal Church (South) in 1910, cried, "After twenty centuries we stand knocking at the door of the Church of God, saying yet, 'My brothers, brothers, won't you take us in?' "[2]

Furthermore, women were vulnerable to loss of even the qualified benefits of outsider status. In the interests of greater efficiency and – no doubt – consolidation of male power, many of the women's societies eventually were merged with the general missionary boards, often without consulting the women and despite their protests. Typically the women were allowed some representation on the consolidated boards, but not enough to give them a decisive voice as women. Even this degree of female representation achieved at the time of merger tended to diminish over time, as men replaced retiring women representatives. Male educators also took over leadership of the training schools begun and led by women. Not infrequently they were merged with other seminaries or closed for lack of funds, particularly during the hard times of the thirties. At these moments of involuntary incorporation many women had to face the fact of powerlessness. Although their public rhetoric was usually muted, their private letters to each other often expressed great outrage and bitterness.[3]

Outsidership, obvious as it was at times, did not define the whole situation. Women of the established denominations, a majority of the membership, constituted a special group. They were the daughters, sisters, nieces, and wives of prominent male laity and clerics. They could claim friends among the mighty. Mostly they were white Anglo-Saxons; they enjoyed abundant social and economic privileges. To use Carroll Smith-Rosenberg's distinction, if they did not wield much actual *power* – except in their separate, outsider groups – they had a great deal of *influence*.[4]

Churchwomen, then, were both insiders and outsiders; they were both *of* the Protestant establishment and yet barred from its inner citadel. In this dual role they suffered many of the disabilities of outsiders, namely, a dearth of power. At the same time they enjoyed some of the advantages of insidership, among them, influence and at least the illusion of power. As halfway members of the establishment they inherited a consciousness of their privileged station and also a concomitant sense of social responsibility; they felt an obligation to exercise whatever influence they could on behalf of the poor and the unchurched. They were often stymied, however, in the full exercise of authority by the strictures that the male establishment imposed, and by their own culturally derived self-doubts and internal inhibitions. Frequently they were forced to employ methods of indirection and content themselves with the attainment of modest goals.

Women of the established denominations, as the most inside of all female outsiders, might be called "friendly" outsiders, as distinguished from the less friendly women who stood more distinctly outside the male-dominated Protestant establishment – Christian Scientists or Pentecostals, for instance. These out-outsiders sometimes held a radically alternative vision to that of the establishment. However important the examination of such women's views, that is not our goal here. Our focus is upon the character of the establishment itself, and upon some of the more subtle aspects of women's outsidership. If wives and daughters of the establishment remained in some stark sense outsiders – and they did, as the next pages will show – that knowledge emphasizes how fundamental gender was in defining who was inside and who was outside the councils of the twentieth-century Protestant church.

Women Ecumenists Outside and Inside the Church

One of the major focuses of twentieth-century churchwomen has been ecumenical cooperation, and in this area a prominent organization, dating from 1941, has been United Church Women.[5] The complexities of women's insider–outsider status are especially evident in the story of this group. Of particular interest is a series of developments in the late forties and the fifties that involved, as so often in the past, the issue of merger. In 1950, after long and careful deliberations, United Church Women joined with several other national interdenominational organizations to form the National Council of Churches. The decision to unite with the other church organizations – to move from outside to inside – involved difficult questions for the women about the nature of their participation in the church, questions that remained unresolved once they had joined the National Council.[6]

The events of this period are revealing precisely because they caused the women a good deal of anguished soul-searching. One might have expected not anguish but rejoicing over their new role in the National Council. Of all churchwomen these ecumenists would least be expected to be interested in prolonging the advantages of outsidership. The cooperation of "all God's people" was their controlling ideal. The ecumenical church movement in which they participated was one of the most politically and socially liberal groups in American Protestantism and would have been expected to give women maximum scope for their talents and energies. And to an unprecedented degree, the women dictated the terms of their entry into the new organization. Inclusion in the National Council should have heralded the realization of their dreams. As the history reveals, it did not; women remained partial outsiders even after they were supposed to have become insiders.

In order to explore the significance of these events we require an understanding of the traditions and styles of operation the women leaders brought with them to the new council. One strand in the UCW past was an eagerness to shed denominational parochialisms in order to accomplish certain cooperative goals, especially those related to missions. As early as 1861 a New York City woman began the interdenominational Union Missionary Society. In succeeding decades women banded together across denominational boundaries to further such aims as the organization of special days of prayer for missions, the preparation of home and foreign missionary study materials, and the establishment of training centers for women missionary publicists and fund-raisers.

Another strand in the story is the existence by the end of World War I of numerous local and regional societies of women, also interdenominational, who shared civic and religious goals. Some of these societies had begun as missionary societies, then had broadened their purview after World War I and become involved in diverse ways in the betterment of their communities. By the thirties leaders of these local groups felt the need for a national umbrella organization to provide guidance, expertise, and coordination. Two national interdenominational groups already in existence, the Council of Women for Home Missions (founded in 1908) and the Federation of Women's Boards of Foreign Missions (1911), proved inadequate because their purposes were more narrowly defined than those of the local groups. The logical solution might have been for the local societies to look for additional guidance to the Federal Council of Churches and its related local councils of churches. However, the latter took a dim view of the local interdenominational organizations, regarding them as an unnecessary duplication of their own efforts; cooperation on equal terms seemed out of the question.

After some experiments with weak coordinating bodies, the United Council of Church Women came into being in 1941. During the first decade the principal activities of the organization included war relief and, at war's end, reconstruction and reconciliation, especially as these em-

The new seal of United Church Women, 1946. Left to right: Mrs. R. W. Hollinger, Mrs. Walter B. Foley, Mrs. Harper Sibley. Religious News Service photo.

phases affected women and children; efforts for peace, including strong support of the United Nations; and the cultivation of harmonious and just racial relations. In the mid-forties the women, through the good offices of a board member, Marie Johnson (whose husband, Charles, was president of Fisk University), received $25,000 from the Rosenwald Foundation to work in the area of race relations. During the same decade the national leadership put the state councils of women on notice that it would recognize only those that were racially integrated. The statistics showed a growth in activity; the budget climbed from $12,000 in 1942 to $185,946 in 1950; subscriptions for *Church Woman,* UCW's journal, rose from 2,235 in 1942 to 13,412 in 1949.[7]

The United Church Women

Because historians (other than UCW's own) have left the women of UCW in relative obscurity – both the leadership and the grass roots – it is difficult to say in detail who they were. Most leaders came from the middle or upper middle class and were college educated. They were primarily from establishment denominations, Episcopalian, Congregationalist-Christian, Presbyterian, Baptist, Disciples, and Methodist. There were two groups, volunteers and paid staff. The volunteers were the more visible, often the ones to gain the positions of leadership available to women in the National Council. They were usually married, the wives of clergymen, professionals, or businessmen who shared their dedication to the church. Supported by their families' or husbands' income, these women had the time and energy to contribute generously to missions, ecumenism, and social action. The salaried workers often needed to support themselves. Typically unmarried women or widows, many of them came to UCW from careers in the YWCA.[8]

In their politics many of these churchwomen embraced liberal Republicanism. Mossie Wyker, president during the fifties, was a friend of Bertha Adkins, a leader in the Republican Party at the time. Dorothy Dolbey, active at the national level of UCW beginning in the fifties, was a reform-minded Republican who voted for Eisenhower and, later, Nixon. Abigail McCarthy, wife of 1968 presidential candidate Eugene McCarthy and a vice president of UCW in the sixties, found these women "apolitical," despite the nature of their interests. Of those who became involved in the McCarthy campaign because of their commitment to peace, she said:

> I think that of any group of women in 1968 the Church Women who took part in the campaign probably went farthest in what they did and took greater personal leaps than women who had always been involved in secular movements or in politics. For the Church Women were primarily apolitical and, if they participated in politics, it would usually be the party in which they had been born. The effort to discern what was actually involved in our foreign policy, what relation it had to Christian principle, to take a stand, to move into active participation really involved a long, spiritual, personal journey for many.[9]

Although McCarthy was describing the political innocence of church-women in 1968, her remarks could be applied to the women of the previous decades as well. Dorothy Dolbey, prominent in Cincinnati politics in the fifties, was unusual among UCW women in her degree of political savvy and involvement.

The women leaders may have been innocents as far as the nitty-gritty of electoral politics was concerned, but obviously they were far from politically dispossessed. In the mid-forties they sent representatives to a White House conference, sponsored by Eleanor Roosevelt, on "How Women May Share in Post-War Policy Making." In 1945, 150 UCW leaders in Washington had tea with the Trumans. During their 1949 board meeting the women heard that a bill dealing with displaced persons was faltering in the Senate:

> As usual with concerned Christian women there was a quick desire to "do something" and a motion was made that women send wires at once to senators urging immediate action. Telegrams were quickly dispatched. . . . The next day we discovered that the bill was reported out of Committee and on to the floor of the senate. We gave thanks for the influence of Christian women.

They had enough pull with the Republicans to secure Eisenhower as a speaker at their Sixth Assembly in 1953. At this time, worried about the effect of McCarthyism on American society, the leadership urged Eisenhower in a personal meeting not to recognize McCarthy. "He agreed by saying that never would he invite him to the White House and he kept his word."[10]

In the South, United Church Women exercised considerable political influence. Dorothy Tilly, a UCW leader active in the Association of Southern Women for the Prevention of Lynching, was accustomed to making her views known in high places. When her businessman husband told her that black children in Atlanta were not benefiting from the federal lunch program, she and a group of women associates visited the school board and had the situation reversed. Tilly was aided in her activities by her friendship with the editor of the *Atlanta Constitution*. "He has often saved space for us in his paper when we were wanting to raise our voices for some cause." Tilly was one of two women appointed to Truman's Committee on Civil Rights.[11]

The kinds of political involvement outlined thus far are loaded with ironies, of course. There are insiders and then there are insiders. The women met with Eleanor Roosevelt, not Franklin. They dispatched telegrams rather than telephoning senators. They had tea with the Trumans, but they did not confer with the president on matters of state. They brought about (or at least thought they had) a sort of social ostracism for Joseph McCarthy rather than taking him on in newspaper columns or the halls of Capitol Hill. In short, they used the means they were familiar with as women.

Whatever pull these women had undoubtedly came partially from their social connections. Among their leaders were Mrs. Norman Vincent Peale, Mrs. Samuel McCrea Cavert, Miss Dorothy McConnell (daughter of Methodist Bishop Francis John McConnell), Mrs. Harold E. Fey (wife of the *Christian Century* editor), Mrs. Harper Sibley (whose husband, a prominent layman, headed the international YMCA), Mrs. Theodore O. Wedel (her husband was canon of Washington Cathedral and president of the Episcopal House of Deputies), Mrs. Francis B. Sayre (Mr. Sayre was a prominent diplomat and Episcopal layman), and Mrs. Allan Knight Chalmers (her husband was a Congregational minister at the Broadway Tabernacle, New York City, and later a professor at Boston University School of Theology). State leaders tended to have a parallel prominence on the local level. Mrs. William G. Bek of North Dakota, for instance, was the wife of a professor and dean at University of North Dakota; Mrs. William G. Dingus of Lubbock, Texas, was a Daughter of the American Revolution.

Despite these obvious elements of insidership, their second-class status as women was frequently at least a minor note in their rhetoric. Georgiana Sibley, one of the early presidents, was well known in the group for her frequent admonition, addressed to the churches, that "only equals can cooperate." An editorial in *Church Woman* in September 1939 (and thus at a time not commonly remembered as a heyday of feminist consciousness) declared:

> Women are ready to stand by the church, to minimize its obvious weaknesses and to emphasize its latent powers; to give to it, to work for it, to pray that it may be a tool of God. Church women form a group of more than 15,000,000 in the U.S.A., yet they are without a voice. The voice of the official church is still largely a man's voice, for what church is governed equally by its men and women members?[12]

Declarations like this notwithstanding, most of the women would have been distressed to be called feminists. In the early fifties, when UCW sponsored a report on the status of women, Mossie Wyker, the president, "thought it wise to include the president of the National Council in the plans so that this would not appear to be a feminist uprising." For fear of the feminist label, they steered away from talk of their "rights" in the church, preferring to speak about their "place," about "enlarged opportunities" for women's service, about a variety of gifts, or about restoring the "wholeness" of the church by means of the inclusion of women. They stressed their roles as wives, mothers, and homemakers. Abbie Clements Jackson, a leader in the African Methodist Episcopal Zion church, the UCW, and the FCC and NCC, traveled away from home so much of the time on church business that she frequently had to engage a housekeeper, yet she described her "primary vocation" as that of "housewife." A tribute to Georgiana Sibley described with admiration how during a meeting in her home she had simultaneously cared for her three grandchildren and conducted an executive session of United Church Women. Mrs. Norman Vincent Peale's autobiography was entitled *The Adventure of Being a Wife*. From other evidence we know she headed important church committees, served as vice-president of the NCC, and even spoke from the pulpit on occasion, but she glossed over these functions in favor of her wifely and maternal role.[13] The women regarded their church activities as extensions of their roles as mothers and homemakers, and as demanding the same kind of care, nurture, and management as families except on a larger scale; their public activities, they thought, grew naturally out of private ones.

If the outsider rhetoric of these women was muted, many were at pains to describe the ways in which women were distinct from men, and special. They regarded themselves as more practical, less given to talking about problems and readier to do something about them. Sibley criticized the church for being "too wordy – substituting words for action." They prided themselves on being able to think small, on being able to operate effectively on "shoe-string financing." And they regarded themselves as out ahead, even of the Federal and National Councils, on many social issues. Women addressed what they regarded as their special concerns: marriage, family life, the problems of employed women, education, and the issue of morality in the media. Occasionally they celebrated the hardship – the affronts and rejections – women had encountered in the past in serving the church – the "lion in the path that our mothers in the faith had to tread," in the words of one churchwoman. In the pages of their publication they highlighted the achievements of women, in both secular and sacred spheres. They dwelled upon positive images of women in the Bible: Mary the mother of Jesus, the Samaritan woman. At times Sibley sounded a millennial note: "Is it by accident that at the same moment 'One World' is struggling to be born, women have been given opportunities to serve and to lead such as have never been known in all history? Is it an accident or is it the hand of God?"[14]

On occasion churchwomen even went so far as to hint that they were superior to men in the religious sphere. UCW's second president, Georgiana Sibley, for instance, quoted a "great Christian layman": "Most women are capable of living nearer to God than most men. Women can be interpreters of God to their fellow men." She added somewhat demurely, "For many years I have pondered this statement. I would not want to argue it now, but what I know is that a deep responsibility has been laid upon women by God Himself." Her successor, Mossie Wyker, wrote in a similar vein,

> We have almost unlimited opportunity to influence the Christian contribution of our husbands in their performance of the world's work. There are leaders in the church today who are baffled at the immature religious thinking of many American men. The men read the newspapers and are versed in "politics"; they know business and industry; they can discuss labor and management. Yet, in their religious experience they are often as children, swayed by any wind that blows across their intellectual paths. . . . We have a double responsibility, not only to grow into mature persons ourselves, but to help our husbands and our children grow also to be spiritually mature.[15]

If this was not a rhetoric of outsidership, it was a rhetoric of distinctiveness, designed to create a sense of sisterhood – not a feminist sisterhood, to be sure, but nevertheless an identity based on gender.

The Merger with the National Council

United Church Women as it emerged during the forties had several characteristics that would affect its functioning in the National Council. First, because it was a creature of the local and regional united groups of women that had willed it into being, it relied upon grassroots support. Leaders had inherited from their missionary society roots a tendency to keep their eyes on the folks at the local level; they realized that their success at fund-raising depended upon their industry in educating, informing, and consulting with the women in local churches. In 1950 the UCW had local councils of churchwomen in 1,800 communities and state councils in forty-eight states, whereas the National Council had local councils of churches in only 875 communities and state councils in forty states.[16]

A second distinctive characteristic of the women's group was its tradition of social activism; they prided themselves on taking positions and making public pronouncements with little regard for what denominational officialdom might say, a luxury denied, they thought, to the cler-

gy in the Federal Council. They suggested that because they had no
ecclesiastical status to lose, they could afford to take unorthodox social,
political, and economic stances. As President Sibley put it, "Women
sometimes have the advantage over men, because they don't have so
much ecclesiastical or legal baggage, and they can go through smaller
cracks in various walls."[17]

A case in point was a pacifist article by Muriel Lester published by
Church Woman in one of its early issues. A UCW leader involved recalled
that

> some of the leading churchmen in the nation wrote telegrams
> begging us to take no such stand since to do so would sever the
> unity of the church and certainly ruin the circulation of the
> magazine. But the committee decided that that was a Christian
> principle and we dare not be false to it. Finally, we presented
> both sides of the question.

She went on to say that other publications ended up emulating their
advocacy of pacifism, "but it was *The Church Woman* which fearlessly led
out in an unpopular cause." Similarly Wyker pointed out that women
had dared to use the word "peace" in the early fifties when it meant
risking being called a communist. The women claimed to be unfazed by
McCarthy, perhaps in part because they were less likely to be the objects
of his attack. When a Methodist minister in Dearborn, Michigan, was
branded as a communist on a local radio station, "the indignant church
women consulted a lawyer, began a telephone campaign, marched on the
broadcasting station and won a well-deserved apology."[18]

The *Christian Century*, itself no friend to ecclesiasticism, seconded the
women's self-ascription. One of its writers described the impressions of
a veteran observer of church conferences who had gone to the UCCW
convention in 1946. He returned uncharacteristically "stirred and heart-
ened," because the women delegates, overwhelmingly lay, "were un-
hampered by ecclesiastical cautioners and unconfused by theological
double talk, and were thus free to devote themselves, directly, forth-
rightly and wholly, to the business of increasing their Christian effectiveness." Three years later, when the UCCW decided to join the NCC, the
Century applauded, saying that the move would be "good for the new
interchurch agency. The United Council [of Church Women] has a pronounced allergy to stuffed shirts and has largely succeeded in keeping its
own activities out of their clutches." Recognizing that the women would
be more vulnerable to "ecclesiastical interference" in the NCC, the
Century added, "it is accepting that risk in the interest of a larger minis-

try. Meanwhile it can be counted on to do its part in preventing the National Council from falling into the hands of male dowagers, who seem to have considerable success in getting themselves elected to represent denominations on interchurch bodies."[19]

A third peculiarity of the UCW, and one that would vex its relationship with the National Council, was its inclusive nature. Any woman who believed in the goals of the local organizations was welcome to join; she did not come as a representative of a denomination, nor did she even have to belong to one. The liberal social goals of many of the local councils of women attracted Unitarians and Universalists, and the heads of several of the local and state councils of women belonged to these denominations. The Federal Council, in contrast, did not permit Unitarians to join, nor would its successor, the National Council. In 1950 UCW included women from eighty-nine denominations, whereas the National Council had only twenty-nine member denominations.[20]

Inside the National Council

Throughout the forties ecumenical leaders had debated the desirability of merging all the national interdenominational agencies, including United Church Women, into a larger, more inclusive council. Finally, between April 1948 and December 1950 the "Planning Committee for the NCCC," consisting of representatives from eight interdenominational agencies, wrestled with the details; the UCW delegation was headed by Marjorie Terrell.

UCW women viewed the emerging National Council with mixed feelings. As ardent ecumenists they regarded the movement for greater unity as a positive project. And their already strong ecumenical inclinations were further bolstered by international developments. The opening assembly of the World Council of Churches in Amsterdam in 1948 seemed to signal that ecumenism's day had dawned; the establishment of the United Nations symbolized growing cooperation in the secular sphere. "This is an age of emphasis on unity and correlation of effort," declared Marjorie Terrell.[21] How could women possibly stand in the way by remaining outside a major ecumenical initiative when they had been invited in?

Cooperation also seemed to offer the opportunity for the UCW to work together more closely with leaders from denominational women's organizations. Because hitherto women had joined local councils of church women as individuals, not as representatives of denominations, the connections with denominational women leaders had remained loose.[22] Not least of all, joining the emerging National Council of Churches would quell the chronic complaint that women with their separate organizations constituted a "church within a church."

On the other hand, the women knew their history well enough to recognize that in the past merger had been destructive of their identities and influence as churchwomen. Even Marjorie Terrell, who worked so hard for ecumenical participation, cautioned, "It is possible that merging with such an all-inclusive organization might hamper our freedom and slow up our advance." The decision whether to cast their lot with the National Council posed a dilemma: It pitted their desire for identity and influence *as women* against their ideals of ecumenism and cooperation. The group's historian, Gladys Calkins, recalling this period, summarized the issues this way; the merger, she said, threatened

> a value that seemed fundamental – women's independent action as a group. Was it possible to safeguard this freedom, which historically had opened up so many opportunities, and still merge in a combined organizational structure? UCCW did not want to be caught in the position of waving the banner of "women for women" within the Church. Yet was it possible to face all the questions that would be necessary, without raising the basic issue of women's place in all policy-making church bodies?[23]

In the end the women tried to have it both ways, by proposing a set of conditions for their membership in the National Council, necessary "to preserve the work of this great laywomen's organization" and "insure the degree of autonomy essential to carrying out our UCCW purpose and projects." They insisted on retaining the right to call their national assemblies and to "organize, develop, and serve local and state councils of church women"; these councils would retain their autonomy. The women also required "representation on the various sections and committees of the National Council, including representation on the governing board and the Executive Committee."[24] What the UCW women desired, in short, was a guarantee of leadership positions in the National Council and, simultaneously, the retention of as much of their former corporate identity as possible. This, they felt, had been achieved in the planning process. The top leaders at the time – including Georgiana Sibley and Mossie Wyker – supported the merger.

In addition to insisting on certain conditions, the women determined to enter the National Council with substantial financial backing. In 1949 they started an "Ecumenical Register." Each woman signer contributed a dollar; by the time the Register was closed in 1951, three hundred thousand dollars had been raised. Approaching life in the National Council with this sum – like a woman entering matrimony with her own sizable bank account – gave the women more confidence that they would be listened to.[25]

The UCW's national leadership distributed abundant information on the proposed merger and arranged and presided over a series of twenty seminars in the states west of the Mississippi. Although reports in *Church Woman* suggested that some UCW members argued vigorously against merger, only a small dissenting minority remained opposed by the time the vote was taken in 1949. In the end only three delegates to the national assembly voted against merger. Many women reported at the time that a decisive element in their thinking was a comment from Marjorie Terrell, head of UCW's merger committee, that "it is only fair to remind ourselves that in the event of a negative decision a Woman's Department will be set up within the National Council in which case the UCCW will find itself outside the main stream of the cooperative ecumenical movement."[26]

Even those who supported the merger anticipated problems. As President Georgiana Sibley warned in 1950, "We must needs accept many disciplines and some frustrations."[27] She and her associates were not disappointed. Some transitions, to be sure, went smoothly, or turned out to entail no readjustment at all. The new name for UCW, the "General Department of United Church Women," emphasized the continuities with the pre-1950 arrangements. Local councils of women were not much affected at all, retaining considerable independence. Initial difficulties seem to have arisen in two areas. One was that of membership on the Board of Managers, the governing body of the General Department of UCW. Almost immediately, the women wanted to add four Unitarians to this board. They were aware that, according to the NCC constitution, prospective members for the UCW Board of Managers who – like the Unitarians – did not belong to the denominations constituting the NCC would have to receive special approval from the National Council's General Board. But the women believed that before agreeing to come aboard they had received assurances that this approval would be merely pro forma.

Immediately after the Constituting Convention that formally established the NCC, however, UCW President Mossie Wyker walked into a meeting of the General Board in time to hear the speaker outline some unexpectedly strict rulings regarding the appointment of members to boards of National Council departments. The promulgation meant that the four Unitarians proposed for membership on the UCW board would not be approved. "What are they doing to us?" Mrs. Wyker is reported

to have "muttered" to a colleague. She protested, but the tougher regulation prevailed; the top leadership "remained adamant." "All must
conform," the women were told.[28]

Probably because she had little choice, Wyker acquiesced in the un-
favorable dictum. As the UCW's historian explains (using a domestic
analogy), Wyker and her associates

> had enough good sense to know that a blueprint gives way once
> the available material, money, and future occupants of a house-
> hold are taken into account! They knew that some of the valu-
> able nods which had given them assurance had no legal standing
> once the "committee" [i.e., the planning committee for the
> NCC] was dismissed.[29]

The UCW leaders were perhaps a bit more successful in getting their
way on another point in contention. Accustomed as they were to being
out in front on social and political issues, they continued in the National
Council context to make up their minds quickly on a given issue and
state their minds publicly. This practice did not sit well with National
Council leaders. Even when they concurred with the women, they still
insisted on the right to veto their public utterances. Once when UCW
took a public stand without consultation, an officer of the National
Council delivered a reprimand. As the UCW historian tells it, the officer

> was always sympathetic to the women, but dutifully reminded
> Mrs. Wyker that . . . public statements were to be cleared
> through the Council officers. Mrs. Wyker apologized profusely:
> "The women wouldn't embarrass the Council for anything. We
> promise not to do it again – well, not until our conscience tells
> us to!" She explained carefully that the women felt the Holy
> Spirit moving through their meeting and were unanimous in
> their decision. "The men never know what to do or say when
> we talk about the Holy Spirit!" she told me once with a chuckle.

Privately, however, Wyker exhibited less optimism. In 1951 she wrote
the National Council's head, Samuel McCrea Cavert, asking if "the
prophetic voices of the old Federal Council had been silenced." She was
probably reacting, as were other social liberals, to the existence in the
early fifties of the National Council's Lay Committee, headed by
wealthy political conservative J. Howard Pew. For several years this
committee exerted a chilling influence on the NCC's social activism.[30]

Dorothy Dolbey, a member of the Board of Managers during this
time, paints a gloomy picture of the women's early participation in the
NCC: "It was difficult to adjust to being 'just a woman's group' in the

eyes of some of the church leaders. . . . In the early days we had to fight every inch of the way for our voice to be heeded and our person to be involved in policy making." An inventory of the gender of delegates and of top leaders in the NCC supports a vision of the group as a male bastion. Of the six vice-presidents at large in 1957, to be sure, two were female (one was Cynthia Wedel, president of UCW), but all the heads of divisions were males. Among the denominational delegates to the General Board, tokenism seems to have prevailed, with one or two women among each denominational group of eight or more. Representation for women had improved somewhat since Federal Council days, but equality still eluded them.[31]

Whatever the disappointments and stresses of life in the NCC, none of the leaders of the fifties publicly expressed the view that it had been a mistake to join the Council. However, President Wyker betrayed some nostalgia for the past: "We now look back rather longingly to the independence, joy, and achievement of our work as the UCCW."[32] Yet they considered the problems to be unavoidable, endemic to the kind of organization they had entered. It would be hasty to view the situation as simply another case of women falling victim to a powerful, essentially male organization. The sense of struggle and the need to protect one's turf seems to have been widespread, even in cases where gender was not apparently involved. The leaders of each of the constituting agencies – mostly male except for the UCW – seem to have felt their agency had something to lose by joining the NCC, and fought to preserve as much automony as possible.

Nor were women totally helpless in the face of male ecclesiasticism and high-handedness. Later generations may feel that Wyker, their leader during much of this time, had to adopt some typically "feminine" wiles in response to criticism. They may also be less than comfortable with the knowledge that UCW leaders tried to recruit as many *wives* of important NCC leaders as possible, not only for their own sakes, but also for whatever influence they might have with their spouses. The women had other resources at their command, however. Wyker herself possessed more than feminine charm and, in fact, presented a disconcerting phenomenon for male clerics with stereotyped views of women. An ordained Disciples of Christ minister, she had not come up through "just another women's group," as conservative males might have put it. As a member of the Board of Managers of the International Convention of Disciples of Christ and as acting president of the Convention in 1952, she was accustomed to presiding over mixed church councils of men and women. In addition, women considered they had several powerful friends among the males: Henry Knox Sherrill (he was the bishop of

Georgiana Sibley, the early president of UCW; this fact the outspoken Sibley would not have let him forget), Samuel McCrea Cavert, and Edwin Espy were considered the women's allies in the struggle against "strict liturgists" like Franklin Clark Fry.[33]

In their struggles to assert themselves in the National Council church-women found reinforcement in the wider society and church. The fifties were not quite as dead a period for feminism as usually portrayed. Simone de Beauvoir's *The Second Sex* had become available in English translation in 1953; and the economic reality was that in 1955, long after veterans had returned from World War II, 31 percent of American women were working. Indeed, a quiet restlessness was abroad among women in the American churches, stimulated in part by the findings of the World Council of Church's Commission on the Life and Work of Women in the Churches. During the late forties and early fifties, a series of studies and articles about women's participation (or rather, lack of it) in the American churches appeared. In 1948 Inez Cavert published *Women in American Church Life;* in 1953 the UCW itself sponsored an examination of women's status that demonstrated how poorly women were represented in the higher councils of the church. That same year Mossie Wyker's gently critical *Church Women in the Scheme of Things* came out.[34] In addition to these inquiries into women's church status, tangible advances were made, as the Methodist Episcopal Church and the Presbyterian Church USA granted them full ordination privileges.

Just as women were adjusting to their ambiguous relation to the National Council, that situation changed significantly when, in the mid-sixties, the unwieldy National Council was reorganized. UCW lost its status as a "General Department," and, along with United Church Men, Faith and Order, Councils of Churches, and Youth Ministries, was included in a new "Division of Christian Unity," headed by Cynthia Wedel, a UCW leader. Dorothy MacLeod, executive director at the time, put the best face on developments, writing in *Church Woman:*

> Yes, it would *seem* we might be losing our identity, our status, our so-called autonomy. Rather we are losing ourselves to find ourselves; we are "accepting the discipline" to become a more integrated part of the whole. We soon will be helping to chart the course for one of the four divisions of the NCC. . . . Ask not what the churches can do for women, but what women, by assuming full participion, can do for Christian unity.

The dramatic rise of Wedel to the leadership of an NCC department made the incorporation of UCW within the Department of Christian

Unity more palatable. If they had lost face on one front, they seemed to have gained it on another.[35]

The course of the new department was ill-starred, however. To begin with, the department lacked a clear identity; groups were put together that did not happen to fit anywhere else. Because the denominations were better geared to support familiar departments of missions and religious education than they were an ill-defined unit called "Christian Unity," the department soon fell on financial hard times and had to be operated from National Council general funds. In 1969 when Wedel resigned from the department, its operations were suspended. UCW, feeling itself financially undercut in the NCC (UCW leaders discovered they were paying considerably more for NCC central services than they would have had to pay for the same services on their own), nursing a "backlog of other grievances," and probably also affected by the resurgence of feminism in the late sixties, decided to pull out of the NCC and resume its autonomous existence. The accession of Wedel, a former president of UCW, to the presidency of the National Council in 1969 seemed a propitious moment for parting. She was sympathetic to UCW's position, and hence the leave-taking could be accomplished "without a real fight."[36]

How should we read the story of women's travails in the National Council? What does it tell us about the character of women's experience as insiders and outsiders and about the nature of the establishment itself? Like Mildred Horton these were women who, relative to most other churchwomen, enjoyed tremendous success and influence. They were both insiders and outsiders and accordingly experienced the advantages and disadvantages of both identities. On the one hand they were much like the Protestant men they married or who fathered them – practical, concerned about moral and ethical questions, optimistic, committed to the principle of voluntarism – and therefore they failed to develop a radically divergent vision of the American church or society. On the other hand, they stood just enough on the peripheries of institutional church life to have a slightly different notion of their mission and the way to accomplish it. Perhaps because of their experiences of marginality they were better able to live up to some of American Protestantism's professed ideals – toleration for divergent religious and political views, empathy for the oppressed and victimized, belief in the value of the laity, responsiveness to the church people at the grass roots. Sometimes, because they had less to lose they seemed braver, more outspoken, more activist than their brethren. The women may, in fact, have helped sway the establishment in a more liberal direction. Other consequences of marginality may have been more problematic. Because they were shut

out from the seminaries of the church and from clerical and scholarly
circles, they sometimes lacked theological sophistication and found it
difficult to engage in a common discourse with male NCC members and
with Europeans of both sexes in the World Council of Churches. Because they remained for the most part outside the centers of power they
sometimes exhibited naïveté about the realities of its uses and underesti-
mated the difficulties involved in bringing about real social change. On
balance, then, and for better or worse, these women confirmed and
affirmed characteristics already present in the male Protestant establishment. They basically agreed with their male counterparts about the social
and religious agenda of the Protestant churches. When a conflict arose
between male and female church groups, it was over the distribution of
power and authority, not over vastly different worldviews.

NOTES

1 Most of the information on Horton, including the quotations, is from Margaret Frakes, "Counselor to Councils," *Christian Century* 69(June 25, 1952):
745–8. See also Ray Tyler Nourse, "College President," in Anne Stoddard
(ed.), *Topflight: Famous American Women* (New York: Thomas Nelson, 1946),
67–85. For Wyker's remark see *National Council Outlook* 1(April 1951): 18.
2 Rosemary Radford Ruether and Rosemary Skinner Keller, *Women and Religion in America* (San Francisco: Harper & Row, 1986), vol. 3, 290.
3 For Presbyterian women see Lois A. Boyd and R. Douglas Brackenridge,
Presbyterian Women in America: Two Centuries of a Quest for Status (Westport,
Conn.: Greenwood Press, 1983), 61ff. See also Elizabeth Howell Verdesi, *In
But Still Out: Women in the Church* (Philadelphia: Westminster Press, 1976).
For Methodists see Section IV, "The Status of Women in Institutional
Church Life," in Rosemary Skinner Keller and Hilah F. Thomas, *Women in
New Worlds: Historical Perspectives on the Wesleyan Tradition* (Nashville, Tenn.:
Abingdon Press, 1981), vol. 1, 217–89. For training schools see Virginia
Lieson Brereton, "Preparing Women for the Lord's Work," in Keller and
Thomas, *Women in New Worlds,* I, 178–99. For the outrage see, e.g., Boyd
and Brackenridge, *Presbyterian Women,* 63.
4 Carroll Smith-Rosenberg, *Disorderly Conduct: Visions of Gender in Victorian
America* (New York: Oxford University Press, 1985), 16.
5 Its original name was United Council of Church Women, but generally I will
refer to it by its post-1950 name, United Church Women, or UCW. After
1966 the organization became known as Church Women United.
6 There are two book-length histories of the organization: Gladys Gilkey Calkins, *Follow Those Women: Church Women in the Ecumenical Movement* (New
York: National Council of Churches, 1961), and Margaret Shannon, *Just
Because: The Story of the National Movement of Church Women United
in the U.S.A., 1941 through 1975* (Corte Madera, Calif.: Omega Books,
1977).
7 For racial matters see Shannon, *Just Because,* 32. For the statistics see Shannon,

Just Because, 24, 50; "The 1949 Board Meeting," *Church Woman* 15(November 1949): 22, 26.

8   One might have expected at least some divergence of vision between these two groups, but the available records are silent on the subject. Dorothy Dolbey, a UCW leader during the fifties and sixties, could recall no sense of conflict. Dorothy Dolbey, in interview with the author, August 1986.

9   Abigail McCarthy, *Private Faces, Public Places* (Garden City, N.Y.: Doubleday, 1972), 301.

10   "The 1949 Board Meeting," 23; remark on McCarthy is in notes sent by Dorothy Dolbey to the author, August 1986.

11   Sarah Cunningham, sketch of Dorothy Tilly, *Church Woman* 32(August–September 1966): 11.

12   For Sibley quote see Mossie Allman Wyker, *Church Women in the Scheme of Things* (St. Louis, Mo.: Bethany Press, 1953), 36; *Church Woman* editorial is quoted in Calkins, *Follow Those Women,* 55.

13   Mildred McAfee Horton, "Where Do We Stand?" *Church Woman* 19 (November 1953): 13; Margaret Frakes, "For Better Human Relations" (sketch of Abbie Clements Jackson), *Christian Century* 69(December 10, 1952): 1433; Mrs. Norman Vincent Peale, *The Adventure of Being a Wife* (Englewood Cliffs, N.J.: Prentice-Hall, 1971).

14   Sarah Parrott, "Action . . . Not Just Words" (sketch of Georgiana Sibley), *Church Woman* 32(December 1966): 18; Calkins, *Follow Those Women,* 39; for "lion" quotation see Wyker, *Scheme of Things,* 26; Mrs. Harper Sibley, "A Program of Work, Harbors of Peace, Wells of Refreshment," *Church Woman* 15(May 1949): 6.

15   Mrs. Harper Sibley, "His Way – Together," *Church Woman* 14(May 1948): 3; Wyker, *Scheme of Things,* 116–17.

16   For women's attention to the local level see Boyd and Brackenridge, *Presbyterian Women,* 64; Shannon, *Just Because,* 57.

17   Parrott, "Action . . . Not Just Words," 18.

18   For pacifist article see Shannon, *Just Because,* 15. Shannon does not give the date of Lester's article; Wyker, *Scheme of Things,* 75, 77.

19   Stanley High, "Enlist the Laymen, Mr. Taft," *Christian Century* 64(February 12, 1947): 203; "Women Join National Council of Churches" (editorial), *Christian Century* 66(October 26, 1949): 1253, 1254.

20   Shannon, *Just Because,* 57.

21   Mrs. William Sale Terrell, "Regarding the Proposed National Council of Churches," *Church Woman* 15(March 1949): 21.

22   After UCW joined the NCC its policy-making Board of Managers included, among others, women representing their denominations in the NCC.

23   Terrell, "Regarding the Proposed NCC," 21; Calkins, *Follow Those Women,* 72–3.

24   Terrell, "Regarding the Proposed NCC," 18; Terrell, "A Progress Report on the Proposed National Council of Churches," *Church Woman* 15(August–September 1949): 20.

25   Dolbey notes, August 1986.

26   Terrell, "A Progress Report on the Proposed NCC," 21. Clearly the leaders of the other merging organizations wanted UCW to join the NCC, because of the women's demonstrated ability to inspire, raise funds, and organize effectively on the local level. See, e.g., William J. Schmidt, *Architect of Unity: A Biography of Samuel McCrea Cavert* (New York: Friendship Press, 1978), 247–8.

27   Mrs. Harper Sibley, "A Glorious Tomorrow," *Church Woman* 16(November 1950): 7.

28   Shannon, *Just Because,* 56–7.

29   Ibid., 57.

30   Shannon, *Just Because,* 59; Schmidt, *Architect for Unity,* 167–8. Wyker is quoted indirectly here.

31   Dolbey notes and interview, August 1986; for the names of delegates, officers, etc., see the National Council yearbooks.

32   *Church Woman* 17–18(1951–2): 7.

33   The assertions about wives of influential leaders and NCC allies come from the author's interview with Dolbey, August 1986.

34   For the numbers of working women see Lois Banner, *Women in Modern America: A Brief History* (New York: Harcourt Brace Jovanovich, 1974), 225–6; The World Council of Churches report was published as Kathleen Bliss, *The Service and Status of Women in the Churches* (London: SCM Press, 1952). Among the critical or semicritical views from this period of women's place in the church, see also Elizabeth Hartsfield, *Women in the Church: A Symposium on the Service and Status of Women among the Disciples of Christ* (Lexington, Ky.: College of the Bible, 1953); Raymond T. Stamm, "The Status of Christian Workers in the Church," *Lutheran Quarterly* 10(May 1958): 139–40; Ursula M. Niebuhr, "Women and the Church, and the Fact of Sex," *Christianity and Crisis* 11(August 9, 1951): 106–10; Betty M. Rice, "Report of Meeting on 'Women and Church,'" *Christianity and Crisis* 11(August 9, 1951): 110–12; Mary Ely Lyman, "Women in the Church," *Church Woman* 17(December 1951): 16–22; Dorothy McConnell, "Women Are Almost People," *Church Woman* 18(December 1952): 15–18; Mildred McAfee Horton, "Second-Class Citizens or Partners in Policy?" *Presbyterian Life,* June 15, 1958, 26–7, 42.

35   Dorothy MacLeod, "Where Is UCW?" *Church Woman* 30(August–September 1964): 38–9; see Shannon's assessment, *Just Because,* 148.

36   The source of information on the leave-taking is Dolbey notes, August 1986. Dolbey suggested to the author in conversation that the UCW had been looking for an opportunity to depart from the NCC for some time (Dolbey interview, August 1986).

SELECT BIBLIOGRAPHY

Boyd, Lois A., and Douglas Brackenridge. *Presbyterian Women in America: Two Centuries of a Quest for Status.* Westport, Conn.: Greenwood Press, 1983.

Calkins, Gladys. *Follow Those Women: Church Women in the Ecumenical Movement.* New York: National Council of Churches, 1961.

Frakes, Margaret. Series of articles on leading churchwomen. *Christian Century* 69(1952): 584–7, 745–8, 872–5, 1088–9, 1433–6; 70(1953): 128–31.

Harkness, Georgia. *Women in Church and Society*. Nashville, Tenn.: Abingdon Press, 1972.

James, Janet W. *Women in American Religion*. Philadelphia: University of Pennsylvania Press, 1980.

Keller, Rosemary Skinner, and Hilah Thomas. *Women in New Worlds: Historical Perspectives on the Wesleyan Tradition*. 2 vols. Nashville, Tenn.: Abingdon Press, 1981, 1982.

Ruether, Rosemary, and Rosemary Skinner Keller. *Women and Religion in America*. 3 vols. San Francisco: Harper & Row, 1981, 1983, 1986.

Ruether, Rosemary, and Eleanor McLaughlin. *Women of Spirit*. New York: Simon & Schuster, 1979.

Shannon, Margaret. *Just Because: The Story of the National Movement of Church Women United in the U.S.A., 1941 through 1975*. Corte Madera, Calif.: Omega Books, 1977.

8

An Enduring Distance: Black Americans and the Establishment

DAVID W. WILLS

The story of the relationship between black Americans and the Protestant establishment during the first two-thirds of the twentieth century is above all a story about distance. Distance here is to be understood, of course, as social and cultural as well as geographic, but the simple fact of physical separation is so fundamental that one must begin by taking its measure.

Initial Considerations

In 1900, 90% of all black Americans lived in the South – the South here being defined, as it was by the United States Bureau of Census, to include the border states of Delaware, Maryland, West Virginia, and Kentucky as well as the states of the Deep South. In this same year, the black population of the United States was about 75% rural. If we think of the northeastern and north central United States as the establishment's heartland and those regions' towns and cities as the geographic centers from which its efforts at cultural hegemony emanated, then it is clear how vast the distance was between black America and the Protestant establishment in 1900. It is important, moreover, not to overestimate how much that distance was reduced during the period under consideration. Beginning during the First World War, it is true, the great migration of blacks out of the rural South brought them to the establishment's doorstep in unprecedented numbers. By 1960 the black population had become 73% urban, reversing the urban–rural ratio of six decades before. Still, the urbanization of black America to a large degree coincided with the suburbanization of white America, and there is every reason to believe that the establishment's own membership was among

168

the most thoroughly suburbanized. In 1960, moreover, the Census Bureau reported that 60% of all black Americans still lived in the South. The most obvious feature, then, of the relationship throughout these years of black America and the Protestant establishment was the distance between them.[1]

This impression is reinforced, but also complicated, when one turns to a second set of numbers, those reflecting religious group membership among American blacks. Throughout this period only a very small percentage of the religiously affiliated black population ever belonged to the core denominations of the Protestant establishment. The census of 1890 reported that of a total black Christian church membership of 2,673,977, membership in the predominantly white "mainline" churches was only 333,645 – about 12½%. Among these denominations, as the following numbers attest, only the Methodist Episcopal Church could count a large black membership:

Methodist Episcopal	246,249
Regular Baptists (northern)	35,221
Disciples of Christ	18,578
Presbyterian (northern)	14,961
Congregationalists	6,908
Methodist Protestant	3,183
Protestant Episcopal	2,977
Presbyterian (southern)	1,568

This situation was not significantly different in 1960. The Methodist Church, with about 375,000 black members, remained the only establishment denomination with a sizable black membership. And although overall figures for 1960 comparable to those of the 1890 census are hard to come by, a reasonable estimate is that by midcentury certainly no more, and probably significantly less, than 10% of black Protestants in the United States belonged to predominantly white denominations. In considering the Protestant establishment's relation to black America, it is clear that what we are examining is a relationship to a population that remained throughout these years removed from it ecclesiastically as well as socially and geographically.[2]

There were, however, important degrees of difference in how far removed from the establishment various forms of organized black religious life were. Although the great independent black Methodist and Baptist denominations were not "insider" churches, they were linked to the establishment both by their historic roots in evangelical Protestantism and by their participation in a range of ecumenical bodies, including the Federal Council and the National Council of Churches. They were, moreover, the numerically preponderant form of organized black religious life in both 1900 and 1960. In 1890, their membership figures were as follows:

Regular Baptists	1,348,989
African Methodist Episcopal	452,725
African Methodist Episcopal Zion	359,788
Colored Methodist Episcopal Church	129,383

The membership figures in the 1962 edition of the *Yearbook of American Churches* show how great the continuity was in the relative size and strength of these bodies:

National Baptist Convention, USA, Inc.	5,000,000
National Baptist Convention of America	2,668,799
African Methodist Episcopal Church	1,166,301
African Methodist Episcopal Zion Church	770,000
Christian Methodist Episcopal Church	392,167

Taken as a group, these churches of what is sometimes known as "the black Protestant establishment" accounted for five-sixths of all black church members in 1890 and probably more than three-fourths in 1960. The establishment's links to these churches, though often fragile and uncertain, constituted its major point of access to the mainstream of black life throughout this period.[3]

Still further removed from the Protestant establishment were black Catholics and the black adherents to Judaism. Black Jews (i.e., Afro-American adherents to Orthodox, Conservative, or Reform Judaism, not blacks who followed some of the Judaistic new religious movements of the time) apparently never accounted for more than a handful of persons during this period. In 1890, there were a mere 14,517 black Catholics; seventy years later, however, that figure approached 700,000, about 3½% of the black population of the United States and a concentration of black Christians rivaling in size any of the black Methodist denominations.[4] This emergence of a significant body of black Catholics might in some ways seem to mark a growing alienation of black Americans from the Protestant establishment. Yet in the same years that blacks were moving in greater numbers into the Catholic church, the Protestant establishment was also moving, with whatever reluctance and misgivings, toward closer collaboration with Catholics and Jews. As a kind of senior partner in a "triple establishment" with Catholicism and Judaism, establishment Protestantism was arguably more in touch with black adherents to those faiths than with blacks belonging to Protestant churches or movements standing more or less entirely outside the boundaries of establishment respectability – above all the members of the black Holiness and Pentecostal churches.

The latter churches also experienced very rapid growth during the first two-thirds of the twentieth century. Most notable among them is the Church of God in Christ. At the time of the 1890 census, its founder, Charles Harrison Mason, was a Baptist preacher and the denomination did not even exist. By 1960, the church claimed 392,635 members and was growing far more rapidly than any other major black religious group. These churches, it seems accurate to say, represented a growing force in Afro-American religious life that was almost completely alienated from the Protestant religious establishment – and sometimes the black religious establishment as well.[5]

The growth of these groups was paralleled, moreover, by the development during these same years of powerful black religious movements outside the sphere of traditional Christianity – or Judaism. A range of groups could be cited here, the most notable being Father Divine's Peace Mission Movement and the National of Islam. The number of persons directly involved in either movement is difficult to establish. Scholarly estimates of Father Divine's constituency have ranged from a few thousand to two million, with the best guess being around 50,000.[6] It is also difficult to assess the actual impact of such groups, since their prominence in the urban ghettos of the North attracted more journalistic and scholarly attention than that usually accorded to the "mainline" black churches, particularly in the South. Still, it is evident that these movements represented a direct challenge to the religious standing of the Protestant establishment in the black world. This challenge, only dimly sensed in 1960, exploded on the establishment like a cultural bombshell in the following decade.

It is possible, then, to think of religiously affiliated blacks as relating to the Protestant establishment in a pattern of five concentric rings. Naming them from the inside out – "inside" being here defined as closeness to the Protestant establishment – they are: (1) blacks belonging to the predominantly white core denominations of the establishment itself; (2) blacks belonging to the major independent black Baptist and Methodist churches; (3) blacks belonging to the junior partner bodies of the "triple establishment," that is, black Catholics and Jews; (4) blacks belonging to "third force" Protestant churches; and (5) blacks belonging to nontraditional, extra-Christian new religious movements. This essay will focus entirely on the inner rather than the outer rings and will sketch the story of the establishment's own "black insiders" and the relationship between the white and black establishments.

The central theme of this story is how black insiders and black establishmentarians experienced, understood, and came to terms with the gap that separated most of the Protestant establishment from most of black America during these decades. To some extent, this is a story of success, of battles fought and won. When the twentieth century opened, the Protestant establishment, largely remote from and generally indifferent to southern segregation, appeared almost entirely inert in its relation to black America. But in the following decades (not least, as we shall see, because of the efforts of the establishment's black insiders), the Protestant establishment increasingly lent its influence to the cause of racial desegregation. The great landmark in this conversion process came in March 1946, when the Federal Council of Churches, in a special meeting held at Columbus, Ohio, renounced "the pattern of segregation in race relations as unnecessary and undesirable and a violation of the Gospel of love and human brotherhood." The Council committed itself and sought to commit member churches to "work for a non-segregated church and a non-segregated society."[7] This pronouncement encouraged changes within the establishment denominations themselves and paved the way for the establishment's significant support for the civil rights movement of the 1950s and 1960s. Yet the story to be told here is also one of failure, of dreams deferred and illusions shattered, of a gap not finally bridged. Even at its best moments, the Protestant establishment tended to disappoint its own black leaders and those of the major black denominations as well. Most strikingly, what appeared in the early 1960s to be a historic triumph "of black and white" together became by the end of the decade a new discovery of the depth of racial alienation in America, an alienation to be found even within the inner circles of the establishment itself.

The Outsider as Insider

Before the emergence on the national scene in the late 1950s of Martin Luther King, Jr., no black American exerted more influence within the inner circles of the Protestant establishment than George Edmund Haynes (1880–1960) or Benjamin E. Mays (1894–1984).[8] Haynes, from 1922 to 1947 the executive director of the Federal Council's Commission on Race Relations, was the first black to hold an executive position in the FCCC. Mays, elected to the Council's vice presidency in 1944, was the first black to hold such a high elective office. Both were present at the special meeting of the Federal Council in Columbus in 1946, and each could reasonably have taken some credit for the Council's historic endorsement of desegregation. Yet both men were, like King, southerners, and each was born and reared in places and circumstances

Portrayal of "a Southern university" used by George E. Haynes as frontispiece for *The Trend of the Races,* 1922. Courtesy of the National Council of Churches.

far removed from the main centers of the Protestant establishment. Haynes was from the river town of Pine Bluff, Arkansas. His father was a laborer and his mother a domestic servant. Benjamin Mays's parents were ex-slaves who farmed rented land in rural Greenwood County, South Carolina. The network of establishment institutions and relationships that each man moved through to reach his eventual place of importance was dense and complicated, but nothing was more important as a route into the establishment for both of these men than the world of higher education.

David Reimers, whose *White Protestantism and the Negro* represents the most recent (1965) general survey of the establishment denominations' twentieth-century engagement with black America, contends that between its late nineteenth century acceptance of southern segregation and its mid-twentieth century conversion to integrationism, "the basic approach of Protestantism to a solution to the race problem . . . consisted in evangelism and Negro education."[9] One consequence was that although establishment denominations generally had very small black constituencies of their own, they were disproportionately influential in black higher education. The northern Baptists, for example, continued to play an important role in southern black education long after 1895, when the bulk of their black coreligionists organized themselves into the National

Baptist Convention. It was at Virginia Union University, one of the schools the northern Baptists helped support, that Benjamin Mays as a freshman in 1916–17 met two faculty members who helped him transfer the following year to their own historically Baptist alma mater, Bates College in Maine. After his graduation from Bates in 1920, Mays went on to earn an M.A. (1925) and a Ph.D. (1935) from another institution of Baptist origins, the University of Chicago. From 1940 to 1967, he served as president of Morehouse College in Atlanta, a black school that had become completely independent of the American Baptist Home Mission Society only in 1935. During Mays's presidency Martin Luther King, Jr., completed his undergraduate work at Morehouse and headed north to Baptist Crozier Seminary for his theological education – to be followed by doctoral study at Methodist Boston University.

Nowhere was this pattern of establishment influence on southern black life more evident than in the educational network of Congrega-tionalism – as is clear from the career of George Edmund Haynes, the valedictorian of the class of 1903 at Fisk University. Fisk crucially opened for Haynes the door to a wider world. After studying at the Fisk Pre-paratory School and then at the university itself, Haynes went on to Yale University, where he earned an M.A. degree in 1904, studying sociology under William Graham Sumner. After a year at Yale Divinity School and two years during which he worked as a field secretary of the Colored Men's Division of the YMCA and attended summer school at the Uni-versity of Chicago, Haynes returned to full-time study as a graduate student in sociology at Columbia University, and in 1912 became the first black to receive a Ph.D. from that school.

Initially, moreover, Haynes hoped to use the very educational net-work that had facilitated his own development as an institutional base for attacking the grave social and economic problems faced by black mi-grants to the nation's major cities. Before he had even completed his dissertation, Haynes had already returned to Fisk with ambitious plans to develop both a department of sociology and the first program in the country for training black social workers. Part of these plans involved his coordinating the work at Fisk with the simultaneous efforts of a group of New York philanthropists and educators who in 1911 founded the Na-tional League on Urban Conditions among Negroes, with Haynes as its first executive secretary.[10] From his post at Fisk, however, Haynes found it impossible to control the development of the Urban League program in New York or sustain the League's support for his plans at Fisk, and in 1918 he abandoned these efforts to accept instead the newly created position of Director of the Bureau of Negro Economics in the United States Department of Labor. The federal government's interest in "the harmonious adjustment of labor relations between whites and negroes" ended, however, with the war that had occasioned it,[11] and Haynes soon found himself back at work for the Protestant establishment.

Like the federal government, ecumenical Protestantism's interest in black Americans was notably increased by its efforts to mobilize the country for war.[12] Although the major black Baptist and Methodist denominations had participated in the Federal Council from the time of its founding in 1908, the FCCC had been slow to develop any specialized work with or on behalf of blacks. Only after the General Conference of the Colored Methodist Episcopal Church petitioned in 1914 for such a program did the Council create the Committee on Negro Churches. Grudgingly authorized at the 1916 quadrennial meeting, in the context of an acrimonious debate over lynching, the Committee began to come into its own only during World War I. Temporarily transformed into the General War-Time Commission's Committee on the Welfare of Negro Troops, it worked to ensure an adequate supply of black chaplains and pressed the War Department to more adequately provide for the general welfare of America's black soldiers. With the war's end, the continuing effects of black migration northward and an alarming series of urban race riots persuaded the Council further to upgrade race relations work, and it was in this context that the Council turned to George Haynes. When the Council began in 1921 to organize the new Commission on Race Relations, Haynes was invited to participate and soon was appointed the Commission's first executive director. According to one account, he was "the only candidate seriously considered for the job."[13]

One of the things that apparently helped clinch his candidacy was his book, *The Trend of the Races*.[14] Published in 1922, this book offered both a wide-ranging assessment of trends on both sides of the color line and a carefully considered prescription for dealing with the problems resulting from those trends. Most important, the book's approach was thoroughly consonant with the kind of program establishment leaders at this point wished to promote. One of the influences that shaped establishment racial attitudes during these years was a tradition of southern inter-racialism rooted in southern progressivism, nurtured by southern Methodist and Presbyterian women, and flowering in the postwar period in the Commission on Interracial Cooperation.[15] Organized early in 1919 under the leadership of southern Methodist preacher Will Alexander and southern Presbyterian layman John Eagan, the southern Commission, like its northern counterpart, has emerged from wartime ecumenical cooperation. The Commission's goals were to improve race relations and better the position of southern blacks without directly challenging segregation. Its leaders, moreover, were actively involved in helping the

George E. Haynes. Courtesy of the Office of History, Presbyterian Church (U.S.A.).

Federal Council launch its own Commission on Race Relations. It was therefore essential that Haynes's views be compatible with those of the southern leaders. *The Trend of the Races* indicated that they were.

Haynes warned his white readers from the outset that black Americans' historic personal and political loyalty and their tolerance and "sustained optimism . . . under . . . oppression" were beginning to fade. Blacks were increasingly likely to feel both racial pride and "resentment" against whites and to believe in the necessity for militant tactics on the part of their leaders. Among these leaders, Haynes discerned three broad tendencies. The "left wing" contained two very different sorts of radicals, the socialists gathered around A. Philip Randolph and the black nationalists associated with Marcus Garvey. The center was "composed of . . . the spiritual descendants of the aggressive abolitionists of a previous generation," a group of fighters "for citizenship rights and full democratic privileges of American life" centering on the NAACP. The "right wing" consisted of those who shared the center's goal of "full justice, manhood rights, and opportunities for Negroes," but who "still [clung] to methods of conciliation and the preaching of cooperation and [turned] a deaf ear to militant methods of agitation."[16]

The prospects for this last group's holding its own in the contest for racial leadership depended in large measure on developments on the white side of the color line – and here Haynes found cause both for concern and hope. Too much determined by the legacy of the past, white opinion persisted in denying blacks the "capacity for full personality." A growing separation of the races reinforced this tendency, for it meant that white people, who seldom dealt with black businessmen or professionals and "rarely enter[ed] the better type of Negro homes," were "accustomed to draw their impressions about Negroes from the crime accounts of white newspapers, from conversations, from observations and reports from their Negro servants, and from what they see of the idle loafers about the streets."[17] This very problem, however, suggested a solution. If one kind of racial contact reinforced prejudice and suspicion, another kind could undermine them. Specifically, Haynes called attention to the increasingly important work of interracial committees. These local or regional bodies brought together black and white leaders committed cooperatively to addressing in very concrete ways racial antipathy and discrimination against blacks. To Haynes, the most hopeful development on the white side of the racial line was an apparent increase in the willingness to participate in such collaborative efforts.

Of the numerous examples of this new phenomenon Haynes provided, the most notable was the southern Commission on Interracial Cooperation. In describing and praising the Commission's work, Haynes nowhere mentioned its working acceptance of segregation. Indeed, nowhere in *The Trend of the Races* did Haynes himself directly attack segregation as such. It is to be remembered, of course, that in characterizing the differences between right and center black leadership, he had insisted they shared a commitment to "full justice" and differed. simply on the means for achieving it. Presumably in his own mind he believed that downplaying a direct critique of segregation was not acquiescing to it but merely seeking its end in a more prudent and realistic fashion.

As executive director of the Commission on Race Relations, Haynes followed the strategy of improving race relations that he had laid down in *The Trend of the Races*. Since, as Reimers has observed, "the denominations themselves generally ignored race relations, aside from missionary and education work," the Commission became the establishment's most advanced agency for confronting racial issues and "provided denominational leaders with an opportunity to explore new approaches to the field . . . later utilized in their own denominations."[18]

The new approach most emphasized by Haynes was, of course, the creation of interracial committees. Under his leadership the Commission immediately began a far-reaching campaign to build a complex structure of such bodies at the local, state, and national levels. But Haynes and the Commission developed a number of other notable programs as well, including the William E. Harmon Awards for Distinguished Achievement among Negroes, the Honor Roll of States Free from Lynching, and – the Commission's best-known program – Race Relations Sunday. Started in 1923, Race Relations Sunday was by the 1940s a fixture in the life of many churches and sometimes even enjoyed the official blessing of a governor's proclamation. An annual flood of pamphlets and brochures accompanied the occasion, and the Commission used the event to highlight specific racial problems. Yet the core of the event remained ritual. On the Sunday preceding Lincoln's birthday, black pastors and choirs traded places with their white counterparts. This ritual of interracial goodwill and civility was both vividly expressive of Haynes's confidence in the transformative power of positive interaction and altogether in keeping with his own deep belief that the universe was on the side of human mutuality.

Such sentiments have always made Race Relations Sunday a target of ridicule from those less inclined to accentuate the positive. In the 1960s, it was widely criticized as a trivial observance that treated a massive institutional injustice as though it were a problem of disharmonious interpersonal relations. It is worth remembering, however, that Race Relations Sunday was sufficiently provocative in the interwar years that the southern Presbyterians refused as late as 1935 to participate in it.[19] For Haynes interracial conciliation, whether ritual or otherwise, was not only an end in itself but also a means to improve black life in very specific, even material ways – sometimes through its capacity to redirect the exercise of government power. Haynes did not, for example, rely on winning the goodwill of lynchers to stop lynching, but lobbied energetically on behalf of federal antilynching legislation. Similarly, he did not expect harmonious interaction with business and labor leaders alone satisfactorily to advance black economic interests. During the early years of the New Deal, he helped organize and chaired the Joint Committee on National Recovery, a combination of twenty-two black religious and other organizations that worked energetically against racial discrimination by the National Recovery Administration, the Agricultural Adjustment Administration, and a wide range of other New Deal agencies.

If Haynes's conciliatory approach sometimes converged with the more assertive tactics of the "center," it remained in sharp opposition to all forms of radicalism. His interracialism naturally set him against all forms of black nationalism even those that were more tactical than ideological.

Haynes also remained deeply suspicious of all efforts to approach black–white relations in America as essentially a problem of class struggle, as was evident in his resistance to popular front collaboration with Communists in the National Negro Congress. Organized in the mid-1930s by John P. Davis, with whom Haynes had worked very closely on the Joint Committee on National Recovery, the National Negro Congress aspired to mobilize the entire black community and sympathetic white allies on behalf of a militant program of "adequate relief, equality of economic opportunity, suppression of lynching, [the] abolition of Jim Crowism," and, most especially, biracial industrial unionism.[20] Its first president was A. Philip Randolph, president of the Brotherhood of Sleeping Car Porters and longtime black socialist. Haynes resisted its creation and declined to attend the first Congress in 1936, instead sending a representative who reported back to him that "the issue was one of the Communists versus the Negro churches, with the masses up for grabs." With so much apparently at stake, Haynes, who had absolutely refused to work with Communists in defense of the "Scottsboro boys," reluctantly agreed to participate, doing what he could to sustain Randolph's leadership in order to keep the organization from falling into more radical hands. By 1940, however, it was clear that this battle had been lost. Randolph, declaring "that the Negro people cannot afford to add to the handicap of being black the handicap of being red," refused to run for reelection as president; Haynes walked out of the Congress, never to return.[21]

Haynes meanwhile persisted in his conciliatory strategy of promoting through the churches an increase in positive interracial contact. In 1943, in the aftermath of a summer of bloody and destructive race riots, he launched a program of interracial clinics. Local events in which a team of outside experts drew together leaders from both races and helped them address amiably but very concretely the sources of racial tension in their communities, these clinics represented a renewal of the emphasis on local interracial committees with which the Commission had begun work twenty years before. They also indicated how things had in some respects come full circle for Haynes. Just as the war to make the world safe for democracy and the aftermath of racial strife had fostered establishment interest in black–white relations and prompted the creation of the Commission on Race Relations, so the war against fascism and its attendant racial strife promoted a new establishment concern to confront domestic racism and led to the Council's historic postwar endorsement of "a nonsegregated church and a nonsegregated society."

The same resurgent interracialism that effected this pronouncement also made possible Benjamin Mays's election in 1944 to the Federal

Council's vice presidency. After graduating from Bates College in 1920, Mays had for a dozen years combined intermittent work on an M.A. and Ph.D. at the University of Chicago Divinity School with service in a variety of organizations, some with strong establishment links. In the early 1920s he taught at Morehouse College in Atlanta and at South Carolina State College, and then served successively as executive secretary of the Urban League in Tampa, Florida, and as a student secretary with the YMCA, supervising its work at black colleges in five southern states. From 1930 to 1932, he collaborated with Joseph W. Nicholson, a minister in the Colored Methodist Episcopal Church, on a major comprehensive sociological study of the black church. Sponsored by the establishment-linked Institute of Social and Religious Research and published in 1933, *The Negro's Church* was one of the most influential works ever published on Afro-American religion.[22] After completing his work at the University of Chicago (he received his Ph.D. in 1935) and turning down a teaching position at Fisk, Mays served for six years as dean of the School of Religion at Howard University. In 1940, he began a twenty-seven-year term as president of Morehouse College.

Mays's election to the vice presidency of the Federal Council both recognized and further promoted his growing role in ecumenical Protestantism internationally. In 1937, he was one of thirteen American delegates to the World Conference of the YMCA in Mysore, India. He had a memorable visit with Gandhi, appreciated the fact that at the conference "members of different races and nations met on a plane of absolute equality," and was elected to the World Committee of the YMCA. That same year he attended the Oxford Conference on Church, Community, and State, beginning an association with the emerging ecumenical movement that led to his election in 1948 to the ninety-person central committee of the new World Council of Churches (WCC). At the Council's Second Assembly in 1954 in Evanston, Illinois, Mays gave a stirring address entitled "The Church Amidst Ethnic and Racial Tension." Described by Mays himself as "moderate," the speech has been credited by at least one observer with helping lead the WCC a decade later toward its controversial Program to Combat Racism.[23]

Mays appreciated the possibility for "fellowship across racial barriers in assembly and worship" that the ecumenical world provided and on that account thought the "national and world gatherings [he had attended] have been more Christian . . . than [the] local ones." He also was aware, however, that "national and world gatherings are not empowered to pass resolutions which are binding on local bodies, and so are not subject to the same pressures." When the 1937 World Conference of the YMCA's Commission on Race condemned segregation based on

Benjamin E. Mays (*center*) with Eugene Carson Blake (*left*) and O. Frederick Nolde, 1958. Religious News Service photo.

race, he observed, it "did not change one iota the segregated practices of the local YMCAs in the United States." When the Federal Council of Churches issued its condemnation of segregation, he may also have had doubts about just what the practical effect would be. President Harry Truman addressed this same meeting of the Federal Council and, in advance of his coming, there had been considerable discussion – in which Mays was not included – about whether the Council's black vice president should be seated on the rostrum with Truman or placed in the first row of the audience with a group of other dignitaries. The latter choice prevailed. Had not one disturbed ecumenical leader caused another chair to be placed on the rostrum and seen that Mays was escorted to it, Mays would not have been on the platform when Truman spoke. The incident seemed to convey a very different message from that contained in the Council's pronouncement.[24]

Still, by voting to renounce "the pattern of segregation in race relations as unnecessary and undesirable and a violation of the Gospel of love and brotherhood" and calling upon its constituency to make this renunciation good by working for a "non-segregated church and a non-segregated society," the Federal Council had indeed taken what Mays himself termed a "giant step."[25] In the context of the emerging consensus that this statement both reflected and fostered, the establishment denominations moved in the 1940s to issue the pronouncements and create the organizational structures that allowed for their increasingly effective responses to the civil rights movement of the 1950s and early 1960s. This belated rejection of segregation, while repositioning the establishment to play a significant role in the postwar battle against southern caste, also, however, raised an awkward question about racial separation within the establishment churches themselves. Just how far inside was the establishment willing to let its own racial outsiders come?

Desegregating the Establishment

In *The Protestant Church and the Negro,* published in 1948, Frank Loescher declared that "the Protestant church in general, by the practices of its congregations and educational institutions, is following the status quo in Negro-white relationships and . . . is not actively furthering the integration of the Negro into American society."[26] Galvanized into action by such critiques and following the suggestions that reformers such as Loescher provided, Protestant racial liberals sought in the ensuing two decades to integrate their churches and colleges. These attempts sometimes showed an insensitivity to the role the establishment denominations' black churches and colleges had played in developing figures like George Edmund Haynes and Benjamin Mays and in providing a context for black autonomy and self-development. The most visible target of their attacks, however, and the one most successfully assaulted, was not local or educational segregation but segregated organizational structures beyond the local level. Especially important here was the extended battle over Methodism's "Central Jurisdiction," which was created in 1939 and did not entirely disappear until 1973.[27]

Methodism's "problem" of how to organize its black membership was, of course, a result of at least intermittently energetic efforts to evangelize blacks from the time of Methodism's eighteenth-century beginnings through the Reconstruction period in the South. With the exception of the Congregationalists, no denomination had come closer than the Methodist Episcopal Church to creating a thoroughly biracial structure – from the congregational level up – in the postwar South. Nevertheless, by 1876 the Methodists had organized black and white members separately not only at the congregational but also at the regional level. Black Methodist congregations thus belonged not to the same conference as nearby white Methodist churches but to special all-black conferences, just as black Presbyterian churches were grouped in black

presbyteries and even black Congregationalists eventually were organized into an all-black "Convention of the South."[28] Such "integration"
as there was structurally, therefore, took place almost entirely at the
national level.

Blacks working within these arrangements tended initially to concentrate their efforts on achieving equality and nondiscrimination, especially
at the national level. Black Methodists, for example, early achieved full
status for black conference delegates at the denomination's quadrennial
General Conference and, after a half century of sometimes bitter struggle, the election of blacks to the episcopate, Robert Jones and Matthew
Clair in 1920. (Four other blacks had earlier been made bishops, but with
the understanding that they were to function as such only in the mission
fields in Africa.)[29] Black Presbyterians had long been represented in the
General Assembly, but no black was elected to a national church board
until 1932, and the denomination's Unit of Work for Colored People did
not have a black chief administrator until 1938. Meanwhile, blacks and
white liberals sought to ensure that national meetings were not held in
cities that imposed Jim Crow practices on the delegates, an effort that
achieved increasing success in the late 1930s and early 1940s.[30]

In this context of seeming progress the reuniting northern and southern Methodists created in 1939 the "Central Jurisdiction," a grouping of
all the church's black conferences in a structure that was separate from
but equal to the four regional jurisdictions into which the white conferences were grouped. This arrangement was a compromise plan. Representatives from the Methodist Episcopal Church, South, had initially
urged northern Methodists to do with their black members what the
southerners themselves had done with theirs between 1866 and 1870,
namely, organize them as a parallel but entirely separate denomination
and send them on their way. Some blacks and northern white liberals
thought, on the other hand, that the time had come for Methodism to
eliminate even the existing structure of separate black conferences. The
Central Jurisdiction plan was defended as a compromise that established
the racial separation the southerners required while extending black participation and power at the national level. But although some blacks
were encouraged by the increase in the number of black bishops and
black representatives on national boards and agencies, most apparently
saw the new plan as a humiliating insult. At the Kansas City meeting of
May 10, 1939, where the plan was adopted, thirty-two black delegates
voted in the negative, and eleven abstained; and according to one account, while the jubilant whites stood to sing "We Are Marching Upward to Zion," the blacks stayed seated and some even wept.[31]

Whatever could be said on behalf of the Methodist reunion plan of

1939, it clearly did not represent a model of "the nonsegregated church," and in the postwar climate of opinion represented by the 1946 Federal Council of Churches, the plan was subject to persistent attack as white Protestantism's most obvious monument to caste. In 1956, the denomination voted to allow local congregations within the Central Jurisdiction to switch to the geographic jurisdiction in their area if both the white and black conferences involved agreed to the transfer. This arrangement allowed for regional "integration" in areas where it was acceptable to whites without in any way challenging southern segregation. Only in 1966, at the height of the civil rights movement "after much agony," was the decision to abolish the Central Jurisdiction made. Even then another seven years elapsed before the old arrangements were entirely eliminated. In that same year, Congregationalists abolished the Convention of the South, and integrated its churches "into new conferences determined by geographical rather than racial factors." Legislated racial segregation, along with institutionalized racial separation above the local level, was finally at an end in the predominantly white churches of the Protestant establishment.[32]

The Black Protestant Establishment

"I have been definitely and proudly involved with the Federal and National Council of the Churches of Christ," Benjamin Mays declared toward the end of his life. But he also said, "I am basically a 'race man.'" At a time when southern segregation was in its death throes and racial integration was the order of the day in the upper reaches of the establishment, it was possible to believe that the black churches either would or should disappear along with Jim Crow and their members become assimilated in predominantly white denominations. From this standpoint, figures like Benjamin Mays were both symbols of the establishment's own liberality and vanguards of the black churches' coming absorption into the Protestant establishment. This, however, is not how Mays understood himself. Pursuing the goals of improved race relations and full justice for black Americans did not for Mays necessarily mean abandoning black consciousness or black institutions. Mays was no radical. He was "always . . . wholly unsympathetic to the Communist ideology" and thought "the dream of black nationalism . . . whether Garvey's or the Black Muslins['] . . . little more than a mirage." But his assessment of the "Black Power" slogan of the mid-1960s was that it was "a blessing if it convinces black people that their strength lies in solidarity, and that black men can never get political and economic power if they are divided and fighting among themselves." He also saw the new movement as deeply resonant with the black churches' longstanding emphasis on the importance of black identity, something that he and Joseph Nicholson had emphasized thirty years before in the *Negro Church*. "The identity Negroes have had in church lo! these many years," he observed, "they now seek everywhere."[33]

There was, indeed, throughout this period, as there had been in the century before, a black Protestant establishment centered on the great black Baptist and Methodist denominations, but also including the black Methodists of the Central Jurisdiction and, to some extent, blacks within the other Protestant establishment denominations as well. George Edmund Haynes, for example, as a black Congregationalist employed by the Federal Council was far removed from the center of the black establishment. Yet throughout his tenure at the Council he retained important working relationships with more mainstream black establishment leaders. During the Depression, for example, when Haynes needed a way to communicate with black farmers in the rural South about the various forms of government assistance available to them, he turned to the black Baptist and Methodist churches, through whose organizations he was able to disseminate the information, sometimes with striking results.[34] It is also to be noted that in spite of his prominent involvement in interracial ecumenism, Benjamin Mays worked most of his life in the context of black institutions. When he went to the First Assembly of the World Council of Churches in 1948, moreover, his official status was that of a delegate from the black National Baptist Convention, U.S.A.

Highly visible figures such as Haynes and Mays were not, of course, the only persons linking the two establishments. The connections between them were manifold, complex, and enormously important. The pattern of dual affiliation, a common though scarcely universal black Baptist practice whereby individuals and congregations aligned themselves simultaneously with both the American Baptist Convention and one of the black Baptist denominations, made it unusually easy for Afro-Americans of this tradition to participate simultaneously in both establishments. The same was true of the black Methodists of the Central Jurisdiction and, in a more limited sense, of those leaders of the major black Methodist denominations who were active in ecumenical organizations such as the Federal and National Councils. All these people provided the establishment with a resource its white leaders seem generally not to have appreciated. Given its general isolation from black America, the establishment was dependent on such bridge figures for its only enduring link, through the major black denominations, with the mainstream of black American life. At no time, of course, was the importance of this connection more evident, if still often unappreciated, than during the civil rights movement, when Martin Luther King, Jr., created an unprecedentedly effective working relationship between the Protestant establishment and the black churches. This collaboration would have been impossible without the persistent bridge-building efforts of an earlier generation.

Relations between the Protestant religious establishment and the black religious establishment were not always collaborative, however, either in King's time or before. Leaders of the major black Baptist and Methodist denominations, especially those from the urban North, often had doubts about the adequacy of Protestant establishment race relations efforts and high hopes about what might be achieved if the black churches could collaboratively mobilize the whole force of the black community. They also simply wished at times to do certain things collectively on their own without white supervision or interference. A striking instance of this tendency was the creation of the National Fraternal Council of Negro Churches. Launched in 1933 when AME bishop Reverdy C. Ransom called together a group of mostly northern black church leaders, and continuing to elect officers into the early 1960s, the Fraternal Council attempted to give the black Protestant establishment organizational form. The main leadership for its work came from the five major bodies among whom its presidency rotated: the National Baptist Convention, U.S.A., Inc., the three independent black Methodist denominations, and the Central Jurisdiction of the Methodist Episcopal Church. Over the course of its history, it drew together black leaders from more than thirteen denominations, including the Church of God Holiness and the Pentecostal Church of God in Christ.[35]

It is important to realize that for the black leaders who worked within it, the black religious establishment itself defined the meaning of being "inside" as much as the Protestant establishment did for its leaders. It is also true that the black establishment depended on its own institutional and personal networks, which differed significantly from those along which George Haynes or even Benjamin Mays moved. This is clear from the career of the Fraternal Council's founder, Reverdy Ransom.[36] An Ohioan, Ransom (1861–1959) grew up in the AME Church and graduated in 1886 from that denomination's leading school, Wilberforce University. He served for twenty-six years as an AME pastor (in Pittsburgh, Cleveland, Chicago, Boston, and New York) and for twelve years as editor of the church's quarterly before being elected to the bishopric in 1924. This immersion in the life of a black denomination seems to have been a matter of deliberate choice. Ransom did an undergraduate year at Oberlin in the early 1880s, but was unhappy at the establishment school and decided to finish at Wilberforce. He also was very active in the black Niagara Movement that helped launch the NAACP, but was never much involved in the interracial NAACP itself. Clearly, he preferred to move primarily within the world of the black church and community rather than pursue a career in a biracial context. There is no reason to believe that this choice was eccentric. The typical AME bishop or the pastors of such great metropolitan black Baptist churches as Olivet in Chicago or Abyssinian in New York did not seem to envy George Haynes his job or Benjamin Mays his ecumenical prominence. Such powerful black churchmen were not dependent on the Protestant establishment as a vehicle for exerting social influence beyond the church. They could do that from their position within the black establishment. Reverdy Ransom, for example, was actively involved in the 1930s in efforts to shift the black vote from the Republican to the Democratic party (George Haynes never left "the party of Lincoln"). Abyssinian's pastor, Adam Clayton Powell, Jr., in 1944 was elected to Congress from Harlem and for more than twenty years was black America's most prominent national political figure.[37] Such examples apparently gave black church leaders confidence about what they could accomplish through their own efforts. They were also persuaded that if the black churches were effectively to serve the general interests of black people, they could not rely entirely on the leadership of the Protestant establishment and its black insiders.

In his autobiography *The Pilgrimage of Harriet Ransom's Son,* Bishop Ransom recalled that most of the black church leaders who initially organized the Fraternal Council were also active in the Federal Council and appreciated its work. He also noted, however, that "some of us clearly saw that this organization could not bring its full influence to bear upon many questions that were vital to Negroes and other minority groups." The official message of the Fraternal Council's Second Annual Convention in 1935 put the point more bluntly. "The hour is at hand," it declared, "when the Negro Church should unite to fearlessly challenge the faithless stewardship of American Christianity by submitting it to the test of political, social, and economic justice, a justice that accepts no peace on the basis of submission, compromise, or surrender."[38]

What Ransom and some others seem to have wanted was a program that was more "left wing" than that proposed by Haynes at the Federal Council. Certainly they were more enthusiastic than Haynes about the National Negro Congress. At the 1935 Annual Convention, the Fraternal Council endorsed the incipient "movement to bring about unified action of Negroes for social and economic justice through a national

Negro Congress." It also enunciated for itself a program similar in many ways to that which soon emerged from the black Congress. Such a program was not out of character for someone like Ransom. As early as 1896, he had predicted that since "social and industrial oppression have been his portion for centuries, . . . the Negro will enthusiastically espouse the cause of socialism." He had also suggested to the AME General Conference in 1936 that "Communism, with all its cruelties, actually tries to practice what it preaches" and therefore could accurately be described as "the only religion left among the white races today that has vitality." Ransom was, moreover, more sympathetic than George Edmund Haynes to racial as well as working-class radicalism. As the editor of the *A.M.E. Review,* his editorials on the Garvey Movement had been relatively sympathetic. The theme of racial solidarity was also strong in the Fraternal Council's early pronouncements.[39]

The National Fraternal Council of Negro Churches never succeeded in becoming the expression of black peoplehood or the bearer of social radicalism that it aspired to be. Through part of the 1940s and 1950s, a Washington Bureau, sponsored by the Council and directed by National Baptist churchman W. H. Jernagin, sought to bring the organized force of the black churches to bear on the work of Congress and the White House. But over the years its policies moderated, and by the heyday of the civil rights movement it was little more than a paper organization, without a significant constituency even in the black churches themselves. Still, as originally conceived by Ransom it represented an impulse, strongest among northern urban churchmen, that surfaced again in the 1960s and 1970s, just at the time the unsettling reality of the black world beyond the "inner rings" was breaking in upon the establishment with unprecedented force. Then, knowingly breaking ranks with Martin Luther King and the Southern Christian Leadership Conference, some northern black churchmen, eager to reshape the black religious establishment into an embodiment of black power radicalism, renewed the tradition of the Fraternal Council. Even some of the ecclesiastical descendants of George Haynes, black insiders with high positions in the National Council of Churches and in the establishment denominations, joined with militants from the black Baptist and Methodist churches to form the National Committee of Black Churchmen. In the judgment of this body, "the American religious establishment" was not to be praised for its belated integrationism but condemned for providing "the moral cement of the structure of racism in this nation." Even within the inner circles, where black America and the world of the Protestant establishment were most closely joined, the painful distance between black and white had not after all been overcome.[40]

NOTES

1 U.S. Department of Commerce, *The Social and Economic Status of the Black Population in the United States: An Historical View, 1790–1978* (Washington, D.C.: U.S. Government Printing Office, n.d.), 13, 15.

2 The relevant figures from the 1890 census are reported in W. E. B. DuBois, *The Negro Church* (Atlanta: Atlanta University Press, 1903), 38; on the number of black members in the Methodist Church in 1960, see Willis J. King, "The Central Jurisdiction," in Emory Stevens Bucke (ed.), *The History of American Methodism,* vol. 3 (New York: Abingdon, 1964), 490; Frank Loescher, *The Protestant Church and the Negro* (New York: Association Press, 1948), 51, estimated that of a probable eight million black church members, only 500,000, about 6½ percent, belonged to predominantly white denominations.

3 DuBois, *The Negro Church,* 38; Benson Y. Landis (ed.), *Yearbook of American Churches: Thirtieth Issue* (New York: National Council of Churches, 1961), 250, 253. The Colored Methodist Episcopal Church changed its name in 1956 to Christian Methodist Episcopal Church.

4 DuBois, *The Negro Church,* 38; Harry V. Richardson, "The Negro in American Religious Life," in John P. Davis (ed.), *The American Negro Reference Book* (Englewood Cliffs, N.J.: Prentice-Hall, 1966), 410.

5 Landis, *Yearbook of American Churches: Thirtieth Issue,* 250.

6 Robert Weisbrot, *Father Divine and the Struggle for Racial Equality* (Urbana: University of Illinois Press, 1983), 68–9.

7 Cited in David M. Reimers, *White Protestantism and the Negro* (New York: Oxford University Press, 1965), 112.

8 There are no major, published biographical studies of either Haynes or Mays, other than Mays's autobiography *Born to Rebel* (New York: Scribner's 1971; reprint, Athens: University of Georgia Press, 1987). On Haynes, see two Ph.D. dissertations: Daniel Perlman, "Stirring the White Conscience: The Life of George Edmund Haynes" (New York University, 1972), and Samuel Kelton Roberts, "Crucible for a Vision: The Work of George Edmund Haynes and the Commission on Race Relations, 1922–1947" (Columbia University, 1974). Chapter 2 of the latter also appears in Randall K. Burkett and Richard Newman, *Black Apostles: Afro-American Clergy Confront the Twentieth Century* (Boston: Hall, 1978), 97–127.

9 Reimers, *White Protestantism,* 95.

10 For Haynes's involvement in the development of the Urban League, see along with the Perlman and Roberts dissertations, Nancy J. Weiss, *The National Urban League, 1910–1940* (New York: Oxford University Press, 1974).

11 Perlman, "Stirring the White Conscience," 129.

12 For the effect of the war on the racial work of the Federal Council and related agencies, see John F. Piper, Jr., *The American Churches in World War I* (Athens: Ohio University Press, 1985), especially Chapter 8.

13 Roberts, "Crucible for a Vision," 95.

14   (New York: Council of Women for Home Missions and Missionary Education Movement of the United States and Canada, 1922).

15   Wilma Dykeman and James Stokely, *Seeds of Southern Change: The Life of Will Alexander* (Chicago: University of Chicago Press, 1962), 43–76. The role of women in the creation of both the Commission on Interracial Cooperation and Federal Council's Commission on Race Relations suggests that establishment females were generally ahead of establishment males on questions of race relations.

16   Haynes, *Trend of the Races,* 82, 86, 14–16.

17   Haynes, *Trend of the Races,* 145, 184.

18   Reimers, *White Protestantism,* 93.

19   Reimers, *White Protestantism,* 91.

20   Perlman, "Stirring the White Conscience," 279. For an account that stresses the centrality to the Congress of industrial unionism, see Raymond Wolters, *Negroes and the Great Depression* (Westport, Conn.: Greenwood Press, 1970), Chapter 13.

21   Roberts, "Crucible for a Vision," 237; Perlman, "Stirring the White Conscience," 282.

22   (New York: Institute of Social and Religious Research, 1933; reprint New York: Arno Press/New York Times, 1969).

23   Mays, *Born to Rebel,* 157, 260: Pearl L. McNeil, "Baptist Black Americans and the Ecumenical Movement," in William J. Boney and Glenn A. Igleheart (eds.), *Baptists and Ecumenism* (Valley Forge, Pa.: Judson Press, 1980), 109. The latter volume is identical with *Journal of Ecumenical Studies* 17(Spring 1980).

24   Mays, *Born to Rebel,* 251, 158 and 253.

25   Mays, *Born to Rebel,* 253.

26   Loescher, *Protestant Church,* 15–16.

27   William B. McClain, *Black People in the Methodist Church: Whither Thou Goest?* (Cambridge, Mass.: Schenkman, 1984), 75–92; Julius Ernest Del Pino, "Black Leadership in the United Methodist Church: A Historical Review and Empirical Study" (Ph.D. diss., Northwestern University 1976), 52–63.

28   Reimers, *White Protestantism,* 56–62; H. Shelton Smith, *In His Image, but . . . : Racism in Southern Religion, 1780–1910* (Durham, N.C.: Duke University Press, 1972), 232–7; A. Knighton Stanley, *The Children Is Crying: Congregationalism among Black People* (New York/Philadelphia: Pilgrim Press, 1979), ix. The situation of black Episcopalians was somewhat different and requires special discussion.

29   Reimers, *White Protestantism,* 71–5; McClain, *Black People in the Methodist Church,* 77. These four were Francis Burns, John W. Roberts, Isaiah B. Scott, and Alexander Camphor. Bishops, of course, were not the only major black Methodist leaders. Mary McLeod Bethune, president of the denomination's Bethune-Cookman College, was also the founder and president of the National Council of Negro Women, director from 1935 to 1943

of the National Youth Administration's Division of Negro Affairs, and a member of Franklin Roosevelt's "black cabinet."

30 Reimers, *White Protestantism*, 103–8.

31 McClain, *Black People in the Methodist Church*, 75–82.

32 McClain, *Black People in the Methodist Church*, 91; Stanley, *The Children Is Crying*, ix.

33 Mays, *Born to Rebel*, 230, 141, 136, 308, 315, 133.

34 Haynes also collaborated closely with leaders of the major black denominations on the Joint Committee on National Recovery. Prominent black Baptist educator and churchwoman Nannie Burroughs, for example, was the organization's treasurer.

35 This organization has received very little scholarly attention. I have relied here primarily on Spurgeon E. Crayton, "The History and Theology of the National Fraternal Council of Negro Churches" (M. Div. thesis, Union Theological Seminary, New York, 1979). A more recent study, Mary R. Sawyer, "Black Ecumenism: Cooperative Social Change Movements in the Black Church" (Ph.D. diss., Duke University, 1986), 105–29, came into my hands too late to be used extensively in the preparation of this essay.

36 I have discussed Ransom's early career in "Reverdy C. Ransom: The Making of an A.M.E. Bishop," in Burkett and Newman, *Black Apostles*, 181–212, and have analyzed the relation of liberalism, black nationalism, and socialism in Ransom's social thought in "Racial Justice and the Limits of American Liberalism," *Journal of Religious Ethics* 6(Fall 1978): 187–220. See also Calvin S. Morris, "Reverdy C. Ransom: A Pioneer Black Social Gospeler" (Ph.D. diss., Boston University, 1982).

37 Martin Kilson, "Adam Clayton Powell, Jr.: The Militant as Politician," in John Hope Franklin and August Meier (eds.), *Black Leaders of the Twentieth Century* (Urbana: University of Illinois, 1982), 259–75.

38 Reverdy C. Ransom, *The Pilgrimage of Harriet Ransom's Son* (Nashville: AME Sunday School Union, n.d.), 296, 299.

39 Roberts, "Crucible for a Vision," 238; Ransom, *Pilgrimage*, 297–8; Reverdy C. Ransom, "The Negro and Socialism," *A.M.E. Church Review* 13(October 1896): 200; and Reverdy C. Ransom, "Quadrennial Sermon to the . . . General Conference, May 6, 1936, New York City: The Church That Shall Survive," in George A. Singleton, *The Romance of African Methodism: A Study of the African Methodist Episcopal Church* (New York: Exposition Press, 1952), 154.

40 "The National Committee of Black Churchmen's Response to the Black Manifesto," in Gayraud S. Wilmore and James H. Cone, *Black Theology: A Documentary History, 1966–1979* (Maryknoll, N.Y.: Orbis Books, 1979), 90. For an account of these developments from the standpoint of a black insider actively involved in shaping them, see Gayraud S. Wilmore, *Black Religion and Black Radicalism*, 2d ed., rev. (Maryknoll, N.Y.: Orbis Books, 1973), 192–219. For a full understanding of the tension involved here between the northern and southern wings of the black Protestant establishment, it is

necessary to take into account the relation of the latter to the southern white
Protestant establishment – a topic that lies outside the scope of this essay.

SELECT BIBLIOGRAPHY

Brooks, Evelyn. "Nannie Burroughs and the Education of Black Women." In
    Sharon Harley and Rosalyn Terborg-Penn, eds., *The Afro-American
    Woman: Struggles and Images,* 97–108. Port Washington, N.Y.: National
    University Publications, 1978.
Burkett, Randall K. *Black Redemption: Churchmen Speak for the Garvey Movement.*
    Philadelphia: Temple University Press, 1978.
    *Garveyism as a Religious Movement: The Institutionalization of a Black Civil Re-
    ligion.* Metuchen, N.J.: Scarecrow Press, 1978.
Garrow, David J. *Bearing the Cross: Martin Luther King, Jr., and the Southern
    Christian Leadership Conference.* New York: Morrow, 1986.
Heilbut, Anthony. *The Gospel Sound: Good News and Bad Times,* rev. ed. New
    York: Limelight Editions, 1985.
Lincoln, C. Eric. *The Black Muslims,* rev. ed. Boston: Beacon Press, 1973.
Newsome, Clarence G. "Mary McLeod Bethune as Religionist." In Hilah F.
    Thomas and Rosemary Skinner Keller, eds., *Women in New Worlds:
    Historical Perspectives on the Wesleyan Tradition,*102–16. Nashville: Ab-
    ingdon, 1981.
Osborne, William. *The Segregated Covenant: Race Relations and American Catholics.*
    New York: Herder & Herder, 1967.
Synan, Vinson. *The Holiness-Pentecostal Movement in the United States.* Grand
    Rapids, Mich.: Eerdmans, 1971, esp. Chapters 3, 5, 7–9.
Thurman, Howard. *With Head and Heart.* New York: Harcourt Brace
    Jovanovich, 1979.
Washington, James M. ed. *A Testament of Hope: The Essential Writings of Martin
    Luther King, Jr.* San Francisco: Harper & Row, 1986.

9

A Wary Collaboration: Jews, Catholics, and the Protestant Goodwill Movement

BENNY KRAUT

Jewish and Catholic relations with Protestants during the first five decades of the twentieth century were marked by serious strains and tensions. In contrast to the more religiously pluralistic atmosphere pervading American culture by the 1960s, noted by Will Herberg in his penetrating *Protestant-Catholic-Jew*,[1] the prevailing Protestant ethos of American culture in prior decades subtly and not so subtly reinforced the outsider status of Jews and Catholics. The two groups frequently were subjected to religious or ethnic bigotry and accusations questioning, if not ridiculing, their American loyalties. Because they maintained religious separateness, affirmed religious "chosenness," and created their own communal organizations, Jews were often branded clannish, ethnocentric, and religiously obstinate.[2] Because they looked for guidance to a foreign pope, acquiesced to a more rigid church hierarchy, and were committed to an expanding parochial school network, Catholics were often attacked as antidemocratic, politically subversive, and alienated from authentic American ideals.[3] These charges had already been leveled against Jews and Catholics in the nineteenth century; they were repeated with varying intensity in every decade of the first half of the twentieth century, although most passionately during the 1920s and 1930s.

American Jews felt themselves to be in a particularly ambiguous situation with respect to American Protestantism. Perhaps more than any other outsider group, they craved insider status. Since the nineteenth century, the Protestant establishment served as a source of social gratification and coalition building for Jewish concerns, and provided Jews with models of social, cultural, religious, and social gospel behavior. Yet, this same establishment, and some of the ideals it espoused, threatened the Jewish position in society. As the largest non-Christian minority in the country, Jews were terribly anxious about the establishment's cultural interpretation of a Christian (i.e., Protestant) America that relegated them to a secondary status as Americans. The overwhelming Protestant spirit of America in the first decades of this century confronted Jews with the need to find some conceptually coherent reasoning that would articulate and reconcile their American and Jewish identities, while concomitantly legitimating their place as equals in a Protestant-dominated country.

American Catholics, the largest and fastest growing Christian body in the United States, were, no less and perhaps even more than the Jews, acutely sensitive to the Protestant aspiration for cultural hegemony. To them, the Protestant flavor of the country, with its deep-seated anti-Catholicism and religiously partisan moral tastes enshrined in public law, was morally offensive, intellectually unjustified, and religiously misguided. Over the years, Catholic spokesmen not only defended Catholic American legitimacy, but also proclaimed Catholic equality and, in many instances, prophesied ultimate religious supremacy in the land.

To be sure, positive interfaith relations in the first half of this century were not entirely absent. Some establishment figures and organizations, in concert with Jewish and Catholic individuals and institutions, worked to foster more harmonious group relations. Protestant leaders called on Jews and Catholics to join in concrete efforts to promote civic and religious goodwill. Protestant scholars and theologians wrote scholarly and popular books discussing other faiths and, together with prominent Protestant politicians, held discussions and established friendships with Jews and Catholics, ultimately spawning greater tolerance and respect among the three religious communities. When Protestants initiated such activities, Jewish communal leaders and thinkers and, to a lesser extent, Catholics, proved responsive, for any establishment moves mitigating social tension and religious friction were generally welcomed.

The persistent difficulty Jews and Catholics had with such Protestant overtures, however, was how to interpret these expressions of inter-religious goodwill against the background of anti-Jewish and anti-Catholic sentiments that emerged simultaneously from other quarters of the establishment. The mixed signals of Protestant disdain and friendship in the first half of the twentieth century, therefore, sparked feelings of tentativeness and ambivalence among Jews and Catholics. Indeed, if any one word can aptly capture their outlook on the establishment in this whole period, it is "ambivalence."

In no decade of the twentieth century were the establishment's mixed signals more apparent than in the 1920s; consequently, in no decade was Jewish and Catholic ambivalence to this establishment more manifest. During the 1920s, Jews and Catholics encountered a Protestantism acting at once at its most aggressive and at its most accommodating. On the one hand, the establishment moved to shore up its cultural and religious hegemony in America. Following World War I, both Jews and Catholics experienced in similar as well as variant ways the sting of Protestant cultural triumphalism. On the other hand, a gradually evolving Protestant goodwill movement arose in the decade after the war. Largely inspired and nurtured by clergy, laypeople, and organizations connected with the Federal Council of Churches of Christ in America (hereafter, Federal Council), this movement in large measure was an offspring of this establishment. The efflorescence of personal and institutionalized civic and religious goodwill tendencies established countervailing trends that served as a corrective to Protestant nativist currents. Demonstrating good will was now projected by a number of establishment leaders as the finest expression of the Protestant and American spirit.

Peering in at the establishment from the outside and fully cognizant of the ugly prejudices of the day, which they attributed to the Protestant majority, Jews and Catholics in the 1920s had to adjust culturally to the establishment's goodwill movement and evaluate the scope and limits of rapprochement. Not without good reason, as we shall see, their responses to Protestant goodwill reflected great uncertainty. Indeed, the goodwill movement engendered in rather salient, even exaggerated fashion, the spectrum of ambivalent Jewish and Catholic feelings toward the establishment that was symptomatic of their reactions to it during the first half-century. Consequently, this case study of Jewish and Catholic reactions to the Protestant goodwill movement of the 1920s, although set within a limited time frame, points to interreligious phenomena in American history with much broader socioreligious significance. By describing the development of this movement, illustrating how Protestants, Jews, and Catholics related to it, and analyzing the reasons for their respective responses, this essay points to the fundamental and paradigmatic perceptions Jews and Catholics held of the establishment in the first sixty years of the twentieth century.

The Goodwill Movement and the Protestant Establishment

American historiography generally depicts the decade of the 1920s as one of disillusionment, isolationism, and nativism, in reaction to the idealism, social gospel, liberalism, and reform of the Progressive Era. Economic historians, moreover, often limn the postwar period as merely an interregnum between the Progressive Era and the depression, whereas historians of American religion reflect on the 1920s as an age of profound

Protestant spiritual depression and decline. To be sure, perceptions of the postwar years as turbulent and replete with prejudice and social cleavage can be readily substantiated. A postwar antiforeigner atmosphere, the Bolshevik scare of 1919–20, Henry Ford's dissemination of the forgery, *The Protocols of the Elders of Zion,* alleging a world Jewish conspiracy, the resurgence of the Ku Klux Klan, the restrictive Johnson-Reed Immigration Act of 1924, and the violent anti-Catholic fervor aroused by Alfred E. Smith's 1928 presidential bid – all justify the standard portrait of the 1920s as an isolationist age punctuated by ethnic and religious bigotry.[4] And yet this decade can also be regarded as an "age of goodwill," and this fresh perspective ought to take its place alongside prevalent historical notions about this period.

A spirit of goodwill of considerable social and religious consequence gained momentum into the 1920s. Despite repeated references in contemporaneous literature to the "goodwill movement," one cannot speak of a centralized, unified movement. One can, however, point to an invigorating general impulse expressed in diverse social activities that promoted civic and political reform. This animating force, channeled into newly proliferating national organizations and local committees, however long- or short-lived, was dedicated to such issues as improving industrial conditions and the quality of urban life, resettling immigrants, and fostering national justice and international peace. Civic-oriented goodwill functions, moreover, brought Protestants, Jews, and Catholics together in constructive coalitions for the commonweal. Indeed, the Federal Council invited the Social Justice Department of the Central Conference of American Rabbis (hereafter, Central Conference) and the Social Action Department of the National Catholic Welfare Conference to participate in joint studies of industrial and labor problems, which not only drew public attention to the issues, but also channeled the moral fervor of the religious conscience into American politics.[5]

Religious goodwill was often a by-product of these civic activities. But the impulse of goodwill also prompted attempts specifically geared to bringing about interreligious understanding and harmonious relations among Protestants, Catholics, and Jews. These efforts sparked new religious organizations and committees seeking to encourage interreligious discussions and to combat prejudice, among them: the Federal Council's Committee on Goodwill between Jews and Christians, the Central Conference of American Rabbis Committee on Goodwill, the American Good Will Union, and the National Conference of Jews and Christians (hereafter National Conference; its name was changed to the National Conference of Christians and Jews only in 1938–39). In later decades, these religious goodwill groups would have been labeled interfaith organizations; in the 1920s, however, that term was not in vogue.

This widespread institutionalization of the goodwill impulse may not

Social gathering at the September 1935 meeting, at Williams College, of the National Conference of Jews and Christians. From Landman, Isaac, ed., *The Universal Jewish Encyclopedia* (New York, 1940), p. 267. Used by permission of the National Conference of Christians and Jews.

have represented the views of the majority, or even large numbers, of Americans. Still, the founding of national organizations, together with civic goodwill dinners and local community goodwill forums, planted new seeds on the American cultural landscape. The term "goodwill" served as a cultural cue in Protestant, Jewish, and some Catholic circles, signaling new sociocultural and religious aspirations. The interreligious goodwill committees that appeared in the 1920s and the organization that outlasted them all, the National Conference of Christians and Jews, were not mere exceptions in a bleak age, but representative of a sociospiritual phenomenon of considerable breadth and force.

The goodwill movement of the postwar era clearly involved, and on different levels embraced, Jews and Catholics. In a few cases, Jews even initiated goodwill activities: Isidor Singer, Jewish intellectual maverick and organizer of the sweeping *Jewish Encyclopedia,* established the universalizing, interreligious Amos Society in 1923; Reform Rabbi Isaac Landman, editor of the *American Hebrew,* in 1927 founded the Permanent Commission on Better Understanding between Christians and Jews.[6] But the primary impetus undoubtedly came from Protestant sources and specifically from the Protestant establishment, as Roger W. Straus, Jewish industrialist and cochairman of the National Conference of Jews and

Christians, declared in 1931.[7] Organizations such as the Federal Council, as well as individuals of the American Protestant cultural, political, and intellectual elite, constituted this establishment. Protestants from most of the mainline denominations participated, as did those from nonmainline churches, as, for example, the Unitarians. Even a very partial list of Protestants actively involved in the goodwill events or organizations is impressive: from the Federal Council, general secretaries Revs. Charles S. Macfarland and Samuel M. Cavert, various presidents including Rev. Frank Mason North, Rev. S. Parkes Cadman, and Bishop Francis J. McConnell, and Administrative Council members such as Revs. Henry A. Atkinson, Alfred Williams Anthony, Arthur S. Lloyd; from the world of education, prominent faculty participants were William Adams Brown, Charles P. Fagnani, and Reinhold Niebuhr at the Union Theological Seminary, George Foot Moore and Roscoe Pound at Harvard, and President W. H. P. Faunce at Brown University; from the political arena, former President Theodore Roosevelt, former Secretary of War Newton D. Baker, and Secretary of State (and future Chief Justice) Charles Evans Hughes. Indeed, a number of individuals belonged to multiple interreligious organizations. Clearly these organized goodwill ventures testified to the overlapping networks of American Protestant elites intersecting the spheres of religion, politics, economics, and education.

A number of factors explain the emergence of a Protestant social and religious goodwill movement. The war itself, although soon followed by a nativist backlash, stimulated a spirit of religious fraternity. Everett R. Clinchy, the first director of the National Conference, attributed the genesis of his interest in people of other faiths to wartime exposure to them. Rabbi Isaac Landman, first Jewish chaplain in World War I, and Rabbi Morris Lazaron, also a chaplain and one of twenty founders of the interfaith Military Chaplains' Association in 1925, became pivotal Jewish leaders in the movement. Similarly, Father Francis P. Duffy, of New York's Church of the Holy Cross, who had served as a chaplain of the 165th Regiment during the war, became a leading Catholic proponent of goodwill activities.[8]

Then, too, in light of postwar discussions fostering international goodwill, some Protestants recognized that improved international relations were contingent on first creating domestic harmony. As Charles Evans Hughes exclaimed in his address to the Hotel Astor Goodwill Dinner in 1926, "Good-will begins at home. While it is a sentiment of common humanity, there will be no international peace unless we first provide domestic peace."[9] Such assertions reflected genuine disgust with the excesses of postwar racial and religious bigotry among some Protes-

tants. In fact, a number of renowned members of the Protestant establishment proclaimed intolerance to be un-Christian and un-American,
and they participated in the promulgation of a variety of pronouncements against American group hatred, such as the December 1920 statement against anti-Semitism by the Church Peace Union, the January
1921 "Christian Protest against Anti-Semitism," and the September
1922 Federal Council proclamation against the grave consequences of
"hooded bands" roaming America.[10] Efforts to eradicate religious intolerance and sow religious goodwill, therefore, were yoked with the quest
for a sound Americanism. Goodwill became a handmaiden of an all-
embracing, postwar Americanist ideology that imagined a spiritually
reinvigorated, socially reformed, united America free of social discord.

But which religious spirit was America to reflect? Postwar Protestant
goodwill advocates naturally reaffirmed the authority of Protestant ideals. Indeed, the crucial source for their sentiment was a resurgence of the
postwar social gospel and evangelical zeal that had its roots in the Protestant evangelical revival of the late nineteenth and early twentieth centuries. At that time, goodwill signified the feelings that individuals and
Protestant mainline churches showed each other as they moved toward
the interdenominational cooperation, unity, and ecumenism that had
revitalized missionary and social gospel endeavors. The postwar millennial euphoria recharged these benevolent feelings, igniting them with the
heady evangelical ardor of mission and service, and linking goodwill to
the sense of selfless Christian mission identified with the true American
spirit. Many Protestant goodwill utterances, therefore, exuded a tacit or
explicit religiocultural triumphalism that interpreted the American and
Allied victory as a victory for Christianity, identifying American nationalism with evangelical Christianity and American democracy with
the Protestant temper.[11] The goodwill movement, therefore, represented yet another sphere of activity in which an important segment of
the Protestant establishment attempted to exercise cultural authority in
America and fashion the nation after its own image. Understandably,
Jews and Catholics were profoundly uncertain and deeply suspicious
about its underlying motivations.

If Protestant goodwill provoked unease among Jews and Catholics,
ironically it had a similar effect, albeit for quite different reasons, on the
Protestant establishment itself. Gradually, some Protestant leaders came
to recognize the difficulty of avowing social and religious goodwill within a newly idealized America that was still seen as Protestant. Protestant
goodwill activities seemed to challenge the latter idea implicitly, for they
pointed to American unity and underlined religious commonalities
rather than differences. The Reverend John W. Herring, executive secre-

tary of the Federal Council's Committee on Goodwill between Jews and Christians and a leading proponent of interreligious activity, wrote Temple Emanu-El's Rabbi Hyman Enelow that the "church itself must take active steps to draw various creeds together in behalf of common ideals."[12] But which "common ideals" might reflect unity within America? The charter of the Reverend Edward L. Hunt's American Good Will Union suggested that all distinct religious groups could conform "to the highest American ideals and standards . . . which thrive in obedience to the Constitution of the United States: The Golden Rule." Frederick Kershner, dean of the College of Religion at Butler College in Indianapolis, asserted, "The essence of the Christian message as I understand it is the ethical gospel of righteousness, goodwill and universal brotherhood; this also, I take it, is the ethical content of Judaism." John Foster Dulles also found agreement among the religions in social ethics, thus rendering their adherents equal participants in the building of America. As he observed, whereas "the great religions differ among themselves in theological concepts, nevertheless when their views are translated into the practical problems of the day, almost complete unanimity can be found."[13] But if Protestants, Catholics, and Jews equally subscribed to an essential American creed – whether this was defined as the Golden Rule, a "gospel of righteousness," or a social ethic dealing with "practical problems," then in what sense of public culture could America be considered a Protestant country?

Protestant cultural hegemony received more systematic attack, especially from Everett R. Clinchy of the National Conference who, in the late 1920s, propounded an ideology of religious or cultural pluralism that anticipated Will Herberg by almost three decades. Notions of cultural pluralism had appeared in print earlier – Horace Kallen, Jewish philosopher, educator, and ideologue of pluralism, had tried to popularize such ideas in 1915 – but they lay dormant until the 1930s. Clinchy, however, did not cite Kallen. Influenced primarily by philosopher John Dewey, and by anthropologists Franz Boas and Clark Wissler (whose *Man and Culture* he cited repeatedly), Clinchy argued that America consisted of three equal "culture groups" – Protestant, Catholic, and Jewish – none of which was more American than the other, none of which was better than the other, and each of which had made substantive contributions to America and was destined to continue to do so. This view, affirming the equality of religions with respect to American culture, also suggested that the continued existence of all three was essential to America. Attempts by one group to win over or to convert another were pointless.[14]

This pluralist orientation emanating from Protestant goodwill leaders was obviously anathema to triumphalists within the Protestant establishment. Anti-Catholicism was still rife, while declarations upholding the religious equality of Judaism had conservative evangelicals seething. The religious goodwill movement challenged not only Protestant cultural authority but, from a conservative perspective, Protestant theological self-understanding as well. To conservative Protestants, propagating the faith was the quintessential ideal, "the heart of Christianity," as Presbyterian Rev. William M. Curry of Philadelphia stressed.[15] To the extent that goodwill seemed to dismiss this goal, it contravened Protestant ideology and represented yet another outward sign of Protestant decline rather than of spiritual advance.

The bitterness within Protestant circles over goodwill and the extent to which it fractured religious consensus is well illustrated by a brief, more focused examination of the contradictory opinions concerning goodwill to the Jews. Conrad Hoffman, executive secretary of the Christian Approach to the Jews of the International Missionary Council from 1927 to 1951, labeled goodwill to the Jews an "appeasement policy." In 1934, Hoffman's Committee on the Christian Approach to the Jews accused the goodwill movement of undermining missions to the Jews, for "the uncompromising good-will approach and its unfortunate effect is paralyzing participating Christian leaders from any positive approach to the Jews."[16] According to the Reverend J. B. Hunley of the Central Christian Church in Walla Walla, Washington, the original intent of Federal Council goodwill activities in relation to Jews had been their Christianization: "No representative of the Federal Council correctly represents the Protestant Churches of America and the world if he takes any other view. . . . When the Federal Council undertook the mission of goodwill to the Jews, it took it for granted, this fundamental faith of [propagating] Christiandom [*sic*]."[17]

Such conservative attitudes enjoyed significant support, and consistently placed Federal Council moderates on the defensive. The Federal Council's Committee on Goodwill between Jews and Christians was never widely popular within the federation itself, and its overtures to Jews were attacked when perceived to be unduly gracious. The *Jewish Telegraphic Agency* in 1929 reported sample criticisms of the Federal Council: The United Presbyterian General Assembly had shown disapproval of the Council's liberal policies, and especially of its goodwill programs, by cutting its Council appropriation in half; a Methodist author had been infuriated when his article on proselytizing was rejected by the Federal Council *Bulletin;* two denominational papers of mainline Protestant groups had attacked Federal Council cooperation with Jews; and the United Presbyterians had threatened to bolt the federation because S. Parkes Cadman, chair of the Federal Council Committee on

Goodwill, had allegedly said more positive things about Jews on his radio program than about orthodox Christians.[18]

Moderate Protestant churchmen generally responded in one of two ways to those who thought goodwill a challenge to Protestantism. Some, such as the Reverend R. A. Carter of the Colored Methodist Episcopal Church of Chicago, dissented from the overevangelical slant given to Protestant self-understanding, and emphasized that true Christianity consisted of "everyday life rather than [the preaching of] a set of dogmas."[19] Others favoring interreligious goodwill tried to reconcile twin commitments to goodwill and evangelical Christianity by eschewing proselytism on pragmatic grounds. But the tension was palpable. The Reverend Robert A. Ashworth of the Baptist Church of the Redeemer in Yonkers, New York, perhaps best illuminated this delicate balance:

> Christianity is in essence a missionizing religion. It seeks to propagate itself. I do not see how Christianity can relinquish that element without irreparable loss. On the other hand, missionary effort which results in ill-will rather than goodwill defeats its own aims. I know no gain great enough to compensate for the loss or destruction of goodwill.[20]

The poignancy of such feelings was expressed by Protestant Episcopal bishop A. S. Lloyd of the Diocese of New York. Despite his wish to have the "veil lifted" from Jewish eyes, he refrained from missionizing because "My Master is a gentleman."[21] Reinhold Niebuhr succinctly portrayed the Protestant dilemma: "Most Christian churches still hold to the position that the Jews ought to be converted, even though they are not busy doing it." Hence any representative of Protestantism, he thought, was placed in a difficult position with respect to the Jews. While Protestantism was "honestly trying to create goodwill between the two groups," Niebuhr declared, "at the same time it [was] anxious not to disavow too overtly the traditional position of the church."[22]

In noting the impact of goodwill on the Protestant establishment itself, one cannot help being struck by a profound irony. The goodwill impulse, translated into a social gospel orientation, was the centripetal force that originally helped forge Protestant unity in the Federal Council, enabling it to transcend denominational and theological differences and to exercise cultural authority in America. However, when channeled into the religious goodwill movement of the 1920s, this same impulse helped precipitate controversy and deepen the divisions within an already disquieted Protestantism, causing some Protestant leaders to dismiss the idea of Protestant cultural preeminence altogether.

Jews, Goodwill, and the Protestant Establishment

American Jews were quite conscious of the pervasive spirit of goodwill in the 1920s. As Rabbi Hyman Enelow of Temple Emanu-El commented sardonically in 1924, "There are so many committees coming into existence for the diffusion of goodwill, that I hope [Jews] won't be killed with kindness before the Messiah has arrived."[23] Jewish leaders were also quite aware that much of this goodwill effort was inspired by the Federal Council. It was to this federation, for example, that Rabbi Leo Franklin, president of the Central Conference of American Rabbis, turned in 1919–20 to solicit support both against missionary activities directed at Jews and against anti-Semitic slanders. His action set the precedent for relations over the next decade and a half between Jewish organizations and the Federal Council, and with some of its leaders outside formal institutional frameworks.

Jewish reaction to the establishment's goodwill movement was mixed: Some individuals and groups were favorably disposed toward it, others were not. Protestants found Jews especially cooperative when goodwill sentiments led to civic actions. On the local level, Jews joined Protestants in thirty of the thirty-six community chests that came into existence in the 1920s. On the national level, the Social Justice Commission of the Central Conference of American Rabbis was a most willing partner with the Federal Council in joint studies and declarations of social, economic, and moral concerns. Reform rabbis in the Central Conference such as Edward Israel, Ferdinand Isserman, and Morris Lazaron, who assumed principal leadership roles on behalf of social justice and who were therefore most attuned to civic and political issues, used the organizational structure and social conscience of the Federal Council as their model. Lazaron, for instance, even tried to establish an International Goodwill Committee in the Central Conference to function much like the Federal Council Commission on International Goodwill, and "for the expressed [*sic*] purpose of closer cooperation with the Federal Council."[24]

Adopting a Protestant agency as a model was typical of social trends in American Jewish history. Since the mid-nineteenth century, the Jewish community, and especially the German-Jewish establishment, had looked upon Protestants as a sociocultural and even religious "significant other." Jews borrowed social customs and religious forms from Protestant models: They created the Jewish Sunday school, transformed the role of the rabbi to a position devoted more to pastoral duties, reformed the nature of the temple services along Protestant lines, founded a Jewish Chautauqua society, and, in the 1920s, established Jewish university pastorates. Furthermore, the Protestant establishment almost always set the

limits for them of the permissible intrusion of the religioethical conscience into the secular world. Except in the area of philanthropy, the
Jewish socioreligious impulse, although independent and based on the
Jewish heritage, expressed itself publicly only after Protestant actions or
initiatives had aroused the Jewish ethical conscience or had given sanction to feelings already held. Hence, the Jewish establishment almost
always lagged behind Protestant social gospel thoughts and deeds. For
instance, the social policy of the Central Conference of American Rabbis
followed and, in a few cases, borrowed directly from Federal Council
initiatives. Protestant invitations to Jews to join in civic, social, political,
and educational goodwill activities in the postwar era, in effect, represented a stimulus for Jews. They could actualize their own ethical ideals
for the betterment of American and world society while building bridges
to the more influential Protestant organizations in the country.

Protestant undertakings specifically aimed at promoting religious
goodwill appealed to many in the Jewish community. Between 1924 and
1927, Jewish establishment groups applauded the creation of the Federal
Council's Committee on Goodwill between Jews and Christians. In December 1924, the Central Conference of American Rabbis was the first to
establish a parallel Committee on Goodwill, and with the Federal Council Committee on Goodwill created a Joint Commission on Goodwill
that lasted until 1929. Other organizations followed suit. The International B'nai B'rith, the Union of American Hebrew Congregations, the
New York Board of Ministers, the National Council of Jewish Women,
and the Synagogue Council of America all established goodwill committees to cooperate with the Federal Council and Central Conference Joint
Commission. In fact, as an explicit sign of their endorsement, the B'nai
B'rith, the Central Conference, and the Union of American Hebrew
Congregations contributed supporting funds to the Federal Council
Committee on Goodwill. When the National Conference of Jews and
Christians was organized in 1927, nine of the initial ten affiliating organizations were Jewish; the entire spectrum of religious orientations as well
as two of the more prominent Jewish secular agencies were repre-
sented.[25]

The attraction to these Protestant-inspired goodwill organizations by
Jewish individuals and groups is easily understood as a blend between
honest conviction as to what was best for America and what was best for
Jews. Jews perceived religious goodwill as an important medium for
defending both the American Jewish community and the integrity of
American Judaism. In the face of widespread social, economic, educational, and religious discrimination, the American Jewish minority felt

itself particularly vulnerable in the 1920s, and its leaders associated this prejudice with Protestantism and its sociocultural offshoots. Whether in the marauding prejudice of the KKK or the more culturally sophisticated quota systems of Ivy League schools, Jews saw sufficient evidence of Protestant bigotry that, to their minds, required specifically Protestant corrective action. Hence, they regarded the establishment's denunciation of group and religious prejudice as an encouraging response to their most urgent needs. Protestant labeling of anti-Semitism as un-American elevated a crucial issue of parochial Jewish concern to the level of an American problem, thus holding out the promise of wider sensitivity to the issue.

Not surprisingly, goodwill goals dovetailed nicely with B'nai B'rith's own Anti-Defamation League's fight against prejudice. In addition to supporting the Federal Council Committee on Goodwill, B'nai B'rith was the largest financial backer of the National Conference of Jews and Christians in this organization's first years of existence. The American Jewish Committee, the pillar of the American Jewish establishment in defending Jewish rights, also acknowledged the advantages of the goodwill movement for Jews. In 1932–3, through the formal auspices of the National Conference, the Committee silently funded the Drew University study of Protestant textbook references to the Jews; this subsidy foreshadowed the numerous publications on intergroup and interfaith relations that it underwrote in subsequent decades.[26] Indeed, goodwill activities became so associated with the defense of Jewish interests that in the early 1930s the American Jewish Committee advised Jews to support the National Conference individually rather than organizationally, lest that group become viewed merely as a front for Jewish interests.

The vocal defense of Jews by people within the Protestant establishment had vital derivative benefits. Goodwill established a framework for recognition of Jews that provided enormous social gratification, reinforcing their sense of sociocultural belongingness in America. In fact, throughout American Jewish history, the degree to which the Protestant religious and political elite could be encouraged to advocate national and international Jewish causes has served the Jews as an index of their acceptance as Americans. This was as true in the later decades of the twentieth century when Jews tried to curry favor with Protestants over causes such as Israel and Soviet Jewry as in the nineteenth century when American Jews galvanized leading Protestants to speak out against the Damascus blood libel of 1840. Apart from their intrinsic merit, therefore, church pronouncements against American anti-Semitism in the 1920s, or the creation in 1926 of the Christian Fund for Jewish Relief in Eastern Europe kicked off by a Yom Kippur appeal in the Cathedral of St. John the Divine, were all of inordinate symbolic significance for the sense of Jewish self-esteem they engendered.[27]

Of even greater consequence, Jews found particularly attractive the hints and sometimes explicit assertions by Protestant goodwill spokesmen of the equality of American religious groups. Therefore, Everett R. Clinchy's conception of American "culture groups," which rejected Protestantism as America's national religion and sketched an image of an America nurtured by three ennobling spiritual traditions, gained Jewish approbation. Clinchy offered Jews one solution to the dilemma of how a small minority could aspire to American religiocultural equality while maintaining its spiritual independence and cultural integrity. Jews regarded this pluralist vision of American culture as compelling since it reaffirmed their most ardent ideological self-conception; over time, they eagerly adopted it. Roger W. Straus, for example, regularly appropriated Clinchy's view, although sometimes reducing the tripartite division of Protestant, Catholic, and Jew into two categories, Christian and Jew. In the 1920s, Jews took note of other culturally pluralist developments; for example, NBC radio's allotment of equal time for Protestant, Catholic, and Jewish talks, and the advocacy by the American Association on Religion in Universities and Colleges of the academic study of all three primary religions. They were especially pleased by the Association's justification of this pursuit, namely, that Catholic, Protestant, and Jewish agencies were "responsible for the moral and religious culture of the University family."[28] Although not solely rooted in the goodwill movement, the idea of Jews, Catholics, and Protestants as equal partners in America was nevertheless given a significant boost by the movement and its spokesmen.

Jews themselves developed other intellectual orientations to justify the assertion of Jewish cultural equality, some of which had been enunciated in the nineteenth century. Pointing to Jewish contributions to the Republic, to the common biblical patrimony of Jews and other Americans, and to the total congruity of biblically rooted ideals of liberty, democracy, and human equality, some Jews contended that American values and classic Jewish socioethical teachings were equivalent, and this equivalence demonstrated the integral role of Jewish spirituality in American culture.[29] Others, like Isidor Singer, through his interreligious Amos Society, projected a universal American religion based on what he considered to be the equivalent prophetic teachings of Amos, Isaiah, and Jesus, rendering American Protestant values synonymous with Jewish ones. Rabbi Samuel Schulman, with his interpretation of the "melting pot" concept, put forth yet another approach. Schulman attributed to

America a set of spiritual values – inalienable human rights guaranteeing individual liberty and church–state separation enshrined in political institutions – that transcended both Christianity and Judaism. Hence, America was not Protestant, and Jews and Christians could "melt" together as equals under the banner of Americanism while retaining separate identities and communities.[30] The thrust of each ideological approach led to the same conclusion: American Jews, although a numerical minority, did not constitute a minority in religion or culture; they were equals.

The goodwill movement's pluralist tendencies, therefore, addressed the most ardent American Jewish expectations. Despite this, however, some Jews remained wary and stayed aloof from its activities, primarily for one reason: They suspected that Protestant religious goodwill simply masked a hidden missionary agenda aimed at their conversion. Such Jewish apprehensions were both appropriate and reasonable. Significant leaders and ideals of the religious goodwill movement were intimately connected to facets of the sustained postwar Protestant drive to Christianize America, either by evangelical dissemination of the individual gospel or by preaching the social gospel.

Following World War I, the home mission boards of Protestant churches, as well as federated mission councils, actively sought to influence new immigrants by directing them to church organizations as soon as they disembarked, preaching and proselytizing in immigrant neighborhoods, and endeavoring to attract unsuspecting newcomers to Christian-oriented settlement houses. Indeed, according to reports of the Synagogue Council of America in 1928–9, missions to the Jews were found in most American urban centers; in New York City alone twenty-eight missions to the Jews existed, over half of them affiliated with mainline Protestant churches. Moreover, periodic public proclamations by church representatives announcing the intent to proselytize Jews elicited a storm of indignation and bitterness. Such proclamations seemed to confirm that Protestant goodwill was a sham, violating, in the words of the eminent Conservative rabbi Israel Goldstein, "the indispensable condition for the promotion of goodwill," namely, the recognition of "the equality of Judaism as a religion." Rabbi Samuel Schulman previously had warned Jewish industrialist Felix Warburg and rabbinic colleagues in 1924 that "there is a subtle attempt in this movement, under the guise of establishing goodwill between Jews and Christians to lead us into an indirect consent to subtle missionary work." By 1929, the Reform Jewish movement, which had been centrally involved with the Federal Council from the outset, also cautioned that preaching goodwill to Jews was a new tactic in missionary efforts. In March 1931, the *B'nai B'rith Magazine* editorialized that John R. Mott, founder of the World's Student Christian Federation and president of the International Missionary Council, could not have it both ways: He could not assert that missionary work to Jews was a duty and simultaneously profess goodwill to Jews, hoping "for a deeper understanding and mutual helpful fellowship between Christians and Jews." To Jewish ears, that was a contradiction in terms.[31]

Antagonism to Protestant missions transcended Jewish denominational lines. Spokesmen for the Orthodox, Reform, and Conservative branches of Judaism, as well as for secular Jewish agencies, lashed out against them. These individuals expressed their resentment in the press, in direct confrontations between rabbis and missionaries, and even in interreligious seminars, such as the St. Louis Good Will Seminar held May 14–15, 1928. No issue agitated Jews more than proselytizing drives. Missionaries implicitly attacked the integrity of American Jews and Judaism, which dredged up tragic historical associations with forced Jewish conversions. In addition, these contemporary approaches to the Jews underscored such painful internal Jewish realities as religious laxity, indifference, and defection; missionaries considerably embarrassed the Jewish community.

Although aggressive missionizing was never a serious threat in terms of numbers converted, to Jews the hostile atmosphere created was one more undesirable outcome of the Protestant triumphalism experienced in the 1920s. Missionary actions reflected Protestant buoyancy and strength, not decline. Jews of the 1920s would not have agreed with later scholarship, based on Protestant sources and introspection, that portrays Protestantism as spiritually depressed at this time. From the Jewish perspective, Protestants exercised cultural power and leverage in society, and the missionaries were important exemplars of this control.

The blatant Protestant cultural triumphalism that alarmed Jews was evident in a 1919 pronouncement of the Bureau of Christian Americanization of the Protestant Episcopal Church. Since, according to a *New York Times* report, only 25 percent of American Jews were affiliated with synagogues, the Bureau took it upon itself as a patriotic duty to bring religion to the "unchurched." What rankled Leo Franklin, president of the Central Conference of American Rabbis, was not so much the fact of missionizing per se – if foolish Jews wished to convert, let them, or so he said – but the implicit premise that Jews really needed Christianity and to be "churched" to become good Americans. Franklin arranged a meeting between representatives of the Central Conference and the Episcopal Board in October 1919 that ostensibly resolved the contentious issue. The Episcopalians denied equating Americanization with Christianization and promised not to say anything in the future that might lead to that impression. The Federal Council issued a similar demurrer in a meeting with Central Conference representatives in March 1920.[32] Nevertheless, much to Jewish dismay, establishment figures such as Bishop William T. Manning continued to reaffirm the legitimacy of converting Jews spiritually adrift, after the Jewish community had had a fair chance with them, for the sake of America as well as for their personal salvation. Many in the Protestant establishment rejected the unequivocal Jewish supposition that Protestants should never approach Jews. Samuel M. Cavert, Federal Council executive secretary and a religious moderate, probably best defined the meaning of missions to many mainline Christians as merely the act of informing people of "a point of view . . . which will add to the rightness of their lives." If Jews could only understand that, he remarked, "they might not be quite so troubled about our missionary emphasis."[33] But Jews for the most part found the distinction between the act of informing and the act of proselytizing problematic and were disinclined to expose themselves to Protestant religious self-affirmations.

Within this social climate, the discomfort of some Jews with Protestant exclamations of goodwill is understandable. The establishment sent out inconsistent signals, so that Jews were not sure whether the motivation for goodwill groups was the American ideal of constructing a prejudice-free society or the Christian ideal of seeking converts. Jewish suspicions were strengthened by the fact that the one Protestant most responsible for so much of the organized religious goodwill movement, former general secretary of the Home Missions Council, Northern Baptist Rev. Alfred Williams Anthony, came from a decided missionary background and had declared at a 1922 meeting with some Central Conference rabbis that he hoped "to help Jews find their messiah." Although Anthony immediately regretted his remark and refrained from any similar comments as he guided the creation of both the Federal Council Committee on Goodwill and the National Conference of Jews and Christians, Rabbi Samuel Schulman, for one, never forgot his slip, and he tried to warn his colleagues about Anthony. Indeed, Anthony subsequently became embroiled in a public controversy in June 1929 with Louis Marshall, president of Temple Emanu-El and of the American Jewish Committee, and arguably the preeminent member of the Jewish establishment, over the Protestant right to try to win Jewish converts. Defending this right, Anthony undermined his credibility in Jewish eyes, again calling into question the entire Protestant goodwill movement.[34]

Jewish reservations about Protestant goodwill did not center solely on Anthony. Jewish leaders knew that the Federal Council was constitutionally dedicated to evangelism and that it enjoyed a cooperative relationship with foreign mission boards and the Home Missions Council. In fact, a number of members of the Federal Council Committee on Goodwill, as well as of the National Conference board, had strong missionary backgrounds, including Frank Mason North, Stanley White, Sidney L. Gulick, Luther Wilson, and Charles E. Burton. It is no wonder, therefore, that the Synagogue Council of America in 1929 expressed dismay with the Protestant goodwill movement "in view of the sanction which the proselytizing program receives at the hands of the leaders of that movement."[35] Such presidents of the Federal Council as S. Parkes Cadman and Francis J. McConnell periodically felt constrained to deny Federal Council missionary aspirations toward the Jews. Everett R. Clinchy himself also had to defend the National Conference against the frequent charge of missionizing, proclaiming religious goodwill an antidote to proselytism rather than its cause.

To be sure, most Jews in the 1920s were not sensitive to the nuances of Protestant social and theological rifts. Nor could they have realistically assessed whether Protestant agencies like the Federal Council were strong or weak. As non-Christian outsiders, they tended to see a single Protestant stream from which flowed energetic currents dedicated to their conversion. This perception brought genuinely moderate Protestants under a general cloud of suspicion. On the other hand, Rush Rhees, president of the University of Rochester, was very much aware of inner Protestant religious debates and acknowledged that the "liberal and reactionary" divisions in the churches caused insuperable difficulties in the promotion of goodwill. He therefore suggested that "quiet cultivation of acquaintances and responsibilities between Jews and Christians would be far more beneficial than any official activities for the same end."[36] Many Jews agreed, but for different reasons. Their apprehension about goodwill's missionary goals led some to disassociate themselves completely from goodwill and led others, like Rhees, to advocate goodwill restricted to common civic endeavors. Still others, such as Louis Marshall and Joseph Proskauer, future president of the American Jewish Committee, recommended that Jews and Christians live up to their own highest ideals in order to actualize goodwill. "Let the Jews become better Jews and the Christians better Christians," Marshall wrote Anthony, "and this will be a happier world. Then genuine goodwill would be ushered into existence automatically without meetings or conferences or discussions."[37]

The ambivalent perceptions Jews had of the Protestant goodwill movement in the 1920s were typical of how Jews viewed the Protestant establishment from the nineteenth century through the first five decades of the twentieth century. Jews appreciated and took advantage of many of the sociocultural blandishments offered by Protestant society. They fervently sought acceptance and approval from the Protestant majority. Indeed, Jewish perception of the establishment depended heavily on how Jews thought the Protestant elite perceived them. Therefore, success or failure in gaining Protestant support for Jewish causes or in forging social networks for Protestant–Jewish interaction in large measure dictated their sense of fraternity or alienation from the Protestant establishment. This explains the appeal of the goodwill movement in the 1920s, with the subsequent desire of Jewish organizations and denominations, except the Orthodox, for continued "interfaith" or intergroup activities. This also explains the bitter Jewish despair and keen disappointment when the Protestant establishment responded inadequately to paramount Jewish issues such as the Holocaust and the precarious plight of Israel just prior to the 1967 Six-Day War.

Jews also recognized the Protestant world to be a source of danger to group survival if, as in the late nineteenth century, Judaism became so closely identified with Unitarianism as to lose its raison d'être,[38] or if, as in the early decades of the twentieth century, Protestant Christianity became so enmeshed with the definition of American culture as to relegate Jews to permanent outsider status. Jews questioned Protestant goodwill in the 1920s because they were unclear whether they were welcomed as insiders or regarded as outsiders who had to be refashioned religiously. They resisted any moves on the part of the Protestant establishment to identify America as Christian or to deny Judaism equal cultural and religious status in American life. This explains the continuing Jewish unease with Christmas, the only national legal holiday rooted in a specific religious tradition, and the cultural atmosphere it sparks every December. It also explains later Jewish vigilance against the growing appeal of the New Right and contemporary evangelical Protestant movements, which not only preached a religious triumphalism, but also aspired to cultural and political authority in America. Jews were less interested in the relationship of this latest evangelical revival to the Protestant establishment, than in gauging the threat that the surge of Protestantism, establishment or not, posed to Jewish security in America.

To be sure, Protestant–Jewish relations have improved significantly since the 1960s. Jews found the establishment to be less hostile, less threatening, and more open. They took heart from the reduction of anti-Semitism, Protestant reevaluation of anti-Judaic references in sacred texts, newly invigorated interfaith dialogues, and the beginnings of Protestant introspection over Christian complicity in the Holocaust. Despite these positive interreligious developments, however, Jews in more recent decades have confronted the same dilemma as did the Jews of the 1920s, wondering whether to welcome the evangelical preaching of goodwill that also denounced anti-Semitism. During the 1970s, the Reverend Jerry Falwell and members of his Moral Majority became leading Protestant proponents of the State of Israel; yet a debate within the American Jewish establishment arose over whether to encourage this support. The suspicion of ultimate evangelical goals was pitted against pragmatic considerations arguing for the acceptance of help in defending Jews regardless of the quarters from which such aid might come. The issue that had marred the Jewish consensus over Protestant goodwill in the 1920s continued to divide American Jews into the 1980s.

Catholics, Goodwill, and the Protestant Establishment

Like American Jews, Catholics were keenly aware of the prevailing spirit of Protestant goodwill. Even more than the Jews, they understood its dramatic ecumenical implications as they witnessed three Protestant-initiated international Christian congresses within less than twenty years: the World Missionary Conference (Edinburgh, 1910), the Universal Christian Conference on Life and Work (Stockholm, 1925), and the World Conference on Faith and Order (Lausanne, 1927). Indeed, the encyclical of Pope Pius XI, *Mortalium animus* (January 6, 1928) expressly forbidding Catholic participation with Protestants in Christian congresses, nonetheless acknowledged in its opening paragraph the contemporary spirit of goodwill compelling moves toward Christian fraternity:

> The will to strengthen and to diffuse for the common good of human society that brotherhood in which we are all closely united by the bonds of a common nature and origin has never perhaps so taken hold of men's minds as in our time.[39]

American Catholics participated in various civic and religious activities involving Protestants and Jews. A few Catholics sat on the board of the Church Peace Union; the National Catholic War Council joined with the Jewish Welfare Board and the Federal Council in Secretary of War Newton D. Baker's chaplaincy program as well as in other activities on behalf of American servicemen. Catholics joined Protestants and Jews in forming the American Committee on the Rights of Religious Minorities, which, on December 24, 1920, issued the first trifaith appeal in American history against "racial prejudice and religious fanaticism." John A. Ryan, director of the Social Action Department of the National Catholic Welfare Conference, and the most influential and sophisticated Catholic advocate of American socioeconomic reform, led Catholics to work with the Federal Council in 1921 against the Open Shop Movement, and in 1923 against the twelve-hour shift in the steel industry. In 1929, along

"Barnstormers" for interreligious understanding, 1933. *Left to right:* Father John E. Ross, the Rev. Everett R. Clinchy, Rabbi Morris Lazaron. From *National Conference of Jews and Christians Bulletin* (December 1933):1. Courtesy of the National Conference of Christians and Jews.

with the Federal Council and the Central Conference of American Rabbis, the National Catholic Welfare Conference cosponsored a Washington Conference on Permanent Preventatives of Unemployment. Catholics joined twenty-seven of the thirty-six community chests founded in the 1920s, and in 1926 Victor J. Dowling, a prominent Catholic jurist, served as coconvener with the Reverend S. Parkes Cadman, of the Christian Fund for Jewish Relief in Eastern Europe.

Catholics sometimes joined interreligious functions, even initiating them on occasion. In 1929, the Calvert Round Table organized a Harvard seminar that involved over five hundred Protestants, Catholics, and Jews discussing prejudice and mutual group perceptions.[40] Judge Dowling, Martin Conboy, and Father Francis P. Duffy represented Catholics on Rabbi Isaac Landman's nine-member Permanent Commission on Better Understanding between Christians and Jews in America. The eminent Catholic historian Carlton J. H. Hayes joined Roger W. Straus and Newton D. Baker as cochairman of the National Conference of Jews and Christians in 1929, and a number of Catholics sat on its board and participated in its various goodwill seminars around the country. Father J. Elliot Ross, who held a Ph.D. from Catholic University and a D.D. from the Papal University in Rome, was intimately involved in religious goodwill. A professor of moral theology, a university chaplain at major universities, and at one time associate director of the School of Religion at the University of Iowa, Ross in 1933 barnstormed the country with the Reverend Everett R. Clinchy and Rabbi Morris Lazaron to help dispel religious prejudice.

Despite this interreligious collaboration, Catholic participation consistently was disproportionately smaller than that of either the Jews or the Protestants, who regularly bemoaned Catholic disinclination to become more involved. Catholics, for example, were the last to join the National Conference of Jews and Christians, and were never enthusiastic activists in the organization. Even with respect to social goodwill efforts, ostensibly less threatening than those of religious goodwill, the National Catholic Welfare Conference joined the Federal Council less frequently than did the Central Conference of American Rabbis. Indeed, John A. Ryan found it necessary to admonish Catholics who grappled with urban and immigrant resettlement issues to become more active in nonpartisan civic affairs, and to work on issues other than those specifically affecting Catholics.

Catholic ambivalence to Protestant goodwill initiatives, particularly religious goodwill, stemmed from complex and interlocking historical factors. Official Catholic Church involvement with Protestants had proved to be a source of tension throughout American Catholic history for cultural as well as doctrinal reasons. The issue of fraternization with Protestants had intensified the nineteenth-century split between Catholic liberals and conservatives over Americanization of the Catholic Church, a schism that erupted with particular vehemence in the Church's Americanist controversy at the close of the century. Interaction with Protestants had been welcomed by liberals such as Bishop John Keane, first rector of Catholic University of Washington, D.C., who, to the utter dismay of conservative Bishop Bernard McQuaid of Rochester, had spoken at the Harvard chapel in 1890. Conservatives were also outraged when Archbishop John J. Kain welcomed the Salvation Army to St. Louis, or when Bishop Lawrence Scanlan of Salt Lake City appeared in public ceremonies with Mormons, and when James Cardinal Gibbons, Archbishop John Ireland, and Bishop Keane participated in the World's Parliament of Religions in 1893. This last action induced the Vatican, displeased with liberal tendencies within the American Church, to formulate an interreligious approach that restricted fraternization with non-Catholics. The 1895 encyclical of Pope Leo XIII, asserting that "unless forced by necessity to do otherwise, Catholics ought to prefer to associate with Catholics," clearly suggested that Catholics should limit their interaction with non-Catholics, interfaith congresses included. But where Catholics necessarily found themselves in discourse with "dissenters from us in matters of Christian faith," the ultimate goal of winning them over to Catholicism must be uppermost in their minds.[41]

The legacy of these papal attitudes at the close of the nineteenth century dampened Catholic interreligious interaction in the twentieth. Pius XI's encyclical promulgated in January 1928, six months after the Lausanne Conference on Faith and Order, unequivocally spelled out doctrinal opposition to interfaith discussions with Protestants. The encyclical asserted that movements, conferences, meetings, and congresses with peoples of different religions might lead one to the totally erroneous conclusion that all religious are equal. "Pan-Christian" bodies that sought to promote Christian unity, moreover, presupposed a lack of church unity, conceding separate status to Christian entities that Catholics proposed to bring back into the fold. Such "ecumenism" utterly contradicted the self-understanding of a Catholicism that saw itself as one unified, indivisible church representing Christ's Mystical Body on earth. There was no need to unite or discuss Christianity with anyone else, the encyclical averred; the only authentic church, the Catholic, had always been united. Others had just broken away from it.

This triumphalist papal decree had a profound impact on American Catholic participation in interreligious goodwill. Catholic reactions to Protestant outreach in the wake of the encyclical reflected and further reinforced both the liberal and the traditionalist impulses within the Church. To be sure, some Catholics were not guided by papal directives on this issue, and simply followed their own inclinations. But for those mindful of the Vatican's religious authority, laymen and clergy alike, interpreting the pope's words became crucial for working out acceptable parameters for Catholic–Protestant interaction.

Commonweal editor Michael Williams's artful response to the early versions of the encyclical strikingly reveals an Americanist liberal posture that insisted on the value of Catholic–Protestant cooperation. Williams concluded that although the pontiff had warned of the dangers of Pan-Christianity, he did not "seek to restrain Catholics from participation with others not of the Faith in works of benevolence and charity not compromising their relationship to the See of Peter." More than most Catholic writers, this liberal layman applauded Protestants for their positive contributions to human virtue and human welfare. Sensing a commonality in Protestant and Catholic Christian morality, Williams frequently advocated Catholic–Protestant social cooperation, believing that "the attainment of common objectives through concordant effort is desirable," since "every genuine manifestation of Christian morals is commendable." Catholics would "continue to feel that Catholics and

Protestants can do ever so much in common," Williams wrote in February 1928, "in that domain of civilization which is lower, indeed, than the highland of faith, but nevertheless dear and indispensable to us all."[42]

Williams's predisposition to Catholic–Protestant cooperation obviously influenced his exegesis, but it is not at all clear that his interpretation can withstand critical scrutiny; for although primarily concerned with interreligious interaction on religious matters, the encyclical seemed en passant to frown upon Catholic–Protestant cooperation in civic goodwill and charitable endeavors as well. The encyclical of 1928 affirmed that although Jesus had preached love for all, he had forbidden "relations with those who do not profess [his] entire and uncorrupted teachings," and since "charity is found in whole and sincere faith, the disciples of Christ must be united by the bond of unity in faith and by it as the chief bond."[43]

Yet another significant example of creative Catholic exegesis of papal attitudes, justifying in this instance Catholic–Protestant religious interaction, is found in a very revealing 1927 essay by J. Elliot Ross. Father Ross described an experimental interreligious discussion group in Fairfield, Connecticut, whose goal was to foster better understanding between Protestants and Catholics. The liberal Ross appeared to have found overwhelming papal support for this type of interreligious exchange, as excerpts from a letter of Pius XI to Italian university students in the spring of 1927 would indicate:

> It is necessary to know and to love one another . . . because the failure of reunion work is often due . . . to the lack of mutual acquaintance between the two sides. . . . Errors, misunderstandings, which persist and are repeated against the Catholic Church . . . seem incredible. But Catholics also sometimes lack a just appreciation of their brethren . . . because they lack acquaintance with these groups.[44]

Acknowledging that the pope's letter referred exclusively to Catholic relations with Eastern Orthodox churches, whose breach from the Roman Church was neither as historically deep nor as theologically profound as was the gulf separating Protestantism from Roman Catholicism, Ross nevertheless insisted that the papal comments were equally applicable to the American scene. American Catholics still could and ought to interact with Protestants to promote better understanding and religious goodwill because, Ross claimed, the pope's decree had prohibited only interreligious discussions on Christian unity, not interreligious activities dedicated to the civic goal of the elimination of religious prejudice.

Ross's ingenious exegesis of this papal text, although casuistry to conservative Catholics, exemplified a much broader social phenomenon. He and like-minded Catholics tended to view religious goodwill functions not as *religious* but as *civic* activities in which different Americans joined to become better acquainted for the common good. Thus, as the official Catholic representative to the National Conference of Jews and Christians goodwill seminar held at Columbia University, January 30–1, 1929, Ross justified Catholic participation because the seminar was "sociological rather than theological," having nothing in common with other theological conferences of the 1920s, "else the ecclesiastical authorities would hardly have approved Catholic participation."[45] Similarly, Carlton J. H. Hayes and other Catholics upheld the propriety of their involvement in the National Conference because it was a civic rather than a religious organization, which gloried in religious diversity rather than promoting fanciful religious unity. Because Jews had been incorporated from its inception, this trifaith organization did not pair off Catholics with Protestants. Hence, Hayes thought, the National Conference could not be misconstrued as seeking a Christian unity in which Catholics would compromise their claim to sole and complete religious truth.

Conservative American Catholics, on the other hand, were alarmed at what they perceived to be the dangerous precedents for Catholic–Protestant interaction. The mutual declaration of principles by the goodwill committees of the Federal Council and the Central Conference of American Rabbis in December 1924 elicited the comment from the Jesuit weekly *America* that "owing to the difficulties regarding joint statements that might touch directly upon religious questions . . . Catholics could evidently not participate."[46] The 1928 encyclical merely reinforced this view. Conservative Catholics also feared that, in addition to compromising Catholic triumphalist claims as articulated in the encyclical, interreligious gatherings might undermine the faith of Catholic participants. As late as 1949, the *American Ecclesiastical Review* replied to a question about the legitimacy of Catholic affiliation with the National Conference of Christians and Jews that "participation on the part of Catholics in this organization is likely to endanger their faith gravely by leading them to think that religious differences are of little account."[47] Interreligious goodwill was dangerous because Catholics might extend the principle of personal tolerance, which the Church upheld, to the principle of doctrinal tolerance, which it did not. This type of conservative Catholic assessment led two bishops to refuse Father Ross permission to speak from the same National Conference platform with the Reverend Mr. Clinchy and Rabbi Lazaron during their revolutionary cross-country tour in 1933. It also explains why, as late as 1955, 22 percent of American

a

Cabinet Meeting—If Al Were President

b

c
Catholics as insiders and outsiders. *a:* Cardinal Gibbons, reviewing a
parade with President Taft and others, Washington, D.C., 1909. *b:* "If
Al were President." A possible Al Smith presidency as depicted in an
anti-Catholic publication (the *Fellowship Forum*) in 1928. Religious
News Service photo. *c:* Bishop Oxnam (*seated, center*) and other Protestant leaders in 1946 preparing for a meeting with President Truman to
protest continued U.S. representation at the Vatican. Religious News
Service photo.

Catholic dioceses "absolutely forbade Catholic participation" in the National Conference of Christians and Jews.[48]

   Official Church policy was only one factor impinging on Catholic–
Protestant goodwill. Protestant and Protestant establishment attitudes
constituted the other side of the coin. Catholics in the 1920s felt the full
weight of Protestant cultural dominance, which, as so often had been the
case in the nineteenth century, they experienced either in the form of
outright anti-Catholic bigotry or cultural antipathy to Catholic values.
The scope of Protestant–Catholic goodwill endeavors was limited by
Protestant concerns over Catholic strength and by internecine Christian
discord endemic in American society since the 1830s. Many Protestants
therefore were simply not eager to make overtures to Catholics. The

Federal Council, for example, did not establish a committee on goodwill between Catholics and Protestants comparable to its Committee on Goodwill between Jews and Christians. Furthermore, much Protestant goodwill to Jews was accompanied by some kind of *mea culpa* for past Christian wrongs. Few apologies were forthcoming in relation to Catholics, whom many Protestants regarded as primarily responsible for most of the religious intolerance of the past. Catholics, on the other hand, found little incentive to become involved in Protestant goodwill in the midst of the Protestant-inspired anti-Catholic social climate of the 1920s. Like the Jews, Catholics' perception of Protestants depended heavily on their sense of how the Protestant establishment perceived them.

Catholics, moreover, assumed the violent anti-Catholic agitation of the 1920s to be representative of American Protestantism. Although not a product of the establishment, the KKK often spoke in the name of all American Protestants, and Catholics were dismayed at the absence of forthright establishment condemnation of this movement. Catholics also were incensed by the Protestant canard charging unwarranted intrusion into American politics, typified by the self-righteous remark made by Henry Sloane Coffin, president-elect of Union Theological Seminary, that Presbyterians had no reason to meddle in politics: "That is what the Roman Catholic Church does. We Protestants object to this." During the heated 1928 presidential campaign, Catholics were infuriated by the crescendo of scare tactics predicting papal rule if Al Smith won and charging inadequate Catholic political loyalty. They not only found Protestant responses to the unseemly attacks tepid, but saw liberals within the Protestant establishment jumping on the anti-Catholic bandwagon. For example, a few weeks before the election, the *Christian Century* referred to the Catholic world as "an alien culture, with a medieval Latin mentality, undemocratic hierarchy and foreign potentate."[49]

Other manifestations of Protestantism's incontrovertible cultural hegemony compounded Catholic disaffection from American culture. Prohibition, to Catholics, institutionalized the moral outlook of a few Protestant mainline denominations. State support for public schools, which Catholics regarded as really Protestant institutions (Bishop McQuaid had accused them of teaching "crypto-Protestantism"), seemed unfair when Catholic schools were denied funding. Frontal assaults in various school controversies against the very legitimacy of parochial schools appeared to Catholics to be flagrant aggression against Catholic religion and culture, as well as a gross violation of church–state separation. Catholics were also quite displeased with the general cultural laxity in moral and family relations stemming, in their view, from the American Protestant elite's immoral social policies. Responding to a 1931 report that the Federal Council, after much study, had approved contraceptives as a valid and moral means of family planning, *America* lampooned the moral myopia of American Protestantism: "A religion that goes into a frenzy against a harmless glass of beer but smiles complacently on divorce that destroys the home and on acts leading to sexual promiscuity – this is not the religion of Jesus."[50] Finally, Catholics felt completely frustrated and angry over their inability to arouse American popular and governmental opinion to intervene in Mexico on behalf of its repressed Catholic Church and oppressed Catholic citizenry. The foreign policy assessment of an essentially Protestant American governmental leadership, as well as Protestant religious establishment, differed from that of the American Catholic Church. Catholics interpreted lack of establishment sympathy on this issue as but another instance of insensitivity to legitimate Catholic needs and a willingness to condone anti-Catholicism.[51]

Catholic alienation from American Protestant culture in the 1920s did not alienate them from America. On the contrary, nourished by prolific institutional and demographic growth, and an awareness of inner Protestant malaise, Catholics evinced a self-confidence and even smugness about the future of American Catholicism. Less allied to nineteenth-century optimism than Protestants, they were less affected by its postwar demise. In contrast to the intellectual and religious skepticism and the moral uncertainty plaguing Protestants, which Catholics understood far better than did Jews, the Catholic church offered its adherents religious continuity and stability, theological certainty, and moral balance. As Michael Williams remarked, "All things, save . . . one thing, the Catholic Church, are in flux."[52]

Catholic lay and clerical spokesmen could not dismiss the still pervasive and obviously powerful Protestant ambience that had made them outsiders to American culture. But in the course of the 1920s, they created an American national myth that wove Americanism and Catholicism together culturally, placing Catholics at the center rather than at the margins of the American story. The elements of cultural integration had been enunciated by nineteenth-century proponents of Catholic Americanization such as Isaac L. Hecker, Orestes Brownson, James Gibbons, and John Ireland. In their writings, as well as in others of that century, Catholic authors in the 1920s often found useful precedents to substantiate their claim of a fruitful, centuries-old, Catholic–American symbiosis. Individual Catholic contributions to the history of America were duly noted: the discoveries of Columbus, the noble missionary work of Spanish friars and French Jesuits among the Indians, the participation of two Catholics in the framing of the Constitution, and the religious toleration first exhibited by Catholic Maryland. More significantly, contemporary Catholic writers pointed to the congruity of American and Catholic ideals in much the same way as Jewish writers found convergence between American and Jewish ideals. Democracy, church–state separation, and American governance, they argued, were rooted in Catholic political theory that recognized the division between spiritual and temporal domains so characteristic of America. Even the Declaration of Independence was indebted to medieval Catholic thought. In fact, Carlton J. H. Hayes maintained that America was "the daughter of the Catholic Church," and that if one studied any institution or ideal commonly regarded as an aspect of true Americanism, one would necessarily conclude that "its embryo and antetype are to be found in Catholic theory and practice."[53]

Little was fundamentally new in the overall content of these claims, but the documentation was new. Protestant success in passing prohibition ultimately was a failure, some Catholics asserted, because this act subverted the cornerstone of American culture, the separation of church and state. Protestants therefore had become poor Americans because of their disloyalty to the country's most precious political legacy. The reasons for this betrayal of American ideals and for Protestantism's current state of religious disarray were one and the same: its religious break from the Catholic Church and consequent cultural break from the Catholic vision of America.[54] This kind of Catholic Americanist rhetoric, while clearly not convincing to Protestants, was an apologetic of great utility in the Catholic world, suggesting that Catholics were not merely cultural equals in America but, in fact, superior. Ironically, notwithstanding the attacks of anti-Americanism to which they were subjected, Catholic thinkers during the 1920s saw themselves as the saviors of American ideals. This supremacist attitude sharply distinguished Catholic apologetics from that of the Jews with respect to Protestant society. Jews in this decade, and indeed throughout the first half of the twentieth century, had sought only cultural equality in Protestant America. In contrast, the conjunction of Catholic tradition with American ideals and polity was visionary, depicting a powerful Catholic impact on American culture in the past and projecting Catholic aspirations to cultural authority in the future.

This triumphalist formulation was characteristic of some of the leading Catholics who engaged in interreligious goodwill, such as Carlton J. H. Hayes, Michael Williams, John A. Ryan, and George Shuster, no doubt fortifying them in discussions with non-Catholics. To be sure, the more liberally inclined Catholics saw hopeful signs on the American horizon; they met Protestants who genuinely welcomed fraternity with Catholics in building American society. As J. Elliot Ross noted after the 1929 National Conference goodwill seminar at Columbia University:

> In spite of the very evident manifestation of bigotry, there is abroad in this country an earnest and rather widespread desire to understand Catholics. I suppose that bigotry is more pictur-esque, and has a greater news value, but I am confident that the determination to be fair is much more important. . . . [The] heart of the American people is fundamentally sound, and we have traveled a long distance from the Know-nothing days.[55]

Had not some Catholics perceived new openness amid the prejudice of the 1920s, Catholic participation in non-Catholic goodwill ventures would obviously have been stillborn. But, as Hayes asserted, the sense of wellness and strength within Catholic ranks suggested that Catholics need not feel defensive as Americans, nor, as Ross remarked, was there any need for timidly holding back in "sullen isolation." "The Catholic Church has nothing to fear from getting out in the open," Ross declared. "Let us court investigation. Let us meet inquirers half-way. A truly Catholic and a truly American spirit has no room for an Achilles sulking in his tent."[56] Confident in their Catholicism and Americanism, as well as in their ability to respond to nativist attacks, some Catholics joined non-Catholics willing to work with them for the common good.

The tentativeness of Catholic responses to Protestant goodwill during this period illustrates the broader phenomenon of Catholic ambivalence to the Protestant establishment as a whole from the nineteenth century through much of the twentieth. Many factors contributing to this am-bivalence remained in place over the decades subsequent to the immedi-ate postwar era. Vatican disassociation from non-Catholic ecumenical movements led the Church to abstain from involvement in the founding of the World Council of Churches in the 1940s.[57] American Protestant anti-Catholicism resurfaced, from time to time, as tensions over specific issues or incidents flared up: American Catholic support for Franco in Spain; the appointment of Myron Taylor as presidential envoy to the Vatican in 1939; the establishment in the 1940s of Protestant and Other Americans United for the Separation of Church and State; and the con-tinued Catholic quest for state funding of parochial schools. Even Carl-ton J. H. Hayes's bid to become president of the American Historical Association in 1944 inspired a backlash because of his Catholicism, al-though he did eventually win the position.

Only by the close of the 1950s did the emerging American pluralist climate, stimulated to no small degree by the diminution of Protestant strength and cultural authority, lead to significant improvements in Protestant–Catholic interaction. These changes were both symbolized and inspired, first, by the initiatives of the engaging Pope John XXIII, whose spirit guided Vatican II's sanctioning of religious dialogues with non-Catholics, and second, by the presidency of John F. Kennedy, which demonstrated that Catholics could work successfully with the political and religious establishment. The public baiting of Catholics sharply declined. In contrast to the 1920s, Catholic–Protestant relations, entering the 1960s, were more positive and hopeful than at any previous time in this century.

Conclusion

Jewish and Catholic reactions to the Protestant goodwill movement were directly influenced by their respective historic relations to Protestantism, by the collective memory of each group's experience in America, and by each group's sense of place in the 1920s. Jewish and Catholic perceptions of Protestant cultural hegemony helped shape their response to Protestant goodwill; but, conversely, the nature of their participation in the movement and specific reservations reveal much about their relationship to the Protestant establishment in general.

As outsiders to the Protestant establishment, Jews and Catholics shared obvious similarities in their involvement in Protestant goodwill. Both religious communities featured prominent proponents and opponents of the goodwill movement. The proponents in each group sought to foster better understanding, as well as to shed the status of cultural outsider in a meliorated, religiously pluralistic American civic society. The differences between Jews and Catholics with respect to Protestant goodwill, however, were more striking than the similarities. As non-Christians, Jews were spared the animus of the triumphal intra-Christian theological rivalry that dated back centuries; on the other hand, although Catholics were not immune to Protestant missionizing, Jews were far more concerned about active Protestant proselytizing. Moreover, in the 1920s Jewish understanding of their place in America differed fundamentally from that of Catholics and was rooted in a collective memory, of almost mythic proportions, of religious liberty and social equality in the New World. American Jews recalled how receptive the country had been to them, how utterly different America had been, in this respect, from the European countries they had fled. The hostile social forces of the 1920s shook their self-confidence dramatically as they felt buffeted by external dangers as well as internal Jewish sociocultural cleavages. Hence, Jews looked at the new Protestant overtures of goodwill from a sense of weakness and hope, rather than strength and communal security. Goodwill held out the promise of an enlarged field of Jewish defense, an enhanced social recognition, and a greater degree of cultural equality. Jewish Americanist ideologies, therefore, whatever their precise outlines, preached cultural equality, not supremacy. To some the goodwill movement appeared to be a good framework to attain these goals. Twentieth-century Jews, unlike some of their nineteenth-century forebears, envisioned neither cultural nor religious triumph; the Chosen People idea, at the core of Jewish spiritual identity, had no supremacist overtones for the future of American culture. With respect to the Protestant establishment, Jews did not seek to displace Protestant influence; they just wanted equal room on the common public bench.

In contrast, for the vastly larger body of American Catholics, the anti-Catholic prejudice of the 1920s triggered a different national memory of American history. They recalled cycles, not mere isolated incidents, of anti-Catholic bigotry. While America had afforded opportunities for Catholic self-expression and development, at times it had seemed to be but the newest locale for resuming centuries-old Catholic–Protestant disputes. Unlike the Jews, however, Catholics in the 1920s, animated by surging growth and Protestant spiritual–cultural upheaval, responded to Protestant aspirations for continued cultural authority with their own vision of cultural superiority. Catholics involved in goodwill sincerely worked for an America that would embrace all three religious groups as equals. But their activities were more frequently undergirded by the hope, or even expectation, of eventual Catholic cultural and religious triumph in America.

If Jews and Catholics felt ambivalence toward the Protestant establishment, they also had mixed feelings about each other. As outsiders, they sometimes found themselves allied in the face of perceived common dangers from Protestant initiatives. Both Jews and Catholics realized that if Protestant culture persisted in rendering one group an outsider, the other's status was equally uncertain. The alliance was therefore mutually advantageous. Thus, Belle Moskowitz, community and political activist and confidante of Governor Al Smith, together with Joseph Proskauer and Father Francis P. Duffy, helped write Smith's response to Charles C. Marshall's *Atlantic Monthly* attack against Catholic political views and allegiances. In 1925, when the state of Oregon attempted legally to mandate elementary public school attendance, in effect prohibiting Catholic schools, the American Jewish Committee filed a brief with the United States Supreme Court on behalf of Catholic parochial school rights. For their part, Catholics spoke out against anti-Semitism at home and abroad, signing petitions against its various manifestations.

The alliance between the groups, however, was fraught with suspicion and distrust that was voiced privately as well as publicly even among their most ardent liberal spokesmen. Felix Adler, religious and social progressive, Jewish founder of the Ethical Culture Movement, was apprehensive about the rise of Catholicism in the 1920s. Rabbi Morris Lazaron, despite his undeniable commitment to interreligious goodwill and to the National Conference, in private letters expressed his disdain for Catholic political and religious positions. He feared "papists and Romanists" as much as Protestants did, and much preferred an alliance of Jews with Protestants rather than have the Jews associated with Catholics and considered just another non-Protestant group.

Catholics, in turn, expressed uncharitable views of Jews in both conservative and liberal Catholic publications. Michael Williams, for example, referred to them as "unwholesome materialists." Some Catholics, moreover, were profoundly dismayed that Jews (except for the Orthodox) sided with Protestants on almost every social value and political issue from which Catholics strenuously dissented: prohibition, the nonsectarian utility of public schools, the teaching of religion primarily at home and not in the school, the ease of divorce, the right to abortion and birth control, and American foreign policy toward Mexico. Indeed, the lack of Jewish support for Catholic positions on Mexico, and in the 1930s on Spain evoked bitterness from John A. Ryan, who lamented his perception of the asymmetry between Catholic concern for German Jews suffering under the Nazis and the apparent lack of Jewish concern for the sorry plight of Catholics in Mexico and Spain. Catholics were both jealous and resentful of the Jews' ability to transform anti-Semitism abroad into a concern of the American Protestant establishment while parallel efforts to place anti-Catholicism on the American public agenda fell on deaf ears. Hence, Jewish complaints over Father Coughlin's vitriolic, anti-Semitic radio diatribes in the late 1930s left many Catholics unmoved; and this, of course, increased Jewish resentment against Catholic leadership.

The bond uniting Jews and Catholics when confronting the Protestant establishment was fragile indeed. Still, some Jews and Catholics in the 1920s arrived at a common realization that the Protestant establishment sought to maintain religiocultural preeminence in America. They also understood that the interreligious goodwill movement, spurred by individuals from within this establishment itself, ultimately pointed to a decline in Protestant cultural hegemony. Jews and Catholics concurred that that would be a desirable end.

NOTES

I would like to thank my colleagues for their informed critical comments: Professors Steven Bowman, Alexandra Korros, Gila Safran-Naveh,

Jonathan D. Sarna, and Mark Silk. The editorial suggestions and technical assistance of my student Norma Davidson were also extremely helpful.

1 Will Herberg, *Protestant-Catholic-Jew* (Garden City, N.Y.: Doubleday Anchor, 1960).

2 See Arnold Eisen, *The Chosen People in America: A Study in Jewish Religious Ideology* (Bloomington: Indiana University Press, 1983).

3 See Paul Blanshard, *American Freedom and Catholic Power* (Boston: Beacon Press, 1949).

4 Among the voluminous secondary literature illustrating this theme, see John Higham, *Strangers in the Land: Patterns of American Nativism 1860–1925* (New York: Atheneum, 1967), esp. 264–99, and Robert T. Handy, *A Christian America: Protestant Hopes and Historical Realities* (New York: Oxford University Press, 1971), 184–225.

5 See Claris Edwin Silcox and Galen M. Fisher, *Catholics, Jews and Protestants* (New York: Harper, 1934), 329–31.

6 See Isidor Singer, *A Religion of Truth, Justice and Peace* (New York: Amos Society, 1924); see Isaac Landman (ed.), *Christian and Jew: A Symposium for Better Understanding* (New York: Horace Liveright, 1929).

7 Roger W. Straus, "The Good Will Movement in the United States During the Year 5691," *Jewish Telegraphic Agency,* September 11, 1931.

8 See Morris Lazaron Papers, American Jewish Archives, Cincinnati, Ohio (hereafter, AJA); also, Francis P. Duffy, "Religious Freedom in America," in Isaac Landman (ed.), *Christian and Jew,* 313–20.

9 *New York Times,* February 24, 1926.

10 See Everett R. Clinchy, "Better Understanding between Christians and Jews," *Universal Jewish Encyclopedia,* II, 257–70, esp. 258–60.

11 See, e.g., Robert T. Handy, *We Witness Together: A History of Cooperative Home Missions* (New York: Friendship Press, 1956), 66–8. Also, Ralph L. Pearson, "Internationalizing the Social Gospel: The Federal Council of Churches and European Protestantism, 1914–1925," *Historical Magazine of the Protestant Episcopal Church* 52(1983): 275–92.

12 Letter of Rev. John W. Herring to Rabbi Hyman Enelow, January 6, 1926, in the Hyman Enelow Papers, AJA.

13 The Good Will Union charter is cited in Everett R. Clinchy, "Better Understanding between Christians and Jews," 260; see letter of Frederick Kershner to Isidor Singer, September 28, 1929, in the Isidor Singer Papers, AJA; Dulles to Rabbi Morris Newfield, January 28, 1943, in the Morris Newfield Papers, AJA.

14 See Everett R. Clinchy, *All in the Name of God* (New York: John Day, 1934).

15 Letter of Rev. William Curry to Isidor Singer, September 24, 1929, Singer Papers, AJA.

16 Minutes of the North American Section of the International Missionary Council's Committee on the Christian Approach to the Jews, November 9, 1934, Presbyterian Historical Society.

17 Letter of Rev. J. B. Hunley to Isidor Singer, September 25, 1929, Singer Papers, AJA.
18 "Goodwill Movement Tested," *Jewish Telegraphic Agency,* June 7, 1929.
19 Letter of Rev. R. A. Carter to Isidor Singer, September 21, 1929, Singer Papers, AJA.
20 Letter of Rev. Robert A. Ashworth to Isidor Singer, September 1929, Singer Papers, AJA.
21 Letter of Bishop A. S. Lloyd to Isidor Singer, September 20, 1929, Singer Papers, AJA.
22 Letter of Reinhold Niebuhr to Isidor Singer, August 30, 1929, Singer Papers, AJA.
23 Letter of Rabbi Hyman Enelow to Rabbi Louis Wolsey, president of the Central Conference of American Rabbis, April 27, 1927, Enelow Papers, AJA.
24 Letter of Rabbi Morris Lazaron to Rev. Sidney L. Gulick, secretary of the Commission on International Justice and Goodwill of the Federal Council of Churches of Christ in America, June 13, 1924, Central Conference of American Rabbis Papers, AJA.
25 See the Annual Report of the Committee on Goodwill between Jews and Christians, November 27, 1925, Enelow Papers, AJA.
26 See the entries of the Executive Committee Minutes of the American Jewish Committee, October 12, 1930, March 22, 1931, May 10, 1931, October 25, 1931. See, too, Naomi Cohen, *Not Free to Desist: The American Jewish Committee* (Philadelphia: Jewish Publication Society of America, 1972), 458–9.
27 See *New York Times,* October 23, 1926, November 13, 15, 22, 1926, and *American Hebrew,* December 4, 1926.
28 Paper by O. D. Foster, associate secretary of the Council of Church Boards on Education, entitled "The American Association of Religion in Universities and Education," which was sent to Rabbi David Philipson. David Philipson Papers, AJA.
29 See Oscar S. Straus, *The Origin of the Republican Form of Government in the United States of America* (New York: Putnam's, 1885).
30 See Samuel Schulman Papers, AJA, for Schulman's ruminations on "melting pot," particularly his letters to the *New York Times,* January 27, 1944, and to John W. Herring, November 19, 1925.
31 See letters of Israel Goldstein to Samuel Schulman, May 27, 1929, and letter of Samuel Schulman to Felix Warburg, Schulman Papers, AJA. On B'nai B'rith and Mott, see the editorial of the *B'nai B'rith Magazine* 45(1931): 190.
32 Franklin's interchange with the Episcopal Church can be traced in the Central Conference of American Rabbis Papers, AJA.
33 Letter of Samuel M. Cavert to Everett R. Clinchy, March 27, 1931, Morris Lazaron Papers, AJA.
34 On Anthony and the Jews, see the Samuel Schulman Papers and the Isidor Singer Papers, AJA; the *Jewish Times,* June 28, 1929; and his letter to C. H.

Sears, December 28, 1927, Alfred Anthony Papers, American Baptist-Samuel Colgate Historical Library, Rochester, N.Y.

35 Minutes of the Synagogue Council of America board meeting, March 12, 1929, Schulman Papers, AJA.

36 Letter of Rush Rhees to Isidor Singer, October 3, 1929, Singer Papers, AJA.

37 Open letter of Louis Marshall to Alfred Williams Anthony, June 19, 1929, published by the American Jewish Committee with other letters between Marshall and Anthony in June 1929, "Good-Will Between Jews and Christians, and Proselytism."

38 Benny Kraut, "The Ambivalent Relations of American Reform Judaism with Unitarianism in the Last Third of the Nineteenth Century," *Journal of Ecumenical Studies* 23(1986): 58–68.

39 Encyclical of Pope Pius XI, "The Promotion of True Religious Unity," trans. Rev. R. A. McGowan, in *Sixteen Encyclicals of Pope Pius XI* (Washington, D.C.: National Catholic Welfare Conference, 1937).

40 See Silcox and Fisher, *Catholics, Jews and Protestants*, 308, 312–14, 320–1, 329–36.

41 See the encyclical of Pope Leo XIII, "Catholicity in the United States," in *The Great Encyclical Letters of Pope Leo XIII* (New York: Benziger, 1903), 332–5, and his apostolic letter to Gibbons, "True and False Americanism in Religion," ibid., 451–2.

42 *Commonweal*, January 25, 1928, 969, and February 1, 1928, 1001. See, too, his *Catholicism and the Modern Mind* (New York: Dial Press, 1928).

43 Encyclical of Pope Pius XI, "The Promotion of True Religious Unity," in *Sixteen Encyclicals*, 11.

44 See J. Elliot Ross, "How Protestants See Us," *Commonweal*, November 30, 1927, 750–2, "How Catholics See Protestants, Part I," *Commonweal*, May 16, 1928, 39–40, and "Part II," May 23, 1928, 68–70.

45 J. Elliot Ross, "Courtesy at Columbia," *Commonweal*, February 20, 1929, 448–50.

46 *America*, January 31, 1925, 384.

47 "The National Conference of Christians and Jews," *American Ecclesiastical Review* 121(1949): 341–2.

48 Cited in Robert D. Cross, *The Emergence of Liberal Catholicism in America* (Cambridge, Mass.: Harvard University Press, 1958), 212.

49 The *Christian Century*, October 18, 1928. The Coffin quotation is found in Edmund A. Moore, *A Catholic Runs for President: The Campaign of 1928* (New York: Ronald Press, 1956), 52.

50 *America*, April 4, 1931, 614.

51 James Hennesey, SJ, *American Catholics* (New York: Oxford University Press, 1981), 222–3, 250–3.

52 See Michael Williams, *Catholicism and the Modern Mind*, 39–40, 188. See, too, William M. Halsey, *The Survival of American Innocence: Catholicism in an Era of Disillusionment, 1920–1940* (Notre Dame, Ind.: University of Notre Dame Press, 1980), esp. 47ff., 70–5.

230   *Benny Kraut*

53 Carlton J. H. Hayes, "Obligations to America," *Commonweal,* December 31, 1924, 201.
54 See, e.g., Michael Andrew Chapman, "Modern Protestant Tendencies," *Catholic World* 118(1923/24): 598–604.
55 J. Elliot Ross, "Courtesy at Columbia," *Commonweal,* February 20, 1929, 449.
56 Ibid., 450.
57 See the memorandum prepared by Henry Smith Leiper, general secretary of the World Conference of Churches, "Relations between the Ecumenical Movement and the Vatican in the Twentieth Century" (n.d.), Presbyterian Historical Society.

SELECT BIBLIOGRAPHY

Bellah, Robert N., and Frederick E. Greenspahn, eds. *Uncivil Religion: Inter-religious Hostility in America.* New York: Crossroad, 1987. The relevant essays are: Jonathan D. Sarna on Jewish perceptions of American Jewish–Christian hostility, Barbara Walter on a century of Protestant anti-Catholicism, and Jay P. Dolan on Catholic attitudes toward Protestants.

Cavert, Samuel M. *The American Churches in the Ecumenical Movement.* New York: Association Press, 1968.

Hutchison, John A. *We Are Not Divided: A Critical and Historical Study of the Federal Council of Churches of Christ.* New York: Round Table Press, 1941.

Kraut, Benny. "Towards the Establishment of the National Conference of Christians and Jews: The Tenuous Road to Religious Goodwill in the 1920s." *American Jewish History* 77(1988): 388–412.

McAvoy, Thomas, T. *The Americanist Heresy in Roman Catholicism.* Notre Dame, Ind.: University of Notre Dame Press, 1963.

Pitt, James E. *Adventures in Brotherhood.* New York: Farrar, Straus, 1955.

Rouse, Ruth, and Stephen Charles Neill, eds. *A History of the Ecumenical Movement, 1517–1948.* Philadelphia: Westminster Press, 1954.

Sheerin, John B. "American Catholics and Ecumenicism." In Philip Gleason, ed., *Contemporary Catholicism in the United States.* Notre Dame, Ind.: University of Notre Dame Press, 1969.

Sklare, Marshall. "The Conversion of the Jews." *Commentary* 56(September 1973): 44–53.

Sussman, Lance J. "Toward Better Understanding: The Rise of the Interfaith Movement in America and the Role of Isaac Landman." *American Jewish Archives* 34(1982): 35–51.

V

External Challenges

The analyses in this section are continuous with those in Part III, and to some extent would have appropriately been pursued there. We consider them separately, and at the end of the volume, for at least two reasons. One is that the challenges of secularization, of religious pluralism, and of conservative evangelicalism were notably comprehensive, cutting across all the items of business, old and new, on the Protestant agenda. The other is that, in our view at least, these were forms of challenge to mainline Protestant hegemony that were recognized as such only at the end of the period we treat, that is, just before and just after the turn into the 1960s. Will Herberg's *Protestant-Catholic-Jew* (1955), Henry Pitney Van Dusen's "Third Force in Christendom" (1958), Harvey Cox's *Secular City* (1965), and a pivotal World Council report called *The Church for Others and the Church for the World* (1967) all appeared in those years. The attention and credence given to all of them signified that the Protestant establishment was ready at last to consider fundamentally changed conceptions of its place in American and world culture.

The challenges themselves, of course, were far from new. To be sure, conservative evangelicalism as an external threat dated only from the time, roughly 1925–35, when fundamentalists had abandoned their efforts to reform the establishment denominations from within; and Mark Silk's analysis begins at that juncture. But, as the essays by R. Laurence Moore and Grant Wacker make clear, the secular and pluralist challenges that came to full consciousness at midcentury had presented themselves as "outside" threats at or before the opening of our era.

231

10

Secularization: Religion and the Social Sciences

R. LAURENCE MOORE

Charles Darwin's *On The Origin of Species* was published in 1859. That event is conventionally remembered as the beginning of a new and perhaps decisive stage in efforts to determine whether traditional Western Christianity could live harmoniously with the accumulating discoveries of the natural sciences. A great deal was at stake, more in fact than can be suggested by any listing of disputed doctrinal points. The issue was not merely whether God or chance determined the order or disorder of nature, but whether a religious faith that salvaged Christianity or a scientific spirit that epitomized secularization was to control the intellectual discourses of the modern world.

In 1865, six years after the publication of Darwin's book, the first organization designed to promote the social sciences appeared in the United States. Although early work in the social sciences was inspired in part by evolutionary theory's possible relevance to human societies, the formation of the American Social Science Association and of other more specialized groups over the next three decades caused little turmoil among Protestant thinkers. Initially few of them bothered to ask whether the infant disciplines of sociology, economics, psychology, and anthropology might pose more troubling questions to the religious imagination than anything contained in Darwin. In fact, many Protestant preachers and laypeople regarded an alliance formed between the "sciences of man" and the social gospel movement of the late nineteenth century as altogether natural. Richard Ely, who played a leading role in professionalizing the academic discipline of economics in the United States, was interested above all in "Christianizing" the social order. In the first issues of the *American Journal of Sociology*, Shailer Mathews, a prominent "modernist" theologian, published a series of articles on "Christian sociology." The first course in sociology offered at Harvard, initiated in the academic year 1891–2, was taught by the Reverend Edward Cummings, the pastor of the South Congregational Church of Boston.

One can extend to considerable length the list of committed Christians deeply involved with the social sciences in the first decades of the twentieth century. Simon Patten's *The Social Basis of Religion* (1911), Carroll D. Wright's *Some Ethical Phases of the Labor Question* (1902), and W. D. P. Bliss's *Encyclopedia of Social Reform* (1897), formed part of the corpus of texts that kept American social science inquiry in harmony with the advocacy of a society modeled, ethically, according to the tenets of Protestant Christianity. This harmony typified American progressivism prior to World War I.

One cannot pinpoint a precise moment when issues began to look more troubling. The work of Durkheim, Troeltsch, Frazier, Spencer, Freud, and Weber, among others, had by the early part of the twentieth century suggested possible sources of friction between the claims of the social sciences and the claims of religious faith. Yet most academic social scientists on this side of the Atlantic were reluctant to acknowledge that friction. Even those interested in establishing a firm and independent base for research wanted social science disciplines that were compatible with enlightened Christianity.

G. Stanley Hall is a good example. One of America's leading psychologists, he had sponsored Freud's only visit to the United States in 1909. In the *American Journal of Religious Psychology and Education,* which he edited from 1904 to 1915, he stated explicitly that he saw nothing demeaning in throwing "the light of psychology" on "Jesus the Christ." He assumed, as William James had assumed, that empirical scrutiny of the regularities of religious phenomena did not undercut their claims to transcendent validity. The presumed audience for his articles included professors and students in seminaries, pastors, religious workers, Sunday school teachers, and those interested in mission work.[1]

The connections linking many educated Protestants in the United States to the social sciences were not seriously disturbed until the 1920s. In the decade that followed World War I, the social science disciplines, as organized in the most prestigious universities, began in a militant way to distance themselves from associations engaged in political advocacy and social reform. Objective empiricism became more and more strongly asserted as the watchword of social science methodology, and the ethical or religious persuasions of the various practitioners were deemed irrelevant to ongoing research.

True, objectivity and empiricism were concepts that Protestant thinkers valued and often invoked in their various efforts to accommodate the

G. Stanley Hall (seated, center) at the Clark University conference held in September, 1909, during the American visit of Freud and Jung (to his right and left respectively). From G. Stanley Hall, *Life and Confessions of a Psychologist* (New York: D. Appleton and Co., 1923), facing p. 335. Used by permission, D. P. Dutton, New York.

natural sciences. But the social sciences presented different and largely unanticipated applications of these concepts. A scientific investigation of natural phenomena was one thing. If the facts proved uncomfortable, as with the assertion that human beings and apes shared an ancestor, those facts could always be given a spiritual significance in a world where God was presumed to be immanent. That in any case was the course taken by a number of Protestant thinkers beginning in the late nineteenth century. The process of having religious behavior and belief themselves subjected to a cold, objective inquiry was something else altogether and required another response.

Although ethical prescription in the service of social policy still counted for something in the 1920s, a neutral model of behaviorist interpretation gained a strong hold on the American social science imagination. Behaviorism suggested that human beings, acting in society, were driven by deterministic and mechanistic forces analogous to those controlling natural processes. Even many social scientists who wished to preserve the claim that humans were capable of creative and rational choices endorsed the notion that humanity's understanding of itself was moving away from transcendent references into the realm of the rational and secular. Such an assumption was bound to alarm Americans who equated progress or national destiny with the authority of a Protestant establishment.

Put bluntly, the newer social science perspective regarded religion as a cultural artifact to be placed for purposes of objective study alongside all the other cultural artifacts that determined or circumscribed human conduct in any time and place. Something called religion might be a constant factor in all human societies. It might have its worthy uses, and some forms of it might clearly be distinguishable from "primitive" forms of magic and animism. But something called Protestant Christianity had to wonder, given the comparative references furnished by the social sciences, whether it could accept its role as just another element of culture, or just another form of religion, without falling victim to the "aimless pluralism" that a merely secular society invited. There was even an indication, already in the 1920s, that religion as a subject of social science scrutiny was going to become a neglected subheading. It would be treated as a curious anachronism, something that would soon disappear, or worse, as a sign of social pathology.

Efforts at Accommodation: The First Phase

Beginning in the 1920s the task of responding to the challenge, or perhaps threat, of the social sciences fell primarily to Protestants who were more or less liberal in their theological orientation. This was true for several reasons. More theologically conservative members of the Protestant establishment kept their eyes fixed on the natural sciences. In countering Darwin, they argued that they were prepared to accept a truly empirical science but not one based on theory and speculation. Using that criterion, they saw little reason to bother with the social sciences, which they regarded, rightly or wrongly, as totally theoretical and subjective.

Beyond that, Protestant conservatives, with the important exception of neo-orthodox thinkers, proved in the long run to be little concerned with defending the credibility of Christian dogma to intellectual elites. Conservatives did not immediately lose their claim to a voice in determining what constituted "intellectual credibility," but their influence at major universities and divinity schools was sharply reduced as a result of the fundamentalist controversies of the 1920s. The more thoughtful among them, J. Gresham Machen, for example, believed that establishment influence was a misguided ambition if it meant giving up every essential of Christianity for fear of giving offense. Liberals, in contrast, tended to rest the future of the Protestant establishment, its claim to

Harlan Paul Douglass. From *Literary Digest* (July 28, 1934):20. Used by permission, Harper & Row Publishers, Inc.

cultural authority, on continued respect from American intellectual leaders, however secular their interests might be. Finally, as heirs of the social gospel, Protestant liberals were naturally interested in preserving bonds between their organizations and the social sciences.

Some modernists, who like Shailer Mathews had embraced a historical understanding of Christianity, continued to suggest that the dangers posed to faith by the social sciences were minimal. They defended the sociological investigation of religion in utilitarian terms. So what if churches were treated as social institutions and were subjected to the same objective analysis that was applied to other institutions? The process did not threaten the integrity of religious belief, which Protestants, unlike Catholics, had always distinguished from the "church." The latter, although ordained by God, was given its social forms by very fallible human agents. Modernists argued that sociological analysis would in fact help individual churches and interdenominational institutions to maximize their social impact.

Harlan Paul Douglass caught on to this last possibility more quickly and with more conviction than most of his contemporaries. A Congregational clergyman who did graduate work in sociology at Chicago and Columbia, Douglass was the research director of the Institute of Social and Religious Research from 1921 to 1933. This organization, funded in part by the Rockefeller Foundation, grew out of the Town and Country Division of the Interchurch World Movement (an organization that had run out of funds in 1920). Douglass organized projects and wrote over the next several decades a series of monographs on urban churches. His interests centered, as did those of most liberal Protestants, on interdenominational cooperation.

Douglass wished his work to encourage what he called "church-manship." This "practical art" involved bringing churches into being where they were most needed, avoiding the duplication of effort in neighborhoods where churches were already congested, and devising the means best suited to serve individual localities. In his efforts Douglass sought help from the social sciences. Such assistance, in his mind, provided the skills needed to compile statistical tables, graphs, and charts, but it also meant the ability to create models for "controlled experiments," and the sophistication to generalize from a large number of case studies.[2] The textual achievement of his enterprise was impressive. Some fifty surveys and ninety volumes were published under the auspices of the Institute of Social and Religious Research, including one genuine masterpiece in American sociology. That was Robert and Helen Lynd's *Middletown,* which appeared in 1929.

The net impact of Douglass's particular efforts to tie social science methodologies to church policy was nonetheless disappointing. Although the demographic work was praised by the Federal Council of Churches and sparked some notable efforts in interchurch cooperation, many Protestants found the research chilling.[3] They were not prepared to discuss churches in a language of statistical description that was normally reserved for more ordinary things, like factory output or cholera epidemics. Douglass worked for the Federal Council of Churches in the late 1930s and early 1940s, but the Rockefeller Foundation, alleging that the Institute of Social and Religious Research was not sufficiently influential, stopped funding it in 1934.

Something of Douglass's intentions was echoed in the 1920s by the veteran American sociologist Charles A. Ellwood. Ellwood had received his Ph.D. from Chicago at the turn of the century and was teaching after World War I at the University of Missouri. In two of his books published in the early 1920s, *The Reconstruction of Religion: A Sociological View* and *Christianity and Social Science,* Ellwood tried to enlist the enthusiasm of social gospel liberals in the cause of sociology. Religion, he argued, with its object of redeeming mankind from a life of sin, needed the scientific spirit and a scientifically tested knowledge of human life to accomplish its work successfully. In his mind, instruction in religion and instruction in the social sciences went hand in glove.

Ellwood's appeal for reconciliation and accommodation was as bold and optimistic as any that one can find in the decade of the 1920s. It rested, however, on the questionable assumption that American sociologists would continue in explicit terms to regard Christianity as laying down the normative terms for a good society. The theme of Jesus the consummate sociologist would inform many essays in establishment Protestant literature for a long time to come; but the professional literature of sociology made less and less mention of the social teachings of Jesus. Ellwood's determined effort at reconciliation, moreover, made it clear that in the marriage of social science and Christianity it was Christianity that had to do most of the adjusting. "Science," he said with approval, "is the outstanding and dominating fact in modern civilization."[4]

However questionable, and however repugnant to Protestant conservatives, Ellwood's argument remained one obvious line for Protestant liberals to pursue. One can find it repeated, for example, in articles published in the 1920s and 1930s in *Christian Education* (renamed in 1953 *The Christian Scholar*), a publication initially of the Council of Church Boards of Education. In its early days, one important inspiration of the Council was Charles Foster Kent, who was until his death in 1925 the Woolsey Professor of Biblical Literature at Yale. The argument that economics and sociology can only be rightly studied from the standpoint of Christian ethics was deemed a sufficient answer to the threat of behaviorism. For most writers who contributed to *Christian Education,* the concern over how to teach the social sciences properly formed part of a larger concern about how to keep Christianity relevant to a college curriculum.

Another journal, *Religious Education,* published by the Religious Education Association, made efforts to keep up with social science literature in the 1920s and 1930s. Its mission was "to present, on an adequate scientific plane, those factors which make for improvement in religious and moral education." The thought was along the lines of Douglass's research justifications, and the journal tried to keep readers current with recent social trends and attitudes, especially ones that could be measured by polls and through interviews. The social sciences, it was suggested, provided useful guides for Christian nurture. John Dewey was quoted extensively, as were other thinkers who had no particular use for institutionalized religion. Even behaviorism, when shorn of its excessive reductionism, was said to provide insights into how to educate children.

Psychology emerged as something of a special case, especially the sort of psychology identified with Freud. The Freudian concept of repression and the Christian concept of sin and guilt may be rooted in a common, and uniquely Western, philosophical tradition; but the remedies to correct neurosis and those to save the unredeemed soul are usually distinguished. They are in fact potentially competitive. In many versions of twentieth-century depth psychology, Christianity confronted a rival that regarded religion as the cause or symptom of an unbalanced psyche.

With the rising popularity of the belief that Christian ministers had an important role to play as "counselors," that is, as servants of mental health, Protestants, again especially liberals, felt obligated to do what they could to effect an alliance between psychological insight and their own views about the causes of human misery. Extensive institutionalized forms of these efforts did not take shape until the 1950s, but the awareness of the need for ministers to be able to distinguish a sinner from a schizophrenic was implanted earlier. Here was a specific area of the social sciences where a pastor was urged to develop at least some expertise or learn to work with people who had expertise. Christian counselors were doubtless well served by these endeavors; at the same time they learned that exchange was almost always a one-way street. The psychologists instructed, and the ministers learned. One writer for the *Christian Century* captured the imbalance well enough when he noted that psychologists did not waste time developing "six sound reasons for believing that psychology will not perish." Trying to prove the ongoing viability of religion was, in contrast, standard fare in Protestant journals.[5]

A fair assessment of the situation on the eve of World War II is that American social scientists had learned to proceed professionally by growing independent of their original clerical allies. Protestant leaders who worried about their diminished role in academia regretted the independence but had no intellectually persuasive way to put the alliance back together. One commentator noted ruefully that college textbooks in sociology generally assumed a dismissive attitude toward religion, pausing only briefly to define it as an emotional attitude toward the unknown and uncontrolled. He implied that students in the social sciences came to regard a successful education as learning to do without religion.[6]

It is symptomatic that the most important use of sociological theory by a Protestant theologian in the period between the wars resulted in a sharp indictment of the institutional arrangements of Protestant denominations. H. Richard Niebuhr's brilliant *The Social Sources of Denominationalism,* published in 1928, was no doubt meant as a corrective. But it suggested how easily, even naturally, the social sciences could be called upon to record the failures of religion. If a dedicated theologian like Niebuhr used sociology to uncover the class structure of organized Christianity, then what could one expect from secular-minded sociologists who attached no particular significance to the moral dilemmas of Protestant Christendom?

Efforts at Accommodation: The Second Phase

The advent of the Second World War provided a rich opportunity to attack science along with many of the "isms" with which it had frequently been associated – pragmatism, relativism, determinism. Surely, many thinkers argued, the destructive course of fascism had proved that an unconditional right and an unconditional wrong were real and substantial entities. Moreover, whatever the limits of rationality, properly educated human beings ought to be able to tell the difference. One sign of the times was a more than usually conscientious effort to do something about the fragmentation of the academic disciplines and to restore, at least among the nations fighting on the right side in global conflict, a moral consensus. One could in this context note any.number of interesting enterprises, but for present purposes we must be content with a few examples that were of special interest to those who continued to think of themselves as part of a Protestant establishment, now almost entirely liberal, theologically, in its self-image and in the image of others.

In 1940, a group of academics with cross-disciplinary interests convened, in New York City, the "Conference on Science, Philosophy and Religion in their Relation to the Democratic Way of Life." The conference became an annual event and regularly attracted a long list of distinguished participants, including social scientists, whose papers and comments were published in substantial volumes. The level of discussion was impressive, and participants did not shrink from controversy in the hope of finding a pedestrian basis for agreement. If religion was ever to reestablish its claim as an equal in the academic hierarchy, not as a phenomenon to be studied in the language of other disciplines but as a discipline whose language affected the assumptions of all the others, here was a forum where the mood and expectations were favorable.

Liberal Protestant thinkers could take heart from a number of papers in the opening conferences since almost everyone was ready to blame the rise of fascism on the reductive elements in science that had resulted in moral indifference. Pitirim A. Sorokin, the Russian-born, Greek Orthodox sociologist who taught at Harvard, launched a full-scale assault on pragmatism, moral relativism, and what he described as an overcommitment to "sensate culture." That culture had to its shame tried to destroy the belief in man "as a bearer of the divine ray in the sensory world, as an incarnation of the charismatic grace." Sorokin gave a resounding endorsement of the "Glory of God" in terms that no other respected social scientist of his generation would have dared.[7]

Other participants clearly questioned whether an attempt to correct reductionist elements in the social sciences, using Sorokin's kind of language, was credible. Everyone wanted to root out of the twentieth-century intellectual world whatever was responsible for Hitler, but could one repeal the twentieth century itself? Could one really assert, without fear of outright rejection, that "religion cannot be regarded as just another aspect of culture, one among many human occupations. . . . Religion is either the supreme human discipline, because it is God's discipline of man, and as such dominates our culture, or it has no place at all"? Mortimer Adler, a professor of philosophy at the University of Chicago, flung that gauntlet in defense of religion, but it had little effect on the discussions in future conferences.[8]

The best efforts at reconciliation concentrated instead on seeking to demonstrate that Christianity and Judaism had formed a moral consensus in the West that was worth considering in absolute, or almost absolute, terms. This remained a touchy subject, for the majority of American social scientists continued to regard religion solely as an artifact of culture. The most that liberal Protestants could hope to wrest from the controversy was a recognition that ethical standards, although historically conditioned, were not indifferently legitimate in every time and place. They also argued that religion, as a subject of objective study, was a phenomenon of such uncommon force, a force empirically demonstrable, that it belonged in a category by itself, one that was off-limits for pragmatists.

America's foremost sociologist of the postwar years, Talcott Parsons, suggested one way to compromise the perspectives of Christians and secularists. Religion, he said, existed and continued to exist because it satisfied important human needs. It dealt with areas of experience that defied rational understanding and control, especially evil and suffering. Although his position left religion in most ways the handmaiden of science – it could only fill in gaps in our knowledge left open by the state of scientific knowledge at a given time – Parsons's functionalism gave a central role to religion and faith in modern society. In whatever age, religion was tied to the fundamental motivations of human behavior and was responsible for the stability of the value patterns in a culture. As a cultural force, religion was almost by definition resistant to change. Hence, science and religion did often conflict. But a society or culture without the special authority or power conferred upon values by religious faith, by the nonrational sentiments of humankind, was more or less unthinkable in Parsons's terms. A social science that proceeded on the assumption that religion was dead or dying deprived itself of a subject crucial to social analysis.[9]

Parsons's analysis suggested that one need not regard a sociology of religion as challenging the metaphysical claims of Christianity. In an introduction to a book written by J. Milton Yinger in 1946, Howard Jensen argued that the empirical approach of the social sciences, although it treated religion as a process of human interaction related to other phases of collective life, implied nothing one way or the other about the "essence of the religious experience" or the "nature of the religious object."[10] Jensen's formulation was an important one. He was not promoting Christian sociology of the old type, but he did mean to make religion a central concern of academic investigation. In the immediate postwar years, this was about the best offer the Protestant establishment could hope to get from academia.

Continued Difficulties

The exigencies of moral commitment stressed in the atmosphere of the war against fascism continued into the cold war era of the 1950s. Although American intellectuals were split on the question of how to deal with communism on the domestic scene, they agreed that communism on the international scene represented the forces of evil. Some religious spokespeople thought the atmosphere of international tension created an opportunity to reestablish the cultural authority of a Protestant establishment. And, in fact, leading Protestants were regularly included as part of imposing public forums convened to clarify moral choices. Even so, Protestants soon found that the mood of the postwar era worked against them in several significant ways. They had difficulty finding the proper voice to address a public they regarded as placing secular concerns above religious ones and valuing religious pluralism more than Protestant hegemony.

Consider, for example, the effort of one committee sponsored by the Department of the Church and Economic Life of the Federal Council of Churches. (The Federal Council merged in 1950 with other organizations to form the National Council of Churches.) Beginning in 1949, the committee was charged with producing a series of studies on Christian ethics and economic life. Funded by the Rockefeller Foundation, six volumes appeared under the auspices of the committee.

The first, published in 1953, comprised conference papers edited by A. Dudley Ward and was devoted to a discussion of the goals of economic life. The fifteen contributors included several economists, a political scientist, a psychologist, and an anthropologist. That representation adequately demonstrated what Theodore M. Greene wrote in the introduction to the volume: Not all American social scientists followed a "positivistic" or "dogmatically anti-metaphysical approach" to their discipline.[11] Most of the contributors had little difficulty integrating ethical questions into their discussions of economics. They argued that ethics would enter a social science perspective one way or the other and that a frank acknowledgment of bias was better than efforts to conceal it behind a posture of objectivity.

Unfortunately, at least as far as religious claims were concerned, the volume implicitly acknowledged something else as well: Ethical discussions need not appeal to religion, and especially the claims of any one religion. Most of the contributing social scientists, as Reinhold Niebuhr noted in his concluding essay, managed to consider the ethical problems of economic life "without explicit recourse to uniquely Christian standards of judgment."[12] Morality might be a welcome leaven in the language of the social sciences, but it no longer produced the Christian sociology that had sustained the Protestant establishment at the beginning of the twentieth century. The social science mentality that dominated the volume eschewed positivism, but the basis for the corrective was secular and humanistic rather than Christian.

The issue, as Protestant conservatives had long argued, was whether the price of public influence was too high. Protestant liberals, acting through the Federal and, later, the National Council of Churches wished to speak out on issues of social concern. Editorials in the *Christian Century* and *Christianity and Crisis* in the postwar years took a stand on virtually every item of political significance – presidential candidates, trade unions, economic policies, atomic energy, foreign alliances, Supreme Court decisions, and racial disputes. The editorial voice was self-assured, one that took its influence for granted. Some wondered, however, whether it was any longer an identifiably Protestant Christian voice. The voice might be intelligent, but could it be distinguished from other intelligent voices that sounded in "every woman's club and every open forum?"[13] The National Council's Committee on the Church and Economic Life produced documents filled with statistics and study questions that would have been serviceable in freshman economics classes. Yet the Christian content that accompanied the material was arguably neither the most interesting nor the most essential part of the lessons.

More promising initially were the short pamphlets, funded in the early 1950s by the Edward W. Hazen Foundation, that were devoted to religious perspectives on the teaching of a number of academic disciplines, including all the social sciences. The series was urged on the foundation by George F. Thomas, who introduced the study of religion as a discipline within the liberal arts curriculum at Princeton University. Each pamphlet was assigned to a distinguished academic known to have strong religious convictions. Kenneth E. Boulding of Michigan wrote the pamphlet on the college teaching of economics, and Talcott Parsons prepared the one on sociology and social psychology. The pamphlets all admirably dispatched their duty of demonstrating the importance of religion in understanding human culture, and they were cited and used. Nonetheless their influence on college teaching was short-lived. They faded away like the efforts of a group called the Faculty Christian Fellowship, organized between 1950 and 1952.

The latter, cooperating with the National Council of Churches and the Committee on Christian Higher Education, formed a sociology committee that hoped to establish regular links with the American Sociological Association. By the end of the 1950s, however, the committee had accomplished almost nothing, and its goal of examining the presumptions and assumptions of sociology in the light of the Christian faith remained a program without a method. Determinism, reductionism, and historical relativism remained assumptions that Protestant leaders of all theological shades rejected, but the main trends in American social science disciplines, despite the calls for reorientation that followed World War II, had not radically departed from what many regarded as overnarrow and empirical studies.

Protestants involved with the National Council of Churches had been misled into imagining that moral relativism had been gravely weakened as a result of the West's brush with fascism and Soviet communism. In a volume edited by Amos Wilder, *Liberal Learning and Religion,* a great deal of collective hope was placed on the purported movement of the social sciences beyond ethical relativism. The United Nations charter was cited as proof of an emerging worldwide consensus about the foundations of a good society. So was the work of Gunnar Myrdal, Elton Mayo, Erich Fromm, and Rollo May. One contributor, who presumed to speak knowingly about the discipline of anthropology, wrote: "The amoralism of ethical relativism finds no support in the serious study of cultural relativity."[14] Similar judgments about the attitudes of individual scholars were not necessarily wrong, but the generalizations they supported were too sweeping and did not accurately project the trajectory of work in the social sciences. A liberal Protestant establishment in search of intellectual respectability had the money and organizations to launch any number of enterprises in the 1950s, but consensus over how to meet contemporary demands for research and expertise seemed more and more elusive.[15]

The Neo-orthodox Alternative

Beginning with *Moral Man and Immoral Society,* published in 1932, Reinhold Niebuhr tried to chart a new intellectual direction for educated Protestants. That book marked Niebuhr's own firm declaration of independence from the Christian liberalism he had embraced earlier. And it was his call upon other Christians to rethink the ways they were trying to accommodate to the scientific and secular perspectives of the twentieth century.

Niebuhr in *Moral Man* was in effect saying that there could be no science of man, not one in any case that could set the conditions for a just and peaceful society. He expressed impatience with the schemes of social planners who with their engineering expertise imagined that they could control the future. According to Niebuhr, human beings acting in society were inevitably irrational, greedy, and sinful. Their self-interested actions were hemmed in only by the naked power that those people with contrary and competing interests could muster. The Christian imagination therefore should not waste its time trying to gain expertise in areas that had little to do with divine justice. Those areas had a relative importance in the secular realm. But the major concern of religion was, or ought to be, the bearing of testimony to the radical disparity between the divine law of Christian love and the utter failure of all human societies to embody it. Niebuhr, as all who heard his powerful voice knew, did not mean this attack on the pretensions of secular knowledge to become a formula for ignorance and social inaction. But he did mean to say that the Christian religion had something to declare that was more powerful than what was embodied in secular knowledge. Without the transcendent and humbling perspective offered by the drama of Christianity and its promise of a redemption from history, all secular knowledge was mechanical, narrow, and sinfully arrogant.

Niebuhr's point of view had made a strong impact on Protestant thinking by the middle of the 1930s. Neo-orthodoxy held that the liberal effort to preserve religion as an ally of science represented a costly and largely futile investment. In article after article and book after book, Protestant writers mulled over the implications of doing head-on battle with the claims of scientists to cultural dominance. An especially sharp debate was joined in the pages of the *Christian Century* in 1943. The antagonists were Charles Clayton Morrison, the long-time editor of the *Christian Century* who subscribed to part of the neo-orthodox position, and Hornell Hart, a sociologist and theologian who defended the cause of Christian liberalism.

Hart's argument was the familiar but still hotly contested one that true science and true religion had no quarrel. Hart conceded that work in the social sciences had weakened the authority of biblical revelation, and that many professional scientists no longer believed in God. But the reason for the declining status of religion was the failure of Protestant clergy to

Charles Clayton Morrison. Religious News Service photo.

preach a credible faith. Scientists and other moderns would make room for religion when it no longer flew in the face of scientific certainties. To these notions, Morrison replied testily: "The assumption of Christian liberalism that Christianity must go over to science in order to win the allegiance of the scientific mind, I utterly reject."[16]

Morrison and others who took this defiant stand were, of course, aware that they might be confused with the very different breed of Protestant fundamentalists who had taken their own firm stand against the scientific imperative. Their position, however, was aimed not at proving scientists wrong but in keeping them in their own sphere. With the social sciences, science had tried to enter the field of human behavior and confront religion in a way that stultified it. Protestants had to draw a line at this point and refuse the insights being offered. They had to confront without embarrassment the scorn of the social scientist who ridiculed Christianity with the question: Why would God select one minor province of the Roman Empire to reveal himself nineteen hundred years ago? The reply had to be: Why not? Christians did not need to challenge the social scientists in their efforts to investigate functions and origins of value systems. Christianity emerged in a specific historical community, and the scenario for that event could bear a secular and historically accurate telling. However, Christians should not be lulled into discounting the claims of faith, which are utterly distinct from the claims of science and historicism. To do that would be to lose sight of Christian values as supreme and transcendent.

Morrison qualified his statement a bit by arguing that the efficacy of Christian values could be demonstrated in historical experience. That was not exactly Reinhold Niebuhr's point, for he had conceded that the historical effect of an action in producing a relatively greater degree of justice in human society did not hinge on its being based on Christian values. But Morrison and Niebuhr were at least agreed in insisting that Christianity lost its force through efforts to translate it into the language of science. Christianity would not usefully affect society in the guise of something called Christian sociology. The idea was from the beginning a misconceived hybrid.

Niebuhr's career suggests that he was on to something. His was the most influential Protestant voice of the post–World War II years, at least in academic communities, because he seemed to provide a means to challenge the intellectual environment of the twentieth century in religious terms that educated people could respect. Rather than being dismissed as an intellectual reactionary, he became the vanguard. His repeated emphasis on sin, irony, and paradox was absorbed into the language of postwar political and theological liberalism and was hailed as introducing a new brand of realism. The best and the brightest applauded him. He was quoted by social scientists in every discipline as a Protestant thinker who was able to meet them convincingly on more or less their own terms.

In this way Niebuhr brought about one important reversal. He did not translate religion into the language of the social sciences. He forced social scientists to translate the Christian concept of sin into one of the guiding assumptions of their disciplines. That was perhaps a difference without much final meaning. What he accomplished by way of public influence may have been merely an alternate path to secularism; many who cited his neo-orthodoxy for its political wisdom had not the slightest use for its theological underpinnings. Nonetheless, at a critical moment of Protestant uncertainty about itself, Niebuhr's views provided some courage.

The Late 1950s and a Look Beyond

As the United States approached the 1960s, Protestant churchmen and -women faced some additional adjustments with respect to the enormous growth of the social science establishment in American universities. The National Council of Churches and other large and ambitious denominational groups increased the number of staff members who were retained to carry out demographic research. In most ways the rhetorical patterns of adjustment that educated Protestants had already established did not vary. Articles in Christian journals continued to employ the term "Christian sociology" and called upon Protestant teachers in social science disciplines to stress the ways in which humankind transcends culture and depends upon a set of normative spiritual values.

Nonetheless, significant splits widened. The people who conducted research projects for the National Council of Churches were not the people who taught in major universities, and these two groups generally came from very different academic backgrounds. The former often had no formal training in the social sciences, and their demographic inquiries were prompted by a set of imperatives that had little in common with the concerns of academic researchers, many of whom were in fact Jewish. The research undertaken for the National Council of Churches had virtually nothing to do with the questions that governed research in the fields of the sociology, psychology, and anthropology of religion.

The division of concerns was certainly predictable, given all that had happened, and probably unavoidable. During the decade of the 1950s, professional social scientists developed an enormous interest in religious phenomena. One can almost refer to an explosion of interest. Books written by, among others, Paul M. Harrison, Robin Williams, J. Milton Yinger, Gerhard Lenski, Marshall Sklare, Thomas O'Dea, and Will Herberg were widely studied. Two professional groups, the Religious Research Association and the Society for the Scientific Study of Religion, were formed in the late 1950s and published journals. Within a few years, another journal was founded that dedicated its pages to the study of religion and mental health.[17]

Protestant leaders who still hoped to influence academic curricula could welcome news that religion was not going to be a neglected subject of academic inquiry. They could also take heart in seeing that the sociology of religion had departed somewhat from its earlier emphasis upon the primitive and marginal aspects of religion. Religion was accorded a place as a normal and probably permanent part of modern world perspectives. Nonetheless, their view of what made religion authoritative in culture remained rather different from that of social scientists.

Peter Berger, a Lutheran and a professional sociologist, made the most impressive effort at the end of our period of study to combine his academic expertise with a Christian witness. His book *The Noise of Solemn Assemblies: Christian Commitment and the Religious Establishment in America,* which was published in 1961, served, like previous work done by H. Richard Niebuhr and Liston Pope, as a criticism of the religious establishment. Berger, however, was buoyed by the notion that a serious Christian perspective was itself a debunking instrument. Christian churches, objectively studied as social institutions, were clearly embedded in society in such a way that they served to enforce unjust social norms. But, Berger went on to argue, sociology enables people to see in clear perspective precisely what Christianity, in its mission on this planet, is *not* all about. The social corruption of churches, once revealed, becomes a call to prophetic arms even if the churches themselves no longer offer much hope for a radicalized Christianity.

For Protestant churchmen and -women to take much cheer from Berger, they had to have a strong faith in the ability of ordinary people to transcend ordinary forms of social involvement. But that was always what they had said in confronting the challenge of the social sciences. Either Christians believed in the transforming power of their religion or they believed in nothing. What was perhaps more encouraging about the work of social scientists interested in religion was their growing desire to study "subjective" experience. What people believe to be true is an important social force. Perception has a "reality" that cannot be undercut with reference to some external arena of supposedly objective data. To view religious belief in that way by no means provides it with a transcendent justification, but from the standpoint of Protestant churchmen it is a major step beyond treating religion invariably as illusion.

Those who tried to maintain the hegemonic claims of Protestant establishment leadership found the postwar years difficult. The social sciences, although not the sole cause of their problems, exposed to them one large problem they could not hope to solve, not in any case without drastically revising their sense of purpose. The social sciences helped to destroy Protestant claims to be the dominant cultural authority in the United States, in part because the functionalist perspective invariably employed when approaching religion acted as an equalizer among competing religious groups. The social sciences in effect endorsed the religious pluralism that had always existed in the United States. In fact, anthropology, the most historically minded of the social sciences, has been influential in promoting the value of parts of the religious imagination in which Protestantism is most deficient – myth, symbol, and ritual. Arguably, the investment that liberal Protestants have made in trying to retain intellectual respectability in the twentieth century encouraged them to jettison those things that social scientists now suggest are essential to the survival of religion in all human cultures. As a result, a lot of Americans, with historical grudges of long standing, have gained additional leverage in their ongoing efforts to take revenge on John Calvin, the Puritans, and the whole concept of a Protestant establishment.

NOTES

1 Hall, "Editorial," *American Journal of Religious Psychology and Education* 1(May 1904): 1–6; Hall, *Jesus, the Christ, in the Light of Psychology* (Garden City: Doubleday, Page, 1917).

2 See, e.g., H. Paul Douglass, *Church Comity: A Study of Cooperative Church Extension in American Cities* (Garden City: Doubleday, Page, 1929), 41–3.

3 On Douglass's assessment of the opposition he encountered from church groups, see Edmund deS. Brunner, "Harlan Paul Douglass," *Review of Religious Research* 1(Summer 1959): 3–16, 63–75.

4 Ellwood, *The Reconstruction of Religion: A Sociological View* (New York: Macmillan, 1923), 3.

5 Goodwin Watson, "What Does Psychology Do to Religion?" *Christian Century* 48(May 6, 1931): 603.

6 Brewton Berry, "Religion and the Sociologists," *Christian Century* 58(October 22, 1941): 1301–3.

7 Sorokin, "The Tragic Dualism of Contemporary Sensate Culture: Its Root and Way Out," in *Science Philosophy and Religion: A Symposium* (New York: Harper, 1941), 106.

8 Adler, "God and the Professors," in *Science Philosophy and Religion*, 131.

9 Parsons, "The Institutionalization of Social Science and the Problems of the Conference," in Lyman Bryson et al. (eds.), *Perspectives on a Troubled Decade: Science, Philosophy, and Religion, 1939–1949. Tenth Symposium* (New York: Harper, 1950), 221–44.

10 "Editorial Note" in J. Milton Yinger, *Religion in the Struggle for Power: A Study in the Sociology of Religion* (Durham, N.C.: Duke University Press, 1946), vii.

11 A. Dudley Ward (ed.), *Goals of Economic Life* (New York: Harper, 1953), 7.

12 Ward (ed.), *Goals of Economic Life*, 438.

13 Reinhold Niebuhr, "Sects and Churches," *Christian Century* 52(July 3, 1935): 887.

14 Walter G. Muelder, "Norms and Valuations in Social Science," in Amos Wilder (ed.), *Liberal Learning and Religion* (New York: Harper, 1951), 123.

15 For one indictment that suggested a dilemma, see D. L. Munby, "A Plea for Economics," *Christianity and Crisis* 11(June 11, 1951): 74–8.

16 "The Scientist and the Christian Gospel," *Christian Century* 60(June 30,

1943): 768. Also see Morrison, "Protestantism and Science," *Christian Century* 63(April 24, 1946): 524–7.
17 Yoshio Fukuyama, "The Uses of Sociology: By Religious Bodies," *Journal for the Scientific Study of Religion* 2(Spring 1963): 195–203; Robert Lee, "The Sociology of Religion. Some Problems and Prospects," *Religion in Life* 30(Spring 1961): 268–78.

SELECT BIBLIOGRAPHY

Bannister, Robert C. *Social Darwinism: Science and Myth in Anglo-American Social Thought*. Philadelphia: Temple University Press, 1978.
Fox, Richard W. *Reinhold Niebuhr: A Biography*. New York: Pantheon, 1985.
Furner, Mary O. *Advocacy and Objectivity: A Crisis in the Professionalization of American Social Science, 1865–1905*. Lexington: University Press of Kentucky, 1975.
Haskell, Thomas L. *The Emergence of Professional Social Science: The American Social Science Association and the Nineteenth Century Crisis of Authority*. Urbana: University of Illinois Press, 1977.
Hutchison, William R. *The Modernist Impulse in American Protestantism*. Cambridge, Mass.: Harvard University Press, 1976.
Matthews, Fred H. *Quest for an American Sociology: Robert E. Park and the Chicago School*. Montreal: Queen's University Press, 1977.
May, Henry F. *Protestant Churches and Industrial America*. New York: Harper & Row, 1947.
Meyer, Donald B. *The Protestant Search for Political Realism, 1919–1941*. Berkeley: University of California Press, 1960.
Mills, C. Wright. *The Sociological Imagination*. New York: Oxford University Press, 1959.
Moore, James R. *The Post-Darwinian Controversies: A Study of the Protestant Struggle to Come to Terms with Darwin in Great Britain and America, 1870–1900*. Cambridge: Cambridge University Press, 1979.
Ross, Dorothy. *G. Stanley Hall: The Psychologist as Prophet*. Chicago: University of Chicago Press, 1972.

11

A Plural World: The Protestant Awakening to World Religions

GRANT WACKER

In the fall of 1893 visitors from all parts of the United States descended upon Chicago to tour the World's Columbian Exposition. Many left with the sights and sounds of one part of the Exposition, the World's Parliament of Religions, still racing through their minds. The Parliament may not have been, as one reporter exclaimed, "the supreme moment of the 19th century," but at the time it must have seemed so. For seventeen days running, thousands of spectators jammed the Hall of Columbus hoping to catch a glimpse of the colorfully garbed savants and swamis who had traveled from all parts of the earth to describe the faiths of their homelands. More significant than the excitement of the moment, however, was that the Parliament marked a turning point in the history of American Protestant perceptions of other religions. For most of those visitors in Chicago, as well as countless men and women who read about the proceedings in hometown newspapers, the Parliament offered their first real exposure to any religion besides Judaism or Christianity.[1]

The Fortress Undermined

Christians had always known, of course, that other highly developed religions existed. Thinkers as diverse as Origen in the second century, Thomas Aquinas in the thirteenth century, and John Calvin in the sixteenth century, had acknowledged that other religions contained elements of genuine revelation. And during the Enlightenment a number of factors such as the global expansion of trade, the spread of Christian missions, and the beginnings of the comparative study of religions heightened ordinary believers' awareness of other faiths. Not until the late nineteenth century, however, did world religions begin to pose a serious theological challenge to Christians in Europe and North America.

a

The reasons why that transformation took place when and where it did are too complex to be unpacked adequately in a short chapter. Suffice it to say that the shift was part of a larger series of tremors that rumbled through the foundations of Western civilization at the turn of the century. In the United States, in particular, rapid social changes such as urbanization and industrialization influenced the way ordinary people viewed other religions. Smokestacks elbowed out steeples. Manmade time and indoor labor replaced work attuned to the rhythm of the seasons. As a result, God's direct presence in everyday life receded into an intangible spiritual realm where all religions increasingly looked alike. Cultural changes also undermined the Christian fortress. The rise of research universities and of scientists as a new cultural elite effectively displaced the clergy as the final arbiters of knowledge. Within the univer-

b
Prominent representatives of Eastern religions at the World's Parliament. *a:* H. Dharmapala, Theravada Buddhist. From John Henry Barrows, *The World's Parliament of Religions* (Chicago: The Parliament Publishing Co., 1893), p. 861. *b:* Swami Vivekananda, Hindu. Later founder of the Vedanta Society. From Barrows, *World's Parliament,* p. 973.

sities, the humanities and the social sciences were rapidly permeated by the notion that all social and cultural phenomena, including all religions, were only human inventions. The emerging discipline of cultural anthropology proved especially destructive to Christian insularity; in its maw the rites and doctrines of Christianity began to bear an uncanny resemblance to the forms of other major religions.[2]

Those broad social and cultural changes eroded but did not topple

Christian absolutism. In the end the fort was brought down by forces closer to home. The latter included biblical higher criticism, the academic study of comparative religions (or the history of religions, as it came to be called), and the delayed effect of missionary interaction with foreign cultures.

The impact of biblical higher criticism was the most direct, or at least the most visible of the three. Professional biblical scholars stimulated the ordinary Protestant's awareness of world religions by casting the history of Israel and early Christianity in developmental and contextual terms. If Christianity, as all religions, had evolved in response to social and cultural pressures, how could the Gospel be timeless and universal? Differently stated, was there any reason to believe that its message was any less timebound, or any less particularistic, than the message of other highly developed faiths?

The rapid growth of scholarly literature on other religions also relativized Christian claims. The first book-length studies by American authors had appeared in the late eighteenth century. By the time of the Civil War stories about the beliefs and practices of remote peoples regularly appeared in general-interest magazines such as the *North American Review*. The work of European scholars Max Müller and Frederick D. Maurice started to circulate in the United States in the 1850s; comparative studies by American Unitarians Samuel Johnson, Thomas Wentworth Higginson, and James Freeman Clarke became available in the 1870s. The impact of those works is difficult to gauge, but undoubtedly they influenced the educated elite. Cornell's president Andrew Dickson White acknowledged, for example, that his belief in Christ's miracles collapsed in the 1850s when he learned that Muslims made similar claims for Muhammad. Another index of the influence of scholarly books about other religions was the almost overnight demise among many believers of the idea of hell. A large minority of conservatives never budged on that matter, but there is considerable evidence that between 1880 and 1910 the majority of preachers simply ceased to talk about it. By 1910, as one historian has put it, it was clear that most Protestants did not want the Chinese to come to California, but "neither did they want them to go to hell."[3]

In addition, there was the cumulative impact of missionary interaction with foreign cultures. That too is difficult to measure, but typically the missionaries' perceptions moved from abhorrence to grudging admiration to varying degrees of approval of the ethical and religious ideals of the peoples among whom they worked. Sometimes individuals, but more often successive generations in a particular place or successive generations sent by a particular board or denomination, followed that pattern. Almost always the solvent that loosened the old absolutist assumptions was the same worrisome question. Was the theological difference between Christianity and other religions absolute or was it one of degree? If the difference was absolute, did that then mean that the missionary was to uproot indigenous faiths regardless of the consequences? If the difference was one of degree, did that then mean that the missionary was to present the Christian message as a better but not necessarily as the exclusive solution to mankind's spiritual needs?

Forms of Response (1890–1930)

Although one might recognize that there were countless forms of response to the challenge posed by world religions, those dominant between 1890 and 1930 can be sorted into three broad categories. I shall label them conservative, liberal, and moderate. Conservatives maintained that Christianity was both unique and exclusive, which meant that it was qualitatively different from all other religions and that it offered the sole avenue to salvation. Liberals denied that Christianity was either unique or exclusive, although they remained certain that it was immeasurably better than the others. Moderates tried to have it both ways, holding that Christianity was superior to all other faiths, and therefore the loftiest road to salvation, but not necessarily the only one. Sociologically, conservatives constituted a large minority of Protestant opinion. Liberals represented a small but highly articulate minority. Moderates, not surprisingly, spoke for the Protestant majority. Until the 1930s, all three groups quite reasonably could claim to be part of the Protestant establishment.

One or two examples illustrate the real-life contours of each position. Conservatives for the most part boycotted the Parliament of Religions, but a few showed up and left no doubt as to where they stood. One contrasted the beauty of the Bible to the "odious stench" of heathen scriptures; another insisted that an "infinite and bridgeless gulf" separated Christianity from other religions; a third described Christianity's attitude toward them as "indiscriminate damnation leaping out like forked lightning." The opinions aired at the Parliament echoed conservative views in general. These were forcefully articulated by Benjamin Warfield, a Presbyterian professor at Princeton Theological Seminary and the premier conservative theologian of the age. In the Bible, Warfield argued, the "heathen religions are uniformly treated as degrading to man and insulting to God." It was true that the human religious appetite

Benjamin Breckenridge Warfield. Courtesy of the Office of History, Presbyterian Church (U.S.A.).

was universal, but God permitted the heathen religions to exist for the same reason that he permitted the Old Testament law: "as a demonstration of their incapacity" to save.[4]

In any consideration of the conservative position, however, two qualifications should be kept in mind. The first is that some individuals who, in most respects, were quite conservative, sometimes proved surprisingly flexible when they confronted the fate of the heathen. That tendency was illustrated by Augustus H. Strong, president of Rochester Theological Seminary and author of a widely used textbook, *Systematic Theology*. Until the human candle was lit by the special revelation of God in Christ, he wrote in 1918 following a worldwide tour of Baptist missions, it emitted a "dim and lurid light . . . touched with the flames of hell." Even so, Strong acknowledged, most religions contained "grains of truth" that missionaries should build upon rather than denigrate. There were sincere seekers after God everywhere, and though they did not know the Christ who saved them, they were saved nonetheless.[5]

The second qualification is, in a sense, the reverse of the first. Some figures who normally steered down the middle of the theological road veered far to the right when other religions swung into view. John R. Mott, general secretary of the World's Student Christian Federation, and widely regarded as a theological moderate, offers a case in point. Other religions, he wrote in 1900, left their adherents in "ignorance and darkness, steeped in idolatry, superstition, degradation and corruption." Although it was true that most religions had existed "many centuries, and in some cases for millenniums," still, sin remained the "supreme obstacle" that blocked their eradication. It alone "benumbed the spiritual sensibilities of the heathen, seared their consciences, hardened their hearts."[6]

The liberal view of world religions stood at the other end of the spectrum. From 1890 to about 1930 liberals consistently affirmed the essential continuity among all religions, or at least among the "high" ones of Buddhism, Confucianism, Hinduism, Islam, and Christianity. But their conception of the exact nature of Christianity's relationship to other faiths evolved considerably. At the Parliament of Religions, for example, Lyman Abbott, editor of the *Outlook*, gave a thumping endorsement to the idea that Christ came "not to create religion but to develop the religion that was already in the human soul." Nonetheless, in Christ the moral relations of men were "better represented" than in any other religion. "We recognize the voice of God in all prophets and in all time," Abbott judged, "but we believe no other revelation . . . equals that which he has made [in this] one transcendental human life."[7]

By 1930 liberal Protestant thinking had moved well beyond Abbott's benign Christian triumphalism. William Ernest Hocking, professor of philosophy at Harvard and an earnest Congregational layman, stands out as the most notable representative of what might be called the fully matured liberal view of other religions. Best known among his numerous works was a collaborative study called *Re-Thinking Missions: A Laymen's Inquiry after One Hundred Years,* published in 1932. The ferocity of the debate that volume provoked has obscured the fact that Hocking did not at that time question the fundamental legitimacy of foreign missions. "At the center," he insisted, "is an always valid impulse of love of men: one offers one's own faith simply because that is the best one has to offer." Nor did he doubt that Christians must refer their "conception of God, of man, and of religion to the teachings and life of Jesus." What Hocking did doubt was that Christianity was either destined or entitled to displace other highly developed religions.[8]

To begin with, Hocking charged, the typical missionary failed to see that modern communications and technology were rapidly creating a unitary world civilization in which the real enemies were not rival faiths

but materialism and secularism. Since the threat was not so much false
religion as no religion at all, Hocking urged Christians to preserve the
"deep-running spiritual life" intrinsic to each culture. That meant, first
of all, that the missionary's first task was not to uproot any religious
tradition but to help men and women of all heritages come to a truer
interpretation of their own faith. The missionary's second task was "far
more difficult": namely, to seek through dialogue with non-Christians a
deepened "grasp of what Christianity actually means." Sharing becomes
real, he insisted, "only as it becomes mutual, running in both directions,
each teaching, each learning . . . each stimulating the other in growth
toward the ultimate goal, unity in the completest religious truth."9

Through the 1920s most Protestants who addressed the relationship
between Christianity and other religions were neither conservatives nor
liberals but moderates. The last evinced a position that was not so much a
compromise between the extremes as a creative – or tortured, depending
on one's point of view – weaving of the two. The moderate missionary
theorists' theological foreign policy expressed itself in several distinct yet
closely related claims.

They acknowledged, at the outset, that most religions offered genuine
knowledge of God. The Apostle Paul himself had written that God had
not left himself without a witness in the non-Christian world, and the
Gospel of John made clear that Christ was the Light that lighted all
humanity. Thus the missionary's initial task was to seek to understand
other religions as fully and sympathetically as possible. Delegates to the
1910 World Missionary Conference in Edinburgh spoke for many moderates on both sides of the Atlantic when they warned that an iconoclastic
attitude was "radically unwise and unjust." It also was unnecessary.
Honest study of other religions only highlighted the incomparability of
Christianity by showing that Christianity avoided their pitfalls and tow-
ered over their strengths.10

Nonetheless – and this was the moderates' second claim – God had
most fully revealed himself in Jesus Christ. Only Christianity could truly
fulfill the spiritual aspirations of other religions. Exactly what "truly
fulfill" meant was open to a considerable range of interpretation. Some
perceived the distance between Christianity and other religions as great
but not infinite. That meant that Christianity served as the standard
against which other religions were measured and the goal toward which
they strove, whether they knew it or not. Since all religions "are the
result of a human longing for communion with some spiritual Being,"
James L. Barton, secretary of the American Board of Commissioners for
Foreign Missions wrote in 1915, "the modern missionary goes out with
the purpose of conserving all true values in the religious thought, life,

and practices of the people. [He] proclaims a sympathetic, constructive gospel." More typically, however, moderate Protestants asserted that the distance between Christianity and other religions was not relative but absolute. God undoubtedly had revealed himself in other faiths, but that revelation was too obscure, too shadowy, to provide salvation in this life or in the life to come. As E. Stanley Jones, a well-known Methodist missionary to India affirmed at the 1928 International Missionary Council, it was a token of weakness to doubt either the absoluteness of Christ *or* the salvific worth of other religions. The more one was convinced of the former the more deeply one would appreciate Christ's work in other religions.[11]

However one construed the gulf between Christianity and other religions, through the 1920s (and, for that matter, through the 1950s) moderate Protestants as a whole saw that once one acknowledged the presence of genuine revelation outside of Christianity, certain results necessarily followed. One was the development of an attitude or approach that might be called "respectful patronization." Explicit vilification of other faiths, which had been common in nineteenth-century missionary literature, steadily diminished among moderates as well as liberals after the turn of the century. James S. Dennis, a Presbyterian missionary and author of an influential three-volume study of Christian missions, spoke for many when he proclaimed at the World's Parliament that Christianity did not seek to "vindicate itself" against other religions but only to "confer its benefits." Christianity could afford to be generous, Dennis cooed, because it spoke with the "consciousness of that simple, natural, incomparable, measureless supremacy which quickly disarms rivalry." A thousand pages of missionary apologetics was captured in Dennis's classic one-liner: Christianity offered other religions the "steel hand of truth encased in the velvet glove of love."[12]

Acknowledging the possibility of genuine revelation outside the confessional boundaries of Christianity entailed a different message as well as a different method. Increasingly, moderates said that their principal concern was to convey the religious faith of Jesus rather than a set of doctrines about him. Again, the exact meaning that these terms bore varied from person to person. For most moderates, it entailed a shift from a Bible-centered, doctrine-oriented message to a Christ-centered, example-oriented message. More precisely, since Jesus uniquely reflected God's nature as self-sacrificing love, missionaries' achievements were to be measured not so much by the number of conversions they scored as by the Christlikeness of their lives. Nowadays, Barton wrote, missionaries increasingly put "Christianity before sect and life before creed." "If a man is saved for the life that now is, he will be abundantly prepared for the life that is to come." For the majority of moderate voices, in short, conversion, defined as a fundamental change of heart, was still important, but less important than the ability to live a Christlike life and to foster the same among others.[13]

Moderates Capture the Establishment (1930–60)

Between 1930 and 1960 the conservative and liberal positions changed remarkably little. Missionary theorists repeatedly used the term "stalemate," and with good reason. The fixity of the conservative stance was reflected in a paper published in 1961 by Harold Lindsell, a Southern Baptist professor at Fuller Theological Seminary and, later, editor of the influential evangelical periodical *Christianity Today*. Anyone who failed to make an explicit affirmation of faith in Jesus Christ, he snapped, regardless of the reason, was headed for eternal damnation. "No other way or road leads to everlasting life." For Lindsell the reason was self-evident: Non-Christian religions were, without exception, "counterfeits of the one true faith." The liberal posture proved equally static. In *Principles of Christian Theology,* a widely used textbook, John Macquarrie of Union Theological Seminary in New York argued that the aim of the church was not to win the world but to "lose itself in the world." Christians' unwillingness to proselytize adherents of other religions grew from the recognition that "wherever the love that springs from reverence for Being is active . . . there christhood (by whatever name it may be called) is laying hold of human life." The practical results of that sort of posture were almost predictable. One former Muslim, who later became a Harvard professor, reported that when he walked into a Methodist mission station in Gambia in the 1960s, and announced that he wanted to convert to Protestant Christianity, the pastor tried to talk him out of it. When he persisted, the pastor urged him to consider converting to Roman Catholicism instead.[14]

In contrast to the immobility of the conservative and liberal outlooks, the moderate position harbored considerable creative ferment. Views that had characterized moderates in the first third of the century persisted, to be sure, but during the middle decades a cluster of new concerns sprung into existence. For analytical purposes we might break this later foreign policy, like the earlier one, into several distinct tenets.

To begin with, there was a growing sense of urgency about the inadequacy of the older persuasions. That mood, which bore the stamp of Continental and British neo-orthodoxy, revealed itself in a mounting inclination to link the challenge of world religions with the threat of secularism and alien political ideologies such as fascism and communism. Nor was the tendency to make those connections limited to ideologues. Serious and influential theologians like Haverford's Rufus Jones and Oberlin's Walter Marshall Horton argued that secularism, fascism, and communism functioned as quasi-religious foes of historic Christianity and should be treated as such.[15]

The sense of urgency was evident in other ways too. One was the developing awareness that the challenge posed by world religions was no longer an academic question that Christians might or might not address as they preferred. At the turn of the century Christianity's right to displace other religions had been simply assumed. By the 1930s thoughtful observers knew that assumption would have to be proved to an increasingly querulous audience at home as well as abroad. The shift was well illustrated by the contrast between the outlook of the 1910 World Missionary Conference in Edinburgh and its successor, the 1928 International Missionary Conference in Jerusalem. Robert E. Speer, general secretary of the Presbyterian Board of Foreign Missions and the premier missions spokesman of the era, attended both meetings. At the first, he judged, the "missionary message in relation to non-Christian religions" remained relatively low on the agenda of concerns. At the latter, it stood uppermost. In 1910 delegates had cheered about the "grandeur" of Christianity marching to the "conquest of the five great religions of the modern world." In 1928, they acknowledged at the outset that the "perplexities on this subject" were so troubling that a fresh inquiry was "urgently needed."[16]

By 1940, the perplexities had deepened. Henry Pitney Van Dusen, president of Union Theological Seminary, declared that nowhere had the "acids of modernity" done more damage than in regard to the rationale for Christian missions. Although Van Dusen never wavered in his commitment to missions, he acknowledged that "beneath all other misgivings was always the basic query whether Christians were justified in striving to loose other peoples from ancient . . . loyalties in order to induct them into a strange and foreign faith." Pearl Buck, more of a liberal than a moderate, nonetheless captured the mood of the era when she warned that if missionaries did not take the moral implications of destroying ancient faiths more seriously, their legacy would prove as evanescent as the "old Nestorian church, a windblown, obliterated tablet upon a desert land."[17]

A second feature of the midcentury foreign policy was a growing inclination to construe the missionary enterprise in therapeutic rather than in imperialistic terms. This was to say that missions brought the consummation rather than the extirpation of other faiths. None of this was wholly new, of course. Since the beginning of the century moderates had stressed the priority of a Christlike life over strict regularity of doctrine. But now, in the midcentury decades, they tended to say that the missionary's task was not to uproot other faiths at all. For too long Christianity's approach to other religions had been needlessly adversarial, as if they were antagonists squaring off for the souls of mankind. Rightly conceived, however, the missionary's aim was simply to share through word and deed the tidings of God's love in Jesus Christ. That did not mean that the absoluteness of Christianity was negotiable, but it did mean that Christianity should be presented as it truly was, not as a culture-entangled religion, but as a supracultural force, a gift, a life, a message of Good News.

Again, Robert E. Speer loomed as the most forceful exponent of that point of view. The idea that Christianity should not be confused with Western civilization, nor with any particular pattern of culture, was by then an old one. Speer's contribution, rather, was to insist that Christianity should not be regarded even as a religion. Properly understood, it was a vital power divinely infused into the human race by Jesus Christ and sustained through the centuries by the church. Thus the church's aim was not primarily to displace other religions, nor to "impose beliefs and practices on others in order to manage their souls in their supposed interests." Its sole aim, rather, was to share with the world a few basic historical facts about what had happened in Palestine many centuries ago, the meaning of those facts, and the life-transforming effects that flowed from their acceptance.[18]

Unfortunately the therapeutic model of the missionary task often left the status of other religions unclear. To what extent did acceptance of Christianity entail denial of one's natal faith? Some writers came close to saying none at all. Articulating what might be called the "anonymous Christians" theme, A. K. Reischauer, an eminent missionary-scholar in Japan, argued that a non-Christian who strove to know the "great things of the Gospel" should be regarded as a "child of God who did not know his Heavenly Father." Walter Marshall Horton similarly insisted that it would be "blasphemy against the Holy Spirit" to doubt that an upright Buddhist brother truly belonged to the Body of Christ. "I would rather have the Spirit without the Name," Horton urged, "than the Name without the Spirit." More commonly, however, mainline theorists admitted that some things would just have to go. Speer allowed that one's birthright tradition might relate to Christianity much as the Old Testament had related to the New. Thus Buddha might play the same role for a Chinese convert as Moses had served for an early Christian. As for

Christ and the ethical and cultural principles directly implied in his teachings, however, there could be no substitute or compromise.[19]

If in the moderates' agenda the status of other religions remained
ambiguous, so too did the status of Christian culture. In the 1920s and
1930s Speer had argued that it was difficult but not impossible to offer a
pure Christianity, free of cultural accretions. The Methodist theologian
Edmund Davison Soper, who succeeded Speer as the leading mis-
siologist of the 1940s, knew better. Soper recognized that one could not
separate Christianity from its cultural clothes, that conversion often entailed painful estrangement from families, and that missions frequently
brought about the destruction of ancient religions and the disruption of
whole cultures. "Has Christianity a message which is not only unique
but indispensable to the welfare of mankind?" If Christians could not
prove their case in both counts, he insisted, there was "no special point in
taking it to others."[20]

In *The Philosophy of the Christian World Mission*, published in 1943,
Soper responded to those challenges by differentiating between the form
and the content of divine revelation. Christianity was indispensable, he
argued, not because of its form, not because God had presented himself
to Christians alone, but because the content of God's revelation in Jesus
Christ, a revelation of undying love, remained unparalleled in other
religions. At one level the church's task was simply to tell the story of
God's love in Christ. At another level, though, there was nothing simple
about it, for that story demanded a costly response from the hearer.
Conversion to Christianity was very much like marriage, in that a man
might continue to appreciate the beauty and virtue of other women – or
in this case other religions – but his final loyalty must be solely to one.
The Christian story was almost as costly for the teller. If missionaries
were to have credibility in the modern world, they would have to pay a
steep price. "Christianity must win its way by clearer thinking, holier
living, and more hopeful dying," Soper warned. "There is no other
way."[21]

Midcentury Protestants were quite certain that the straightforward
proclamation that God had done something in history, that he had recon-
ciled the world to himself in Jesus Christ, avoided the perils of religious
imperialism on one side and of syncretism on the other. Thus Charles
Forman, professor of missions at Yale Divinity School, wrote in 1957
that the Christian missionary aimed not to disrupt other cultures but
only to tell men and women everywhere that the war was over, that
"God has done what is necessary to overcome the separation, and men
need only . . . rejoice." Forman was one of many writers who believed

that when the good news was presented in this form, it would not destroy other cultures but fortify and thereby help them resist Western technological and economic imperialism.[22]

The most important feature of the new missions foreign policy, finally, was a mounting inclination to reassess the biblical and theological warrants that traditionally had been used to justify Christian absolutism. One approach, represented by L. Harold De Wolf, a Methodist theologian at Boston University, was to argue that in numerous ways Christianity itself was the product of an amalgamation of Judaism with various pagan religions and philosophies of the ancient Near East. Ernst Benz, a German Lutheran church historian widely read in the United States, propounded another approach. Christian intolerance of other religions, he contended, grew not so much from Scripture as from Christianity's thousand-year life-and-death struggle with Islam. The physical and ideological bloodiness of that confrontation had left irreparable wounds that had poisoned Christianity's attitude toward other religions ever since.[23]

One of the most learned and forceful critics of Christian absolutism was Wilfrid Cantwell Smith, a United Church of Canada clergyman and professor of Islamic Studies at McGill and Harvard universities. Smith argued that the first two great challenges to Christian thought, Hellenistic philosophy in the second century and agnostic science in the nineteenth, would prove minor compared to the challenge of religious diversity in the twenty-first century. In Smith's mind parochialism was the critical problem. Christian attitudes toward other faiths were usually rooted in abstractions and stereotypes rather than in first-hand knowledge. Did Christians come to the view that other religions were false after they had thoroughly studied them? After they had forged friendships with their adherents? Or was it not the case, Smith demanded, that Christian absolutism usually functioned as the presupposition rather than the product of extended contact with non-Christians?[24]

However one answered that question, Smith judged that the Bible itself did not, on balance, warrant intolerance toward other faiths. He admitted that the New Testament did contain exclusivistic passages that were "not to be treated lightly or casually compromised . . . for the sake of friendly relations with other groups." But conformity to the whole of the biblical message should draw Christians to the other half of the gospel, to the moral half, which commanded reconciliation with all mankind. If God is the kind of God Jesus Christ revealed him to be, "How is it possible to hold a firm, deep, vibrant Christian faith . . . without knowing that God meets other men in other ways?"[25]

During the midcentury decades, conservative, liberal, and moderate

Wilfrid Cantwell Smith. Courtesy of Harvard University News office.

Protestant attitudes toward world religions took different institutional forms and experienced quite different fates. For reasons that remain debatable, conservatives managed to translate theological stasis into sociological vigor. After World War I, they broke away or were driven from the older independent and denominational foreign mission boards. Once outside the establishment, they steadily gathered strength. By 1960 conservatives controlled more than four-fifths of the personnel and financial resources of American missions abroad. Yet raw numbers did not necessarily spell cultural authority. Whether conservative foreign missions, and the ideology that supported them, constituted a direct counterestablishment, or simply another establishment following its own cultural agenda, remained unclear.

Liberals suffered the opposite fate. Their syncretist inclinations proved to be the kiss of death, not only for their presence on the mission field, but also for their influence upon the older mission boards. In many ways the liberal perspective on world religions both culminated and self-destructed with Hocking's work in the 1930s. A handful of theologically radical writers, such as Archibald G. Baker at the University of Chicago Divinity School, and disillusioned missionaries themselves, such as Pearl Buck, endorsed Hocking's ideas, but not many others did so. Through the 1950s, in any event, the ideas espoused by liberal missionary theorists may have resonated in the walnut-paneled classrooms of the old-line seminaries, but they played wretchedly in Peoria.

In the end, only moderates like Speer, Soper, and Smith, who struggled to be true to the evangelical impulse of Christian faith yet not transgress the living heart of other traditions, were able to fuse theological integrity with ethical accountability. Not everyone liked the result. Conservatives smelled heresy and liberals still heard the echo of imperialism. But a great middle band of Protestants thought the moderate synthesis made sense. By 1960 the moderate attitude toward other religions had become as normative as the cultural power and authority of the Protestant establishment itself.

The Academic Study of World Religions

So far we have examined Protestant perceptions of world religions primarily through the eyes of theologians and mission theorists. There was, however, another important tributary that influenced Protestant thinking after World War II: the work of the professional historians of world religions. Although most of those scholars were self-professed Protestants of one stripe or another, they influenced the perceptions of theologians, missiologists, and ordinary believers primarily through their writings and rapidly expanding visibility in college and university classrooms.

Postwar trends encouraged that development in multiple ways. American troops returning from the Orient, a new inclination to esteem pluralism as a positive cultural value, the development of area studies and foreign language programs in the universities, and growing fascination in popular culture with Oriental music, art, cuisine, and literature undoubtedly prompted common folk to take world religions more seriously. At the same time, an extensive institutional scaffolding provided a reliable base of support for world religion scholarship. Mission conferences such as the International Missionary Council meetings in Edinburgh, Jerusalem, and Madras, in 1910, 1928, and 1938; interfaith conventions like the League of Neighbors, the Union of East and West, and the Fellowship of Faiths; semifictional and journalistic portraits of world religions in popular media, such as Edwin Arnold's continually reprinted *Light of Asia,* Pearl Buck's prize-winning novel *Fighting Angel, Life* magazine's *The World's Great Religions* series, and Public Television's "Religions of Man" documentaries, all contributed to the new attitudes. Religious emissaries to the United States such as Swami Vivekananda in the 1890s, Abdul-Baha in the 1910s, Rabindranath Tagore in the 1920s, as well as scholar-advocates like D. T. Suzuki and Sarvepalli Radhakirshnan in the 1950s, also played a vital role.

By far the most important of those institutional developments, however, was the growth of secular religious studies departments in nonsectarian private and public colleges and universities. Admittedly, church-related colleges and seminaries made valuable contributions too. The work of missionary scholars such as Kenneth J. Saunders in India and A. K. Reischauer in Japan, missionary journals like the *Chinese Recorder* and *Moslem World,* and missiology chairs at Yale, Union, Princeton, Chicago, and Southern Baptist Seminary, immediately come to mind. But by and large, the disciplined, systematic, and empathetic study of world religions was the product of secular religious studies departments. The establishment of endowed chairs and lectureships such as the Haskell Lectures at the University of Chicago in 1894, professional societies like the National Association of Bible Instructors in 1909 (becoming the American Academy of Religion in 1963), learned journals such as *Numen* and *History of Religions* in 1954 and 1961, and resident centers for the study of world religions at major universities like McGill and Harvard in 1951 and 1964, securely rooted the discipline in the academic world.

A final supporting development that should be noted was the surge of interest in religion within the social sciences. That trend, which started in the 1880s, became particularly noticeable after World War I. The list of luminaries was long. One thinks, for example, of psychologists William James, Edwin Starbuck, and Erik Erikson; sociologists Talcott Parsons, Will Herberg, and Milton Yinger; anthropologists Ruth Benedict, Margaret Mead, and Robert Redfield. Some of those figures were personally religious, but most clearly were not. Rather, their contribution lay in their ability to construe religion as an enduring feature of society, culture, and personality. Many social scientists ultimately reduced religion to another realm that supposedly was more fundamental – economic struggle, sexual sublimation, or whatever. Yet, on balance, they helped thoughtful Protestants see that all religions, including Christianity, were inextricably woven into their respective cultural systems, and that all religions played functionally similar roles within their respective social settings.

Although social scientists helped foster awareness of religion as an enduring force in human affairs, the men and women who studied the actual religions of mankind – Islam, Buddhism, Hinduism, and so forth – undoubtedly exerted a greater influence. As noted earlier, in the United States the comparative study of world religions reached back to the late eighteenth century, but objectivity would not be the first word one would use to describe most of the works published before World War II. Titles like *Doomed Religions* (1884) and *Error's Chains* (1884) were more graphic than most, but in substance not atypical. Although a few scholars did achieve a measure of objectivity, anything approaching genuine impartiality was out of the question. James Freeman Clarke's *Ten Great Religions: An Essay in Comparative Theology,* first published in 1871 and reissued eighteen times (most recently in 1975), still ranks as the most widely read scholarly survey of world religions in American history. Even so, the most remarkable feature of Clarke's survey of the world's great religions was that Christianity was not one of them. Pious Unitarian that he was, Clarke considered Christianity not a religion at all, but the product of a direct supernatural revelation, the standard against which all other religions should be compared and the ideal toward which they were evolving.

Another cardinal feature of world religion scholarship before 1940 was the persistent tendency, even among careful observers, to evaluate other faiths by Christian criteria. Robert Ernst Hume's *The World's Living Religions,* first published in 1924 and frequently reprinted, illustrates the point. Although Hume had been a missionary himself, his volume provided a window into the Protestant mind precisely because it purported to be not a missionary tract but a scholarly and objective overview of the major faiths. And in a way it was, for it offered detailed expositions of the beliefs propounded by each of the world's major religions, buttressed with long extracts from each one's sacred literature. Yet that was precisely the problem. The work betrayed a peculiarly Protestant assumption that the most important feature of a religion was the normative principles expressed in its originating documents rather than its ever-evolving assumptions, rituals, and ethos. Hume's comparisons were patronizing in other ways as well. At the end of each chapter he enumerated each religion's strengths and weaknesses. Not surprisingly, each proved to be strong insofar as it resembled mainline Protestant Christianity, weak insofar as it departed from that norm.[26]

The explicit and implicit invidiousness of world religion scholarship diminished considerably after World War II. There was, for example, a rising determination to avoid prejudicial terminology. Paul Hutchinson, a *Christian Century* editor and prominent Methodist theologian, noted in the introduction to *Life* magazine's coffee-table anthology *The World's Great Religions,* that we all tend to "mock the unfamiliar in other men's faith." Therefore the volume would avoid terms like "heathen," "idolatry," and "superstition" because they were smear words one would never apply to one's own faith. Those years also witnessed a growing recognition that all religions existed as a response to universal spiritual needs. In order to understand the religions of man, Huston Smith wrote in his immensely popular textbook of that title, one must regard their followers as persons "confronted with problems like ourselves," pilgrims "struggling to see something that would give help and meaning to their lives." Or as Paul Hutchinson put it, all religions have "supplied answers to . . . the great questions aroused in every human mind by the mystery of life, all have brought strength to bear its sorrows, all have shed light on the path of conduct, all have furnished assurance in the presence of death."[27]

The tempering of the old invidiousness became especially evident in the deepening conviction that the scholar's first and final obligation was to burrow inside the "faiths of other men" in order to understand them in their own terms. Yet two quite distinct sets of enemies seemed to wait in ambush. One was the "positivist" scholars who assumed that all responsible observers would restrict their inquiries to antiseptically value-free descriptions of the data and their explanatory theories to the functional relationships between religious behavior and the environing society. The second set consisted of the Christian apologists who, in the words of University of Chicago Divinity School dean Joseph M. Kitagawa, studied other religions "much as the commander of an invading army investigates enemy territory, and with much the same motivations."[28] As things turned out, however, two of the most learned and, through their students, influential scholars of the postwar years made it their special business respectively to confront those threats. The first protagonist was Joachim Wach, a devout Lutheran and (later) Episcopal layman who taught at the University of Chicago from 1945 until his untimely death in 1955. The second was Wilfred Cantwell Smith.

In Wach's mind, one shortcoming of the positivists' supposedly value-free, functionalist account of religious phenomena was that it led to an "unsatisfactory relativism incapable of contributing to the eternal quest for 'truth.'" But another and more serious shortcoming was that it simply failed to achieve its aim. Truly to understand a religion, he argued, one had to begin by empathetically entering into its "central intuition." That was the fundamental prerequisite for grasping the inner meaning of any religion's outward expressions. Differently stated, understanding another religion required something like a religious musicality. "There must resound in each of us something of the ecstatic, the spectral, the unusual – something of that which to us, the children of another age, of another race, and of other customs, appears strange."[29]

Wach hoped, in short, that students of world religions would cultivate methodological principles appropriate to the "austerity and sacred depth" of their subject. All authentic religious expressions were rooted in divine revelation, and divine revelation was found outside as well as inside the boundaries of Christianity. "Unless all existence is a medium of Revelation," he judged, quoting William Temple, "no particular revelation is possible." Nothing better captured the multivalent quality of Wach's legacy to the study of world religions than his admonition that "in the Incarnation . . . the supreme love of God is revealed unambiguously, as nowhere else. . . . [Yet] it will also take Africans and Indians, Chinese and Japanese to apprehend this truth fully."[30]

Wilfred Cantwell Smith fought the war for a more veracious understanding of world religions on a different front. He grappled with the Christian apologists (and a good many non-Christian ones too) who purported to study the "faiths of other men" by treating those faiths as concrete, frozen things known as religions. In Smith's mind the shortcoming of most religion scholars was that they resembled flies crawling around on the outside of a goldfish bowl, incessantly observing but never really knowing how the goldfish themselves perceived the world. The problem was that religions, as such, did not exist. What existed, and what scholars were obliged to study, was "religious persons . . . something interior to persons . . . qualities of personal living." Hence the proper object of study was "not merely tradition but faith, not merely the overt manifestations of man's religious life, but that life itself."[31]

How was that to be done? Besides the usual methods of religion scholarship – historical, social scientific, and phenomenological – Smith urged students to personalize their subjects, to regard them not as objects, nor even as subjects, but as collaborators in a common quest for truth. This required a "dialogic" approach, talking with, not to, persons of other cultures, always asking if our interpretations of their faith were sound. "No statement about a religion is valid unless it can be acknowledged by that religion's believers," Smith averred. If they could not recognize their own portrait, then it was "not their faith." Scholars could not leave it there, of course. Analysis also was necessary. A large part of Smith's legacy was his ability to persuade generations of doctoral students that their task was "to construct statements about religion that are intelligible within at least two traditions simultaneously": the tradition of academic discourse about a given religion, and the tradition of the religion itself."[32]

The Establishment in Perspective

After surveying the Protestant establishment's changing perceptions of world religions between 1890 and 1960, several conclusions about that period and one or two comments about the shape of things in the mid-1980s now seem warranted.

As for conclusions regarding the earlier period, it is clear, first, that the problem of religious pluralism rarely emerged by itself. Almost always it became entangled with other concerns such as the "manifest destiny" of Western civilization in the 1890s, the threat of secular materialism in the 1920s, the rise of political paganisms in the 1930s, and the peril of atheistic communism in the 1950s. That habit of jumbling religious, cultural, and political categories continued to plague the enterprise. If mainline Protestants in the 1980s instinctively turned to secular authorities such as psychiatrists to explain the appeal of the "New Religions," or to TV newscasters to account for the insurgence of Shi'ite "fundamentalism," missiologists and historians of religion should not have been too surprised. To a great extent, they had only themselves to blame, for they had set the precedent.

A second conclusion is that the establishment's encounter with world religions was, even by its own standards, rather anemic. Over the years Protestant thinkers aggressively tackled problems of epistemology, ecumenism, biblical criticism, and social ethics, but rarely religious pluralism. Not even missiologists gave it much attention, and when they did, rhetorical imprecision – always a vocational hazard among theologians – often got hopelessly out of hand. When so distinguished and saintly a scholar as Joachim Wach could describe conversion to Christianity as not a rejection but a "transvaluation" of one's natal faith, it may have been time to go back to the dictionary.[33]

Still another weakness was the gap – often yawning into a chasm – between the ideal of empathetic understanding and the actual performance. One example suffices. In 1940 a Protestant leader, just returned from a world tour of missions, judged that "one of the most striking points of contrast" between Christianity and other religions was that the latter lacked the "power to purge themselves of extraneous, cheap and unworthy elements." Other religions contained elements of "high aspiration," he admitted, "but these are so overlaid . . . with tawdry, the spurious, the vicious that [they] have very generally been hopelessly diluted and contaminated." The writer was not a stereotypically narrowminded fundamentalist, but Henry Pitney Van Dusen, who in most respects was rightly regarded as a man of broad learning and generous sympathies.[34]

Finally, it is worth noting that old chestnuts kept reappearing, even among writers who scrupulously sought to avoid them. In his introduction to *Life* magazine's survey of the world's religions, Paul Hutchinson concluded: "Each great religion . . . attempts to save man from . . . the City of Destruction. All will accomplish that purpose [as] they inspire man 'to do justly, and to love mercy, and to walk humbly with . . . God.'" The words were classic, and the sentiment unimpeachable, but for anyone outside the mainline Protestant tradition, Hutchinson's formula hardly constituted a definition of salvation.[35]

Having said all this, one also must recognize that after World War I mainline Protestants did make increasingly serious efforts to come to terms with the salvific worth of other religions. Conservatives never even tried. No one should be surprised, for one of the principal reasons the latter dropped out of the Protestant establishment was to maintain a firm stand precisely on that issue. However one might judge the theological validity of the respective positions, the contrast was striking. As late as 1950 the conservative China Inland Mission officially reaffirmed its long-standing view that the ultimate fate of the heathen would be "eternally conscious suffering," a position that was (and remained) virtually universal among such groups.[36]

As for the shape of things in the mid-1980s, something like terminal ambiguity had come to shroud the Protestant establishment's relation to the foreign mission enterprise. Many of the older boards continued to exist, to be sure, but overseas missions had become almost exclusively a conservative preserve. The very idea of moderate or mainline, not to mention liberal, foreign missions seemed almost anachronistic, like a musty brown-tone photograph of someone's Victorian grandmother. Yet one could argue that broad public support for humanitarian programs such as the Marshall Plan, the Peace Corps, and world famine relief marked the culmination, not the demise, of the mainline effort to share one's faith without violating the integrity of other people's religions and cultures.

No such ambiguity shrouded the scholarly study of world religions. That endeavor clearly had come to be a purely academic enterprise. Many – perhaps most – of the scholars who entered the field had been trained in the premier seminaries of the Protestant establishment, and many publicly identified themselves with a mainline Protestant church. Yet most world religion scholars strove to frame their questions in scrupulously nonsectarian terms. Some observers believed that trend betokened an erosion of the establishment's influence upon the universities in particular and upon American culture in general. And with good reason. The day had long since passed when it could be assumed, as

Robert E. Speer and his generation had done, that the critical study of world religions would automatically deepen Christian commitment.

Even so, a new generation of scholars was coming into place who well understood that even if world religious pluralism was here to stay, that did not necessarily mean that one's own faith commitments were nothing but a tissue of "preferences." In itself that was not much of a warrant for proclaiming the Christian message in non-Christian cultures. But the back gate was left ajar. If the faith to which the Protestant establishment bore witness was constrained by limitations of perspective, it also was illumined by an unwavering conviction that in Christ God had redeemed the world. Of course that idea was hardly new. The Puritans had said as much, and as far as that goes, so had the Apostle Paul.

NOTES

I wish to thank Lydia Hoyle, Winthrop Hudson, Charles Long, George Marsden, Mark Noll, James Sanford, Richard Seager, and the members of the Department of Religion, Miami University, Oxford, Ohio, who critiqued an earlier version of this essay.

1 Walter R. Houghton (ed.), *Neely's History of the Parliament of Religions* (Chicago: F. T. Neely, 1893), 35. Throughout this essay I have used "world religions" and "other religions" to refer to all religions except Judaism and Christianity. Whether Protestants considered Judaism another religion or merely an incomplete form of Christianity is a tangled problem I have scrupulously avoided.

2 My understanding of the impact of modernization and secularization has been informed by James Turner, *Without God, Without Creed* (Baltimore: Johns Hopkins University Press, 1985), 114–21, 150–9.

3 I owe the reference to White in this paragraph and to the *North American Review* in the preceding paragraph to Turner, *Without God*, 154–5. The quip is from Paul A. Varg, "Motives in Protestant Missions, 1890–1917," *Church History* 23(1954): 72.

4 The first three spokesmen were Joseph Cook, David James Burrell, and William Cleaver Wilkinson. Cook and Burrell are in J. W. Hanson (ed.), *The World's Congress of Religions* (Cincinnati: E. W. Curtis, 1893), 142, 887. Wilkinson is in *Neely's History*, 763. The Warfield sermon comes from *False Religions and the True* (1903), in Samuel G. Craig (ed.), *Biblical and Theological Studies* (Philadelphia: Presbyterian and Reformed, 1968), 565, 569.

5 Strong, *A Tour of the Missions* (Philadelphia: Griffith & Rowland, 1918), 202–8.

6 Mott, *The Evangelization of the World in This Generation* (1900; New York: Student Volunteer Movement, 1904), 17, 36, 38.

7 Abbott in *Neely's History*, 192, 196.

8   Hocking et al., *Re-Thinking Missions* (New York: Harper, 1932), 4, 55.

9   Ibid., 37–8, 44–6.

10   World Missionary Conference, *The Missionary Message in Relation to Non-Christian Religions* (Edinburgh: Oliphant, Anderson & Ferrier, 1910), 267.

11   Barton, "The Modern Missionary," *Harvard Theological Review* 8(1915): 4; Jones in International Missionary Council, *The Christian Life and Message in Relation to Non-Christian Systems of Thought and Life* (New York: IMC, 1928), 289–90.

12   Dennis in John Henry Barrows (ed.), *The World's Parliament of Religions*, 2 vols. (Chicago: Parliament, 1893), II:1254–5. I owe this reference to Richard Seager.

13   Barton, "Modern Missionary," 2, 16.

14   Lindsell in Gerald H. Anderson (ed.), *The Theology of the Christian Mission* (New York: McGraw-Hill, 1961), 246–7; Macquarrie, *Principles of Christian Theology* (New York: Scribner's, 1966), 393. The convert anecdote is from Lamin Sanneh, "Christian Missions and the Western Guilt Complex," *Christian Century*, April 8, 1987, 330.

15   Jones in *Christian Life*, 230–73; Horton, "Between Hocking and Kraemer," International Missionary Council, *The Authority of the Faith* (New York: IMC, 1939), 137–49.

16   Speer in *Christian Life*, 278, v; John A. Mackay, "Christianity and other Religions," in Arnold S. Nash (ed.), *Protestant Thought in the Twentieth Century* (New York: Macmillan, 1951), 288.

17   Van Dusen, . . . *For the Healing of the Nations* (New York: Scribner's, 1940), 5, 7; Buck, "The Laymen's Mission Report," *Christian Century*, November 23, 1932, 1436.

18   Speer, *Finality*, 280–8; *Christian Life*, 405.

19   Reischauer in *Christian Life*, 284–5; Horton, "Hocking and Kraemer," 139; Speer, *The Finality of Jesus Christ* (Westwood, N.J.: Fleming Revell, 1933), 335, 347.

20   Soper, *The Philosophy of the Christian World Mission* (New York: Abingdon-Cokesbury, 1943), 16, 226.

21   Ibid., 203.

22   Forman, *A Faith for the Nations* (Philadelphia: Westminster Press, 1957), 60.

23   De Wolf in Anderson (ed.), *Theology*, 199–204; Benz, "The Theological Meaning of the History of Religions," *Journal of Religion* 41(1961): 1–16.

24   Smith in William G. Oxtoby (ed.), *Religious Diversity* (1960; New York: Harper & Row, 1976), 9, 17.

25   Smith, "Christianity's Third Great Challenge," *Christian Century*, April 27, 1960, 506, 508.

26   Hume, *The World's Living Religions*, rev. ed. (1924; New York: Scribner's, 1953).

27   Both Hutchinson quotations are in Sam Welles (ed.), *The World's Great Religions* (New York: Time, 1957), 1; Smith, *The Religions of Man* (1958; New York: Harper & Row, 1965), 13.

28   Kitagawa in Mircea Eliade and Kitagawa (eds.), *The History of Religions: Essays in Methodology* (Chicago: University of Chicago Press, 1959), 15.

29 Wach, "The Place of the History of Religions in the Study of Theology," *Journal of Religion* 27(1947): 160; "Introduction," in Joseph M. Kitagawa (ed.), *The History of Religions* (Chicago: University of Chicago Press, 1967), 6, 12.
30 Wach in Kitagawa (ed.), *History* (1967), 5; Wach in Joseph M. Kitagawa (ed.), *Understanding and Believing* (New York: Harper & Row, 1968), 70, 85.
31 Smith in, respectively, Oxtoby (ed.), *Religious Diversity*, xxii; Eliade and Kitagawa (eds.), *History,* 35; and Joseph M. Kitagawa, "Humanistic and Theological History of Religions," *Numen* 27(1980): 206.
32 Smith in Eliade and Kitagawa (eds.), *History,* 42, 52.
33 Wach in Kitagawa (ed.), *Understanding,* 83.
34 Van Dusen, *Healing,* 205–6.
35 Hutchinson in Welles (ed.), *Great Religions,* 8.
36 The China Inland Mission quotation is from M. Searle Bates, "The Theology of American Missionaries in China," in John K. Fairbank (ed.), *The Missionary Enterprise in China and America* (Cambridge, Mass.: Harvard University Press, 1974), 154.

SELECT BIBLIOGRAPHY

Ahlstrom, Sydney E. *The American Protestant Encounter with World Religions.* Beloit, Wis.: Beloit College, 1962.
Barrows, John Henry, ed. *The World's Parliament of Religions: The Columbian Exposition of 1893.* 2 vols. Chicago: Parliament, 1893.
Barton, James L. "The Modern Missionary." *Harvard Theological Review* 8(1915): 11–17.
Forman, Charles W. "A History of Foreign Mission Theory in America." In R. Pierce Beaver, ed., *American Missions in Bicentennial Perspective.* South Pasadena, Calif.: William Carey Library, 1977.
Hocking, William Ernest, et al. *Re-Thinking Missions: A Laymen's Inquiry after One Hundred Years.* New York: Harper, 1932.
Hutchison, William R. *Errand to the World: American Protestant Thought and Foreign Missions.* Chicago: University of Chicago Press, 1987.
Kitagawa, Joseph M. "The History of Religions in America." In Mircea Eliade and Joseph M. Kitagawa, eds., *The History of Religions: Essays in Methodology.* Chicago: University of Chicago Press, 1959.
Kitagawa, Joseph M., ed. *Understanding and Believing: Essays by Joachim Wach.* New York: Harper & Row, 1968.
Sharpe, Eric. *Comparative Religion: A History.* New York: Scribner's, 1975.
Smith, Wilfred Cantwell, "Christianity's Third Great Challenge." *Christian Century,* April 27, 1960, 505–8.
Speer, Robert E. *The Finality of Jesus Christ.* Westwood, N.J.: Fleming H. Revell, 1933.
Williams, George Huntston, "The Attitude of Liberals in New England Toward Non-Christian Religions, 1784–1885." *Crane Review* 9(1967): 60–89.

12

The Rise of the "New Evangelicalism": Shock and Adjustment

MARK SILK

"Sectarianism receives new lease on life," announced the *Christian Century*'s May 19, 1943, editorial on the formation of the National Association of Evangelicals for United Action (NAE). The leaders of the new organization claimed that the great majority for whom the Federal Council of Churches "has presumed to speak" were misrepresented by the policies of that body. Nonsense, snapped the nondenominational weekly. "Every kind of conservatism" within the NAE could be found in bodies belonging to the Federal Council of Churches (FCC) – "and this not in suppressed minorities or in inarticulate and misrepresented majorities, as the 'evangelicals' say, but in the personnel of every part of the organizational structure from top to bottom." As the *Century* saw it, the NAE's founders clearly desired not representation within a united Protestantism but control of part of Protestantism's divided house.[1]

Thus did the New Evangelicalism of Boston pastor Harold Ockenga and Chicago theologian Carl Henry first strike the Protestant establishment, whose chief preoccupation during and just after World War II was institutionalizing ecumenism, what with the Federal Council of Churches about to grow into the National Council (NCC) and the World Council aborning. Efforts on the part of disaffected conservatives to organize in opposition could hardly fail to raise establishment hackles.

The Antiestablishment Gauntlet

The National Association of Evangelicals was not the only such organizational undertaking. The year before, Carl McIntire, a preacher from Collingswood, New Jersey, had established the American Council of Christian Churches (ACCC). A student at Princeton Theological

Carl McIntire. Copyright Francis Laping. Used by permission.

Seminary in the late twenties, McIntire had followed his teacher, the fundamentalist Presbyterian divine J. Gresham Machen, when the latter crossed into Pennsylvania to found Westminster Seminary. In McIntire, however, a native strain of American antiestablishmentarianism ran so pure that within a few years he broke with Machen and founded his own denomination. The American Council, too, manifested his radically oppositional character, becoming a kind of ecclesiastical *doppelgänger* to the establishment's ecumenical bodies; whithersoever they went to meet, there would the American Council go, compelling the Federal Council or National Council or World Council to issue warnings to press and public not to labor under any confusion about which was which and what was what. Living to vituperate and harass, McIntire and his fundamentalist followers classically embodied the paranoid style in American politics during the postwar period.

If the American Council represented the parodic termination of the fundamentalist–modernist battles of the twenties and early thirties, the National Association of Evangelicals expressed the ambition of the next generation. After the Scopes trial of 1925, the fundamentalist tide had ebbed swiftly from the mainline denominations: the Presbyterians and Northern Baptists, both of which had been threatened with takeover, extruded their fundamentalists. As far as could be told from within establishment citadels, fundamentalism had become a throwback, part of the folkways of those "upland primates" on whom Mencken had reported with such relish from Dayton, Tennessee. But the throwback survived and prospered, and not only in mountain hollows. Across the country alternative institutions – congregations, Bible schools, publishing houses – sprang into being outside the mainstream denominations. Anyone turning the radio dial in the thirties would come across many voices preaching fundamentalist faith.

By the forties, this world had produced a new breed of conservatives, anxious to wipe away the stigma of fundamentalism (they eschewed the term) but confident that their old-time religion represented a cure for whatever ailed America. This, however, would require cooperation, a coordination of effort, a united evangelical front. And already there was a divided house. As Carl Henry, the New Evangelicalism's preeminent theological voice, put it in 1947:

> The force of the redemptive message will not break with apostolic power upon the modern scene unless the American Council of Churches and the National Association of Evangelicals meet at some modern Antioch, and Peter and Paul are face to face in a spirit of mutual love and compassion. If, as is often remarked, the Federal Council of Churches is the voice of Protestant liberalism in America, Protestant evangelicalism too needs a single voice.[2]

Was this more than pious rhetoric? Given McIntire's style, an amalgamation of the American Council and the National Association of Evangelicals would seem to have been neither possible nor desirable; the NAE was better positioned to counter the FCC on its own.

The seriousness of its threat to the establishment remained to be seen. In 1948, committees of both the Reformed Church in America and the United Presbyterian Church (not to be confused with the 1958 Presbyterian amalgamation of the same name) met to study the relative merits of remaining in the Federal Council or switching to the NAE. The same year, the question of membership in the FCC was put before presbyteries of the Presbyterian Church in the United States. Yet none of the three chose to run up different interdenominational colors, and it was

Carl F. H. Henry. Religious News Service photo.

soon plain that the NAE was not about to give mainline ecumenism a head-to-head run for its money. There were, however, other ways of doing battle.

In April of 1953, for example, as National Council panjandrum G. Bromley Oxnam, the Methodist bishop of Washington, prepared to defend himself against charges of Communist fellow-traveling before the House Un-American Activities Committee, the NAE annual convention passed a resolution supporting government investigations of ideologically suspect religious leaders. Day in and day out, the NCC was denounced as an ominous superchurch by *United Evangelical Action,* the official NAE organ, under the editorship of James DeForest Murch. But unlike the American Council the NAE did not seek to burn all bridges to the establishment. The *Christian Century* put it this way: "The [ACCC] insists that its members must not only repudiate and denounce apostasy (i.e., the National Council), but also separate from it. The NAE settles for repudiation and denunciation." The point was that the NAE sought the membership not only of whole denominations, but also of individuals, schools, missions, and congregations whose parent denominations belonged to the National Council; it was, in effect, bent on raiding behind NCC lines – and not least in the matter of fund-raising. In the mid-fifties, the Reverend J. Kenneth Miller, a Long Island minister who served on the United Presbyterian Church's World Service Committee, sent a couple of dunning letters he had received from NAE organizations to H. J. McKnight, a fellow committee member (and United Presbyterian representative to the NCC Joint Department of Stewardship and Benevolence). Miller complained of the NAE's ethics in trying to siphon funds from a denomination that possessed its own benevolent and interchurch bodies. Ecclesiastical punctilio was not his only concern. "This N.A.E. outfit," he wrote of the World Evangelical Fellowship in 1956, "has influence in this Synod."[3]

Yet it was not through such sallies or through denunciation or, for that matter, through the influence of its neofundamentalist theologians that the New Evangelicalism disturbed the course of the Protestant mainstream. Rather, the disturbance came through the reemergence on the national religious scene of urban mass revivalism. The man responsible, of course, was Billy Graham, the North Carolina farm boy who, by the mid-1950s, had become perhaps the most famous Protestant in the world. Nothing better displays the character of the Protestant establishment during the celebrated postwar religious revival than its divided response to Graham, and to the evangelism for which he stood.

The Headway of Billy Graham

Ever since his 1949 Los Angeles crusade Graham had basked in a glowing secular press; but cooler temperatures prevailed in the pages of the *Christian Century*. The *Century* duly noted Graham's presence at the NAE conventions of 1951, 1952, and 1953; it was decidedly noncommittal on the effects of his 1951 Seattle crusade. Certainly the journal did not share the enthusiasm that greeted Graham's speech before the 1952 Southern Baptist Convention – especially when "the most popular young evangelist of the day . . . mopped his brow and cried, 'When this convention voted earlier this week not to affiliate with any other group, I thanked God.'" The vote in question was to ratify a committee report that, among other things, attacked both the World and the National Council of Churches; it was, said the editorial correspondent, "the most perverse, únbrotherly and dangerous pronouncement made by any Southern Baptist Convention in many years." Yet barely two years later, with Graham playing to overflow houses across the Atlantic, came the following words:

> In London as in America, Billy Graham is revealing himself as extraordinarily teachable and humble, considering that he is surrounded with the fevered adulation of crowds so much of the time. He will learn a great deal in London, and will, if he keeps up the growth which has characterized his last three years, put what he learns to good use for Christ and the church.[4]

How to explain the change of heart?

Only a month before, Graham had ventured into Union Theological Seminary and, after speaking in chapel for forty-five minutes and answering questions in the Social Room for another thirty, had come away with one of the greatest ovations in that institution's memory. News of the encounter may well have reached the *Century*'s editors in Chicago; in any event, their new view of Graham mirrored what John Bennett had to say in "Billy Graham at Union," in the May issue of the *Union Seminary Quarterly Review*. To explain the applause, Union's dean of faculty pointed to Graham's evident sincerity and magnetism, his verbal adroitness, and the simple relief of his audience at finding him not as bad as they feared. Yet underneath it all, said Bennett, there was reason to think that Graham was "breaking the pattern" of the crude and mercenary evangelist: "Many of us gained the strong impression that he can be used for highly constructive Christian purposes in the churches and in the nation."

For Bennett, "breaking the pattern" meant that Graham understood the limits of mass evangelism and the importance of financial propriety. It also meant, at least he hoped it did, that Graham's grasp of "biblical truth" would be sufficient to correct his enthusiasm for America's "culture religion" (e.g., his inability to understand the laughter that greeted his pointing to the American Legion's back-to-God campaign as a sign of a national return to religion); and that his "ecumenical outlook and strategy" (the word "ecumenical" recurred often in his remarks) might "deliver him from the worst effects of Fundamentalism." In any case, Graham's use of the Bible did not represent a "hard Fundamentalism," and there was evidence that he was "growing" in his social outlook. "I am," Bennett concluded, "publishing this article with some hesitation":

> I do not like to set myself up as a judge of Billy Graham in this way and I do not want this record of my surprise to seem pa-

John C. Bennett. Religious News Service photo.

tronizing. It is a fact that until his visit to Union I had classed
him as a fundamentalist and socially reactionary evangelist and
had dismissed him as a possible constructive force in the American Church. On the other hand there is a chance that this article
may be too optimistic and hence misleading. . . . When all is
said, I believe that his coming to Union was a very good lesson
for us. It may have helped us to realize more vividly, what we
should have known from Church History, that God can work
powerfully through men who do not meet all our specifica-
tions.[5]

The Galahad of the New Evangelicalism had won a provisional seat at
the establishment's Round Table.

The effects could be discerned in the establishment's great ecumenical
institutions. In August of the same year, at the Second Assembly of the
World Council of Churches in Evanston, Illinois, no phase of the program received more attention than the report of Section II, "The Mission

of the Church to Those Outside Her Life"; extra time was allotted for comment on the delicate question of how to pursue a united evangelism. In the spring, meanwhile, the National Council had appointed Berlyn Farris, an old-fashioned evangelical Methodist from Wichita, as executive director of its Department of Evangelism. Having declared, in May, that "today's climate for the evangelistic work of the churches is the most favorable we've had in America in the last 20 years," Farris spelled out, in a year-end report, just what he had in mind for the nation's cities:

> Let us dream a moment. Suppose in a given city a National Christian Teaching Mission would first go in to make a gigantic survey, establish the mood of evangelism in every church in the city and prepare the way for a great movement of evangelism. Following that would be an organized prayer program which would be extended into every block of the entire city. A Visitation Evangelism program would come in, following the spiritual development which would undoubtedly bring hundreds of persons into the acceptance of Jesus Christ and the fellowship of the Church. This would be followed by a great program of preaching with an evangelist who could proclaim nightly the saving power of Jesus Christ.
>
> This would be a revival in the truest sense of the word, not only winning persons to the acceptance of Christ for the first time, but a deepening of the spiritual life of the multitudes of the city. This would then be followed by a program of stewardship, encouraging the people to tithe, to attend church, to pray, and to serve. Thus the whole community would be awakened and the Church and Christian life of the community would be deepened. This is a dream, to be sure. But isn't it the sort of stuff that reality is made of?

With hopes that this would be "one of the greatest evangelistic periods in our history," Farris and his staff persuaded NCC leaders in early 1955 to create a commission to study the need and place of evangelism in contemporary Protestantism, and its role in the work of the National Council of Churches.[6]

A case can be made that during the mid-fifties a kind of evangelical excitement took hold in mainline Protestantism that harked back to the days before Scopes, when "the evangelization of the world in this generation" was a goal establishmentarians could happily embrace. With liberalism (read: modernism) on the run in the loftiest theological circles, those who professed The Fundamentals were no longer so easily dismissed: by his classic revivalist's willingness to ignore doctrinal and institutional barriers in gathering his forces, Graham proved capable of enlisting the support of sophisticated clergy as well as layfolk throughout the mainline denominations. It was also the hour of the American Century (as proclaimed by Henry Luce, the China missionary's son), and the country was pleased to think of itself as on the march against dark, atheistic powers at loose in the world. Why not a return to the yoked advance of American power and American religion? I do not want to overstate the case. There were many in high Protestant places who wanted no part of revivalistic religion. But their very criticism of Graham stirred up an opposition that bore witness to a New Evangelical appeal within even the most forbidding bastions of the establishment.

Neibuhr versus Graham

The most important criticism issued from Reinhold Niebuhr, than whom no Protestant theologian was more thoroughly inoculated against the seductions of evangelistic enthusiasms. He fired first from his own journal, *Christianity and Crisis,* in a March 5, 1956, editorial responding to news that Billy Graham would be coming to New York. "We dread the prospect," he wrote:

> Billy Graham is a personable, modest and appealing young man who has wedded considerable dramatic and demagogic gifts with a rather obscurantist version of the Christian faith. His message is not completely irrelevant to the broader social issues of the day but it approaches irrelevance. For what it may be worth, we can be assured that his approach is free of the vulgarities which characterized the message of Billy Sunday, who intrigued the nation about a quarter century ago. We are grateful for this much "progress."

Niebuhr's central concern was that by "presenting Christianity as a series of simple answers to complex questions" Graham would only strengthen the modern inclination to dismiss the gospel as irrelevant to contemporary life.[7]

Niebuhr's editorial "we," however, presumed too much, for two issues later a sharp rejoinder from editorial board member Henry P. Van Dusen, the president of Union Theological Seminary, appeared in the letters column. Calling his editor's opposition to Graham "thoroughly unscriptural" for ignoring apostolic recognition of "diversities of gifts" and "differences of operations," Van Dusen emphasized the need to present the masses with a "more readily digestible form" of the gospel than the "'strong meat' of a sophisticated interpretation":

> Dr. Niebuhr prefers Billy Graham to Billy Sunday. There are
> many, of whom I am one, who are not ashamed to testify that
> they would probably never have come within the sound of Dr.
> Niebuhr's voice or the influence of his mind if they had not been
> *first* touched by the message of the earlier Billy. Quite probably
> five or ten years hence there may appear in the classrooms and
> churches of Billy Graham's severest critics not a few who will be
> glad to give parallel testimony to his role in *starting* them in that
> direction.[8]

Niebuhr next carried the attack to the pages of the *Christian Century,*
where in May he rather more gently took Graham to task for biblical
literalism and pietistic moralism. In a mannerly reply, E. G. Homrighausen, dean of Princeton Seminary and head of the NCC's Department
of Evangelism, charged Niebuhrian neo-orthodoxy with being "hesitant
and weak in calling persons to a positive faith":

> I have, frankly, been disappointed in its inability to lead the way
> in the revival or rebirth or restoration of a relevant Protestantism
> in the local church. And if men like Graham have arisen and are
> being heard by the thousands, it may be that what he is and says
> in sincerity ought to be said in a better way by the neo-orthodox
> with all their accumulation of intelligence about the Bible and
> history and personality in our times.

Niebuhr came back, in August, with his "Proposal to Billy Graham,"
which, with Bennettian hopefulness, urged Graham to raise high the
banner of racial justice and "become a vital force in the nation's moral
and spiritual life." That drew "A Proposal to Reinhold Niebuhr" from
the New Evangelical theologian E. J. Carnell; Carnell's proposal was
that Niebuhr let his "Yes" to Billy Graham resound ("dialectically") as
loudly as his "No." Niebuhr's increasingly moderated stance toward
Graham had its institutional analogue. In the summer of 1956, Episcopal
bishop John S. Higgins of Rhode Island, a member of the NCC's policy
committee, sent a private letter to NAE president Paul Petticord explor-
ing the possibility of rapprochement between the two umbrella organizations. Petticord had the bad taste to make Higgins's letter public, de-
nouncing the feeler at a meeting of the World Evangelical Fellowship;
but then, much to the approval of the *Christian Century,* Paul S. Rees, a
past NAE president, cordially informed Bishop Higgins of his eagerness
to participate in informal conversations to that end.[9]

The importunate note that crept into establishmentarian discourse in
1955 and 1956 had to do, more than anything else, with the impending

New York crusade: Preparations for it, according to the *Christian Century*, were "so extensive that they threaten to overrun every other church activity." Those raising questions were begging for "a diversified campaign so that a fuller, more accurate account of Protestant Christianity will be given the great community." Given that the big money would be withdrawn if Drs. Niebuhr, Tillich, or Bennett were featured "even in smaller tents" (!), might not Dr. Graham be "more explicit about his ecumenicity"?[10] Conceivably it was not the gospel, but the establishment, that Graham threatened to render irrelevant in Gotham. In the event, the NCC's Department of Evangelism joined the bandwagon; H. H. McConnell, the deputy executive director, took on the responsibility of directing the follow-up program of "visitation evangelism." Yet even before Graham stood up to address his first Madison Square Garden crowd on May 15, 1957, the bloom was coming off the rose for McConnell's boss, Executive Director Berlyn Farris.

At the NCC General Board meeting on May 1 and 2, the Commission to Study Evangelism presented its report. Farris and members of his staff had served as consultants to the twenty-three-member commission, which included such diverse figures as Georgia Harkness, E. G. Homrighausen, and Norman Vincent Peale; but the report itself was largely the work of Robert Calhoun of Yale, a man of no great evangelical enthusiasm, and it embodied a barely disguised neo-orthodox critique of the whole American revivalist tradition. Thus: Original sin condemned society for all time to the status of "a living corporate web of wrong action and impulse that no human being can escape." The evils of the day were not faithlessness and bad morals but the idols of a modern civilization more complex than what went before. Evangelism was the business of God and the entire Church: although preachers possessed a special role, the itinerant exhortation of mass audiences was an uncertain thing:

> Such preaching is revivalism, a method that involves both possible values and very real perils for evangelism, to which it can at best make substantial contributions, of which at worst it can be a gross caricature, and with which in any event it is not to be identified. Revivalists can indeed, under God, be evangelists of power; but it is not their distinctive method that makes them so.[11]

According to the minutes of the meeting, various suggestions were offered toward making the document more conventionally evangelical. One discussion group "asked for a more positive description of revivalism as it relates to evangelism"; in the final, printed version, the phrase "possible values and very real perils" was changed to "possible values and possible perils." Nowhere was there either the rallying cry or the institutional specifics that Farris had had in mind. A week later, in his report to the managers of his department, he bravely called the report "stimulating, challenging, and thought-provoking," adding, "It won't answer all the questions, but it will build fires under our thinking." A month later, citing the department's ongoing shortage of funds, he suddenly announced his resignation, effective July 1, to become director of district evangelism for the Board of Evangelism of the Methodist Church.[12]

But the event that really turned the tide was the New York crusade itself. As even *Life* put it in its July 1 issue:

> Billy Graham opened his New York crusade in high hopes that it would "soon be like a mighty river through the city." But after 37 days of his 66-day stand in Madison Square Garden, the river has not been mighty. New Yorkers have talked surprisingly little about Billy – unlike his smash hits in London and Los Angeles, where he was the talk of the town.

Graham was simply not as much a force to be reckoned with as had been hoped – or feared. Besides this, the manifest nature of the crusade, with its well-oiled mechanisms of conversion, its well-scrubbed and well-mannered audiences, inspired a new establishmentarian line on Graham, evident in the *Christian Century*'s three stiff editorials on the crusade but most bluntly put in the piece contributed to *Life* by Reinhold Niebuhr:

> Graham is honest and describes the signers of his decision cards as "inquirers" rather than "converts." It would be interesting to know how many of those attracted by his evangelistic Christianity are attracted by the obvious fact that his new evangelism is much blander than the old. For it promises a new life, not through painful religious experience but merely by signing a decision card. Thus a miracle of regeneration is promised at a painless price by an obviously sincere evangelist. It is a bargain.

Graham had previously been charged with excessive acquiescence in America's culture-religion, and the long-term effects of his revivals had long been questioned. But in contrast, say, to Peale, he had always been credited with offering up a good strict version of traditional American Protestantism. Now he was merely another dispenser of postwar piety, purveying the things of the spirit on the cheap.[13]

Graham himself turned the other cheek. "I have read nearly everything Mr. Niebuhr has written, and I feel inadequate before his brilliant

Billy Graham in Times Square on the night before the beginning of his New York City "crusade," 1957. Copyright Cornell Capa and Magnum Photos, New York. Used by permission.

mind and learning," he told journalist Noel Houston. He continued his pursuit of good but not overclose relations with the NCC. In December of 1957, for example, he wrote to General Secretary Roy G. Ross expressing thanks that his greetings had been extended to the NCC's General Assembly; apologizing for not being able to attend in person ("due to extensive dental work and one or two speaking commitments"), applauding the choice of Edwin T. Dahlberg as president ("I have admired him for many years"), and mentioning his recent collaboration with the Department of Evangelism's H. H. McConnell ("a very warm friend"). As far as the establishment was concerned, however, New York was Graham's high-water mark. After that, there were no more expectations that revivalism, Billy style, might really make a difference. The difference was to be sought elsewhere.[14]

Beyond the Pale

In 1958, in what is surely one of the few *Life* articles ever regularly cited in scholarly footnotes, Henry P. Van Dusen identified a "Third Force" in Christianity (alongside Catholicism and Protestantism) composed of Adventists, Pentecostals, Jehovah's Witnesses, and other often-despised "fringe" groups; growing by leaps and bounds, it was no less than "the most extraordinary religious phenomenon of our time." Van Dusen had observed these churches firsthand during a three-month visit to the Caribbean three years before. Now he celebrated their "direct biblical message"; its promise of "an immediate, life transforming experience of the living-God-in-Christ" was, he said, "far more significant to many individuals than the version of it normally found in conventional churches." Van Dusen stressed, above all, that followers were expected to "practice an active, untiring, seven-day-a-week Christianity." Sympathetic enough to the New Evangelicalism to have served on Billy Graham's New York committee, he nonetheless drew no connection between the Third Force and the NAE, although five of the Third Force groups listed at the end of his article – the Assemblies of God, the Church of God (based in Cleveland, Tenn.), the International Church of the Foursquare Gospel, the Pentecostal Church of God in America, and the Pentecostal Holiness Church – in fact constituted nearly two-thirds of the NAE's total membership. It was as though the NAE *as such* had become too conventional, as though the vitality of the Third Force had to lie in its independence from any sort of religious consensus. In *The New Shape of American Religion* (1959), Martin Marty took more or less this tack. After blaming Billy Graham for his "failure to become unpopular with people outside the churches," he looked for help from the "protesting intransigents" of the Third Force: "The square pegs that do not fit the round holes of eroded religious expression might call us all to a higher witness."[15]

Soon, however, new challenges were in the air, challenges that stifled all establishmentarian yearning after life-transforming religion on America's spiritual periphery, challenges that cast the New Evangelicals even further beyond the pale. On the evening of September 12, 1960, John Fitzgerald Kennedy stood up in the ballroom of the Rice Hotel in Houston to address that city's ministerial association. For months Kennedy had been trying to lay the issue of his Catholicism to rest, but to no avail; and it was clear whence the bulk of the opposition came. In April 1960 the NAE had resolved to oppose the election of any Roman Catholic as president of the United States. On September 4, a front-page article in the *New York Times* announced that "in Texas and throughout the South, the issue between the Southern Baptists and Senator Kennedy has been joined." On September 8, a new organization calling itself the National Conference of Citizens for Religious Freedom had charged that the Democratic candidate would be unable "to withstand the determined efforts of the hierarchy of his church . . . to breach the wall of separation between church and state." Although this group had as its putative leader Norman Vincent Peale (and also included Charles Clayton Morrison, the former editor of the *Christian Century*), it was preponderantly a New Evangelical affair starring founding father Harold Ockenga, the NAE's public affairs secretary Clyde W. Taylor, Daniel Poling of the *Christian Herald*, and L. Nelson Bell, an editor of *Christianity Today* and Billy Graham's father-in-law. Theirs was the constitutency to whom Kennedy appealed when he went down to Houston.

"I believe," said the candidate, "in an America where the separation of church and state is absolute – where no Catholic prelate would tell the President (should he be Catholic) how to act, and no Protestant minister would tell his parishioners for whom to vote." For those who had followed his remarks on the religious issue, most of what he had to say was familiar, but there was one significant alteration of substance:

> If the time should ever come – and I do not concede any conflict to be remotely possible – when my office would require me to either violate my conscience, or violate the national interest, then I would resign the office, and I hope any other conscientious public servant would do likewise.[16]

Significantly, one hundred Protestant, Catholic, and Jewish leaders had that very day issued their "Statement on Religious Liberty in Relation to the 1960 National Campaign," which covered, in a few more words, the identical ground:

> No citizen in public office dare be false either to his conscience or to his oath of office. Both his conscience and his oath impose responsibilities sacred under the law of God. If he cannot reconcile the responsibilities entailed by his oath with his conscience, then he must resign, lest he fail his nation and his God.[17]

Here was the establishmentarian voice of America, joined in interfaith union to insist on the right of citizens of all faiths to run for the highest office in the land. Not, to be sure, that the Protestant establishment – engaged in running skirmishes with the Catholic Church throughout the postwar period – had been entirely unambivalent about this. Back in May, in *Look,* Bishop Oxnam and the current NCC president, Eugene Carson Blake, had expressed reservations about having a Roman Catholic in the White House. But by the fall, hostility to the *principle* of a Catholic president rested largely with the Protestant antiestablishment.

The hostility was not, at least in the establishment's eyes, merely a matter of anti-Catholic prejudice and *odium theologicum*. As John Bennett wrote a few days after Kennedy's Houston speech:

> Those who take the leadership in this Protestant attack on the Roman Church as a campaign issue are also persons who would not support a liberal Democrat no matter what his religion; . . . the opposition on the religious issue centers in that part of the country where the opposition is equally strong on the issue of civil rights and on the economic philosophy of Senator Kennedy and his platform.[18]

Shades of Scopes: The evangelicals were now simply to be ranged among the forces of darkness in the South. The forces of light, meanwhile, were banding together.

In mid-January 1963, a conference was convened at Chicago's Edgewater Beach Hotel by the NCC's Department of Racial and Cultural Relations, the Social Action Commission of the Synagogue Council of America, and the Social Action Department of the National Catholic Welfare Conference. Six hundred and fifty-seven delegates from these and sixty-seven other religious and religiously affiliated groups turned out for four days of speeches and workshops. Marking the one hundredth anniversary of Lincoln's Emancipation Proclamation, the National Conference on Religion and Race was neither one more exercise in "interfaith dialogue" nor, like the National Conference of Christians and

Jews, ecumenism in the breach. For the first time in American history, central bodies of Protestantism, Catholicism, and Judaism had joined together for the purpose of spearheading a nationwide social reform – specifically, "to increase the leadership of religion in ending racial discrimination in the United States."[19] It was something very like a new American religious establishment.

And it did not need Billy Graham. In 1964, in response to an inquiry from a Mrs. H. J. Van Dort of Spring Valley, California, on the relations of Graham and the NCC, Executive Director Colin Williams stated tersely, "My understanding is that Dr. Graham has spoken at National Council of Churches gatherings but has not been officially involved in National Council activities. His denomination is not a member church of the National Council of Churches." Politics had become the heart of the matter. The following year, in a lead editorial titled "Demythologizing Neoevangelicalism," the *Christian Century* charged Graham with speaking "out of both sides of his mouth," at once repudiating socially activist Christians for "sidetracking the Gospel" and yet stressing the importance of taking stands on the issues of the day. The real issue was, said the editorial, *which stands?* In recent months the neo-evangelicals themselves had made it clear that their oft-professed reluctance to engage in secular politics was just a disguise for all the stands that were bad: capital punishment, right-to-work laws, "military maximalism," and so on. "Now that we are all admitting that we are playing the same game it will be possible to ask whose detail of ecumenical policy and whose program of social concern is more likely to be congruent with Christian norms, more productive of human good." Congruent? Imbued with the spirit of reform, the establishment was now prepared to see the evangelical opposition as arrayed on the side of reaction, and even as unchristian.[20]

Some years before, in an article much taken to heart by NCC activists like Mississippian Will Campbell, the Louisiana Catholic writer Walker Percy had claimed that Southern society, for all its churchiness, was not really Christian; or at least that its upper-class leaders were not. They were, rather, citizens of the ancient Stoic type, who until recently had looked after Negroes as an act of *noblesse oblige,* and presided over a genteel community of manners based on their own self-esteem and the "extraordinary native courtesy and dignity" of the Negroes. But now, said Percy, that time was over; the Negro was demanding his rights and the Southern gentleman, joining a White Citizens Council or simply lapsing into silence, was happy to let him "taste the bitter fruits of his insolence." How different was the Christian scheme of things, where what the Stoic found intolerable simply became "the sacred right which must be accorded the individual, whether deemed insolent or not."

Archbishop Rummel of New Orleans had declared segregation a sin (this was 1956); sooner or later Southerners would have to face up to their Christian heritage and answer him. "And the good pagan's answer is no longer good enough for the South."[21]

When Percy returned to the theme in 1965, some significant updating was required; in the wake of the collapse of "Stoic excellence," the southern Negro had acquired a new ally. He was not, however, the upper-class Christian for whom Percy had hoped – southern Christendom had still not faced up to "the single great burning issue in American life." He was "the liberal humanist, who is more likely than not, frankly post-Christian in his beliefs." Midway through the decade, the white wing of the civil rights movement had ceased to be the preserve of the churches; as an example, Percy pointed to the Mississippi Summer Project of 1964, which, despite the sponsorship of the National Council, had drawn mostly nonreligious volunteers. If the South's professed Christians had stumbled, what then of these good pagans? They were certainly doing God's work. Yet Percy, the traditional-minded believer, was not prepared to say that the answer of "the Cambridge-Berkeley axis" was good enough for the South. There were other theologically inclined souls, however, who did not shrink from breaking down the wall that kept such representatives of "the victorious technological democratic society" outside the commonwealth of faith.[22]

As it happened, 1965 witnessed the biggest theological commotion to hit America since the Scopes trial of forty years before. On October 17, the *New York Times* published an article headed "'New' Theologians See Christianity without God." Hard on its heels came Ved Mehta's *New Yorker* pieces on "The New Theologian," which discovered much the same thing. This journalistic coincidence gave birth to a full-fledged media event that achieved its apotheosis in red and black on *Time*'s April 8, 1966, cover: IS GOD DEAD? Suddenly a few junior theology professors unhappy with supernaturalist religion found themselves scandalizing clergy and laity across the country. To what end? Taken up with ongoing matters of academic theology, the death-of-God theologians – Thomas Altizer, William Hamilton, Gabriel Vahanian, and Paul Van Buren – did not address themselves to how religion was going outside the ivory tower. A more worldly spiritual politics could nonetheless be detected in their preoccupation with adapting faith to the present human condition – a condition they assumed (without discussion) to be implacably secular. This politics was made explicit in Harvey Cox's 1965 bestseller, *The Secular City*.

Cox, a young assistant professor of theology and culture, ebulliently announced the good news that secularization, far from being the enemy of religion, actually represented "an authentic consequence of biblical faith." Christians should therefore "support and nourish" a process that disenchanted nature, desacralized politics, and deconsecrated values. Growing up in rural Pennsylvania had immunized Cox to Protestant nostalgia for small-town churchly community; his book celebrated "technopolis," where the living was free and mobile and the style pragmatic and profane. To be "where the action is," as he put it, the church needed to behave accordingly – coolly promoting social progress while exorcising prejudice and hidebound, unsecular thinking. And if he stopped short of proclaiming the death of God, Cox did declare a moratorium on "God talk." Since, in the secular city, "the political was replacing the metaphysical as the characteristic mode of grasping reality," it was only right for religious folk to drop theology and pick up urbanology. But Cox had no intention of tearing down the tabernacle and stealing away into the secular night. Not only did he expect the church to be "God's Avant-Garde"; by his clever paradox of the secular-as-religious, he did away in an instant with Percy's troublesome post-Christians. The victorious technological democratic society was simply the latest product of the factory of faith. The church and the Cambridge-Berkeley axis were gathered under the Coxian umbrella, where there was neither secular nor sacred, but only one great and good pan-ecumenical enterprise.

But what of the conservative evangelicals, including those Baptists among whom Cox had been raised? In describing the church as "cultural exorcist," Cox warned that the "real ecumenical crisis" was not between Catholics and Protestants, but between "traditional and experimental forms of church life." Was this a warning to the new post-Christian Christians not to lose touch with their roots? Not at all. Cox was simply serving notice on "leaders in the established traditional forms" that they had to "learn to appreciate the value of the innovators and maintain communication across the newly threatening abyss." It was the establishment itself that needed to get with the action. The evangelical anti-establishment did not signify at all.

In his famous "Letter from Birmingham Jail," Martin Luther King, Jr., wrote, "If today's church does not recapture the sacrificial spirit of the early church, it will lose its authenticity, forfeit the loyalty of millions, and be dismissed as an irrelevant social club with no meaning for the twentieth century." Yet even should the church fail, he stated, the civil rights struggle would triumph. "We will win our freedom because the sacred heritage of our nation and the eternal will of God are embodied in our echoing demands." The prophetic mission of America itself would carry the day. A few years later, William McLoughlin, who had earlier seen Billy Graham as the standard-bearer of a "Fourth Great Awakening," asserted that the evangelical Third Force had made little headway in winning over American Protestantism between 1957 and 1965, and he argued that any such possibility was now "extremely unlikely." The real "third force in Christendom," he said, was "the pietistic spirit of American culture itself – not only the American sense of mission which leads it into world leadership for the containment of Communist expansion in the name of democratic freedom for all men, and not only the sense of charity or stewardship which leads it into giving economic assistance in billions of dollars each year to help others to help themselves, but the sense of religious commitment and ideals that Americans inscribe [*sic*] to democracy and their way of life." The age of civil religion had (briefly) arrived.[23]

Thus, from World War II to the war in Vietnam, the New Evangelicalism provided the establishment with a foil against which to define its concerns. It was The Other – first an antiecumenical other and then a spiritually conventional other, a politically reactionary other, and a disappearing unsecular other. Later, when the Protestant center stage came to be occupied by the likes of Jerry Falwell and Pat Robertson, establishmentarians would tend to see the evangelicals outside their ranks as a hegemonic other. For a short span of the postwar era, however, thought was given to the possibility that evangelicalism was not an adversary of the establishment but an ally. That may seem to have been the last hurrah of an earlier day, but if anything like a Protestant establishment is to survive, it is worth wondering whether it could not happen again.

NOTES

This essay was originally written for the Harvard-Lilly Endowment Protestant establishment project. Major portions of it appear in my *Spiritual Politics: Religion and America Since World War II* (New York: Simon & Schuster, 1988).

1   *Christian Century* 60(1943): 596, 614.
2   Carl F. H. Henry, *The Uneasy Conscience of Modern Fundamentalism* (Grand Rapids, Mich.: Eerdmans, 1947), 81.
3   *Christian Century* 70(1953): 550; 68(1951): 536; J. Kenneth Miller, correspondence with H. J. McKnight, 1954, 1956, Presbyterian Historical Society, Philadelphia, Pa.
4   *Christian Century* 68(1951): 536; 69(1952): 543; 70(1953): 551; 69(1952): 494–6; 68(1951): 814; 71(1954): 357.
5   John C. Bennett, "Billy Graham at Union," *Union Seminary Quarterly Review* 9(May 1954): 9–14.
6   *National Council Outlook* 4(June 1954): 19; Berlyn V. Farris, "Report to the

Joint Department of Evangelism of the National Council of Churches,"
Archives of the National Council of Churches, Presbyterian Historical Society, Philadelphia, Pa. (hereafter, NCA).

7   *Christianity and Crisis* 16(March 5, 1956): 18.

8   Ibid. 16(April 2, 1956): 40.

9   *Christian Century* 73(1956): 640–2, 848–9, 921–2, 1197–9, 1045.

10 Ibid. 72(1955): 1076.

11 "Report of the General Board's Commission to Study Evangelism," Document of Record #505 (1957), in possession of National Council of Churches, New York, N.Y.

12 *The Good News of God: The Nature and Task of Evangelism* (New York:
National Council of Churches, 1957), 20; "Report by the Executive Direc-
tor to the Board of Managers of the Central Department of Evangelism,"
May 8, 1957, NCA.

13 *Life* 43(July 1, 1957): 87, 92.

14 Noel Houston, "Billy Graham," *Holiday* (February 1958); letter in NCA.

15 *Life* 44(1958): 122; see also Van Dusen's "Caribbean Holiday," *Christian
Century* 72(1955): 946–8; for NAE membership at the time, see *Christianity
Today* 9(1958): [425]; Martin Marty, *The New Shape of American Religion*
(New York: Harper, 1959), 21, 89.

16 *New York Times,* September 13, 1960.

17 *New York Times,* September 12, 1960.

18 *Christianity and Crisis* 20(September 19, 1960): 126.

19 Mathew Ahmann (ed.), *Race: Challenge to Religion* (Chicago: 4 Regnery,
1963), v.

20 Letter in NCA; *Christian Century* 73(1965): 1115–16.

21 Walker Percy, "Stoicism in the South," *Commonweal* 64(1956): 343–4.

22 Walker Percy, "The Failure and the Hope," in Will D. Campbell and James
Y. Holloway (eds.), *The Failure and the Hope* (Grand Rapids, Mich.:
Eerdmans, 1972), 25, 28, 17.

23 Martin Luther King, Jr., *Why He Can't Wait* (New York: New American
Library, 1964), 100; William G. McLoughlin, "Is There a Third Force in
Christendom?" in McLoughlin and Bellah (eds.), *Religion in America*
(Boston: Houghton Mifflin, 1968), 66.

SELECT BIBLIOGRAPHY

Eckhardt, A. Roy. *The Surge of Piety in America: An Appraisal*. New York:
Association Press, 1958.

Fox, Richard Wightman. *Reinhold Niebuhr: A Biography*. New York: Pantheon,
1985.

Frady, Marshall. *Billy Graham: A Parable of American Righteousness*. Boston: Little, Brown, 1979.

Henry, Carl F. H. *The Uneasy Conscience of Modern Fundamentalism*. Grand
Rapids, Mich.: Eerdmans, 1947.

McLoughlin, William G. *Billy Graham: Revivalist in a Secular Age.* New York: Ronald Press, 1960.

McLoughlin, William G., ed. *Religion in America.* Boston: Houghton Mifflin, 1968.

Marsden, George M. *Fundamentalism and American Culture: The Shaping of Twentieth-Century Evangelicalism, 1870–1925.* New York: Oxford University Press, 1980.

Marty, Martin. *The New Shape of American Religion.* New York: Harper, 1959.

Nash, Ronald H. *The New Evangelicalism.* Grand Rapids, Mich.: Eerdmans, 1963.

Silk, Mark. *Spiritual Politics: Religion and America Since World War II.* New York: Simon and Schuster, 1988.

VI

Conclusion

IV

Conclusion

13

Discovering America

WILLIAM R. HUTCHISON

In a comparative study published in the 1960s, the English historian E. R. Norman dislodged some long-standing assumptions about the differences between the British and the Americans with respect to religion's place in the civic order. The usual assumption, itself an article of faith among the Americans, had been that the British and other Europeans were burdened with establishments of religion whereas Americans, at least since the Massachusetts disestablishment of 1833, had been gloriously free of them.

In fact, as Norman demonstrated, the Anglican establishment, based on a multitude of laws and customs, from the 1820s onward had lost so many of its legislated privileges that it virtually ceased, over the next fifty years, to be that formidable embodiment of an *ancien régime* that we Americans had so loved to hate. In the United States, during the same era, the officially and proudly non-established Protestant churches had managed to maintain and in some ways enhance their position of special responsibility and preferred status.[1]

Firsthand observations by nineteenth-century European travelers – the friendly as well as the querulous ones – nearly always led to similar conclusions about the American situation. Almost without exception (but also without much comprehension from American readers), those commentators noticed that, whatever its other effects, legal separation had in no essential way diminished Protestantism's preferred status. A writer for *Fraser's Magazine* in 1835 went further by suggesting that the much-touted "voluntary principle" had not really been tested in the United States, since "voluntaryism there possesses the features of a state establishment." A British Congregationalist delegation, the same year, noted with admiration that although the Americans had "no law for the regulation of the Sabbath . . . public sentiment secures its sanctification better than with us." John Henry Newman, less admiringly, criticized Americans for boasting that "their Church is not, like ours, enslaved to the civil power." That was technically true, he added, yet the churches in America were enslaved to the laity, "and in a democracy what is that but the civil power in another shape?"[2]

The people, in other words, could and did serve as guarantors for a given ordering of religious life. And while "the people" might signify an overwhelming or more modest majority, that phrase could just as well refer to a dominant minority or plurality – those who had inherited and been able to maintain social and political control.

That brings us to the purpose of this brief foray into nineteenth-century comparisons. Among the numerous similarities between the American form of religious establishment and those known to other societies, one that has seemed increasingly relevant to the writers of this book is the persistence of both, long beyond the time when either could be based upon clear numerical superiority. As early as the famous "religious census" of 1851, the established church in the United Kingdom was maintaining its majority status by a hair – just a percentage point. Its American counterpart, if that means the totality of American Protestantism, was never to come so close to actual minority status. Yet Protestants were reduced from their nearly complete statistical dominance in the colonial and Revolutionary periods, to something like a 4-to-1 position in 1840, and then, by 1860, to the more modest advantage – just above or below 60% – that Protestantism has held ever since.[3] And if one focuses, as we have done, on the so-called mainline denominations as the real analogue to an established church, one could say that the American religious establishment represented a minority of the population by the early years of the twentieth century.

The point is not to press the British or any other analogy, nor to contend about statistics that could be variously generated and interpreted. The point is that the persistent discussions, arguments, and heartburnings, throughout the twentieth century, about the "decline" of Protestantism (mainline or otherwise) might have been both less confused and more productive had we more often begun by recognizing the truly monumental decline of 1790 to 1860. In the great new democracy where the religious establishment's legitimacy did depend peculiarly upon popular preferences and support, this rapid restructuring of the American population constituted a Protestant "decline" of such proportions as to make twentieth-century realignments seem little more than mild, long-overdue adjustments.

Surely, in any comparative assessment that sets its benchmark further back than a selectively remembered "only yesterday," the striking thing about the cultural authority of twentieth-century Protestantism is not its diminution but its persistence; not the moral and institutional "declensions" that many perceived in each of the decades spanned by these essays, but the continuation of a degree of religious and cultural hegemony significantly out of proportion to Protestant or mainline strength in the American population.

To point this out is not to say that such institutional and ideological persistence was a freak occurrence – something to be wondered at. Numbers are not everything, and even those most scornful of inherited cultural hegemonies will not necessarily desire, much less expect, strict conformity between population patterns and the distribution of cultural authority. What is more, like the persistence of less benign oligarchies (those based, for example, squarely upon race or gender), the twentieth-century perdurance of a Protestant establishment can be explained readily enough by the circumstances under which the nation was settled and its dominant culture founded. Counterfactual history is fun, and often therapeutic, and one might usefully project the results had Maryland or Pennsylvania, rather than Massachusetts and Virginia, provided the strongest formative influences in the emerging American culture. But that, of course, is not how it happened.

If immigration and a changed population structure in the nineteenth century did not undermine Protestant hegemony or even greatly affect it, one can find adequate explanations in such realities as geographic distribution and the entrenchment of social classes. Roman Catholic immigrants did not simply cluster in a few cities, but settled throughout the country and countryside.[4] They were, nonetheless, underrepresented in most communities and unevenly distributed – for generations, grossly so – across the lines of caste and class and educational attainment.

Like most other forms of persisting hegemony, moreover, this one was also justified, or at least kept in power, by its patently wide-ranging services to the society. That is a point too easily lost amid all the analysis (of which, quite properly, much appears in this book) of lights that failed and agendas that were at least partially defensive or self-serving. During the twentieth-century decades surveyed here, both the leaders and the more thoughtful constituents of the Protestant establishment did see themselves as burdened and honored with special responsibilities for education and cultural formation and social amelioration. More broadly, they saw themselves as appointed by ancient warrant to the moral guidance, and in some ways to the governance, of their society.

Given their real situation (rather than the one they frequently imagined) in a changed twentieth-century America, their accomplishments were far from negligible. If Protestant social planners can be faulted, as

William McGuire King in particular does, for failing to understand and articulate the grounds of their own programs; if religious statesmen and bureaucrats found it hard to disentangle institutional altruism from institutional defense and self-perpetuation (Robert A. Schneider); if even the most open-minded fell short of true mutuality in relation to other forms of faith (Benny Kraut, Grant Wacker); and if the more daring or prophetic failed to carry their constituents with them (Edwin S. Gaustad, Dorothy Bass), certainly these are failings one detects just as readily among others – new elites as well as traditional ones – with pretensions to service and leadership in a society.

One of the prerequisites for historical realism, after all, for assessing historical actors "as they really were," is some allowance for naive altruism. If most people and institutions are too corrupt to be entirely selfless, most are also not smart enough, or reflective enough, to be entirely devious. Whatever the failures and the mixed motives, there would seem to be little justification, in the case before us, for viewing the achievements of a Protestant goodwill movement or a Protestant social gospel as mere persiflage. Still less would there be adequate ground for discounting the contributions of day-to-day preaching and teaching and human assistance.

On a larger canvas, one can acknowledge much validity in a retrospective view that this writer has disparaged when presented in exaggerated or facile forms, namely, that the "mainline Protestantism" of this pre-1960s era served broadly to provide and articulate moral norms for American society, and that it has since abdicated that function or lost the power to perform it.

That kind of assessment was overdone, if not done to death, in the early 1980s, as many commentators seriously exaggerated the earlier strength and efficacy of mainline religion – discovering virtues in Eisenhower-era religion, for example, that had escaped their notice during that expansive time. Around 1980, critics of the activistic, formerly admired, sixties contrasted them with preceding decades when God had been in his heaven, real religion had resounded in the public square, and Reinhold Niebuhr had appeared on the cover of *Time*. Looking further back, those lamenting our fractured modern condition contrasted *that*, far too simplistically, with a supposed earlier state of moral consensus and societal cohesion.[5]

Once such roseate views of the past have been relinquished, however,[6] the more fundamental point survives: that the pre-sixties Protestant establishment did offer a specifically religious – indeed quasi-ecclesiastical – matrix for common social values, and that a religious matrix of that sort was difficult to construct, or even envisage, in a society that by the 1980s had been led (or dragged) to a substantially new awareness of its own diversities.

To speak thus of a new level of awareness, after midcentury, concerning American diversity and Protestantism's "real situation" is also to imply that the establishment's earlier authority (however one eventually estimates that) had been based in part on illusions – that this emperor, if not unclothed, had not been so well fitted out as he and others imagined. And surely that is one conclusion to be drawn from the essays in this volume. It would seem that, although "discovering America" may not have been on the Protestant agenda, that experience was the subtext and consequence of many items on that agenda.

Although such observations may seem belittling (to be told one has been self-deluded is more humiliating than to be told one is wicked), they may also lead to more favorable assessments of the establishment's ideals and accomplishments. Judgments about Protestant effectiveness or success will vary with the level of expectation (whether their expectations or ours). Insofar as the establishment's goal, consciously or otherwise, was the old dominance and authority, accomplishments were at best modest. But insofar as one sees the Protestantism of this period as already more denominational than establishmentarian in nature, already "a church among churches," the achievements will appear in a different and more positive light. More bluntly: Protestantism as a congeries of working, serving, churches was far more successful than "Protestantism as establishment."

What of the Protestant establishment today, and in the future? These authors were not asked to serve as prophets, or even as commentators on current affairs; so any suggestions along those lines should be understood as extrapolation rather than summary. But certainly the distinction I have just been pressing, between an "establishment" standard for evaluation and a more modest "large-denomination" standard, is even more appropriate as one assesses the present or looks to the future.

I have suggested earlier that much contemporary discussion of "the decline of mainline Protestantism" has been superficial, that historical inspection reveals not so much "decline" as natural, overdue adjustment to the facts of American life. But one can also, of course, raise questions about the extent and genuineness of this adjustment. Has the Protestant establishment now lost its coherence and force, or not? As Mark Silk remarks, the lack of any great or intrinsic hostility between old-line churches and "mainstream evangelicals" can lead one to wonder, at least, "whether it could not happen again." Liberal–evangelical alliances, powerful in the first years of this century, could easily become so again.

Even apart from such possibilities, one should look carefully at some of the cases in point most commonly cited to illustrate the alleged Protestant demise. Despite widespread expectations (and even beliefs) to the contrary, for example, electoral results in the 1980s did not clearly depict a passing of the torch from the old-line denominations to movements on the religious right. The groups traditionally overrepresented in national politics, although they perhaps "lost" in relation to Catholics and Jews, showed little slippage in favor of other brands of Protestant. Thus the United States Congress after the 1984 elections appeared, in religious terms, much like its predecessors. It included, for example, sixty-seven Episcopalians and one Pentecostal.[7]

Similar observations would be appropriate in many other areas. The sharp decline in the numbers of mainline foreign missionaries seems telling until one considers the numbers of mainline church people – many times more than in the past – whose forms of overseas service in the 1980s would be hard to distinguish from those undertaken by mainline missionaries of the 1930s.[8] The momentous decline in direct denominational sponsorship of higher education, as discussed by Dorothy Bass, must be weighed against an equally astounding rise, under generally liberal auspices, in the study of religion in secular institutions (Grant Wacker). As for the media: Although Dennis Voskuil records an undeniable increase in the attention given to non-establishment religion, one might also want to ask where the writers and broadcasters were inclined to turn, after this change, for facts and opinions concerning the non-established. I believe we would find, at least with respect to "Protestant" news and stories, that in general they continued to consult and quote sources within the old-line establishment.

Whether such observations mean simply that the old-line churches have continued to carry substantial weight in American society, or mean that they can still claim the position of "establishment," can be debated; but I am strongly inclined to the first of those views. Although the traditional Protestant denominations, and their influence, have survived better than is commonly supposed, "Protestantism as establishment" has indeed declined – as reality, but even more as rhetoric.

More precisely, the rhetoric of establishment ("We're Number One . . . we write the agenda") has by and large been abandoned by the only plausible Protestant aspirants to new-establishment status. In the event that "mainstream" evangelicals and liberals do coalesce into a newly effective force, it is not they, I think, who will be heard still chanting the slogans of a return to "Protestant America."

NOTES

1   E. R. Norman, *The Conscience of the State in North America* (Cambridge: Cambridge University Press, 1968), Chapter 1.

2   *Fraser's Magazine* 12(November 1835): 579; Andrew Reed and James Matheson, *A Narrative of the Visit to the American Churches by the Deputation for the Congregational Union of England and Wales,* 2 vols. (New York: Harper, 1835), II, 191; [John Henry Newman], "The Anglican Church," *British Critic and Quarterly Theological Review* 26(1839): 281.

3   Elie Halévy, *The Age of Peel and Cobden: A History of the English People, 1841–1852* (London: Ernest Benn, 1947), 340–2: Edwin S. Gaustad, *Historical Atlas of Religion in America* (New York: Harper & Row, 1962), 110–11, 163. Gaustad's nineteenth-century figures compare Protestant church membership with that of the Roman Catholics. One must, of course, consider "cultural" Protestants and Catholics, other non-Protestants, and different ways of counting "members." My own estimate attempts to do this.

4   Gaustad, *Atlas,* 108.

5   For an introduction to the discussion surrounding these historical issues, see William R. Hutchison, "Past Imperfect: History and the Prospect for Liberalism," *Christian Century* 103(January 1–8 and 15, 1986): 11–15, 42–6.

6   In general they have been. See, e.g., Wade Clark Roof, "The Third Disestablishment and Beyond," in Dorothy C. Bass et al., *Mainstream Protestantism in the Twentieth Century: Its Problems and Prospects* (Philadelphia: Presbyterian Church, USA, 1986), 27–37; and the historical chapter (2) in Robert N. Bellah et al., *Habits of the Heart: Individualism and Commitment in American Life* (Berkeley: University of California Press, 1985).

7   *Christianity Today* 29(January 18, 1985): 61–4.

8   For a fuller discussion, see William R. Hutchison, *Errand to the World: American Protestant Thought and Foreign Missions* (Chicago: University of Chicago Press, 1987), 176–209.

Index

314   *Index*